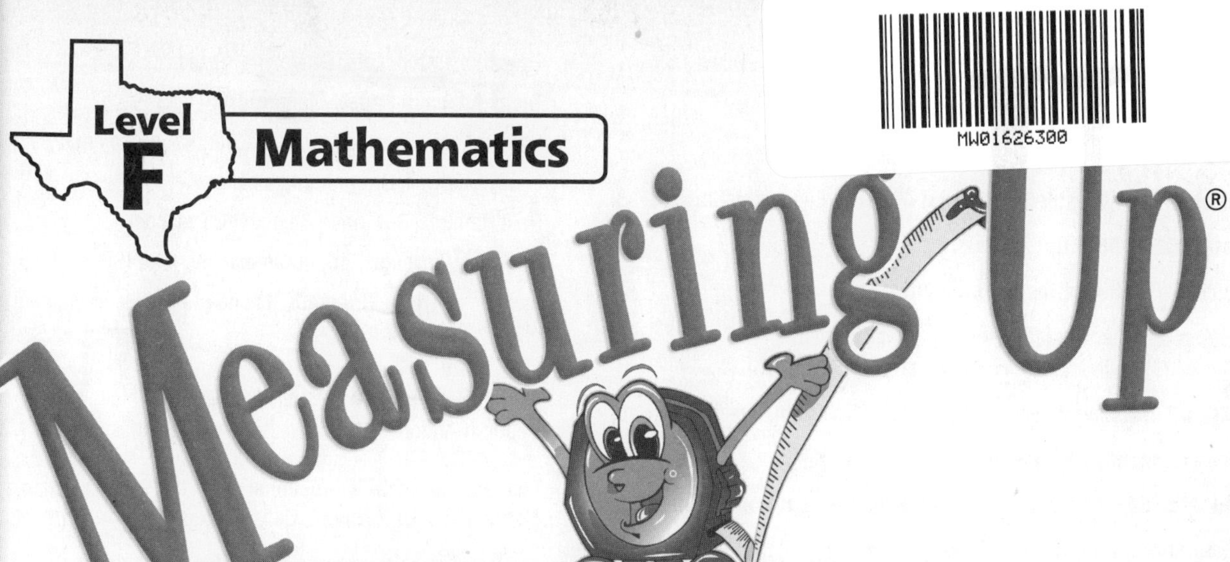

Measuring Up™ to the Texas Essential Knowledge and Skills

and Success Strategies for the TAKS

This book is customized for Texas and the lessons cover ALL TEKS. The Measuring Up® program includes instructional worktexts, Diagnostic Practice Tests, and Measuring Up e-Path® which are available separately.

800-822-1080
www.PeoplesEducation.com

Executive Vice President and Chief Creative Officer: Diane Miller

Vice President, Product Development: Steven Jay Griffel

Editorial Development: Gramercy Book Services, Inc.

Assistant Vice President, Editorial Director: Eugene McCormick

Mathematics Director: April Barth

Executive Mathematics Editor: Martha Torn

Editors: Janet A. Burgess, Rosemary McLaughlin, Michelle Missaggia, Mark Perry

Editorial Assistants: Eliot Hoffman, Tom Robinson, Joseph Schwab

Vice President of Marketing: Victoria Ameer Kiely

Vice President of Production and Manufacturing: Doreen Smith

Production Director: Nicole Dawson

Project Manager: Tara Bernstein

Production Editor: Hugh Haggerty

Production Assistant: Eileen Turano

Designer: Jodi Notowitz

Director of Editorial Services: Lee Shenkman

Copy Editor: Dee Josephson

Proofreaders: Josh Gillenson, Donna Mattina

Photo Researcher/Permissions Manager: Kristine Liebman

Technical Art: Bob J. Eckhardt, Ismael Feliciano, Yadiro Henriquez, Matthew Hjembo, Ken Owens, Sharon MacGregor

Cover Design: Cynthia Mackowicz, Michele Sakow, Yadiro Henriquez

Developmental Editing:
Educational Concepts, Grapevine, Texas

Texas Advisory Panel, Elementary:

Lee Brenner, 4th grade math teacher, Katy Elementary, Katy, Texas

Shelly Caldwell, 3rd grade teacher

Raul Ramirez, 3rd grade Bilingual/GT teacher

Denise J. Clevenger, 4th grade teacher, Islet ISD, El Paso, Texas

Kathryn K. Travis, 3rd grade teacher, Epps Island Elementary, Klein ISD, Houston, TX

Texas Advisory Panel, Middle School:
Deborah Andrews, middle-school mathematics teacher, Mansfield, Texas

Mildred Savannah, Instructional Specialist Middle Schools, Dallas ISD, Mathematics Department, Dallas, Texas

Larry Ward, Mathematics Supervisor, Corinth, Texas

Cynthia L.Worley, Mathematics and Science Specialist, Dallas, Texas

Texas Advisory Panel, High School:

Rene Garcia, grade 9–12 math teacher

Julie Merrill, mathematics consultant

Peoples Education, Inc.
299 Market Street
Saddle Brook, New Jersey 07663

ISBN 978-1-4138-3583-0
ISBN 1-4138-3583-X

Printed in the United States of America.

20 19 18 17 16 15 14 13 12 11

Measuring Up® Contents

These lessons cover 9 TEKS.

TEKS in bold are assessed on the TAKS.

CHAPTER 2 Decimals

CHAPTER 3 Fractions

These lessons cover 9 TEKS.

CHAPTER 4 Patterns, Relations, and Functions

TEKS in bold are assessed on the TAKS.

CHAPTER 5 Ratio, Proportion, and Percent

CHAPTER 6 Geometry and Spatial Reasoning

TEKS in bold are assessed on the TAKS.

CHAPTER 7 Measurement

These lessons cover 8 TEKS.

CHAPTER 8 Perimeter, Area, and Volume

These lessons cover 9 TEKS.

CHAPTER 9 Probability

TEKS in bold are assessed on the TAKS.

CHAPTER 10 Statistics

Correlation to the Texas Essential Knowledge and Skills

This worktext is customized to the Texas Essential Knowledge and Skills and provides complete practice for the TAKS.

The correlation chart shows how Measuring Up® is vertically aligned to the TEKS because the lessons are customized for the TEKS. To see our complete vertical and horizontal alignment for the Measuring Up® program, visit www.TXStandardsHelp.com. As the lesson for each student expectation is completed, place a (✓) to indicate Mastery or an (✗) to indicate Review Needed.

Chapter 1: Understanding Numbers and Operations with Whole Numbers

	Review Skill											
	Mastered Skill											
	Lessons	1	2	3	4	5	6	7	8	9	10	B
TEKS 6.1	**Number, operation, and quantitative reasoning.** The student represents and uses rational numbers in a variety of equivalent forms.											
(C)	Use integers to represent real-life situations.	○	○	○	○	○	○	○	★	✓	✓	B
(D)	Write prime factorizations using exponents.	○	○	○	○	★	✓	✓	✓	✓	✓	B
(E)	Identify factors including common factors and greatest common factor	○	○	○	★	✓	✓	✓	✓	✓	✓	B
(F)	Identify multiples of a positive integer and common multiples and the least common multiple of a set of positive integers.	○	★	✓	✓	✓	✓	✓	✓	✓	✓	B
TEKS 6.2	**Number, operation, and quantitative reasoning.** The student adds, subtracts, multiplies, and divides to solve problems and justify solutions.											
(C)	Use multiplication and division of whole numbers to solve problems including situations involving equivalent ratios and rates.	○	★	★	★	✓	★	✓	✓	✓	✓	B
(D)	Estimate and round to approximate reasonable results and to solve problems where exact answers are not required.	○	○	○	○	○	○	★	✓	✓	✓	B
(E)	Use order of operations to simplify whole number expressions (without exponents) in problem solving situations.	○	○	○	★	✓	✓	✓	✓	✓	✓	B
TEKS 6.11	**Underlying processes and mathematical tools.** The student applies Grade 6 mathematics to solve problems connected to everyday experiences, investigations in other disciplines, and activities in and outside of school.											
(A)	Identify and apply mathematics to everyday experiences, to activities in and outside of school, with other disciplines, and with other mathematical topics.	★	✓	✓	✓	✓	✓	✓	★	✓	✓	B
(B)	Use a problem-solving model that incorporates understanding the problem, making a plan, carrying out the plan, and evaluating the solution for reasonableness.	○	○	○	○	○	○	○	○	★	★	B
(C)	Select or develop an appropriate problem-solving strategy from a variety of different types, including drawing a picture, looking for a pattern, systematic guessing and checking, acting it out, making a table, working a simpler problem, or working backwards to solve a problem.	○	○	○	○	○	○	○	○	★	★	B

Chapter 2: Decimals

	Review Skill											
	Mastered Skill											
	Lessons	11	12	13	14	N/A	N/A	N/A	N/A	N/A	B
TEKS 6.1	**Number, operation, and quantitative reasoning.** The student represents and uses rational numbers in a variety of equivalent forms.										
(A)	Compare and order non-negative rational numbers.	★	✓	✓	✓						B
TEKS 6.2	**Number, operation, and quantitative reasoning.** The student adds, subtracts, multiplies, and divides to solve problems and justify solutions.										
(B)	Use addition and subtraction to solve problems involving fractions and decimals.	○	★	★	✓						B
(D)	Estimate and round to approximate reasonable results and to solve problems where exact answers are not required.	✓	★	★	✓						B
TEKS 6.11	**Underlying processes and mathematical tools.** The student applies Grade 6 mathematics to solve problems connected to everyday experiences, investigations in other disciplines, and activities in and outside of school.										
(A)	Identify and apply mathematics to everyday experiences, to activities in and outside of school, with other disciplines, and with other mathematical topics.	✓	✓	✓	★						B
(B)	Use a problem-solving model that incorporates understanding the problem, making a plan, carrying out the plan, and evaluating the solution for reasonableness.	✓	✓	✓	★						B
(C)	Select or develop an appropriate problem-solving strategy from a variety of different types, including drawing a picture, looking for a pattern, systematic guessing and checking, acting it out, making a table, working a simpler problem, or working backwards to solve a problem.	✓	✓	✓	★						B

Building Stamina® ○ Standards to be covered

★ Standards covered ✓ Standards previously covered

TEKS in bold are assessed on the TAKS.

Chapter 3: Fractions

		15	16	17	18	19	20	N/A	N/A	N/A	B
	Review Skill										
	Mastered Skill										
TEKS 6.1	**Number, operation, and quantitative reasoning.** The student represents and uses rational numbers in a variety of equivalent forms.										
(A)	Compare and order non-negative rational numbers.	✓	★	★	✓	✓	✓				B
(B)	Generate equivalent forms of rational numbers including whole numbers, fractions, and decimals.	★	★	★	★	★	✓				B
TEKS 6.2	**Number, operation, and quantitative reasoning.** The student adds, subtracts, multiplies, and divides to solve problems and justify solutions.										
(A)	Model addition and subtraction situations involving fractions with objects, pictures, words, and numbers.	❍	❍	❍	★	★	✓				B
(B)	Use addition and subtraction to solve problems involving fractions and decimals.	✓	✓	✓	✓	★	✓				B
(D)	Estimate and round to approximate reasonable results and to solve problems where exact answers are not required.	✓	✓	✓	★	★	✓				B
TEKS 6.11	**Underlying processes and mathematical tools.** The student applies Grade 6 mathematics to solve problems connected to everyday experiences, investigations in other disciplines, and activities in and outside of school.										
(A)	Identify and apply mathematics to everyday experiences, to activities in and outside of school, with other disciplines, and with other mathematical topics.	✓	✓	✓	✓	✓	★				B
(B)	Use a problem-solving model that incorporates understanding the problem, making a plan, carrying out the plan, and evaluating the solution for reasonableness.	✓	✓	✓	✓	✓	★				B
(C)	Select or develop an appropriate problem-solving strategy from a variety of different types, including drawing a picture, looking for a pattern, systematic guessing and checking, acting it out, making a table, working a simpler problem, or working backwards to solve a problem.	✓	✓	✓	✓	✓	★				B
(D)	Select tools such as real objects, manipulatives, paper/pencil, and technology or techniques such as mental math, estimation, and number sense to solve problems.	❍	❍	❍	❍	❍	★				B

Chapter 4: Patterns, Relations, and Functions

		21	22	23	24	N/A	N/A	N/A	N/A	N/A	B
	Review Skill										
	Mastered Skill										
TEKS 6.4	**Patterns, relationships, and algebraic thinking.** The student uses letters as variables in mathematical expressions to describe how one quantity changes when a related quantity changes.										
(A)	Use tables and symbols to represent and describe proportional and other relationships such as those involving conversions, arithmetic sequences with a constant rate of change, perimeter, area.	★	✓	★	✓						B
(B)	Use tables of data to generate formulas representing relationships involving perimeter, area, volume of a rectangular prism, etc.	❍	❍	★	✓						B
TEKS 6.5	**Patterns, relationships, and algebraic thinking.** The student uses letters to represent an unknown in an equation.										
(A)	The student is expected to formulate equations from problem situations described by linear relationships.	❍	★	★	✓						B
TEKS 6.11	**Underlying processes and mathematical tools.** The student applies Grade 6 mathematics to solve problems connected to everyday experiences, investigations in other disciplines, and activities in and outside of school.										
(A)	Identify and apply mathematics to everyday experiences, to activities in and outside of school, with other disciplines, and with other mathematical topics.	✓	✓	✓	✓						B
(B)	Use a problem-solving model that incorporates understanding the problem, making a plan, carrying out the plan, and evaluating the solution for reasonableness.	✓	✓	✓	★						B
(C)	Select or develop an appropriate problem-solving strategy from a variety of different types, including drawing a picture, looking for a pattern, systematic guessing and checking, acting it out, making a table, working a simpler problem, or working backwards to solve a problem.	✓	✓	✓	★						B

B **Building Stamina®**
★ Standards covered
❍ Standards to be covered
✓ Standards previously covered

TEKS in bold are assessed on the TAKS.

Chapter 4: Patterns, Relations, and Functions (continued)

Review Skill										
Mastered Skill										
Lessons	21	22	23	24	N/A	N/A	N/A	N/A	N/A	B
TEKS 6.12 **Underlying processes and mathematical tools.** The student communicates about Grade 6 mathematics through informal and mathematical language, representations and models.										
(A) Communicate mathematical ideas using language, efficient tools, appropriate units, and graphical, numerical, physical, or algebraic mathematical models.	★	★	✓	✓						B
(B) Evaluate the effectiveness of different representations to communicate ideas.	○	○	○	✓						B
TEKS 6.13 **Underlying processes and mathematical tools.** The student uses logical reasoning to make conjectures and verify conclusions.										
(A) Make conjectures from patterns or sets of examples and nonexamples.	★	✓	✓	✓						B

Chapter 5: Ratio, Proportion, and Percent

Review Skill										
Mastered Skill										
Lessons	25	26	27	28	29	N/A	N/A	N/A	N/A	B
TEKS 6.2 **Number, operation, and quantitative reasoning.** The student adds, subtracts, multiplies, and divides to solve problems and justify solutions.										
(C) Use multiplication and division of whole numbers to solve problems including situations involving equivalent ratios and rates.	✓	★	✓	✓	✓					B
TEKS 6.3 **Patterns, relationships, and algebraic thinking.** The student solves problems involving proportional relationships.										B
(A) Use ratios to describe proportional situations.	★	★	★	✓	✓					B
(B) Represent ratios and percents with concrete models, fractions, and decimals.	★	✓	✓	★	✓					B
(C) Use ratios to make predictions in proportional situations.	○	○	★	✓	✓					
TEKS 6.11 **Underlying processes and mathematical tools.** The student applies Grade 6 mathematics to solve problems connected to everyday experiences, investigations in other disciplines, and activities in and outside of school.										
(A) Identify and apply mathematics to everyday experiences, to activities in and outside of school, with other disciplines, and with other mathematical topics.	✓	✓	✓	✓	★					B
(B) Use a problem-solving model that incorporates understanding the problem, making a plan, carrying out the plan, and evaluating the solution for reasonableness.	✓	✓	✓	✓	★					B
(C) Select or develop an appropriate problem-solving strategy from a variety of different types, including drawing a picture, looking for a pattern, systematic guessing and checking, acting it out, making a table, working a simpler problem, or working backwards to solve a problem.	✓	✓	✓	✓	★					B
(D) Select tools such as real objects, manipulatives, paper/pencil, and technology or techniques such as mental math, estimation, and number sense to solve problems.	✓	✓	✓	✓	★					B

Chapter 6: Geometry and Spatial Reasoning

Review Skill										
Mastered Skill										
Lessons	30	31	32	33	34	35	36	N/A	N/A	B
TEKS 6.6 **Geometry and spatial reasoning.** The student uses geometric vocabulary to describe angles, polygons, and circles.										
(A) Use angle measurements to classify angles as acute, obtuse, or right.	★	★	✓	✓	✓	✓	✓			B
(B) Identify relationships involving angles in triangles and quadrilaterals.	○	★	★	★	✓	✓	✓			B
(C) Describe the relationship between radius, diameter, and circumference of a circle.	○	○	○	○	★	✓	✓			B
TEKS 6.7 **Geometry and spatial reasoning.** The student uses geometry to identify location in two dimensions.										
(A) Locate and name points on a coordinate plane using ordered pairs of non-negative rational numbers.	○	○	○	○	○	★	✓			B

B **Building Stamina®** ○ Standards to be covered

★ Standards covered ✓ Standards previously covered

TEKS in bold are assessed on the TAKS.

Chapter 6: Geometry and Spatial Reasoning (continued)

		30	31	32	33	34	35	36	N/A	N/A	B
	Review Skill										
	Mastered Skill										
TEKS 6.8	**Measurement.** The student solves application problems involving estimation and measurement of length, area, time, temperature, capacity, weight, and angles.										
(A)	Estimate measurements (including circumference) and evaluate reasonableness of results.	★	✓	✓	✓	✓	✓	✓			B
(B)	Select and use appropriate units, tools, or formulas to measure and to solve problems involving length (including perimeter), area, time, temperature, volume, and weight.	★	✓	✓	✓	✓	✓	✓			B
(C)	Measure angles.	★	✓	✓	✓	✓	✓	✓			B
TEKS 6.11	**Underlying processes and mathematical tools.** The student applies Grade 6 mathematics to solve problems connected to everyday experiences, investigations in other disciplines, and activities in and outside of school.										
(A)	Identify and apply mathematics to everyday experiences, to activities in and outside of school, with other disciplines, and with other mathematical topics.	✓	✓	✓	✓	✓	✓	★			B
(B)	Use a problem-solving model that incorporates understanding the problem, making a plan, carrying out the plan, and evaluating the solution for reasonableness.	✓	✓	✓	✓	✓	✓	★			B
(C)	Select or develop an appropriate problem-solving strategy from a variety of different types, including drawing a picture, looking for a pattern, systematic guessing and checking, acting it out, making a table, working a simpler problem, or working backwards to solve a problem.	✓	✓	✓	✓	✓	✓	★			B

Chapter 7: Measurement

					40	41	42	N/A	N/A	N/A	B
	Review Skill										
	Mastered Skill										
TEKS 6.4	**Patterns, relationships, and algebraic thinking.** The student uses letters as variables in mathematical expressions to describe how one quantity changes when a related quantity changes.										
(A)	Use tables and symbols to represent and describe proportional and other relationships such as those involving conversions, arithmetic sequences (with a constant rate of change), perimeter and area.	✓	✓	★	★	✓	✓				B
TEKS 6.8	**Measurement.** The student solves application problems involving estimation and measurement of length, area, time, temperature, volume, weight, and angles.										
(A)	Estimate measurements (including circumference) and evaluate reasonableness of results.	★	★	★	★	★	✓				B
(B)	Select and use appropriate units, tools, or formulas to measure and to solve problems involving length (including perimeter), area, time, temperature, volume, and weight.	★	★	★	★	★	✓				B
(D)	Convert measures within the same measurement system (customary and metric) based on relationships between units.	★	★	★	✓	★	✓				B
TEKS 6.11	**Underlying processes and mathematical tools.** The student applies Grade 6 mathematics to solve problems connected to everyday experiences, investigations in other disciplines, and activities in and outside of school.										
(A)	Identify and apply mathematics to everyday experiences, to activities in and outside of school, with other disciplines, and with other mathematical topics.	✓	✓	✓	✓	✓	★				B
(B)	Use a problem-solving model that incorporates understanding the problem, making a plan, carrying out the plan, and evaluating the solution for reasonableness.	✓	✓	✓	✓	✓	★				B
(C)	Select or develop an appropriate problem-solving strategy from a variety of different types, including drawing a picture, looking for a pattern, systematic guessing and checking, acting it out, making a table, working a simpler problem, or working backwards to solve a problem.	✓	✓	✓	✓	✓	★				B
(D)	Select tools such as real objects, manipulatives, paper/pencil, and technology or techniques such as mental math, estimation, and number sense to solve problems.	✓	✓	✓	✓	✓	★				B

B **Building Stamina**®
★ Standards covered
○ Standards to be covered
✓ Standards previously covered

TEKS in bold are assessed on the TAKS.

Chapter 8: Perimeter, Area and Volume											
	Review Skill										
	Mastered Skill										
	Lessons	43	44	45	46	47	N/A	N/A	N/A	N/A	B
TEKS 6.4	**Patterns, relationships, and algebraic thinking.** The student uses letters as variables in mathematical expressions to describe how one quantity changes when a related quantity changes.										
(A)	Use tables and symbols to represent and describe proportional and other relationships such as those involving conversions, arithmetic sequences (with a constant rate of change), perimeter and area.	★	✓	★	✓	✓					B
(B)	Use tables of data to generate formulas representing relationships involving perimeter, area, volume of a rectangular prism, etc.	★	✓	★	★	✓					B
TEKS 6.6	**Geometry and spatial reasoning.** The student geometric vocabulary to describe angles, polygons, and circles.										
(C)	Describe the relationship between radius, diameter, and circumference of a circle.	✓	★	✓	✓	✓					B
TEKS 6.8	**Measurement.** The student solves application problems involving estimation and measurement of length, area, time, temperature, volume, weight, and angles.										
(A)	Estimate measurements (including circumference) and evaluate reasonableness of results.	★	★	★	✓	✓					B
(B)	Select and use appropriate units, tools, or formulas to measure and to solve problems involving length (including perimeter), area, time, temperature, volume, and weight.	★	★	★	✓	✓					B
TEKS 6.11	**Underlying processes and mathematical tools.** The student applies Grade 6 mathematics to solve problems connected to everyday experiences, investigations in other disciplines, and activities in and outside of school.										
(A)	Identify and apply mathematics to everyday experiences, to activities in and outside of school, with other disciplines, and with other mathematical topics.	✓	✓	✓	✓	★					B
(B)	Use a problem-solving model that incorporates understanding the problem, making a plan, carrying out the plan, and evaluating the solution for reasonableness.	✓	✓	✓	✓	★					B
(C)	Select or develop an appropriate problem-solving strategy from a variety of different types, including drawing a picture, looking for a pattern, systematic guessing and checking, acting it out, making a table, working a simpler problem, or working backwards to solve a problem.	✓	✓	✓	✓	★					B
TEKS 6.13	**Underlying processes and mathematical tools.** The student uses logical reasoning to make conjectures and verify conclusions.										
(A)	Make conjectures from patterns or sets of examples and nonexamples.	✓	✓	✓	★	✓					B
(B)	Underlying processes and mathematical tools.	❍	❍	❍	★	✓					B

Chapter 9: Probability											
	Review Skill										
	Mastered Skill										
	Lessons	48	49	50	51	52	N/A	N/A	N/A	N/A	
TEKS 6.3	**Patterns, relationships, and algebraic thinking.** The student solves problems involving proportional relationships.										
(C)	Use ratios to make predictions in proportional situations.	✓	✓	✓	★	✓					B
TEKS 6.9	**Probability and statistics.** The student uses experimental and theoretical probability to make predictions.										
(A)	Construct sample spaces using lists, tree diagrams, and combinations.	★	★	✓	✓	✓					B
(B)	Select and use appropriate units, tools, or formulas to measure and to solve problems involving length (including perimeter and circumference), area, time, temperature, capacity, and weight.	❍	❍	★	★	✓					B
TEKS 6.11	**Underlying processes and mathematical tools.** The student applies Grade 6 mathematics to solve problems connected to everyday experiences, investigations in other disciplines, and activities in and outside of school.										
(A)	Identify and apply mathematics to everyday experiences, to activities in and outside of school, with other disciplines, and with other mathematical topics.	✓	✓	✓	✓	★					B
(B)	Use a problem-solving model that incorporates understanding the problem, making a plan, carrying out the plan, and evaluating the solution for reasonableness.	✓	✓	✓	✓	★					B

B **Building Stamina**®
❍ Standards to be covered
★ Standards covered
✓ Standards previously covered

TEKS in bold are assessed on the TAKS.

Chapter 9: Probability (continued)

		48	49	50	51	52	N/A	N/A	N/A	N/A	B
	Review Skill										
	Mastered Skill										
(C)	Select or develop an appropriate problem-solving strategy from a variety of different types, including drawing a picture, looking for a pattern,systematic guessing and checking, acting it out, making a table, working a simpler problem, or working backwards to solve a problem.	✓	✓	✓	✓	★					B
(D)	Select tools such as real objects, manipulatives, paper/pencil, and technology or techniques such as mental math, estimation, and number sense to solve problems.	✓	✓	✓	✓	★					B

Chapter 10: Statistics

		53	54	55	56	57	58	59	N/A	N/A	B
	Review Skill										
	Mastered Skill										
TEKS 6.10	**Probability and statistics.** The student uses statistical representations to analyze data.										
(A)	Draw and compare different graphical representations of the same data.	○	○	○	○	○	★	✓			B
(B)	Use median, mode, and range to describe data.	★	✓	✓	✓	✓	✓	✓			B
(C)	Sketch circle graphs to display data.	✓	✓	✓	✓	★	✓	✓			B
(D)	Solve problems by collecting, organizing, displaying, and interpreting data.	○	★	★	★	★	✓	✓			B
TEKS 6.11	**Underlying processes and mathematical tools.** The student applies Grade 6 mathematics to solve problems connected to everyday experiences, investigations in other disciplines, and activities in and outside of school.										
(A)	Identify and apply mathematics to everyday experiences, to activities in and outside of school, with other disciplines, and with other mathematical topics.	✓	✓	✓	✓	✓	✓	★			B
(B)	Use a problem-solving model that incorporates understanding the problem, making a plan, carrying out the plan, and evaluating the solution for reasonableness.	✓	✓	✓	✓	✓	✓	★			B
(C)	Select or develop an appropriate problem-solving strategy from a variety of different types, including drawing a picture, looking for a pattern, systematic guessing and checking, acting it out, making a table, working a simpler problem, or working backwards to solve a problem.	✓	✓	✓	✓	✓	✓	★			B
(D)	Select tools such as real objects, manipulatives, paper/pencil, and technology or techniques such as mental math, estimation, and number sense to solve problems.	✓	✓	✓	✓	✓	✓	★			B
TEKS 6.12	**Underlying processes and mathematical tools.** The student communicates about Grade 6 mathematics through informal and mathematical language, representations, and models.										
(B)	Evaluate the effectiveness of different representations to communicate ideas.	✓	✓	✓	✓	✓	★	✓			B

B **Building Stamina**®

★ Standards covered

○ Standards to be covered

✓ Standards previously covered

TEKS in bold are assessed on the TAKS.

To the Student:

How do you get better at anything you do? You practice! Just like with sports or other activities, the key to success in school is practice, practice, practice.

This book will help you review and practice mathematics strategies and skills. These are the strategies and skills you need to know to measure up to the Texas Essential Knowledge and Skills, or TEKS, for your grade. Practicing these skills and strategies now will help you do better in your work all year.

This Measuring Up® book has ten chapters divided into two parts. Part 1 provides practice with addition, subtraction, multiplication, division with whole numbers, decimals, and fractions, as well as reviewing patterns, ratio, proportion, and percent. Part 2 provides practice with geometry, measurement, probability and statistics. Each part gives you practice in using your thinking skills.

Each lesson consists of four main sections:

- **Focus on TEKS** introduces the TEKS skills covered in the lesson. Important vocabulary is introduced to help you learn to speak mathematically as you communicate your understanding of math concepts!
- **Guided Instruction** shows you the steps and skills necessary to solve problems.
- **Apply the TEKS** helps you practice important TEKS concepts and skills.
- **TAKS Practice** gives you practice in answering test-type questions.

Next spring, you will take the *Texas Assessment of Knowledge and Skills (TAKS)*. There are many chances throughout Measuring Up® for you to practice for the test. At the end of each chapter, the end of each part, and the end of the book is a **Building Stamina®** section. Each **Building Stamina®** contains both multiple-choice and open-ended griddable questions. Many of these questions are more difficult and will help you prepare for taking tests.

Taking the TAKS will be an important step forward. It will show how well you measure up to the TEKS. It is just one of the many important tests you will take.

Have a great year!

To Parents and Families:

All students need mathematics skills to succeed. Texas educators have created grade-appropriate standards called the Texas Essential Knowledge and Skills, or TEKS, for mathematics. The TEKS describe what all Texas students should know at each grade level. Students need to meet these standards, as measured by the *Texas Assessment of Knowledge and Skills*, or *TAKS* test, given in the spring.

The TAKS is directly related to the TEKS. The TAKS emphasizes higher-level thinking skills. Students must learn to consider, analyze, interpret, and evaluate instead of just recalling simple facts.

Measuring Up® will help your child review the TEKS and prepare for all mathematics exams. It contains:

- **Lessons** that focus on practicing the TEKS
- **Guided Instruction,** in which students are shown the steps and skills necessary to solve a variety of mathematical problems
- **TAKS Practice,** which shows how individual TEKS can be understood through multiple-choice and open-ended griddable questions
- **Building Stamina®,** which gives practice with more difficult multiple-choice and open-ended griddable questions that require higher-level thinking

For success in school and the real world, your child needs to be successful in mathematics. Get involved! Your involvement is crucial to your child's success. Here are some suggestions:

- Make sure your home shows that mathematics is important. Involve everyone in activities that require mathematics, such as mixing recipes and balancing checkbooks. Note how mathematics is used when you are out with your family. Allow students to help with shopping and working out sales tax and tipping.
- Help to find appropriate Internet sites for mathematics.
- Discuss how mathematics is used in financial and banking matters, in careers such as engineering, architecture, and medicine, in space exploration, and other real-life applications.
- Invite your student to write and talk about what he or she has learned in math class.
- Encourage your child to take the time to review and check his or her homework. Just solving a problem is not enough. Ask your student whether or not his or her answers are reasonable and then to justify the answers.

Get involved! Work this year to ensure your child's success. Mathematics skills are essential for success through your student's life.

What's Ahead in Measuring Up™

This book was created for Texas students. Each lesson and question will help you master the TEKS and do well on the TAKS. It will also help you do well on other mathematics exams you take during the school year.

About the TAKS Test

Texas educators have set up standards for mathematics. They are called the Texas Essential Knowledge and Skills, or TEKS, for mathematics. They spell out what all students at each grade level should know. Texas educators have also created a statewide test for mathematics. It is called the *Texas Assessment of Knowledge and Skills*, or *TAKS*. It shows how well students have mastered the TEKS. TAKS questions go along with the TEKS and meet the following TAKS objectives:

Mathematics Objectives

Objective 1	The student will demonstrate an understanding of numbers, operations, and quantitative reasoning.
Objective 2	The student will demonstrate an understanding of patterns, relationships, and algebraic reasoning.
Objective 3	The student will demonstrate an understanding of geometry and spatial reasoning.
Objective 4	The student will demonstrate an understanding of the concepts and uses of measurement.
Objective 5	The student will demonstrate an understanding of probability and statistics.
Objective 6	The student will demonstrate an understanding of the mathematical processes and tools used in problem-solving.

Format of the TAKS

The *Texas Assessment of Knowledge and Skills* for mathematics has two types of test items:

- multiple-choice questions
- open-ended, griddable-response questions

Many questions include a graph, a number line, a coordinate grid or another type of graphic, which is used to solve the problem. Measuring Up® gives you practice in reading and using these types of graphics. Some other questions will ask you to use a formula to solve a problem. A Mathematics Chart like the one you will use during the test is provided for you on pages 286–287 of this book.

Measuring Up® on Multiple-Choice Questions

A multiple-choice question has two parts. The first part is the question, or stem. The second part is the answer choices. These have letters in front of each possible answer. After you solve the problem, you circle the correct answer.

Example:

1. Find the missing term,

$$\frac{2}{8} = \frac{4}{a}$$

A 1

B 8

(C) 16

D 32

By working out the problem you can see that the answer is C, so that is the letter you should circle.

Another type of multiple-choice question includes "Not Here" as an answer choice. You will have to work the problem carefully, then check whether the correct answer is one of the answer choices. If the correct answer is not given, then "Not Here" will be the correct answer choice.

Example:

2. The addresses on the first four houses on Main Street are shown below. If the pattern continues, what is likely to be the number of the next house?

2006 2012 2018 2024 ?

F 2026

G 2028

H 2032

(J) Not Here

You probably noticed that the answer should be 2030 and it is not given. So J is the correct answer choice.

Here are some strategies for solving Multiple-Choice Questions:

- Circle or underline the key information in the problem. Cross out any information in the problem that is not needed.
- Draw a diagram or picture of a problem if possible.
- Try to work out the problem without looking at the answer choices. Once you have solved the problem, compare your answer with the answer choices. If your answer is not one of the choices, you know you are wrong. Then rework the problem.
- Some questions will be more difficult than others. The problem may require an extra step. Or, you may need to look for which answer does not apply. If the question seems too difficult, go to the next problem and come back to it later.
- Even if you don't know the answer, you can make a good guess based on what you know and get the question right.
- Check and double-check your answers before you turn in the test. Be sure you circled the answer you wanted.

Measuring Up® on Open-Ended Griddable Questions

Some test questions will have a grid for you to complete. For these questions you will need to find a numeric answer, fill it in on a chart, then fill in a bubble for the correct digit for each place value.

Example:

3. The cost of a trumpet is $1,279. The sales tax is $102.32. What is the total cost of the trumpet?

Record your answer and fill in the bubbles on the grid below. Be sure to use the correct place value.

1	3	8	1	.	3	2
0	0	0	0		0	0
●	1	1	●		1	1
2	2	2	2		2	●
3	●	3	3		●	3
4	4	4	4		4	4
5	5	5	5		5	5
6	6	6	6		6	6
7	7	7	7		7	7
8	8	●	8		8	8
9	9	9	9		9	9

The answer is $1,381.32. Notice how to mark your answer.

Here are some strategies for solving Open-Ended Griddable Questions:

- Work the problem carefully. Because you do not have the answer choices as a way to check yourself, it is important to take your time and solve the problem correctly.
- Once you have an answer, carefully write it into the chart using place values. Then fill in the bubble for the correct digit in each column.
- After you finish the test, look back at all the griddable questions and check that the bubbles are filled in correctly in each column.

Higher-Level Thinking Skills 

Higher-level thinking skills are important on the TAKS. When you use higher-level thinking skills, you do more than just recall information. On the TAKS, some questions ask you to find and continue a pattern, understand and use information in a table or graph, or use a number line. Instead of adding or subtracting to solve a problem, you may need to solve a two-step problem and use both operations. In Measuring Up® the higher-level thinking skills questions are starred.

Measuring Up® with Building Stamina®

A special feature of Measuring Up® is **Building Stamina®**. It was created to give you practice and build your confidence for taking hard tests. The more you practice answering hard questions, the more prepared you will be to succeed. At the end of each part and the end of the book is a longer **Building Stamina®**. These review all of the TEKS covered in the lessons.

Tips to Measure Up

There are some general test preparation tips you can use to succeed. Here are a few useful tips:

- Get a good night's sleep the night before the test.
- Eat a good breakfast.
- Think positively.
- Once you have finished the test, look back at each item to make sure you marked the best answer.

You will learn a lot in Measuring Up®. You will review and practice the TEKS. You will practice for the TAKS. Finally, you will build your stamina to answer tough questions. You will more than measure up. You'll be a smashing success!

Part 1 Number, Operation, Patterns, Relationships, and Algebraic Thinking

Chapter 1 Understanding Numbers and Operations with Whole Numbers
In Chapter 1 you will study and practice:

- how to compare and order non-negative rational numbers;
- how to add and subtract to solve problems and justify solutions;
- how to identify multiples and common multiples;
- how to multiply to solve problems and justify solutions;
- how to identify factors including common factors;
- how to write prime factorization using exponents;
- how to divide to solve problems and justify solutions;
- how to estimate and round to approximate reasonable results;
- how to identify and apply mathematics to real-life situations;
- how to simplify numerical expressions using the order of operations;
- how to select and identify problem-solving strategies.

★ **Building Stamina®**: This section gives you a chance to sharpen your skills with operations and whole numbers, and to strengthen your test-taking abilities.

Chapter 2 Decimals
In Chapter 2 you will study and practice:

- how to compare and order non-negative rational numbers;
- how to use addition to solve problems involving decimals;
- how to use subtraction to solve problems involving decimals;
- how to work backwards to solve problems involving decimals.

★ **Building Stamina®**: This section gives you a chance to sharpen your skills with decimals, and to strengthen your test-taking abilities.

Chapter 3 Fractions
In Chapter 3 you will study and practice:

- how to generate equivalent forms of rational numbers including fractions;
- how to generate equivalent forms of rational numbers including fractions and mixed numbers;
- how to generate equivalent forms of rational numbers including fractions and decimals;
- how to compare fractions and mixed numbers;
- how to add fractions and mixed numbers;
- how to subtract fractions and mixed numbers;
- how to solve a difficult problem by working a simpler problem.

★ **Building Stamina®**: This section gives you a chance to sharpen your skills with fractions, and to strengthen your test-taking abilities.

Chapter 4 Patterns, Relationships, and Functions

In Chapter 4 you will study and practice:

- how to use a table and symbols to represent and describe relationships; involving proportional reasoning;
- how to generate an equation from a problem situation;
- how to write a formula to represent relationships involving perimeter and area from a table of data;
- how to use the data in tables to solve problems.
- ★ **Building Stamina®**: This section gives you a chance to sharpen your skills with patterns, relationships, and functions, and to strengthen your test-taking abilities.

Chapter 5 Ratio, Proportion, and Percent

In Chapter 5 you will study and practice:

- how to represent ratios with concrete models, fractions, and decimals;
- how to represent equivalent ratios and ratios as rates;
- how to use ratios to describe proportional relationships;
- how to represent percents with concrete models, fractions, and decimals;
- how to solve problems with a Guess and Check strategy.
- ★ **Building Stamina®**: This section gives you a chance to sharpen your skills with ratio, proportion, and percent, and to strengthen your test-taking abilities.

Focus on TEKS

Lesson 1 Add and Subtract Whole Numbers

TEKS 6.2D Estimate and round to approximate reasonable results and solve problems where exact answers are not required.
TEKS 6.11A Identify and apply mathematics to everyday experiences.

You can add to find how many in all. You can subtract to compare or to find how many are left.

Guided Instruction

Problem 1

Texas Stadium, home of the Dallas Cowboys, has a capacity of 65,675. Gillette Stadium, home of the New England Patriots, has a seating capacity of 68,756. Which stadium has the greater capacity? How much greater?

Compare the numbers. Then subtract the lesser number from the greater number.

Step 1 Compare 65,675 and 68,756.
Which number is greater? ________________

Step 2 Line up the digits in both numbers by matching place values. Subtract the ones. Regroup 1 hundred as 10 tens. Then subtract the tens.

```
      15
  68,756
− 65,675
```

Step 3 Continue subtracting from right to left. Regroup as needed. Place a comma after the thousands in your answer.

```
     615
  68,756
− 65,675
      81
```

Solution Which stadium has the greater capacity? How much greater?

____

Another Problem

Problem 2

One weekend, 45,652 people attended a game in Texas Stadium. The next weekend, 51,018 attended a game there. To the nearest thousand, about how many people attended the two games?

Estimate and add to find the total.

Step 1 Round each number to the nearest thousand.
45,652 rounds to 46,000. 51,018 rounds to 51,000.

```
  46,000
+ 51,000
```

Step 2 Add the rounded numbers.

Solution About how many people attended the two games? ________________

Apply the TEKS

Estimate. Then find each sum or difference.

1. 2,317 + 4,539

2. 8,306 − 2,178

3. 72,492 − 5,608

4. 56,829 + 6,005 + 3,377

5. 712,738 + 415,555

6. 945,526 − 129,666

7. 854,002 − 6,119

8. 642 + 3,920 + 246,983

Use the table for Problems 9–11.

Theme Park Attendance Last Year

Theme Park	Number of Adults	Number of Children
Woody's Wild West	327,880	424,982
Sam's Sea Show	356,901	398,251
Hawaiian Holiday	85,362	15,977

9. What was the total attendance at Sam's Sea Show last year?

____

10. How many more adults than children went to Hawaiian Holiday last year? ___________________

11. Which park had the greater total attendance last year, Woody's Wild West or Sam's Sea Show? How much greater?

____

Explain how you found your answer.

____

____

____

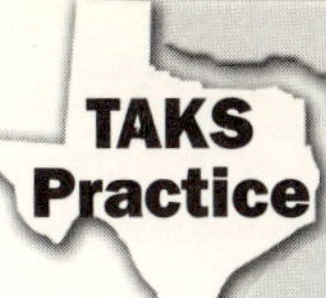

TAKS Objective 1 The student will demonstrate an understanding of numbers, operations, and quantitative reasoning. **TEKS 6.2D**

TAKS Objective 6 The student will demonstrate an understanding of the mathematical processes and tools used in problem solving. **TEKS 6.11A**

DIRECTIONS Read each question. Then circle the letter for the correct answer.

1 Mount McKinley is 20,320 feet high. It is 6,792 feet higher than which of these peaks?

A Gannet Peak, 13,804 feet

B Kings Peak, 13,528 feet

C Wheeler Peak, 13,161 feet

D Borah Peak, 12,662 feet

2 One weekend, 322,284 people saw the movie *Wrap Up* on Saturday. There were 540,078 people who saw the movie on Sunday. About how many people saw the movie that weekend?

F 960,000

G 860,000

H 760,000

J 220,000

3 A factory manager has $300,000 to spend on new equipment. If he buys a $257,356 gasket machine, which other piece of equipment can he buy?

A A $42,500 widget welder

B A $45,200 basic bolt maker

C A $52,400 pneumatic hammer

D A $65,030 laser level

Which expression does NOT have the same sum as the others?

F 15,369 + 62,663

G 47,932 + 41,942

H 25,005 + 53,027

J 38,544 + 39,488

The amounts earned by four university fundraisers are shown in the table below.

Fundraiser	Amount Earned
Alpha	$158,329
Beta	$162,368
Chi	$144.008
Omega	$137,699

Which two fundraisers earned a total of $302,337?

A Alpha and Beta

B Beta and Omega

C Chi and Alpha

D Omega and Chi

For which pair of numbers is the difference greatest?

F 793,261; 109,993

G 793,261; 376,310

H 793,261; 443,226

J 793,261; 583,553

Focus on TEKS

Lesson 2 Multiples and Common Multiples

TEKS 6.1F Identify multiples of a positive integer and common multiples and the least common multiple of a set of positive integers.
TEKS 6.2C Use multiplication of whole numbers to solve problems.

You can multiply a number by 1, 2, 3, and so on to find multiples of a number.

A **multiple** of a number is the product of that number times any whole number other than zero. A **common multiple** is a number that is a multiple of two or more given numbers. A **least common multiple (LCM)** is the least number that is a common multiple of two or more given numbers.

Guided Instruction

Problem 1 On its 16th anniversary, Theater 16 is giving a prize with every 16th ticket sold. Todd's ticket is number 136. Will he get a prize?

Look for multiples of 16.

Step 1 Complete the chart to find multiples of 16.

1 × 16	2 × 16	3 × 16	4 × 16	5 × 16	6 × 16	7 × 16	8 × 16	9 × 16
16	32	48						

Step 2 Compare 136 to the multiples of 16. Is 136 a multiple of 16? ___________

Solution Will Todd get a prize? ____________

Problem 2 Anna winds her grandfather clock every 6 days and her grandmother clock every 4 days. If she winds both clocks today, in how many days will she next wind both clocks?

Look for multiples that are common to both numbers, then find the least common multiple (LCM).

Step 1 Find multiples of 6. What are the first ten multiples of 6?

____

Step 2 Find multiples of 4. What are the first ten multiples of 4?

____

Step 3 Look for common multiples, numbers that are multiples of both 6 and 4. What numbers are common multiples of 6 and 4? ________________

Step 4 Find the least common multiple, the least number that is a common multiple of both numbers. What is the least common multiple? ____________

Solution In how many days will Anna next wind both her grandfather clock and her grandmother clock? ______________

Apply the TEKS **Write the first six multiples of each number.**

1. 3

____

2. 6

____

3. 15

____

4. 20

____

5. 12

____

6. 9

____

Circle the common multiples of the two numbers. Then find the least common multiple.

7. 3 and 9 3 6 9 12 18 24 27 30

least common multiple: ________

8. 6 and 15 12 18 30 45 54 60 72 75

least common multiple: ________

9. 12 and 8 16 24 32 36 40 48 56 60

least common multiple: ________

Solve each problem.

10. Lucy is surveying every fifth person who comes out of the grocery store. Mr. Watkins is the 72nd person out of the grocery store. Will he be surveyed? ___________

11. If Brian touches every 6th fence post and Carla touches every 9th fence post, what is the number of the first fence post both will touch? ___________

12. There are 8 party plates in a package. There are 12 party napkins in a package. What is the least number of plates and napkins you can buy to get one napkin for each plate? How many packages of each will you buy?

____

Explain how you solved the problem.

____

____

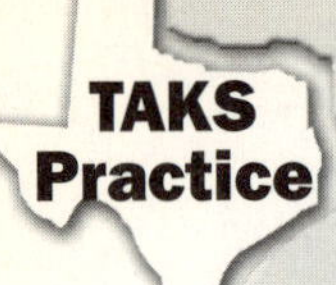

TAKS Objective 1 The student will demonstrate an understanding of numbers, operations, and quantitative reasoning. TEKS 6.1F, **6.2C**

DIRECTIONS Read each question. Then circle the letter for the correct answer.

1 Which number is a common multiple of both 8 and 12?

A 16

B 40

C 48

D 54

2 Tina needs 16 inches of ribbon for each May basket she makes. Which package of ribbon should she buy so she has no ribbon left over?

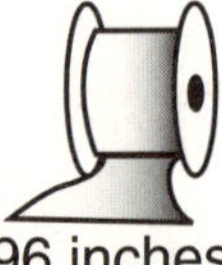

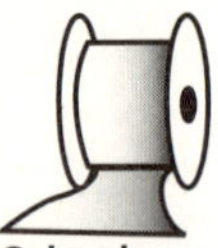

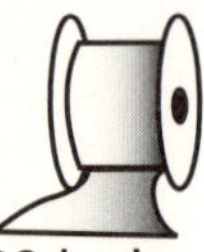

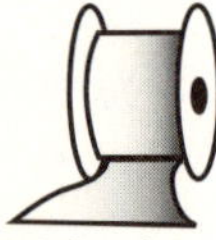

What is the least common multiple of 4, 6, and 8?

A 8

B 12

C 16

D 24

4 Paul tests every 5th appliance that comes off the assembly line and Marsha tests every 9th appliance. Which gives the numbers of appliances that will be tested by both?

F 14 and 59

G 20 and 45

H 45 and 90

J 54 and 72

Robert waters his orchid plant every 5 days and his African violet every 6 days. If he waters both plants on May 1, on what date will he next water both plants?

A May 6

B May 11

C May 26

D May 31

6 70 is a common multiple of which pair of numbers?

F 3 and 5

G 5 and 7

H 7 and 9

J 20 and 35

Focus on TEKS

Lesson 3 Multiply Whole Numbers

TEKS 6.2C Use multiplication of whole numbers to solve problems.

You can multiply to find how many in all.

The answer when you multiply is called the **product**.

The numbers you multiply to get the product are called **factors**.

When multiplying by 3-digit numbers, the product after multiplying by ones, after multiplying by tens, or after multiplying by hundreds is called a **partial product**.

Guided Instruction

Problem

There are 145 students in the sixth grade. They want to go on a class trip. The cost for each student will be $234. How much money does the sixth grade need to earn so that everyone can go on the trip?

Multiply to find the total.

Step 1 Multiply by the ones. Regroup as needed.
What two numbers did you multiply?

____

What is the partial product?

____

$$\begin{array}{r} \$234 \\ \times\ 145 \\ \hline \end{array}$$

Step 2 Multiply by the tens. Regroup as needed.
What two numbers did you multiply?

____

What is the partial product?

____

$$\begin{array}{r} \scriptstyle \not{1}\not{2} \\ \$234 \\ \times\ 145 \\ \hline 1170 \end{array}$$

Step 3 Multiply by the hundreds. Regroup as needed.
What two numbers did you multiply?

____

What is the partial product?

____

$$\begin{array}{r} \scriptstyle \not{1}\not{1} \\ \scriptstyle \not{1}\not{2} \\ \$234 \\ \times\ 145 \\ \hline 1170 \\ 9360 \end{array}$$

Step 4 Add the partial products. Insert a comma between the hundreds and thousands place. Write the dollar sign.

Solution

How much money does the class need to go on the trip? ____________

Apply the TEKS **Find each product.**

1. $\begin{array}{r} 45 \\ \times\ 37 \\ \hline \end{array}$

2. $\begin{array}{r} 82 \\ \times\ 37 \\ \hline \end{array}$

3. $\begin{array}{r} 416 \\ \times\ 77 \\ \hline \end{array}$

4. $\begin{array}{r} 538 \\ \times\ 49 \\ \hline \end{array}$

5. $\begin{array}{r} 638 \\ \times\ 334 \\ \hline \end{array}$

6. $\begin{array}{r} 579 \\ \times\ 146 \\ \hline \end{array}$

7. $\begin{array}{r} 2{,}573 \\ \times\ \quad 357 \\ \hline \end{array}$

8. $\begin{array}{r} 1{,}605 \\ \times\ \quad 532 \\ \hline \end{array}$

9. 89 × 86

10. 57 × 195

11. 738 × 558

Solve each problem.

12. Each of the new benches in a botanical garden cost $380. What is the total cost of 455 new benches? ____________________

13. There are 1,244 seats in a concert hall. If the concert hall is filled for each of 18 concerts, what is the total number of people who attended the concerts? ____________________

14. There are 365 days in a year. There are 24 hours in a day. There are 60 minutes in an hour. How many minutes are there in a year? ____________________

15. If you multiply two three-digit numbers, what is the greatest product you can get? ____________________

Explain how you found your answer.

____

____

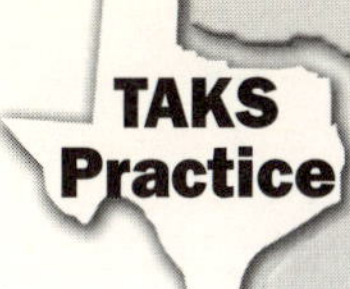

TAKS Objective 1 The student will demonstrate an understanding of numbers, operations, and quantitative reasoning.
TEKS 6.2C

DIRECTIONS Read each question. Then circle the letter for the correct answer.

1 There are 144 pencils in a gross. A school district ordered 325 gross of pencils. How many pencils is that?

- **A** 46,800
- **B** 45,744
- **C** 5,850
- **D** 4,550

2 An airplane ticket to Japan costs $1,019. How much will it cost for the 18 members of a baseball team to fly to Japan?

- **F** $9,171
- **G** $18,119
- **H** $18,342
- **J** $91,062

3 Which of the following statements is true?

- **A** $413 \times 225 < 3{,}261 \times 28$
- **B** $413 \times 225 = 3{,}261 \times 28$
- **C** $413 \times 225 > 3{,}261 \times 28$
- **D** $413 \times 28 > 3{,}261 \times 225$

4 For which of these multiplication expressions will the product be odd?

- **F** 756×441
- **G** $4{,}326 \times 96$
- **H** 667×792
- **J** $7{,}213 \times 55$

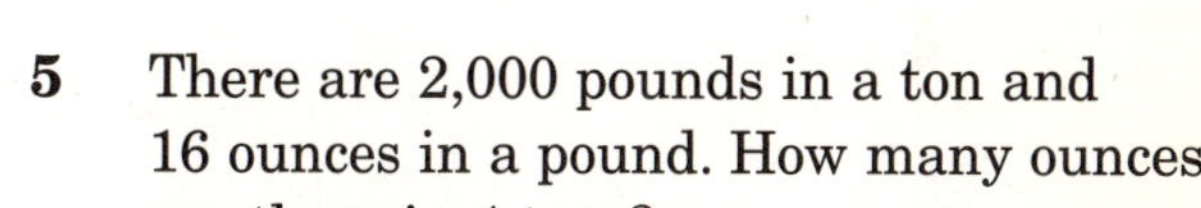

5 There are 2,000 pounds in a ton and 16 ounces in a pound. How many ounces are there in 4 tons?

- **A** 80,000
- **B** 128,000
- **C** 160,000
- **D** 328,000

6 Which of the following has the greatest product?

- **F** 436×162
- **G** 277×229
- **H** 307×198
- **J** 119×558

Focus on TEKS

Lesson 4 Factors and Common Factors

TEKS 6.1E Identify factors of a positive integer, common factors, and the greatest common factor of a set of positive integers.
TEKS 6.2C Use division of whole numbers to solve problems.

You can divide to find the factors of a number.

Factors are numbers multiplied together to get a product. A **common factor** is a number that is a factor of two or more given numbers. The **greatest common factor (GCF)** of two or more numbers is the greatest whole number that is a factor of each of the numbers.

Guided Instruction

Problem 1 Grace has 8 lilies and 12 roses. She wants to use all the flowers to make bouquets so that each has an equal number of lilies and each has an equal number of roses. How many bouquets can she make? Describe them.

You can divide to find the factors of both numbers. Then look for common factors to decide how many bouquets to make.

Step 1 Find the factors of 8. What numbers can evenly divide 8?

____

Into how many bouquets can 8 flowers be divided so that each bouquet has the same number of flowers? _______________

Step 2 Find the factors of 12. What numbers can evenly divide 12?

____

Into how many bouquets can 12 flowers be divided so that each bouquet has the same number of flowers? _______________

Step 3 Look for factors that are common to both 8 and 12. What numbers are factors of both 8 and 12? _______________

Solution How many bouquets can Grace make? _______________

____

Problem 2 Find the greatest common factor (GCF) of 28 and 52.

Step 1 Find the factors of both numbers.

28: _______________

52: _______________

Step 2 List the factors from least to greatest and circle the common factors.

28: _______________

52: _______________

What is the greatest whole number that is a factor of each of the numbers? _____

Solution The GCF of 28 and 52 is _____.

Apply the TEKS **List the factors for each number. Find the common factors for each pair of numbers. Then find the greatest common factor.**

1. Factors of 9 ____________

Factors of 12 ____________

Common factors ____________

Greatest common factor ________

2. Factors of 10 ____________

Factors of 4 ____________

Common factors ____________

Greatest common factor ________

3. Factors of 15 ____________

Factors of 18 ____________

Common factors ____________

Greatest common factor ________

4. Factors of 7 ____________

Factors of 8 ____________

Common factors ____________

Greatest common factor ________

5. Factors of 20 ____________

Factors of 24 ____________

Common factors ____________

Greatest common factor ________

6. Factors of 16 ____________

Factors of 6 ____________

Common factors ____________

Greatest common factor ________

Write true or false for each statement.

7. Two is a factor of all even numbers. ________

8. Any number that has 2 as a factor also has 4 as a factor. ________

9. Any number that has 4 as a factor also has 2 as a factor. ________

10. One is a common factor for any pair of numbers. ________

Solve each problem.

11. If you use all the cards in a standard deck of 52 cards, how many equal groups of cards can be made? How many cards will be in each group?

____

____

12. Riverdale School Chorus has 48 sixth graders and 64 fifth graders. For the Spring Concert, the fifth and sixth graders will be in separate rows with an equal number of students in each row. What is the greatest number of students that can be in a row? ________

13. There are 15 trumpets and 20 violins in the orchestra. Into how many groups can the orchestra be divided so that there are the same number of trumpets in each group and the same number of violins in each group? ________ Explain how you found your answer.

____

____

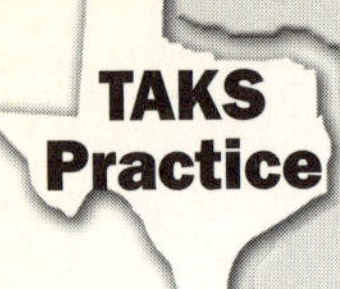

TAKS Objective 1 The student will demonstrate an understanding of numbers, operations, and quantitative reasoning.
TEKS 6.1E, 6.2C

DIRECTIONS Read each question. Then circle the letter for the correct answer.

1 Which lists all of the factors of 42?

- **A** 1, 2, 3, 6, 7, 14, 21, 42
- **B** 3, 7, 21, 42
- **C** 1, 6, 7, 42
- **D** 3, 6, 7, 14

2 Which of the following are common factors of 24 and 36?

- **F** 1, 2, 3, 4, 6, 8, 9, 12, 18, 24, 36
- **G** 1, 2, 3, 6, 8, 12, 18, 24
- **H** 1, 2, 3, 6, 8, 12, 18
- **J** 1, 2, 3, 4, 6, 12

3 There are 21 boys and 24 girls in a club. How many committees can be formed so there are the same number of boys on each committee and the same number of girls on each committee?

- **A** 3
- **B** 4
- **C** 6
- **D** 7

4 Any number that has 6 as a factor also has which of these numbers as factors?

- **F** 1 and 5
- **G** 2 and 3
- **H** 3 and 4
- **J** 5 and 6

5 Bill has 24 baseball cards, 18 football cards, and 30 basketball cards. Into how many groups can he divide the cards so that each group will have the same number of cards for each sport?

- **A** 4
- **B** 6
- **C** 8
- **D** 12

6 Which number is the greatest common factor of 16 and 24?

- **F** 16
- **G** 8
- **H** 4
- **J** 2

Focus on TEKS

Lesson 5 Prime Factorization

TEKS 6.1D Write prime factorizations using exponents.

You can write a composite number as the product of prime numbers.

A **prime number** is a whole number greater than 1 *with only two factors*, itself and one. A **composite number** is a whole number greater than 1 *with more than two factors*. A composite number written as the product of prime numbers is called the **prime factorization** of the number. The prime factorization of 56 is $2 \times 2 \times 2 \times 7$. Using exponents, the prime factorization of 56 is $2^3 \times 7$. This can also be written as $2^3 \cdot 7$.

An **exponent** tells how many times a number is used as a factor. $2^3 = 2 \times 2 \times 2$ (exponent: 3)

Guided Instruction

Problem What is the prime factorization of 180?

You can draw a factor tree to find the prime factorization of a number.

Step 1 Write 180 as the product of two factors.
Are the two factors prime? ________

180
20 × ____

Step 2 Write each factor as the product of two factors.
Are all of the factors prime? ________

180
20 × 9
4 × ____ 3 × ____

Step 3 Continue writing each factor as a product of two factors until all of the factors are prime numbers.
Circle the prime factors.

180
20 × 9
4 × 5 3 × 3
2 × ____

Step 4 Write a multiplication to show the prime factorization.
List the factors in order from least to greatest.

____

Step 5 When a factor is repeated, you can write the product using exponents.
How can you write 2 × 2 using exponents? ________
How can you write 3 × 3 using exponents? ________

Solution What is the prime factorization of 180? ______________________

Apply the TEKS

Tell whether each number is prime or composite.

1. 15 ____________

2. 17 ____________

3. 26 ____________

4. 29 ____________

5. 77 ____________

Complete each factor tree.

6. 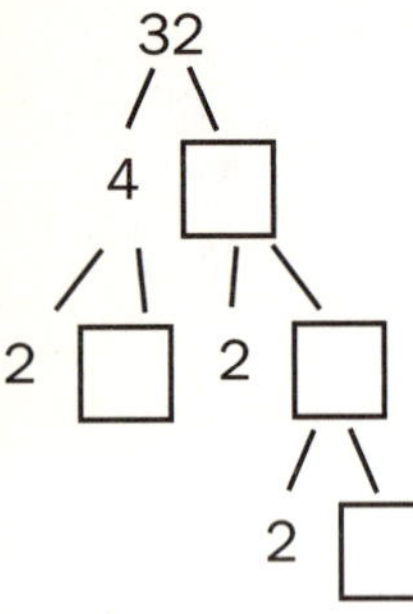

7. 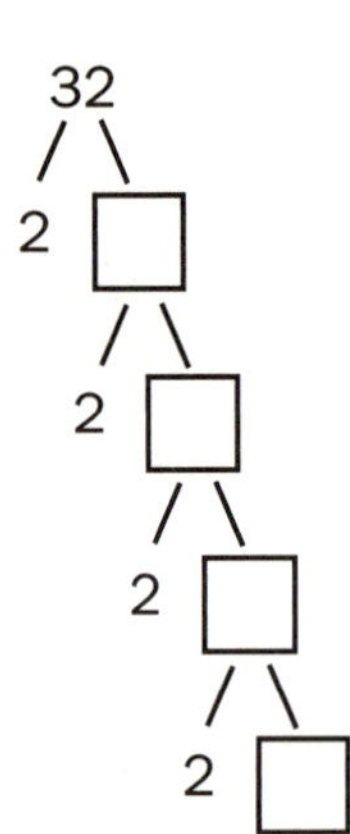

8. 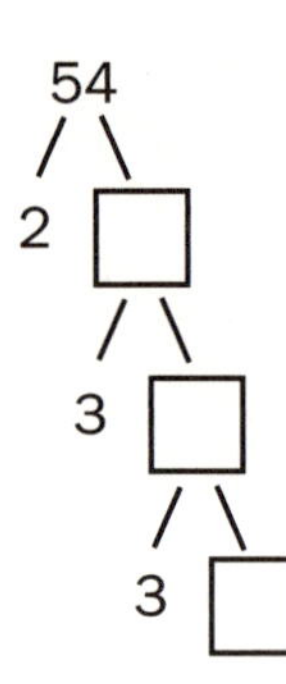

9. 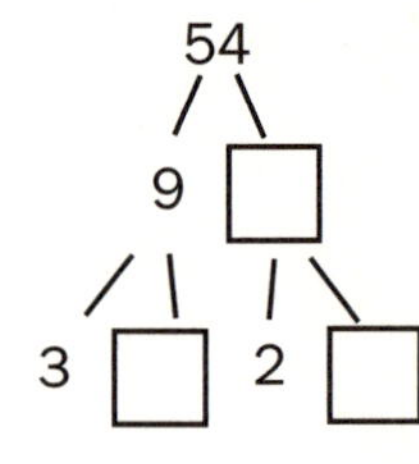

Draw a factor tree for each number. Then write the prime factorization for the number. Use exponents when possible.

10. 16

prime factorization: ____________

11. 40

prime factorization: ____________

12. 63

prime factorization: ____________

13. 150

prime factorization: ____________

14. 70

prime factorization: ____________

15. 98

prime factorization: ____________

Use exponents to write the prime factorization of each number. Draw a factor tree if you want to.

16. 81 ____________

17. 144 ____________

18. 400 ____________

19. 1,350 ____________

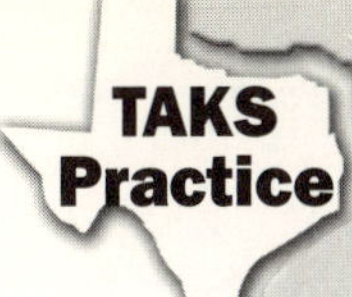

TAKS Objective 1 The student will demonstrate an understanding of numbers, operations, and quantitative reasoning.
TEKS 6.1D

DIRECTIONS Read each question. Then circle the letter for the correct answer.

1 Which is the prime factorization of 45?

A $2^3 \cdot 5$

B $3^2 \cdot 5$

C $9 \cdot 5$

D $3 \cdot 5^2$

2 Which is another way to write $3 \times 5 \times 5 \times 5 \times 7 \times 7$?

F $3 \cdot 5^7$

G $5^3 \cdot 7^3$

H $1 \cdot 3^5 \cdot 2^7$

J $3 \cdot 5^3 \cdot 7^2$

3 $2^3 \times 3^2$ is the prime factorization for which number?

A 24

B 48

C 72

D 108

Which is NOT a prime factorization?

F $2^3 \cdot 3 \cdot 5^2$

G $4^2 \cdot 5^3$

H $2 \cdot 7 \cdot 11$

J $2 \cdot 3 \cdot 5^3 \cdot 13$

Which is NOT a factor tree for 24?

A

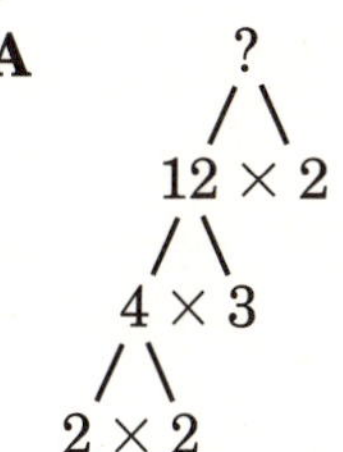

B

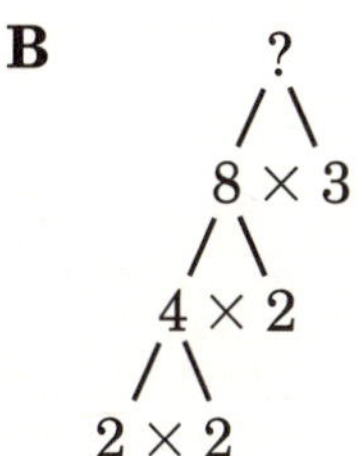

C

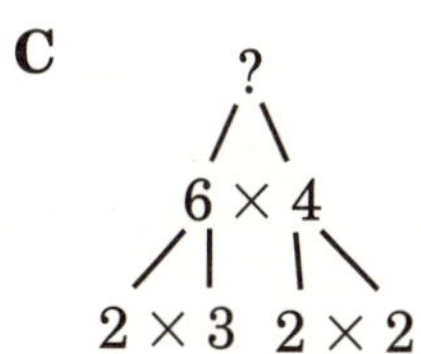

D

?

3×9

3×3

Focus on TEKS

Lesson 6 Divide Whole Numbers

TEKS 6.2C Use division of whole numbers to solve problems.

You can divide to find how many in each group or how many groups.

In a division problem, the number you divide is the **dividend**. The number you divide by is the **divisor**, and your answer is the **quotient**. A **remainder** is the amount left over after dividing. The remainder is always less than the divisor.

Guided Instruction

Problem One year a music store sold 3,224 used CDs. What is the average number of used CDs that were sold in each of the 52 weeks that year?

To divide greater numbers by one-digit or multi-digit divisors, repeat these steps: divide, multiply, subtract, compare, and bring down.

60
50)3,000

Step 1 Estimate the quotient.
Use your estimate to decide where to place the first digit of the quotient. The first digit of the quotient should be in the _________ place.

```
       6
52 )3,224
  − 3 12
      10
```

Step 2 Divide the tens. Write the number in the tens place of the quotient. Multiply the divisor by the number of tens in the quotient. Subtract.

Compare. 10 < 52

```
       6
52 )3,224
  − 3 12↓
      104
    −____
```

Step 3 Bring down the next digit in the dividend. Divide the ones. Write the number in the ones place of the quotient. Multiply the divisor by the number of ones in the quotient. Subtract. If the difference is zero, there is no remainder.

Solution What is the average number of used CDs the store sold each week? _________

Other Examples

A

```
       682 R1
34 )23,189
  − 204
     278
   − 272
      69
    − 68
       1
```

Repeat these Steps:
Divide
Multiply
Subtract
Compare
Bring Down
Write the remainder, if any, in the quotient.

B

```
      2,330 R19
23 )53,609
  − 46
     76
   − 69
      70
    − 69
      19
```

Apply the TEKS **Find each quotient. If there is a remainder, write *R* and the remainder after the quotient.**

1. 752 ÷ 32

2. 648 ÷ 72

3. 951 ÷ 28

4. 449 ÷ 64

5. $41\overline{)4{,}521}$

6. $62\overline{)3{,}410}$

7. $83\overline{)45{,}261}$

8. $45\overline{)82{,}395}$

Solve each problem.

9. A theater troop has 672 costumes. Twelve costumes are stored in each clothing bag. How many bags are needed? ____________

10. Troy got a loan of $7,632 for a used car. If he repays the loan in 24 equal payments, how much will each payment be? ____________

11. Each of the 22 sections of a stadium has the same number of seats. The total number of seats in the stadium is 67,848. How many seats are in each section? ____________

12. 315 people are going on a bus trip. Each bus holds 28 people. How many buses are needed? ____________

Explain your reasoning.

____

____

____

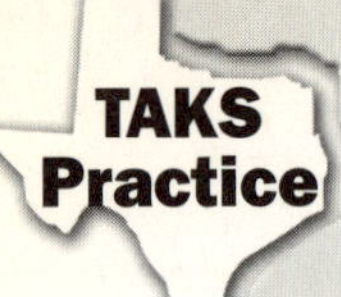

TAKS Objective 1 The student will demonstrate an understanding of numbers, operations, and quantitative reasoning.
TEKS 6.2C

DIRECTIONS Read each question. Then circle the letter for the correct answer.

1 Beth drove 2,880 miles in 60 hours. What is the average number of miles she drove per hour?

Record your answer and fill in the bubbles on the grid below. Be sure to use the correct place value.

				.		
0	0	0	0		0	0
1	1	1	1		1	1
2	2	2	2		2	2
3	3	3	3		3	3
4	4	4	4		4	4
5	5	5	5		5	5
6	6	6	6		6	6
7	7	7	7		7	7
8	8	8	8		8	8
9	9	9	9		9	9

What is the greatest possible remainder for a divisor of 76 and a dividend of any number?

F 67

G 70

H 75

J 76

Barbara needs one roll for each of the 387 people who are coming to a banquet. How many packages of 24 rolls should she buy?

A 8

B 16

C 17

D 24

Stan worked 38 hours one week and 18 hours the next week. He earned a total of $1,456. How much does he earn per hour?

F $26

G $32

H $38

J $81

For which division expression is the reminder 37?

A 949 ÷ 19

B 1,666 ÷ 33

C 2,362 ÷ 40

D 2,809 ÷ 42

6 One week a factory produced 16,380 wheels. The wheels are shipped in boxes of 18. How many boxes of wheels were shipped that week?

F 91

G 901

H 910

J 1,000

Focus on TEKS

Lesson 7 Estimating

TEKS 6.2D Estimate and round to approximate reasonable results and to solve problems where exact answers are not required.

You can estimate when you do not need an exact answer.

Guided Instruction

Problem 1

Grace is renovating her kitchen. She plans to buy a refrigerator that costs $887, a dishwasher that costs $479, and a microwave oven that costs $129. About how much money does she need to purchase these three appliances?

You can round each amount to the nearest $100 to estimate the total.

Step 1 Round numbers with tens digits 1, 2, 3, 4 down to the nearest hundred dollars. Round numbers with tens digits 5, 6, 7, 8, 9 up to the nearest hundred dollars.

What is 887 rounded to the nearest hundred? ____________

What is 479 rounded to the nearest hundred? ____________

What is 129 rounded to the nearest hundred? ____________

Step 2 Find the sum of the rounded numbers.

What is the sum of 900 + 500 + 100? ____________

Solution

About how much money does she need to purchase these three appliances?

____

Problem 2

One year 4,177 cans of food were eaten by cats at the humane society. About how many cans of cat food is that per week?

You can use compatible numbers to estimate the quotient.

Step 1 Think of a basic fact that can help you estimate 4,177 ÷ 52.

[4,1] 77 ÷ [5] 2

What basic fact is close to 41 ÷ 5? ____________

Step 2 Use the basic fact and place value. Estimate the quotient.

What is 40 ÷ 5? ____________

What is 4,000 ÷ 50? ____________

Solution

About how many cans of cat food did the humane society use each week? ____________

Apply the TEKS **Estimate to decide if the solution to each problem is reasonable. Write *yes* if the answer is reasonable and *no* if it is not reasonable.**

1. 563 + 294 = 700 ________

2. 4,562 − 1,727 = 2,835 ________

3. 77 × 83 = 6,391 ________

4. 5,581 ÷ 8 = 67 R5 ________

5. 428 × 36 = 1,548 ________

6. 3,389 ÷ 77 = 44 R1 ________

7. 1,253 + 891 = 3,144 ________

8. 1,893 − 531 = 362 ________

Estimate to answer each problem.

9. When Sandy visited India, 47 Indian rupees equaled one U.S. dollar. Sandy paid 1,463 rupees for a small statue. About how many U.S. dollars was that?

____

10. Nick spends $38 a week for lunches. About how much does he spend each year for lunches?

____

11. A factory has an order for 4,120 bolts. So far 1,877 bolts have been produced. Is the order more or less than half completed?

____

12. The Spanish club has 33 members. The club is planning its trip to Mexico. Bus tickets cost $48 for each student. Meals and other expenses will cost another $48 per student. About how much money will the trip cost the club?

____

Explain how you found your answer.

____

____

____

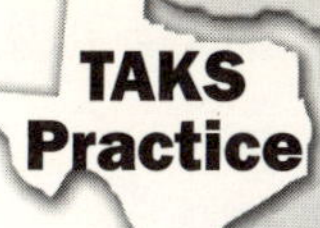

TAKS Objective 1 The student will demonstrate an understanding of numbers, operations, and quantitative reasoning.
TEKS 6.2D

DIRECTIONS Read each question. Then circle the letter for the correct answer.

1 Rhonda has 18 weeks to save $489 for her ticket to Alaska. If she saves $20 per week, which statement is true?

A Rhonda will have more than enough money for the trip.

B Rhonda will have exactly enough money for the trip.

C Rhonda will not have enough money for the trip.

D Rhonda will need another $10 for her ticket.

2 Ms. Parks needs 1,512 award pins. If pins come in boxes of 48, about how many boxes will she need to buy?

F 30

G 50

H 150

J 300

3 Ben exchanged 175 U.S. dollars for Japanese yen. The exchange rate was 119 yen for each dollar. Which is the best estimate of the number of yen Ben received?

A 2,000

B 10,000

C 17,500

D 20,000

4 The chart below shows the cost of items at the local store. Gloria has $100.

Shirts	$33 each
Hats	$12 each
Belts	$21 each
Coats	$49 each

Which group of items can she buy?

F 4 shirts

G a hat, 2 shirts, a coat

H 3 shirts, a belt

J 2 belts, 4 hats

5 If the Wilsons drive at an average speed of 48 miles per hour, about how many hours will it take them to drive 330 miles?

A About 60

B About 6

C About 4

D About 3

6 There were 8,215 books checked out of the library on Monday. On Tuesday there were 6,429 books checked out. Which is the best estimate of how many more books were checked out on Monday than on Tuesday?

F 1,000

G 1,300

H 2,000

J 3,000

Focus on TEKS

Lesson 8 Integers

TEKS 6.1C Use integers to represent real-life situations.

TEKS 6.11A Identify and apply mathematics to everyday experiences, to activities in and outside of school, with other disciplines, and with other mathematical topics.

You can use positive and negative integers to represent real-life situations.

The set of **integers** is the set of whole numbers and the opposites of the nonzero whole numbers; that is, . . . −3, −2, −1, 0, 1, 2, 3, . . .

Positive numbers are numbers greater than zero. **Negative numbers** are numbers less than zero. Zero is neither positive nor negative.

Negative Integers	Positive Integers
6 feet below sea level ⟶ −6	temperature rose 7 degrees ⟶ +7
a drop of 3 degrees ⟶ −3	5,000 feet above sea level ⟶ +5,000
a loss of 4 yards ⟶ −4	a gain of 4 yards ⟶ +4

Guided Instruction

Problem 1

The highest recorded temperature for Texas occurred on August 12, 1936 in Seymour. The temperature was one hundred twenty degrees Fahrenheit. The lowest recorded temperature for Texas occurred on February 8, 1933 in Seminole. The temperature was 23 degrees below zero Fahrenheit. What integers represent these temperatures?

You can show that an integer is positive by writing a + sign in front of it.
You can show that an integer is negative by writing a − sign in front of it.
If an integer other than zero does not have a sign, it is assumed to be positive.

Step 1 Write a positive integer that describes the highest recorded temperature in Seymour. ____________

Step 2 Write a negative integer that describes the lowest recorded temperature in Seminole. ____________

Solution

What is the highest recorded temperature for Texas? ____________

What is the lowest recorded temperature for Texas? ____________

Problem 2

At noon, the temperature in Crawford was 74°F. Two hours later, the temperature had increased 13°F. During the next 5 hours, the temperature decreased 10°F. What expression represents the change in temperature?

Step 1 Use positive and negative integers to represent each temperature.

temperature at noon ____________

temperature at 2 P.M. increased by 13°F ____________

temperature at 7 A.M. decreased by 10°F ____________

Step 2 Write an expression to represent the change in temperature.

____

Solution

What expression represents the change in temperature? ____________

Apply the TEKS **Write an integer to represent each situation.**

1. 68 degrees above zero

____

2. 3 degrees below zero

____

3. 77 feet below sea level

____

4. 12 feet above sea level

____

5. gaining 6 points in a game

____

6. a 14-foot drop

____

7. a $30 loss

____

8. earnings of $28

____

Solve each problem.

9. A fish is located ten feet below sea level. What integer can you write to represent the location of the fish? _____________

10. Alison is recording each play in a football game. What integer can she write to represent a loss of nine yards? _____________

11. A baby gained four pounds. What integer can you write to show the change in the baby's weight? _____________

12. Rose withdrew $100 from her savings account. What integer can she write to represent the withdrawal? _____________

13. A diver descends 14 feet below the surface of the water. She wants to photograph a school of fish that are 25 feet below her. Write an expression that can be used to find the depth of the school of fish. _____________

14. A repairman got on an elevator 3 floors above ground level. The elevator went down 2 floors, went up 14 floors, and then went down 6 floors. Then the repairman got off the elevator. Write an expression that can be used to find the floor of the building on which the repairman last stopped. _______________________

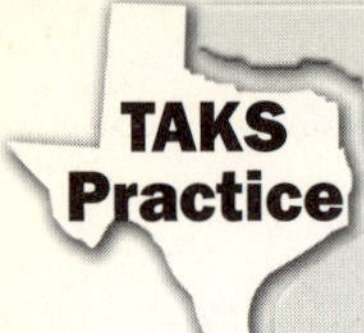

TAKS Objective 1 The student will demonstrate an understanding of numbers, operations, and quantitative reasoning.
TEKS 6.1C

TAKS Objective 6 The student will demonstrate an understanding of the mathematical process and tools used in problem solving.
TEKS 6.11A

DIRECTIONS Read each question. Then circle the letter for the correct answer.

1 Victoria's savings decreased by forty-three dollars. Which integer represents the decrease?

A 43

B −43

C +43

D −34

2 Which integer can be used to show a gain of twenty-four tons?

F +24

G +20

H −20

J −24

3 Which expression is NOT be represented by −20?

A A loss of 20 points

B 20 degrees below zero

C Driving 20 miles

D An elevation 20 feet below sea level

4 During a storm, the Chanagua River rose 4 feet and then later dropped 5 feet and then 1 foot to its current depth. Which expression can be used to find the change in the depth of the river?

F $4 - 5 + 2$

G $-4 + 5 - 1$

H $-4 - 5 + 1$

J $4 - 5 - 1$

5 Joe's score in a game was −4. On his next turn he got 4 points. Then he lost 2 points. Which expression can be used to find Joe's total score?

A $8 - 2$

B $4 + 4 + 2$

C $-4 + 4 - 2$

D $4 - 4 + 2$

6 During one week, José made a deposit of 200 dollars, a withdrawal of 40 dollars, a withdrawal of 70 dollars, and a deposit of 20 dollars. Which expression can be used to find the change in José's balance during the week?

F $-200 + 40 + 70 - 20$

G $200 - 40 - 70 + 20$

H $-200 - 40 - 70 + 20$

J Not Here

Focus on TEKS

Lesson 9 Order of Operations

TEKS 6.2E Use order of operations to simplify whole number expressions (without exponents) in problem solving situations.

You can use the order of operations to simplify a numerical expression.

Order of Operations

1. Work within parentheses.
2. Multiply or divide in order from left to right.
3. Add or subtract in order from left to right.

A **numerical expression** is a combination of numbers and symbols for the operations of addition, subtraction, multiplication, or division.

Guided Instruction

Problem 1 Use the order of operations to simply the expression: $3 + 4 \times (5 \times 2)$

Follow the order of operations.

Step 1 Work within parentheses.

$3 + 4 \times (5 \times 2) = 3 + 4 \times$ ________

Step 2 Multiply or divide from left to right.

$3 + 4 \times 10 = 3 +$ ________

Step 3 Add or subtract from left to right. ________

Solution Use the order of operations to simply the expression: $3 + 4 \times (5 \times 2)$ ______

Another Example

Simplify the expression.	$90 - 18 \div (9 - 6)$
Work within the parentheses	$90 - 18 \div 3$
Multiply or divide from left to right.	$90 - 6$
Add or subtract from left to right.	84

Guided Instruction

Problem 2

Patsy collects rare coins. She bought 4 coins at a convention. Her collection had already contained 15 times that number of coins. Before placing all of her coins into albums, she divided them equally into 2 envelopes. How many coins did Patsy put into each envelope?

Write the expression. Then use the order of operations to simplify.

Step 1 Write the numerical expression to represent the problem.

(new coins bought at convention + coins already in collection) ÷ number of envelopes

↓ ↓ ↓

$(4 + 15 \times 4) \div 2$

Step 2 Work within the parentheses.

First, multiply.

$(4 + 15 \times 4) \div 2 = (4 +$ ________ $) \div 2$

Then, add.

$(4 + 60) \div 2 = ($ ________ $\div 2)$

Step 3 Next, divide.

$64 \div 2 =$ ________

Solution

How many coins did Patsy put into each envelope? ______

Another Example

Simplify the expression.	$3 \times 4 - (16 \div 4)$
Work within the parentheses.	$3 \times 4 - (4)$
Multiply	$12 - 4$
Subtract.	8

Apply the TEKS **Simplify each expression.**

1. $40 \div 8 + 2$ ________

2. $40 \div (8 + 2)$ ________

3. $400 + 3 + 9 \times 5$ ________

4. $90 - (2 + 3) - 15 \div 5$ ________

5. $30 \div 5 \div 3 + 8$ ________

6. $180 \div 6 - 2 + 6 \times 2$ ________

7. $50(2 + 5) - (5 + 4)$ ________

8. $200 - 2(8 - 3)$ ________

9. $(9 + 6)50 \div 6$ ________

10. $96 + 32 - 240 \div 8$ ________

11. $(62 + 38)4 - 100 \div 5$ ________

12. $108 \div (5 + 4) \div (10 + 2)$ ________

Place parentheses to make each sentence true.

13. $480 \div 8 \div 2 + 2 = 15$ ________________

14. $35 + 5 \times 9 - 3 = 240$ ________________

15. $8 \times 20 + 2 - 12 = 164$ ________________

16. $44 - 72 \div 12 - 3 = 36$ ________________

17. $90 \div 3 - 9 + 5 \times 2 = 2$ ________________

18. $8 + 8 \times 8 - 8 \div 8 = 8$ ________________

Solve each problem.

19. Elgin had \$35 in his wallet. He bought 6 cards at \$2.50 each and 4 pens at \$3.25 each. After he paid and put the change in his wallet, he found another \$6 in his pocket. The numerical expression to model how much money Elgin had left is: $35 - (6 \times 2.50) - (4 \times 3.25) + 6$.

    Simplify the numerical expression to find out how much money Elgin had left. __________

20. Hannah simplified the expression $9 + 4 \times (8 \times 8 - 30)$ as follows:

$$9 + 4 \times (8 \times 8 - 30) = 9 + 4 \times (64 - 30)$$
$$= 9 + 4 \times 34$$
$$= 13 \times 34$$
$$= 442$$

    a. What error did she make in simplifying the expression?

    ____

    ____

    b. What is the value of the expression when it is correctly simplified? __________

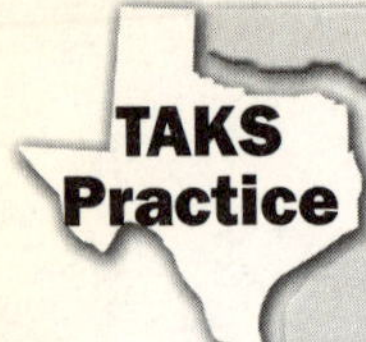

TEKS 6.2E

DIRECTIONS: Read each question. Then circle the letter for the correct answer.

1 Which expression below does NOT have the same value as $48 - 8 \times 3$?

A $8 \times (9 - 6)$

B $(4 + 2)4$

C $72 \div (9 \div 3)$

D $72 \div 9 \div 3$

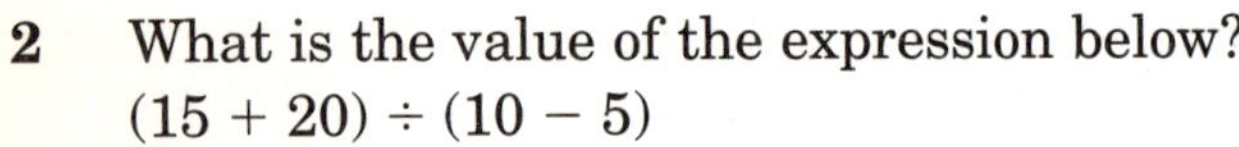

2 What is the value of the expression below?
$(15 + 20) \div (10 - 5)$

F 5

G 7

H 9

J 12

3 Which expression below has a value of 1?

A $(4 + 20) \div 4 - 40 \div 8$

B $7 + 42 \div 6 - 54 \div 9$

C $(40 + 80) \div (3 \times 5)$

D $(75 + 25) \div (5 - 1)$

4 What is the value of the expression below?
$98 - 2 \times 7 + 5 \times 5$

F 3,385

G 445

H 109

J 89

5 To find the value of $450 \div (90 - 5 \times 4)$ using the order of operations, you would first—

A divide 450 by 90

B subtract 5 from 90

C multiply 5 by 4

D divide 450 by 70

6 As you simplify each expression below, which one requires finding the quotient of 80 divided by 2?

F $4 + 6 \times 8 \div 2$

G $2 \times 5 \times 8 \div 2$

H $(2 + 5) \times 8 \div 2$

J $4 + (6 \times 8) \div 2$

Focus on TEKS

Lesson 10 PROBLEM-SOLVING STRATEGY: Make a Model to Act It Out

TEKS 6.11B Use a problem-solving model that incorporates understanding the problem, making a plan, carrying out the plan, and evaluating the solution for reasonableness.

TEKS 6.11C Select or develop an appropriate problem-solving strategy to solve a problem.

You can use models to act out a problem and solve it. Use the problem-solving guide on page 288 to help you.

Guided Instruction

Problem

What are all of the possible ways the 12 members of a band can line up in rows so that all of the rows are the same length? Describe the ways.

Understand the problem.

What are you trying to find?

____

Make a plan.

You can arrange cubes to model the ways people can line up in equal-length rows. Then record the number of rows.

Solve the problem.

Start with 1 row. Decide if 12 people can line up in 1 row with no one left over. If so, record 1. Repeat for 2 rows, 3 rows, 4 rows, and so on. What number of equal-length rows can 12 people make?

____

____

Check your answer.

You can use division to check that you found all of the possible ways. What whole numbers divide 12 evenly?

____

Did you include all of the whole number factors of 12 in your list of equal-length rows?

____

Apply the TEKS

Use models to solve each problem.

Workspace

1. Brian has 6 erasers and 9 pencils. He wants to use all the erasers and all the pencils to make boxes with the same number of erasers in each box and the same number of pencils in each box. How many boxes can he make? ________

2. Arrange the digits 1–9 in a square so the sum of each row, column, and diagonal is 15.

1 2 3 4 5

6 7 8 9

3. Which 5 toothpicks can you remove and have three squares remaining?

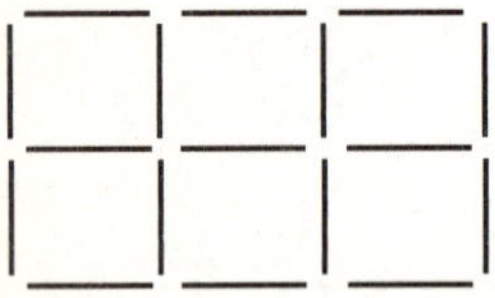

4. Arrange these figures in 3 rows and 3 columns so that no row or column has 2 figures the same color or the same shape.

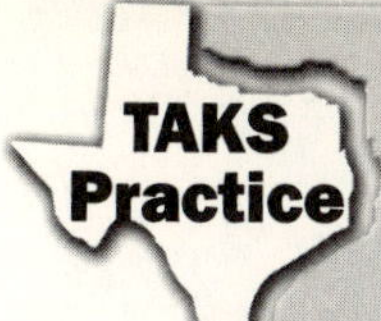

TAKS Objective 6 The student will demonstrate an understanding of the mathematical processes and tools used in problem solving.
TEKS 6.11B, 6.11C

DIRECTIONS Read each question. Then circle the letter for the correct answer.

1 When you put blocks in rows that each have the same number, you form a rectangle. Which set of blocks can be arranged in only one way to form a rectangle?

A 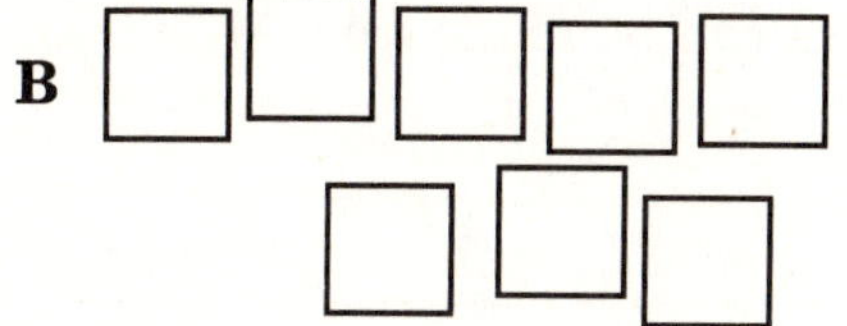

B 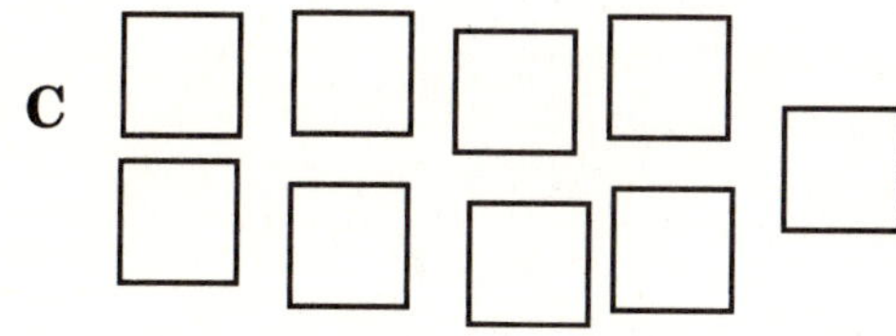

C

D

2 Wayne has 16 pumpkin plants and 12 corn plants. He wants to use all the plants to make rows of plants. Each row is to have the same number of pumpkin plants and the same number of corn plants. How many of each kind of plant will be in each row?

F 3 pumpkin, 4 corn

G 3 pumpkin, 2 corn

H 4 pumpkin, 3 corn

J 4 pumpkin, 2 corn

3 How many times do you need to fold a sheet of paper to make 16 same-size sections?

A 3

B 4

C 5

D 6

4 Which of these shapes can be made with only pieces like this:

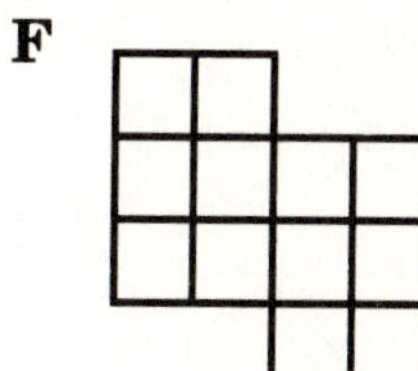

F

G

H

J

Building Stamina®

DIRECTIONS Read each question. Then circle the letter for the best answer. If the answer is not here, mark "Not Here."

1 The Wright family is driving from Dallas, Texas to Portland, Maine, a distance of about 1,875 miles. If they take 15 days to make the trip, how many miles will they drive per day?

Record your answer and fill in the bubbles on the grid below. Be sure to use the correct place value.

				.		
0	0	0	0		0	0
1	1	1	1		1	1
2	2	2	2		2	2
3	3	3	3		3	3
4	4	4	4		4	4
5	5	5	5		5	5
6	6	6	6		6	6
7	7	7	7		7	7
8	8	8	8		8	8
9	9	9	9		9	9

2 Which is the prime factorization of 54?

F $5^{10} \cdot 4$

G $5 \cdot 10 \cdot 4$

H $2^2 \cdot 3^2$

J $2 \cdot 3^3$

3 Which lists all of the common factors of 15 and 18?

A 1, 2, 3, 5, 6, 9, 15, 18

B 1, 2, 3, 5, 6, 9

C 1, 3, 5, 6

D 1, 3

4 Jonathan does 12 sit-ups each morning. Which is the best estimate of the number of sit-ups he does in a year (365 days)?

F 3,000

G 4,000

H 35,000

J 40,000

5 How many different length and width rectangles can be made from 16 cubes?

A 1

B 2

C 4

D 5

6 What is the value of the expression $3 + 7 \times (2 + 3)$?

F 50

G 38

H 20

J 15

7 A scout troop has 150 boxes of candy bars to sell. Each box contains 12 candy bars. If all the bars are sold and each of the 25 members of the troop sells the same number of candy bars, how many bars will each scout sell?

Record your answer and fill in the bubbles on the grid below. Be sure to use the correct place value.

				.		
0	0	0	0		0	0
1	1	1	1		1	1
2	2	2	2		2	2
3	3	3	3		3	3
4	4	4	4		4	4
5	5	5	5		5	5
6	6	6	6		6	6
7	7	7	7		7	7
8	8	8	8		8	8
9	9	9	9		9	9

8 The table below shows the attendance at three fairs.

Festival	Attendance
Apple	562,626
Lilac	538,933
Garlic	564,005

How many more people attended the Garlic Festival than the Apple Festival?

F 25,072

G 23,693

H 1,379

J Not Here

9 There are 36 stuffed animals in a box. There are 15 boxes in a flat. If a toy store ordered 21 flats, how many stuffed animals did they order?

A 540

B 756

C 10,800

D 11,340

10 Teresa plans to exchange 375 American dollars for Korean won during her trip to Korea. The exchange rate is 1,230 Korean won for each American dollar. Which is the best estimate of the number of Korean won that Teresa will get for her 375 American dollars?

F 4,000

G 40,000

H 400,000

J 4,000,000

11 Brian wants to give the same number of prizes to each of the 15 guests at his party. Which box of prizes should he buy so he has no leftovers?

A Box of 60 prizes

B Box of 50 prizes

C Box of 36 prizes

D Box of 18 prizes

12 54 is a common multiple of which pair of numbers?

F 3 and 8

G 6 and 8

H 6 and 9

J 4 and 27

13 For which number is $5 \cdot 3^2 \cdot 2^2$ the prime factorization?

A 75

B 120

C 180

D 300

14 Hannah practices the piano every other day and the cello every 3rd day. How often does she practice both instruments on the same day?

F Every 3 days

G Every 6 days

H Every 9 days

J Every 12 days

15 A jellyfish is 16 feet below the surface of the water. It moves up 3 feet, then down 1 foot. Again, it moves up 3 feet, then down 1 foot. Which expression can be used to find the current depth of the jellyfish?

A $-16 + 3 + 1 + 3 - 1$

B $16 - 3 - 1 - 3 + 1$

C $16 + 3 - 1 - 3 - 1$

D $-16 + 3 - 1 + 3 - 1$

16 Last year, a car dealership sold 362,463 cars and 255,720 trucks. How many vehicles did it sell in all?

F 618,183

G 617,183

H 517,183

J 106,743

17 How many triangles will be formed if you fold a square sheet of paper four times?

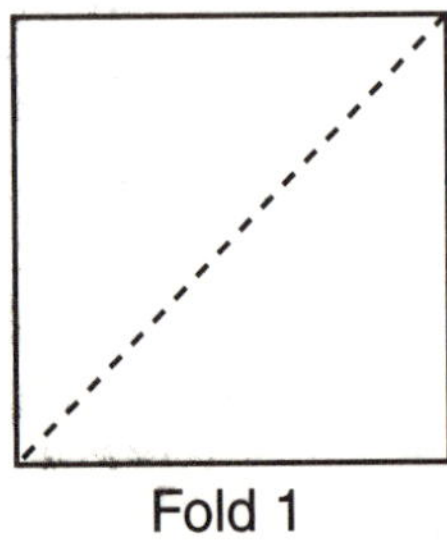

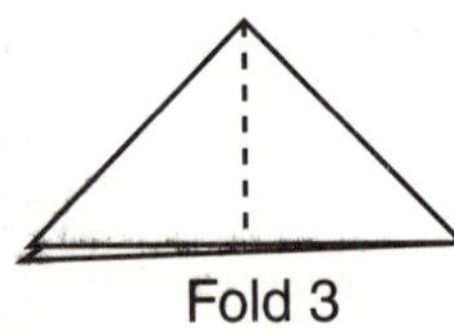

A 4

B 8

C 16

D 20

18 Which expression is NOT represented by -8?

F Gaining 8 points

G 8 degrees below zero

H A decrease of $8

J 8 feet below sea level

19 Carrie has 24 flower stickers, 32 animal stickers, and 12 flag stickers. If Carrie puts the same number of flower stickers on each page, the same number of animal stickers on each page, and the same number of flag stickers on each page of her notebook, how many pages will have the three kinds of stickers on them?

A 3

B 4

C 6

D 8

20 Numa's alarm clock rings every 8 minutes. Michelle's rings every 10 minutes. If both alarm clocks ring at the same time, in how many minutes will they both ring again at the same time?

F 8 minutes

G 10 minutes

H 40 minutes

J 80 minutes

21 Mr. Torres's class is playing a math game. During Round 1, Team A received 15 points for a correct answer, lost 5 points for an incorrect answer, gained 7 points for a tie answer, then lost 10 points for calling out an answer out of turn. Which expression can be used to find how many points Team A has at the end of Round 1?

A $15 - 5 + 7 - 10$

B $-15 + 5 - 7 - 10$

C $15 - 5 + 7 + 10$

D Not Here

22 Riverside Middle School is taking 425 people to a museum on a field trip. If each bus holds 37 people, how many buses will the school need?

F 10

G 11

H 12

J Not Here

23 There are 45 students in the chorus. The director made copies of his music book for each student. If the director used 1,215 sheets of paper, how many pages are in the book?

Record your answer and fill in the bubbles on the grid below. Be sure to use the correct place value.

				.		
0	0	0	0		0	0
1	1	1	1		1	1
2	2	2	2		2	2
3	3	3	3		3	3
4	4	4	4		4	4
5	5	5	5		5	5
6	6	6	6		6	6
7	7	7	7		7	7
8	8	8	8		8	8
9	9	9	9		9	9

24 90 is the least common multiple of which pair of numbers?

A 15 and 30

B 12 and 18

C 5 and 18

D 9 and 15

Focus on TEKS

Lesson 11 Compare and Order Decimals

TEKS 6.1A Compare and order non-negative rational numbers.

You can use place value to compare decimals.

Use the symbols for greater than (>), less than (<), and equal to (=) to compare decimals.

Guided Instruction

Problem 1 In a 200-meter race, Heidi finished in 28.4575 seconds. In the same race, Charlene finished in 28.4558 seconds. Who had the faster time?

Compare and order decimals by comparing the place values of the digits.

Step 1 Write the times in the place-value chart. Compare digits from left to right.

Tens	Ones	.	Tenths	Hundredths	Thousandths	Ten Thousandths
2	8	.				
2	8	.				

What is the first place in which the digits are NOT equal? ________________

Step 2 Use <, >, or = to compare the numbers.

7 thousandths is greater than 5 thousandths, so 28.4575 ◯ 28.4558

Solution Who had the faster time? ____________

Another Example

Compare 0.2, 0.20, 0.28, and 0.23.

Compare decimals using a number line.

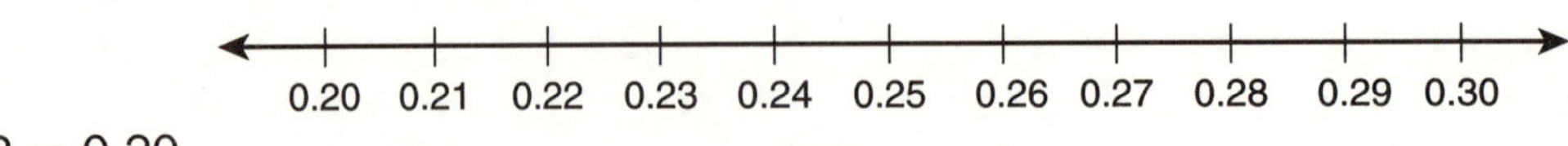

0.2 = 0.20

0 hundredths is less than 3 hundredths: 0.20 < 0.23

3 hundredths is less than 8 hundredths: 0.23 < 0.28

So, 0.2 ◯ 0.20 ◯ 0.23 ◯ 0.28

Guided Instruction

Another Problem

Problem 2

During baseball season, Hank's batting average was 0.329. Kevin's average was 0.327, and Charles's average was 0.330. Order the averages from least to greatest.
Note: Usually batting averages are expressed as decimals without the zero in the ones place.

Use a place-value chart to order the decimals.

Step 1 Write the batting averages in the place-value chart.
Compare digits from left to right.

Ones	.	Tenths	Hundredths	Thousandths
	.			
	.			
	.			

What is the first place in which the digits are NOT equal? ________________

Step 2 When you find the first digits that are not equal, compare them to find the greatest number.

There are ________ hundredths in 0.329.

There are ________ hundredths in 0.327.

There are ________ hundredths in 0.330.

Which of the three is the greatest number? ___________

Step 3 Compare the remaining two numbers to decide which is greater.
Compare thousandths.
Which is the greater number, 0.329 or 0.327? ___________

Step 4 Write the numbers in order from least to greatest.

________ < ________ < ________

Solution

What are the batting averages of the players in order from least to greatest? ________, ________, ________

Apply the TEKS **Write >, <, or =. Use a place-value chart if you want to.**

1. 15.099 ◯ 15.11

2. 12.5460 ◯ 12.56

3. 7.2 ◯ 7.1498

4. 0.684 ◯ 0.694

Write *true* or *false*.

5. 0.556 is less than 0.566. ________

6. 12.345 < 12.3550 ________

7. 7.09 is greater than 7.90. ________

8. 0.65 > 0.650 ________

Write the decimals in order from least to greatest.

9. 0.919; 0.090; 0.890; 0.999 ________________________________

10. 8.822; 7.888; 7.982; 8.812 ________________________________

11. 6.85; 0.68; 0.685; 68.5 ________________________________

12. 0.0035; 0.003; 0.037; 0.307 ________________________________

Write a decimal to make each statement true.

13. 8.555 > ______________ > 8.187

14. 0.3 = ______________

15. 0.345 < ______________ < 0.388

16. 3.203 > ______________ > 3.023

Solve each problem.

17. Four gymnasts are in a competition in which the highest possible score is 10. Three of the gymnasts have completed their performances, and their scores are 9.61, 9.65, and 9.60. What score, to the nearest hundredth, must the last gymnast get in order to win the competition? ______________

18. The Morales family traveled 45.66 miles Saturday, 45.06 miles Sunday, and 45.65 miles Monday. Order the distances they traveled from least to greatest.

____

Explain how you found your answer.

____

____

____

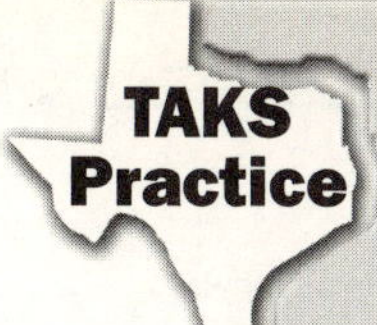

TAKS Objective 1 The student will demonstrate an understanding of numbers, operations, and quantitative reasoning.
TEKS 6.1A

DIRECTIONS Read each question. Then circle the letter for the correct answer.

1 A surveyor determines the area of four properties. Which property has the greatest area?

A Property A: 5.555 acres

B Property B: 5.500 acres

C Property C: 5.550 acres

D Property D: 5.505 acres

2 The table below shows the protein content of different flavors of yogurt.

Flavor	Protein (in grams)
Citrus	4.33
Cranberry	5.11
Peach	2.93
Banana	4.85
Strawberry	6.37
Kiwi	4.89

Which shows the flavors in order from least protein to most protein?

F Peach, citrus, cranberry, kiwi, banana, strawberry

G Peach, citrus, strawberry, cranberry, kiwi, banana

H Peach, citrus, banana, kiwi, cranberry, strawberry

J Strawberry, cranberry, kiwi, banana, citrus, peach

3 A baseball team manager lists the batting averages of four players on the team. Which list shows their batting averages in order from greatest to least?

A 0.298, 0.336, 0.283, 0.332

B 0.336, 0.332, 0.283, 0.298

C 0.283, 0.298, 0.332, 0.283

D 0.336, 0.332, 0.298, 0.283

Susie's best long jump this season was 4.02 meters. Her worst long jump for the season was 3.72 meters. Which of the following could NOT be the distance of any of her long jumps during this season?

F 4 meters

G 3.81 meters

H 3.79 meters

J 3.7 meters

In a gymnastics competition, four of the five participants have completed their performances. Their scores are 9.61, 9.66, 9.64, and 9.60. The highest score wins. Which is the least possible score that will enable the last participant to win the competition?

A 9.68

B 9.67

C 9.65

D 9.64

Focus on TEKS

Lesson 12 Add Decimals

TEKS 6.2B Use addition to solve problems involving decimals.

TEKS 6.2D Estimate and round to approximate reasonable results and to solve problems where exact answers are not required.

You can add decimals to find how many or how much in all.

Guided Instruction

Problem A national collegiate triathlon championship consists of a 0.932-mile swim, a 24.9-mile bike ride, and a 6.21-mile run. What is the total distance of the triathlon?

When you add decimals, align the digits according to their place values.

Step 1 Align the decimal points.
Use zero as a place holder if necessary.

$$\begin{array}{r} 0.932 \\ 24.9\mathbf{00} \\ +\ \ 6.21\mathbf{0} \\ \hline \end{array}$$

Step 2 Add. Place the decimal point in the sum.

$$\begin{array}{r} 0.932 \\ 24.900 \\ +\ \ 6.210 \\ \hline \end{array}$$

Step 3 Estimate to see if your answer is reasonable.
Round each addend to the nearest whole number.
Then add the rounded numbers.

0.932 rounds to ⟶ 1

24.9 rounds to ⟶ 25

6.21 rounds to ⟶ + 6

Compare your result to your estimate.

________ is close to ________, the estimated sum.

So the answer is reasonable.

Solution What is the total distance of the triathlon? ____________________

Apply the TEKS

Add.

1. 47.7 + 5.236 + 0.8 = __________

2. 2.566 + 4.5 + 5.66 = __________

3. 0.0002 + 0.444 + 6.709 = __________

4. $35.67 + $123.55 + $67.88 = __________

5. 0.55 + 0.66 + 0.009 = __________

6. $125.44 + $89.89 + $23.45 = __________

7. 4.7 + 8.8 + 0.45 = __________

8. 0.381 + 0.0002 + 37.708 = __________

Solve each problem.

9. Janet took a pedometer with her on a March of Dimes walk so she could measure the distance she traveled. When she reached Checkpoint A, she had walked 7.38 miles. She then walked 3.91 miles to the finish line. How many miles did she walk in all? ______________

Use the table to answer Problems 10–12.

Nancy used a pedometer to keep track of how far she walked every week in August.

Walking Distance in Miles	
Week 1	6.94
Week 2	12.73
Week 3	9.3
Week 4	10.25

10. During which two weeks did Nancy's distance total about 17 miles? __________

11. Estimate how far Nancy walked in August. __________________

12. Nancy walked 20.7 miles during the month of September. How many miles did she walk during August and September combined? __________________

Explain how you found your answer.

____

____

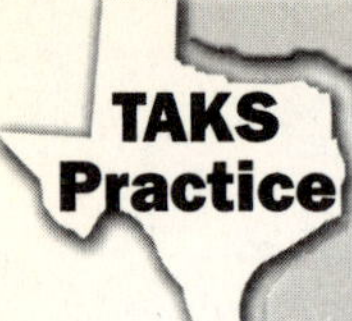

TAKS Objective 1 The student will demonstrate an understanding of numbers, operations, and quantitative reasoning.
TEKS 6.2B, 6.2D

DIRECTIONS Read each question. Then circle the letter for the correct answer.

1 A relay race consisted of three sections. Team A finished the first section in 124.5 seconds, the second section in 165.98 seconds, and the third section in 89.243 seconds. How much time did it take Team A to run the race?

A 124.5 seconds
B 238.84 seconds
C 379.723 seconds
D 479.783 seconds

2 Kyle helped his mom weigh potatoes at the grocery store. The red potatoes weighed 6.42 pounds. The Yukon Gold potatoes weighed 15.87 pounds. How much did the potatoes weigh together?

F 21.29 pounds
G 22.29 pounds
H 22.39 pounds
J 222.9 pounds

3 You have $332.45 in your savings account. You make deposits of $23.45 and $312.47. What is the new balance?

A $312.47
B $523.49
C $667.27
D $668.37

4 A national triathlon championship for athletes who are 11 to 14 years old consists of a 0.114-mile swim, a 6.2-mile bike ride, and a 1.2-mile run. What is the total length of the triathlon?

F 5.444 miles
G 6.484 miles
H 7.514 miles
J 77.514 miles

5 Your friend buys a blouse for $28.95, a pair of sandals for $39.95, and a pair of shorts for $19.90. How much do the three items cost?

A $88.80
B $87.70
C $78.80
D $77.70

6 You buy shoes for $31.99, shoelaces for $1.09, and a shirt for $9.89. After buying these items, you also buy some socks. If you spend about $47 in all, which could be the price of the socks?

F $4.93
G $3.93
H $2.93
J $1.50

Focus on TEKS

Lesson 13 Subtract Decimals

TEKS 6.2B Use subtraction to solve problems involving decimals.

TEKS 6.2D Estimate and round to approximate reasonable results and to solve problems where exact answers are not required.

You can subtract decimals to solve problems.

Guided Instruction

Problem The mass of a substance is 8.3 kilograms. After the water evaporates from it, its mass decreases to 3.617 kilograms. How much of the substance's original mass was water?

When you subtract decimals, align the digits according to their place values.

Step 1 Align the decimal points.
Use zero as a place holder if necessary.

$$\begin{array}{r} 8.3\mathbf{00} \\ -\ 3.617 \\ \hline \end{array}$$

Step 2 Subtract. Place the decimal point in the difference.

$$\begin{array}{r} 8.300 \\ -\ 3.617 \\ \hline \end{array}$$

Step 3 Estimate to see if your answer is reasonable.
Round each mass to the nearest whole number.
Then subtract the rounded numbers.

8.3 rounds to ⟶ 8

3.617 rounds to ⟶ – 4

4

Compare your result to your estimate.

__________ is close to __________, the estimated difference.
So the answer is reasonable.

Solution How much of the substance's mass was water? ____________________

Apply the TEKS

Subtract.

1. 265.3 − 121.44 = _______
2. 703.02 − 98.86 = _______
3. 0.6 − 0.17 = _______
4. 8.004 − 2.572 = _______
5. 1.04 − 0.999 = _______
6. 12.1 − 8.879 = _______
7. 5.56 − 2.3 = _______
8. 7.42 − 3.2 = _______
9. 6.18 − 1.71 = _______
10. 8.0006 − 6.9 = _______
11. 65.23 − 37.68 = _______
12. 4.056 − 2.345 = _______

Solve each problem.

13. The average annual rainfall in Jackson is 14.85 inches. In Milton, the average annual rainfall is 48.61 inches. On average, how many more inches of rain does Milton receive each year than Jackson? _______________

14. Jill saved $56.42 from her summer earnings. She wants to spend $16.99 on a new CD and $8.99 on a tape. After she buys the CD and the tape, how much money will she have left? _______________

Use the table to answer Problems 15–16.

City	Average Annual Rainfall (in inches)
City A	265.25
City B	202.10
City C	196.50

15. What is the difference in annual rainfall between City B and City C? _______________

16. Which two cities have a difference in annual rainfall of about 63 inches?

____

Explain how you found the answer.

____

____

____

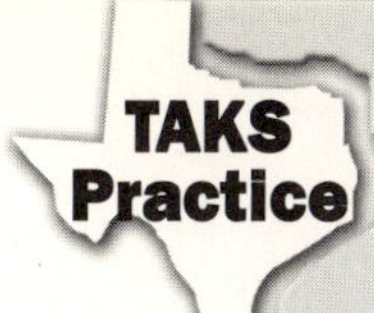

TAKS Objective 1 The student will demonstrate an understanding of numbers, operations, and quantitative reasoning.
TEKS 6.2B, 6.2D

DIRECTIONS Read each question. Then circle the letter for the correct answer.

1 Casey places a dish on a scale. Its mass is 12.988 grams. When she adds a powdered chemical to the dish, its total mass increases to 13.2 grams. What is the mass of the chemical?

A 0.122 gram

B 0.188 gram

C 0.212 gram

D 1.788 grams

2 The table below shows some average precipitation values (measured in inches) for four U.S. cities.

City, State	Annual
Boston, MA	41.51
Dallas-Fort Worth, TX	33.70
New Orleans, LA	61.88
San Francisco, CA	19.70

What is the difference between the average annual precipitation in Dallas-Fort Worth and San Francisco?

F 53.4 inches

G 14.4 inches

H 14 inches

J 5.97 inches

3 What is the difference between 24.034 and 19.098?

A 4.936

B 4.964

C 5.064

D 5.936

4 Your goal is to walk 10 miles every week. The data shown are the number of miles you have walked so far this week.

Day	Distance (in miles)
Sunday	1.3
Monday	1.8
Tuesday	2.1
Wednesday	1.6
Thursday	1.5
Friday	1.1

How many more miles will you have to walk Saturday to complete your goal?

F 0.6 mile

G 1.6 miles

H 6.6 miles

J 9.4 miles

5 The regular price of a TV is $1,291.99. You buy it on sale for $681.99. Which is the closest estimate of the amount you saved?

A $400

B $600

C $800

D $2,000

Focus on TEKS

Lesson 14 PROBLEM-SOLVING STRATEGY: Work Backwards

TEKS 6.11A Identify and apply mathematics to everyday experiences, to activities in and outside of school, with other disciplines, and with other mathematical topics.

TEKS 6.11B Use a problem-solving model that incorporates understanding the problem, making a plan, carrying out the plan, and evaluating the solution for reasonableness.

TEKS 6.11C Select or develop an appropriate problem-solving strategy from a variety of different types, including working backwards to solve a problem.

You can work backwards to solve problems.
Use the problem-solving guide on page 288 to help you.

Guided Instruction

Problem

Natalie and five of her friends went to an ice-cream shop. Each person ordered a single-scoop cone with sprinkles. Their bill for $8.86 included $0.52 sales tax. How much does one single-scoop cone with sprinkles cost before tax?

Understand the problem.

What does the problem ask you to find? ______________________

Make a plan.

Think about what you need to find out to solve the problem.
Start with what you know and work backwards.

Solve the problem.

What is the total cost of the cones? ____________
How much of that cost is tax? ____________

Subtract the tax from the total cost to find how much the cones cost before tax. ____________
How many people had ice-cream cones? ____________

Divide the cost of the cones before tax by the number of cones purchased.
What is the cost of each cone? ____________

Check your answer.

Work forward to see whether your answer is reasonable.
Start with the cost of 1 cone. ____________

Multiply that cost by 6. ____________

Add the tax. ____________

Check that the result matches the total cost in the problem.

Apply the TEKS **Solve each problem. Use the work-backwards strategy.**

Work Space

1. Your friend plays a video game for ten minutes and then you take over. You continue the game and double the current score by crossing a rickety bridge. Next, you earn 30 points twice for collecting treasure. Then, you lose 15 points for slipping while climbing a mountain. You finish with 155 points. How many points did you start with?____________

2. You have $320 in your savings account. You started with $100 and then saved $10 per week. For how many weeks did you save? ____________

3. Your dog has a total of 335 points after 4 agility course events. The dog earned 77 points in the last event, 95 points in the third event, and 84 points in the second event. How many points did your dog earn in the first event? ____________

4. You have $4.25 at the end of a school day. You spent $2.75 for lunch. After lunch, a friend gave you $1.50 that he owed you. How much money did you have before lunch? ____________

5. What number belongs in the blank?

   $(\_\_\_\_\_\_ \div 5) \times 9 + 42 = 150$

6. To get from the bus stop to the park, you walk 2 blocks north, then 3 blocks west, and then 1 block north. Which point on the map below represents the bus stop? ____________

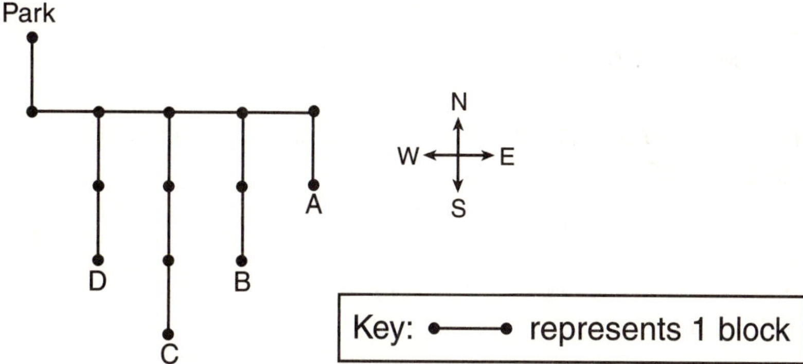

7. Your friend can make 3 sandwiches per minute. In 10 minutes, your friend can make 10 sandwiches more than you can. How many sandwiches per minute can you make? ____________

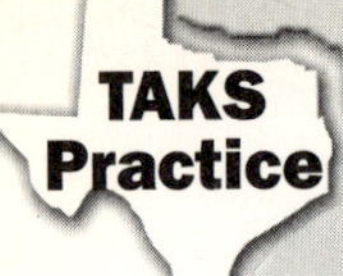

TAKS Objective 6 The student will demonstrate an understanding of the mathematical processes and tools used in problem solving.

TEKS 6.11A, 6.11B, 6.11C

DIRECTIONS Read each question. Then circle the letter for the correct answer.

1 You are playing a role in a school play that begins at 7:30 P.M. It takes you 5 minutes to get into costume, 35 minutes to do your makeup, and 20 minutes to fix your hair. By what time should you start getting ready?

A 5:00 P.M.

B 6:30 P.M.

C 6:45 P.M.

D 7:15 P.M.

2 Today is Tuesday. You had a track meet 3 days ago. Your friend's party was 8 days before the track meet. Your piano recital was 2 days before the party. On which day of the week was the recital?

F Monday

G Tuesday

H Wednesday

J Thursday

3 Judy buys three CDs in a set for $29.98. She saved $6.44 by buying the set instead of buying the individual CDs. If each CD costs the same amount, how much does each of the CDs cost when purchased separately?

A $12.14

B $13.24

C $14.44

D $16.14

4 Keesha went to the movies with her brother and spent $15.00. The tickets cost $4.50 each. She bought a box of popcorn and 2 drinks. The drinks cost $1.50 each. How much did the popcorn cost?

F $1.50

G $2.00

H $2.75

J $3.00

5 Legends Car Hire charges $1.25 for the first mile traveled and then $0.35 for each additional mile. Horatio spent $2.30 on a ride. How many miles did he travel?

Record your answer and fill in the bubbles on the grid below. Be sure to use the correct place value.

				.		
0	0	0	0		0	0
1	1	1	1		1	1
2	2	2	2		2	2
3	3	3	3		3	3
4	4	4	4		4	4
5	5	5	5		5	5
6	6	6	6		6	6
7	7	7	7		7	7
8	8	8	8		8	8
9	9	9	9		9	9

Building Stamina®

DIRECTIONS Read each question. Then circle the letter for the best answer. If the answer is not here, mark "Not Here."

1 The table shows the mass of some gerbils.

Gerbil	Mass (grams)
Edgar	77.0113
Fluff	77.0212
Scamp	77.0033
Scruff	77.0250

Which list shows the gerbils from greatest to least mass?

A Scruff, Fluff, Scamp, Edgar

B Scruff, Fluff, Edgar, Scamp

C Scamp, Edgar, Scruff, Fluff

D Edgar, Scruff, Fluff, Scamp

2 Which decimal is greater than 0.84 and less than 0.845?

F 0.741

G 0.82

H 0.843

J 0.847

3 Which is the least number between 2.5 and 3 that can be written using the digits 1, 2, 4, and 6?

A 2.146

B 2.164

C 2.614

D 2.641

4 Which statement below is true?

F $2.94 > 2.9 < 2.8$

G $5.796 < 5.802 < 5.656$

H $8.55 < 9.111 < 9.229$

J $5.796 > 5.802 < 9.111$

5 The table shows the winning times for a swim race.

Year	Time(seconds)
1999	54.50
2000	54.64
2001	54.93
2002	55.61
2003	54.79
2004	55.01

In which year was the winning time the third fastest?

A 2000

B 2001

C 2003

D 2004

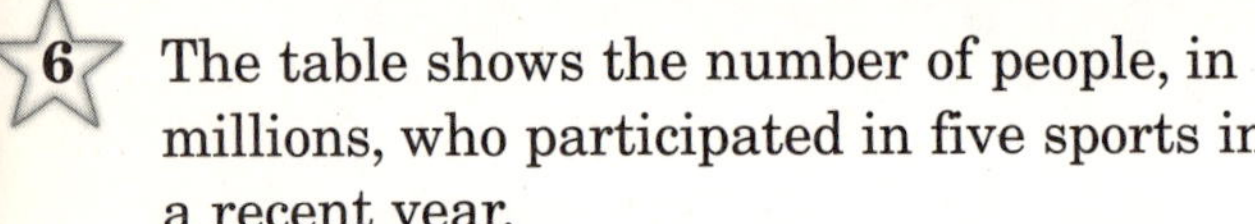

6 The table shows the number of people, in millions, who participated in five sports in a recent year.

Activity	Males	Females
Bicycling	22.9	20.6
Golf	21.8	5.7
Hiking	14.9	12.3
Soccer	8.2	4.9
Swimming	27.0	31.3

About how many more people swam than played soccer?

F About 55 million

G About 45 million

H About 29 million

J About 8 million

7 Al buys a pair of pants for $28.99 and a tie for $12.99. After buying these items, he buys lunch. He spends a total of about $50 in all. Which of the following could be the price of his lunch?

A $20.02

B $11.02

C $8.02

D $4.02

8 Niko mixes 0.25 cup of milk, 0.33 cup of water, and 0.01 cup of vanilla. When he mixes the ingredients, how much liquid does he have?

F 0.35 cup

G 0.55 cup

H 0.59 cup

J 1.14 cups

9 Which addition expression has a sum greater than $20 and less than $25?

A $4.22 + $10.85 + $8.97

B $4.50 + $8.75 + $4.50

C $5.05 + $17.86 + $9.22

D $6.32 + $9.63 + $1.45

10 The table below shows how much the Colon family spent when they attended a football game.

Item	Cost
Admission	$75.75
Popcorn	$12.75
Drinks	$9.50
Hot Dogs	$18.50
Souvenirs	$25.75

Which statement below is true?

F The Colon family spent $10 more on hot dogs than popcorn.

G The Colon family spent a total of $28.00 on hot dogs and drinks.

H The Colon family spent more on souvenirs than they spent on hot dogs and drinks.

J The Colon Family spent about $100 in all.

11 Martha makes $100 each week at her after-school job. What is the amount of her paycheck after the following deductions?

Federal Income Tax	$11.53
Social Security Tax	$6.27
Medicare Tax	$1.45
State Income Tax	$4.13

A $77.62

B $76.62

C $23.38

D $22.38

12 Which subtraction expression has the least difference?

F 40.08 – 9.56

G 40.8 – 9.56

H 41.8 – 19.56

J 41.8 – 29.4

13 What is the difference between 25.01 and 18.88?

Record your answer and fill in the bubbles on the grid below. Be sure to use the correct place value.

				.		
0	0	0	0		0	0
1	1	1	1		1	1
2	2	2	2		2	2
3	3	3	3		3	3
4	4	4	4		4	4
5	5	5	5		5	5
6	6	6	6		6	6
7	7	7	7		7	7
8	8	8	8		8	8
9	9	9	9		9	9

14 At a department store, Kathleen buys a sweater for $49.95, a dress for $52.99, and a hat for $13.49. She gives the clerk two $50 bills and a $20 bill. How much change should she receive?

F $3.57

G $4.43

H $4.57

J $6.43

15 Which expression does NOT have a value of 3.24?

A 8.14 + 2.36 – 7.26

B 8.14 + 9.36 – 14.26

C 8.14 + 9.6 – 14.56

D 8.4 + 2.6 – 7.76

16 At the end of a board game, Alice has 57 game dollars. During the game, she won 200 dollars, lost 150 dollars, won 25 dollars, lost 10 dollars, and lost 35 dollars. How much money did Alice have at the start of the game?

F $18

G $27

H $37

J $49

17 Mrs. Smith lends pencils to her students. One day, she gave out 7 pencils in the morning, collected 5 before lunch, and gave out 3 after lunch. At the end of the day, she had 16 pencils. How many pencils did she have at the start of the day?

A 8

B 10

C 21

D 24

18 Jim took a cab ride from his home to the theater. The cab charged a set rate for the first mile, and $1.25 for each additional mile. The cab traveled 3 miles. Jim paid the cab driver $5.00. This included a tip of $1.10. What was the rate charged by the cab for the first mile?

F $1.40

G $2.10

H $2.65

J $3.60

19 Aaron plans to study in the library after school and then take part in a race that starts at 4:00 P.M. It takes him 5 minutes to change his clothes and 10 minutes to get to the track. Before the start of the race, Aaron needs to meet with his coach for 10 minutes and stretch for 15 minutes. When should he leave the library?

A 2:45 P.M.

B 3:10 P.M.

C 3:20 P.M.

D 3:45 P.M.

20 At the end of the day, Carly has $3.02. During the day, her brother Ralph gave her the $2.10 he owed her. She then spent $3.56 for lunch. How much money did Carly have at the beginning of the day?

Which statement below describes the steps you could use to solve the problem?

F Add $2.10 to $3.02. Then subtract $3.56 from the sum.

G Add $2.10 to $3.56. Then subtract $3.02 from the sum.

H Add $2.10 to $3.56. Then subtract the sum from $3.02.

J Add $3.56 to $3.02. Then subtract $2.10 from the sum.

Focus on TEKS

Lesson 15 Equivalent Fractions

TEKS 6.1B Generate equivalent forms of rational numbers including fractions.

You can use equivalent fractions to solve problems.

Equivalent fractions are fractions that name an equal amount. To find equivalent fractions, you can multiply (or divide) the numerator and denominator by the same nonzero number. This does not change the value of the fraction because you are simply multiplying (or dividing) by 1.

Guided Instruction

Problem

Henry has a collection of miniature airplanes. Of the planes, $\frac{4}{15}$ are 767s, $\frac{22}{45}$ are 747s, and $\frac{8}{30}$ are L1011s. Which of these three groups have an equal number of planes?

Use equivalent forms of the fractions to see which are equal.

Step 1 Determine if the fractions of the planes that are 767s and 747s are equivalent fractions.

What fraction of the collection are 767s? ________

What fraction of the planes are 747s? ________

To find a fraction equivalent to $\frac{4}{15}$ with a denominator of 45, multiply the numerator and the denominator of $\frac{4}{15}$ by 3.

$$\frac{4 \times 3}{15 \times 3} = \frac{\square}{45}$$

So $\frac{4}{15}$ is equivalent to ________. It is not equivalent to $\frac{22}{45}$.

Step 2 Determine if the fractions of the planes that are 767s and L1011s are equivalent fractions.

What fraction of the planes are L1011s? ________

To find a fraction equivalent to $\frac{8}{30}$ with a denominator of 15, divide the numerator and the denominator of $\frac{8}{30}$ by 2.

$$\frac{8 \div 2}{30 \div 2} = \frac{\square}{15}$$

So $\frac{8}{30}$ is equivalent to ________.

Solution

Which of these three groups have an equal number of planes?

____

Apply the TEKS Name the fractions modeled. Then use the models to tell whether the fractions are equivalent.

1. 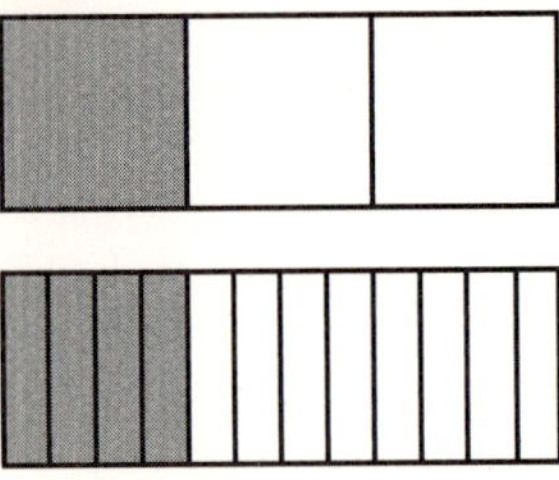

2. 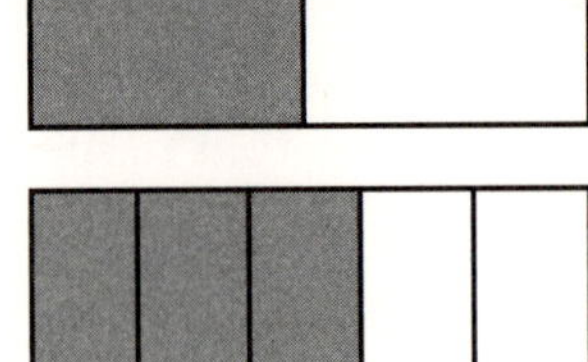

3. 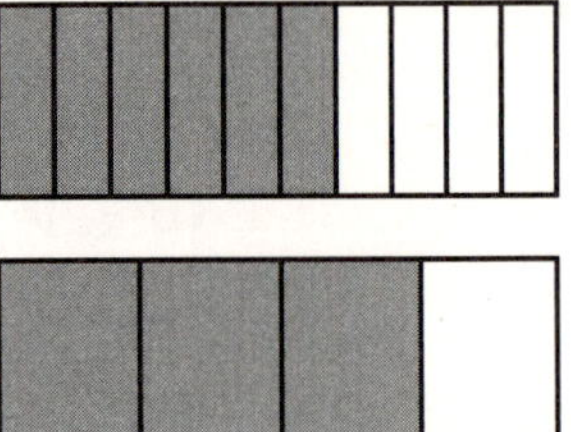

_______________ _______________ _______________

Tell what number the numerator and denominator of the first fraction can be multiplied or divided by to get the second fraction.

4. $\frac{2}{4}, \frac{16}{32}$ ________ 5. $\frac{3}{8}, \frac{15}{40}$ ________ 6. $\frac{42}{60}, \frac{7}{10}$ ________ 7. $\frac{75}{100}, \frac{3}{4}$ ________

Write three equivalent fractions for each fraction.

8. $\frac{3}{10}$ ____________________ 9. $\frac{7}{8}$ ____________________

10. $\frac{6}{9}$ ____________________ 11. $\frac{16}{20}$ ____________________

Identify the fraction in each set that is NOT equivalent to the other fractions.

12. $\frac{4}{7}, \frac{14}{28}, \frac{28}{56}, \frac{7}{14}$ ____________________ 13. $\frac{72}{81}, \frac{8}{9}, \frac{24}{27}, \frac{36}{42}$ ____________________

14. $\frac{8}{32}, \frac{4}{16}, \frac{16}{56}, \frac{1}{4}$ ____________________ 15. $\frac{18}{21}, \frac{24}{64}, \frac{6}{7}, \frac{36}{42}$ ____________________

Solve each problem.

16. Jack bought $\frac{3}{4}$ pound of chopped veal. Mary bought $\frac{5}{8}$ pound of chopped veal. Arnold bought $\frac{12}{16}$ pound of chopped veal. Which two people bought an equal amount of meat? ______________________________

17. James correctly answered 14 of the 20 questions on his test. Bill correctly answered 8 of the 10 questions on his test. Fran correctly answered 40 of the 50 questions on her test. Which two students correctly answered an equal fraction of their test questions? Explain your answer.

____

____

____

____

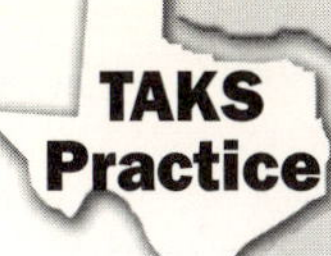

TAKS Objective 1 The student will demonstrate an understanding of numbers, operations, and quantitative reasoning.
TEKS 6.1B

DIRECTIONS Read each question. Then circle the letter for the correct answer.

1 In which set are all the fractions equivalent?

A $\frac{1}{4}, \frac{2}{8}, \frac{3}{15}, \frac{4}{24}$

B $\frac{1}{2}, \frac{2}{4}, \frac{6}{8}, \frac{5}{10}$

C $\frac{6}{16}, \frac{9}{24}, \frac{3}{8}, \frac{12}{32}$

D $\frac{7}{16}, \frac{3}{8}, \frac{1}{4}, \frac{9}{16}$

Use the model below to answer Questions 2–3.

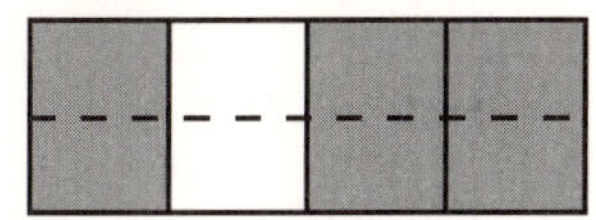

2 Which two equivalent fractions name the shaded part of the model?

F $\frac{3}{5}, \frac{7}{10}$

G $\frac{3}{4}, \frac{6}{8}$

H $\frac{4}{5}, \frac{6}{10}$

J $\frac{4}{6}, \frac{9}{12}$

3 Which two equivalent fractions name the unshaded part of the model?

A $\frac{1}{4}, \frac{2}{8}$

B $\frac{1}{5}, \frac{3}{10}$

C $\frac{2}{5}, \frac{5}{10}$

D $\frac{4}{8}, \frac{2}{3}$

4 In which list are all the fractions equivalent to $\frac{4}{7}$?

F $\frac{8}{14}, \frac{12}{16}, \frac{16}{20}$

G $\frac{8}{14}, \frac{12}{21}, \frac{16}{28}$

H $\frac{14}{17}, \frac{24}{27}, \frac{34}{37}$

J $\frac{16}{28}, \frac{20}{32}, \frac{24}{36}$

5 A survey was taken of 60 sixth-grade students at Jefferson Middle School, of which 48 voted that they wanted the spring dance to be semiformal. Larry said that the results of the survey showed that $\frac{4}{5}$ of the sixth-grade students wanted the spring dance to be a semiformal. Maria stated that the results showed that $\frac{12}{15}$ of the sixth grade wanted the spring dance to be semiformal. Evan stated that the survey showed that $\frac{9}{20}$ of the sixth grade wanted the spring dance to be semiformal. Which students were correct?

A Maria and Evan

B Larry and Evan

C Maria and Larry

D Not Here

Focus on TEKS

Lesson 16 Fractions and Mixed Numbers

TEKS 6.1A Compare and order non-negative rational numbers.

TEKS 6.1B Generate equivalent forms of rational numbers including whole numbers and fractions.

You can write a fraction greater than 1 as a mixed number, and you can write a mixed number as a fraction.

An **improper fraction** has a numerator greater than or equal to its denominator. A **mixed number** is made up of a whole number and a fraction.

Guided Instruction

Problem

Heidi built a fort with a ceiling that was $\frac{21}{4}$ feet high. Marvin is $5\frac{3}{4}$ feet tall. Can Marvin stand up in Heidi's fort?

You can rewrite either of two measures in order to compare them.

Step 1 Rewrite the height of the ceiling as a mixed number.

What is the height of the fort's ceiling? ______________

Divide the numerator of the fraction by the denominator. $4\overline{)21}$

What is the quotient? __________ $-$ ____

What is the remainder? __________

The quotient is the whole-number part of the mixed number.
The remainder is the numerator and the divisor is the denominator for the fraction part of the mixed number.

Write the mixed number. __________

Step 2 Compare the mixed number heights.

Marvin's Height Ceiling's Height

$5\frac{3}{4}$ ◯ $5\frac{1}{4}$

Solution

Can Marvin stand up in Heidi's fort? Explain.

____

Another Example

Marvin is $5\frac{3}{4}$ feet tall. Rewrite Marvin's height as an improper fraction.

Then compare the improper fractions.

Multiply the denominator of the fraction by the whole number. $5 \times 4 =$ __________

Then find the sum of this product and the numerator of the fraction. $20 + 3 =$ __________

Write the fraction. The numerator is the sum.

Use the same denominator of the fraction. __________

Compare the fractional heights.

Marvin's Height Ceiling's Height

$\frac{23}{4}$ ◯ $\frac{21}{4}$

Apply the TEKS **Rewrite each fraction as a mixed number.**

1. $\frac{5}{2}$ ________ 2. $\frac{9}{5}$ ________ 3. $\frac{7}{2}$ ________ 4. $\frac{9}{4}$ ________

5. $\frac{34}{7}$ ________ 6. $\frac{64}{7}$ ________ 7. $\frac{29}{6}$ ________ 8. $\frac{90}{7}$ ________

Rewrite each mixed number as an improper fraction.

9. $2\frac{5}{8}$ ________ 10. $2\frac{3}{5}$ ________ 11. $7\frac{1}{2}$ ________ 12. $6\frac{7}{8}$ ________

13. $8\frac{7}{12}$ ________ 14. $7\frac{3}{4}$ ________ 15. $5\frac{9}{10}$ ________ 16. $6\frac{5}{9}$ ________

Compare using $>$, $<$, or $=$.

17. $3\frac{4}{7}$ ◯ $\frac{25}{7}$ 18. $2\frac{3}{13}$ ◯ $\frac{23}{13}$ 19. $1\frac{5}{8}$ ◯ $\frac{15}{8}$

Order the numbers from *greatest* to *least*.

20. $\frac{33}{7}$ $3\frac{3}{7}$ $\frac{51}{14}$ ________ 21. $\frac{11}{8}$ 2 $1\frac{7}{8}$ ________

22. $\frac{14}{5}$ $1\frac{4}{5}$ $4\frac{1}{5}$ ________ 23. $2\frac{3}{8}$ $\frac{11}{4}$ $2\frac{1}{2}$ ________

Shade the small square that shows a fraction or mixed number that is NOT equivalent to any of the other fractions or mixed numbers.

24.

$\frac{5}{2}$	$\frac{23}{6}$	$\frac{30}{7}$
$\frac{17}{3}$	$2\frac{1}{2}$	$5\frac{2}{3}$
$\frac{25}{8}$	$4\frac{2}{7}$	$3\frac{5}{6}$

25.

$\frac{24}{7}$	$7\frac{11}{12}$	$\frac{121}{8}$
$11\frac{3}{5}$	$15\frac{1}{8}$	$3\frac{3}{7}$
$\frac{66}{5}$	$\frac{95}{12}$	$13\frac{1}{5}$

Solve each problem.

26. Jim's washing machine uses $25\frac{2}{3}$ gallons of water. Write the number of gallons as an improper fraction. ________

27. Flushing a toilet uses $\frac{28}{5}$ gallons of water. Write the number of gallons as a mixed number. ________

28. Betsy is $5\frac{1}{6}$ feet tall. Jack is $\frac{35}{6}$ feet tall. Ned is 5 feet 2 inches tall. Who is the tallest person? Explain your answer.

____

____

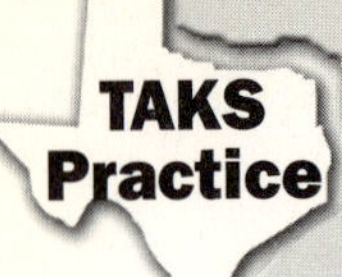

TAKS Objective The student will demonstrate an understanding of numbers, operations, and quantitative reasoning.
TEKS 6.1A, 6.1B

DIRECTIONS Read each question. Then circle the letter for the correct answer.

1 Which mixed number is equivalent to $\frac{32}{3}$?

A $3\frac{2}{3}$

B $8\frac{1}{3}$

C $9\frac{1}{3}$

D $10\frac{2}{3}$

2 A jewelry box is $4\frac{5}{8}$ inches wide. What is its width expressed as an improper fraction?

F $\frac{20}{8}$ in.

G $\frac{32}{8}$ in.

H $\frac{37}{8}$ in.

J $\frac{37}{5}$ in.

A cooking class served $5\frac{1}{8}$ loaves of garlic bread. Each complete loaf was sliced into 8 equal slices. How many slices of bread did they serve?

Record your answer and fill in the bubbles on the grid below. Be sure to use the correct place value.

				.		
0	0	0	0		0	0
1	1	1	1		1	1
2	2	2	2		2	2
3	3	3	3		3	3
4	4	4	4		4	4
5	5	5	5		5	5
6	6	6	6		6	6
7	7	7	7		7	7
8	8	8	8		8	8
9	9	9	9		9	9

A recipe calls for $2\frac{1}{2}$ cups of flour. A different recipe calls for $\frac{26}{4}$ cups of flour. Which number falls between these two measurements?

F 5

G 10

H 15

J 21

Which does NOT show an improper fraction and its equivalent mixed number?

A $\frac{5}{3}, 1\frac{2}{3}$

B $\frac{7}{6}, 1\frac{1}{6}$

C $\frac{9}{4}, 2\frac{1}{4}$

D $\frac{21}{5}, 3\frac{4}{5}$

Which shows the number of hours that 67 minutes are equal to?

F $6\frac{7}{10}$ hours

G $\frac{67}{10}$ hours

H $\frac{17}{60}$ hour

J $1\frac{7}{60}$ hours

Focus on TEKS

Lesson 17 Fractions and Decimals

TEKS 6.1A Compare and order non-negative rational numbers.

TEKS 6.1B Generate equivalent forms of rational numbers including fractions and decimals.

You can use division to write a fraction as a decimal and you can use place-value to write a decimal as a fraction.

A **decimal** is a number that has one or more digits to the right of a decimal point. A fraction is in **simplest form** when the numerator and denominator have no common factors other than 1. To compare and order fractions and decimals, change the numbers so they are all in the same form.

Guided Instruction

Problem The students in sixth grade are growing plants. Sam's plant is $\frac{3}{8}$ inch tall. Jim's plant is 0.4 inch tall. Fran's plant is $\frac{1}{4}$ inch tall. Whose plant is the tallest? Whose plant is the shortest?

Write all of the heights as fractions using *like* denominators and compare.

Step 1 Change the decimal 0.4 into a fraction. The first place to the right of the decimal point is the tenths place. Read 0.4 as 4 tenths. Write 4 tenths as a fraction.

$0.4 = \frac{\_\_}{10}$

Step 2 Choose a common denominator for the fractions. The least common denominator of 4, 8, and 10 is __________.
Write equivalent fractions using the common denominator.

$\frac{3 \times 5}{8 \times 5} = \frac{\_\_}{40}$ $\frac{4 \times 4}{10 \times 4} = \frac{\_\_}{40}$ $\frac{1 \times 10}{4 \times 10} = \frac{\_\_}{40}$

Step 3 Compare the fractions. Since they have the same denominator, compare the numerators.
Which fraction has the greatest numerator? __________

Which fraction has the least numerator? __________

Step 4 Write the fractions in order from greatest to least. ________________________

Solution
Whose plant is the tallest? ___________________________

Whose plant is the shortest? ___________________________

Another Example

You can change a fraction to a decimal by dividing the numerator by the denominator.

$\frac{3}{8} = 3 \div 8 = 8\overline{)3.000}$ = 0.375

$\frac{1}{4} = 1 \div 4 = 4\overline{)1.00}$ = 0.25

You can show the values from the problem above in order from *greatest* to *least* as decimals: 0.4, 0.375, 0.25.

Or you can show the values in their original form in order from *greatest* to *least*: 0.4, $\frac{3}{8}$, $\frac{1}{4}$.

Apply the TEKS

Match each fraction with its decimal equivalent.

1. $\frac{7}{8}$
2. $\frac{19}{20}$
3. $\frac{7}{25}$
4. $\frac{3}{5}$

A 0.28

B 0.45

C 0.6

D 0.875

E 0.95

Write the decimal equivalent for each fraction.

5. $\frac{2}{5}$ ______ **6.** $\frac{1}{8}$ ______ **7.** $\frac{7}{20}$ ______ **8.** $\frac{2}{25}$ ______

9. $\frac{3}{4}$ ______ **10.** $\frac{13}{25}$ ______ **11.** $\frac{39}{50}$ ______ **12.** $\frac{17}{40}$ ______

Write an equivalent fraction in simplest form for each decimal.

13. 0.3 ______ **14.** 0.78 ______ **15.** 0.65 ______ **16.** 0.32 ______

17. 0.025 ______ **18.** 0.005 ______ **19.** 0.48 ______ **20.** 0.075 ______

Compare using >, <, or =.

21. 0.58 ◯ $\frac{5}{8}$ **22.** $\frac{17}{50}$ ◯ 0.34 **23.** 0.615 ◯ $\frac{6}{15}$

Order the numbers from *least* to *greatest*.

24. $\frac{4}{5}$ 0.85 0.45 ______

25. 0.7 $\frac{3}{8}$ $\frac{3}{4}$ ______

26. $\frac{3}{20}$ 0.32 $\frac{1}{5}$ ______

Use the information below to solve Problems 27–29.

Paper products occupy 0.225 of the Hampton landfill. Glass products occupy $\frac{11}{50}$ of the landfill.

27. What fraction of the landfill is occupied by paper products? ______

28. Write the fraction of the landfill occupied by glass products as a decimal. ______

29. Which product occupies more of the landfill? Explain your answer.

______

______

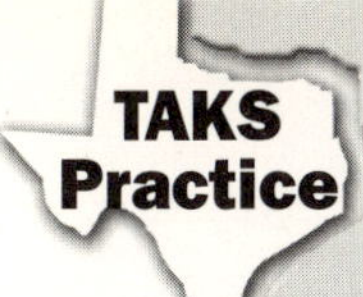

TAKS Objective 1 The student will demonstrate an understanding of numbers, operations, and quantitative reasoning.
TEKS 6.1A, 6.1B

DIRECTIONS Read each question. Then circle the letter for the correct answer.

1 Which is equivalent to 0.72?

A $\frac{36}{25}$

B $\frac{19}{25}$

C $\frac{18}{25}$

D $\frac{72}{10}$

2 Which decimal is greater than $\frac{21}{25}$?

F 0.85

G 0.84

H 0.825

J Not Here

3 In a sixth grade class of 36 students, 9 students walk to school. Which decimal represents the fraction of the class that does NOT walk to school?

Record your answer and fill in the bubbles on the grid below. Be sure to use the correct place value.

				.		
0	0	0	0		0	0
1	1	1	1		1	1
2	2	2	2		2	2
3	3	3	3		3	3
4	4	4	4		4	4
5	5	5	5		5	5
6	6	6	6		6	6
7	7	7	7		7	7
8	8	8	8		8	8
9	9	9	9		9	9

Use the table and information below to to answer Questions 4 and 5.

The table below shows the number of grams of protein, fat, and carbohydrates in a serving of two different meals. The serving size of each meal is 200 grams.

	Meal	
	Macaroni and Cheese	Ravioli
Protein	22 g	24 g
Fat	26 g	18 g
Carbohydrates	41 g	38 g

4 Protein is what fraction of a serving of ravioli?

F $\frac{1}{24}$

G $\frac{3}{25}$

H $\frac{2}{5}$

J $\frac{6}{25}$

5 Which decimal represents the fat in one serving of macaroni and cheese?

A 7.69

B 0.26

C 0.13

D Not Here

Focus on TEKS

Lesson 18 Add Fractions and Mixed Numbers

TEKS 6.1B Generate equivalent forms of ratiional numbers.

TEKS 6.2A Model addition situations involving fractions with pictures, words, and numbers.

TEKS 6.2B Use addition to solve problems involving fractions.

TEKS 6.2D Estimate and round to approximate reasonable results and to solve problems where exact answers are not required

You can add fractions and mixed numbers to solve problems.

When adding fractions or mixed numbers with *like denominators*, add the numerators. The denominator stays the same. When adding fractions or mixed numbers with *unlike denominators*, use the LCD (least common denominator) to find equivalent fractions or mixed numbers with like denominators. The **least common denominator (LCD)** is the least common multiple (LCM) of the denominators of two or more fractions.

Guided Instruction

Problem One day, Kate spent $1\frac{1}{2}$ hours doing exercises and $1\frac{2}{3}$ hours riding her bike. How many hours did Kate spend on these activities?

Add. $1\frac{1}{2} + 1\frac{2}{3}$

Step 1 Use the least common multiple (LCM) of 2 and 3 to find the LCD.

Multiples of 2: 2, 4, ______, ...

Multiples of 3: 3, ______, ...

So the LCD of $\frac{1}{2}$ and $\frac{2}{3}$ is ______.

Step 2 Write equivalent fractions using the LCD, 6.

$\frac{1 \times 3}{2 \times 3} = \frac{\square}{6}$ $\frac{2 \times 2}{3 \times 2} = \frac{\square}{6}$

Step 3 Add the fractions, then add the whole numbers.

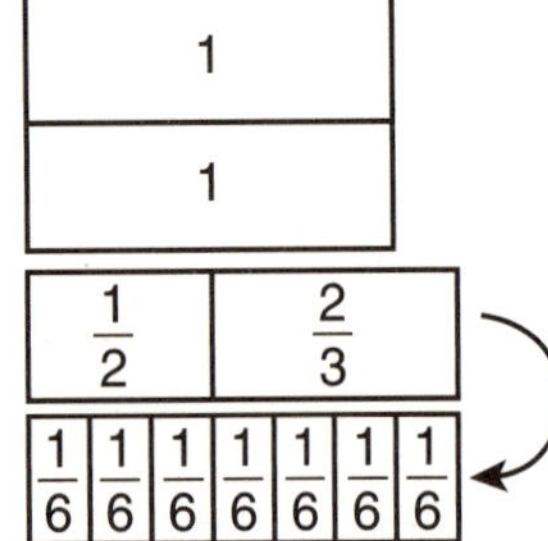

$$\begin{array}{rcr} 1\frac{1}{2} & = & 1\frac{3}{6} \\ +\,1\frac{2}{3} & = & +\,1\frac{4}{6} \\ \hline \end{array}$$

Step 4 Change the improper fraction to a mixed number. Then add the mixed number to the whole number.

$\frac{7}{6} = \frac{6}{6} + \frac{1}{6} = 1\frac{1}{6}$

So $2\frac{7}{6} = 2 + 1\frac{1}{6} =$ ______

Solution How many hours did Kate spend doing these activities? ______

Apply the TEKS **Add. Write each fraction or mixed number in simplest form.**

1. $\frac{2}{9} + \frac{1}{3} =$ ______________

2. $\frac{5}{8} + \frac{1}{2} =$ ______________

3. $\frac{7}{8} + \frac{3}{4} =$ ______________

4. $1\frac{1}{8} + 4\frac{3}{4} =$ ______________

5. $4\frac{2}{3} + 3\frac{1}{4} =$ ______________

6. $2\frac{1}{6} + 5\frac{1}{4} =$ ______________

Find the sum. Write each mixed number in simplest form.

7. $1\frac{4}{9} + 3\frac{1}{3} =$ ______________

8. $6\frac{3}{4} + 3\frac{1}{5} =$ ______________

9. $4\frac{7}{8} + 5\frac{1}{4} =$ ______________

10. $3\frac{3}{5} + 7\frac{7}{10} =$ ______________

11. $5\frac{5}{9} + 8\frac{2}{3} =$ ______________

12. $7\frac{3}{4} + 7\frac{5}{6} =$ ______________

13. $4\frac{2}{3}$
$2\frac{1}{6}$
$+ 3\frac{5}{6}$

14. $6\frac{1}{2}$
$4\frac{3}{4}$
$+ 9\frac{1}{8}$

15. $8\frac{3}{4}$
$1\frac{1}{3}$
$+ 7\frac{3}{4}$

Solve the problem.

16. Leanne planned to hike $4\frac{1}{4}$ miles along a nature trail. She hiked $1\frac{2}{3}$ miles before resting for $\frac{3}{4}$ hour. Then she hiked another $2\frac{1}{4}$ miles. Did Leanne meet her goal? ______________ Explain your answer.

____

____

____

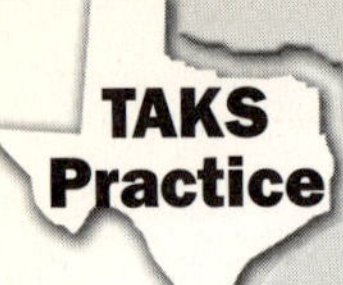

TAKS Objective 1 The student will demonstrate an understanding of numbers, operations, and quantitative reasoning.
TEKS 6.1B, 6.2A, 6.2B, 6.2D

DIRECTIONS Read each question. Then circle the letter for the correct answer.

1 Two boards are nailed together. One board is $\frac{3}{4}$ inch thick. The other board is $\frac{5}{6}$ inch thick. What is their combined thickness?

A $\frac{7}{10}$ in.

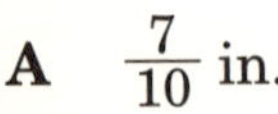

B $\frac{4}{5}$ in.

C $1\frac{7}{12}$ in.

D $1\frac{3}{4}$ in.

2 Yesterday, Ellen worked from 9:30 A.M. to noon. After taking one hour for lunch, Ellen worked until 4:15 P.M. How many hours did she work yesterday? Which number sentence shows how to solve the problem?

F $2\frac{1}{2} + 3\frac{1}{4} = n$

G $2\frac{1}{2} + 4\frac{1}{4} = n$

H $2\frac{3}{4} + 3\frac{1}{2} = n$

J $3\frac{1}{2} + 3\frac{1}{4} = n$

3 Dawn jogged $3\frac{7}{10}$ miles on Monday, $2\frac{1}{2}$ miles on Tuesday, and $2\frac{1}{5}$ miles on Wednesday. About how many miles did she jog altogether?

A 5 mi

B 6 mi

C 7 mi

D 9 mi

4 The sum of $2\frac{5}{12}$ and $4\frac{1}{2}$ is between —

F 5 and 6

G 6 and 7

H 7 and 8

J 8 and 9

5 The fraction bars show that the sum of $\frac{1}{2}$ and $\frac{1}{3}$ is the same as —

1											
$\frac{1}{4}$	$\frac{1}{4}$	$\frac{1}{4}$									
$\frac{1}{3}$	$\frac{1}{3}$										
$\frac{1}{12}$	$\frac{1}{12}$	$\frac{1}{12}$	$\frac{1}{12}$	$\frac{1}{12}$	$\frac{1}{12}$	$\frac{1}{12}$	$\frac{1}{12}$	$\frac{1}{12}$	$\frac{1}{12}$	$\frac{1}{12}$	$\frac{1}{12}$

A the sum of $\frac{1}{6}$ and $\frac{2}{6}$

B the sum of $\frac{1}{6}$ and $\frac{3}{6}$

C the sum of $\frac{2}{6}$ and $\frac{2}{6}$

D the sum of $\frac{3}{6}$ and $\frac{2}{6}$

Focus on TEKS

Lesson 19 Subtract Fractions and Mixed Numbers

TEKS 6.1B Generate equivalent forms of rational numbers.
TEKS 6.2A Model subtraction situations involving fractions with pictures, words, and numbers.
TEKS 6.2B Use subtraction to solve problems involving fractions.
TEKS 6.2D Estimate and round to approximate reasonable results and to solve problems where exact answers are not required.

You can subtract fractions and mixed numbers to solve problems.

When subtracting fractions or mixed numbers having *like denominators*, subtract the numerators. The denominator stays the same. When subtracting fractions or mixed numbers with *unlike denominators*, use the LCD (**least common denominator**) to find equivalent fractions or mixed numbers with like denominators.

Guided Instruction

Problem Larry has a piece of leather $2\frac{3}{4}$ inches long. He cuts off $1\frac{2}{3}$ inches to use in a project. What is the length of the leather Larry has left?

Subtract. $2\frac{3}{4} - 1\frac{2}{3}$

Step 1 Use the least common multiple of 4 and 3 to find the LCD.

Multiples of 4: 4, 8, ______, ...
Multiples of 3: 3, 6, 9 ______, ...

So the LCD of $\frac{3}{4}$ and $\frac{2}{3}$ is ________.

Step 2 Write the equivalent fractions using the LCD, 12.

$\frac{3 \times 3}{4 \times 3} = \frac{\square}{12}$ $\qquad$ $\frac{2 \times 4}{3 \times 4} = \frac{\square}{12}$

Step 3 Subtract the fractions, then subtract the whole numbers.

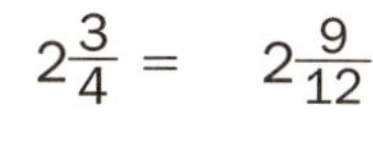
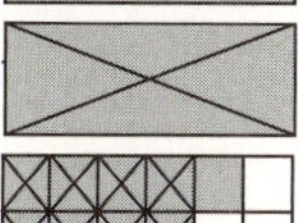

$$\begin{array}{rcr} 2\frac{3}{4} & = & 2\frac{9}{12} \\ -\ 1\frac{2}{3} & = & -\ 1\frac{8}{12} \\ \hline \end{array}$$

Step 4 Check by estimation. Round to the nearest whole number.
The answer is reasonable because it is close to the estimate of 1.

Solution What is the length of the piece of leather that remains? ____________

Other Examples

A. You may need to regroup before subtracting.

$$\begin{array}{r} 5\frac{1}{3} \\ -\ 2\frac{2}{3} \\ \hline \end{array} \longrightarrow \begin{array}{r} 4\frac{4}{3} \\ -\ 2\frac{2}{3} \\ \hline 2\frac{2}{3} \end{array}$$

B. Some differences may need to be written in simplest form.

$$\begin{array}{r} 9\frac{7}{8} \\ -\ 1\frac{3}{8} \\ \hline 8\frac{4}{8} = 8\frac{1}{2} \end{array}$$

Apply the TEKS **Subtract. Write each fraction or mixed number in simplest form.**

1. $\frac{5}{9} - \frac{1}{3} =$ ____________

2. $\frac{5}{8} - \frac{1}{2} =$ ____________

3. $\frac{7}{16} - \frac{1}{4} =$ ____________

4. $2\frac{2}{3} - \frac{1}{4} =$ ____________

5. $2\frac{5}{9} - 1\frac{1}{6} =$ ____________

6. $3\frac{1}{4} - 1\frac{1}{2} =$ ____________

Find the difference. Write in simplest form.

7. $6\frac{4}{5} - 1\frac{1}{2} =$ ____________

8. $14\frac{7}{9} - 8\frac{2}{3} =$ ____________

9. $5\frac{1}{8} - 1\frac{3}{4} =$ ____________

10. $12\frac{3}{5} - 4\frac{7}{10} =$ ____________

11. $7\frac{7}{16} - 1\frac{3}{16} =$ ____________

12. $2\frac{3}{8} - \frac{5}{6} =$ ____________

13. $15\frac{1}{3} - 13\frac{5}{6}$

14. $8\frac{1}{2} - 3\frac{7}{8}$

15. $21\frac{5}{9} - 16\frac{1}{6}$

Solve each problem.

16. You and your friend enter frogs in a frog-jumping contest. Your friend's frog jumps $15\frac{1}{4}$ feet. Your frog jumps $16\frac{2}{3}$ feet. How much farther does your frog jump? ____________

17. Carol promised her mother that she would spend $4\frac{1}{2}$ hours practicing playing the piano. She started at 9 A.M. and stopped at 11:15 A.M. How many more hours must Carol continue practicing to do what she promised?

____

Explain your answer.

____

____

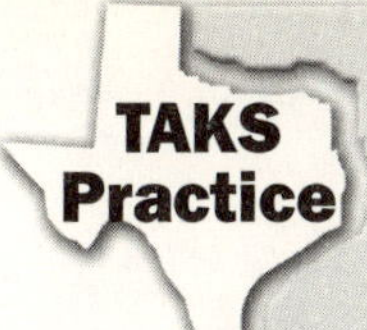

TAKS Objective 1 The student will demonstrate an understanding of numbers, operations, and quantitative reasoning.
TEKS 6.1B, 6.2A, 6.2B, 6.2D

DIRECTIONS Read each question. Then circle the letter for the correct answer.

1 Jim put $\frac{2}{3}$ ounce of lemon juice in a measuring cup. After he added some water, the measure showed $\frac{7}{8}$ ounce. How much water did Jim add?

A $1\frac{23}{24}$ oz $\frac{23}{24}$

B $\frac{7}{8}$ oz

C $\frac{5}{12}$ oz

D $\frac{5}{24}$ oz

Lee has a $2\frac{1}{4}$-yard length of fabric. She buys another length of $3\frac{7}{8}$ yards. She uses a 5-yard length to decorate her room. Which number sentence can be used to find how many yards of fabric are left?

F $(2\frac{1}{4} + 3\frac{7}{8}) - 5$

G $(5 + 2\frac{1}{4}) - 3\frac{7}{8}$

H $(5 + 3\frac{7}{8}) - 2\frac{1}{4}$

J Not Here

The sides of a triangle measure a total of $17\frac{1}{6}$ feet. The lengths of two of the sides are $6\frac{2}{3}$ feet and $4\frac{3}{4}$ feet. Which statement below correctly describes the length of the third side of the triangle?

A It is less than 2 feet long.

B It is between 3 and 4 feet long.

C It is greater than 5 feet long.

D It is greater than 12 feet long.

Kerri works out $1\frac{2}{3}$ hours each day. Ahmad works out $1\frac{1}{2}$ hours each day. Franklin works out $2\frac{1}{6}$ hours each day. Which statement below is true?

F Ahmad works out $\frac{1}{3}$ hour less than Franklin each day.

G Ahmad works out $\frac{1}{6}$ hour less than Kerri each day.

H Franklin works out $\frac{5}{6}$ hour more than Kerri each day.

J Kerri works out $\frac{1}{4}$ hour less than Franklin each day.

The fraction bars show that the difference between $\frac{3}{4}$ and $\frac{2}{3}$ is the same as—

1											
$\frac{1}{4}$	$\frac{1}{4}$	$\frac{1}{4}$									
$\frac{1}{3}$	$\frac{1}{3}$										
$\frac{1}{12}$	$\frac{1}{12}$	$\frac{1}{12}$	$\frac{1}{12}$	$\frac{1}{12}$	$\frac{1}{12}$	$\frac{1}{12}$	$\frac{1}{12}$	$\frac{1}{12}$	$\frac{1}{12}$	$\frac{1}{12}$	$\frac{1}{12}$

A the difference between $\frac{9}{12}$ and $\frac{8}{12}$

B the difference between $\frac{9}{12}$ and $\frac{6}{12}$

C the difference between $\frac{11}{12}$ and $\frac{6}{12}$

D the difference between $\frac{11}{12}$ and $\frac{8}{12}$

Focus on TEKS

Lesson 20 PROBLEM-SOLVING STRATEGY: Work a Simpler Problem

TEKS 6.11A	Identify and apply mathematics to everyday experiences.
TEKS 6.11B	Use a problem-solving model that incorporates understanding the problem, making a plan, carrying out the plan, and evaluating the solution for reasonableness.
TEKS 6.11C	Select or develop an appropriate problem-solving strategy.
TEKS 6.11D	Select tools such as real objects, manipulatives, paper/pencil and technology or techniques such as mental math, estimation, and number sense to solve problems.

Use the strategy of solving a simpler problem to solve problems.
Use the problem-solving guide on page 288 to help you.

Guided Instruction

Problem

Your school is collecting money for a local charity. On the first day, a 1-dollar bill is placed in a jar. On the second day, two 1-dollar bills are added to the jar. On the third day, three 1-dollar bills are added to the jar. If this pattern continues, how much money will be in the jar after 100 days?

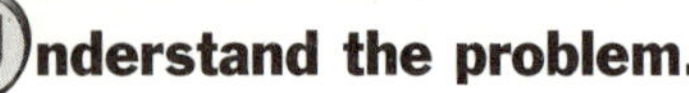

Understand the problem.

You know on each of 100 days, the number of 1-dollar bills in the jar increases by 1. What do you need to find?

____

Make a plan.

Solve a simpler problem using fewer days. Look for a method you can use with the actual problem.

Solve the problem.

$7

$1 + $2 + $3 + $4 + $5 + $6 = ?

$7

$7

First, find the total amount of money after only 6 days. Pair the numbers as shown to help find the total number of dollar bills.

How many number pairs are there? __________

This represents half the number of days.

What is the sum of each pair? __________

Find the total amount by multiplying the number of pairs by the sum of each pair. __________ × __________ = __________

So the amount after 6 days is __________.

Now apply this method to the actual problem.

How many number pairs will there be for 100 days? __________

What is the sum of the first and last number? __________

What can you multiply to find the total number of dollar bills?______________

How much money will be in the jar after 100 days? __________

Check your answer.

Look back at the problem. To help you check the method, try a second small number, such as 10 days. Ten days means 5 pairs. The sum of the first and last number is 11.

So 5 × 11 = __________

Find the actual sum:

1 + 2 + 3 + 4 + 5 + 6 + 7 + 8 + 9 + 10 = __________

Does the product match the sum? __________

Apply the TEKS **Solve each problem using a simpler problem.**

1. Mr. Smith is stacking cans in the grocery store. All the cans are the same size. He wants to stack the cans in rows so that each row has 1 more can than the row above it, as shown at right. How many cans will he stack in 15 rows?

Workspace

Simpler problem

How many cans in 5 rows? Pair the first and last rows. Continue pairing until there are no more pairs of rows.

How many pairs of rows? ___________

How many are in each pair? ___________.

How many cans are in the middle row? ___________

Notice that this is $\frac{1}{2}$ the sum of the number of cans in each pair of rows. Total number of cans in 5 rows:

(2 × ________) + ________ = ________

Actual problem

Total number of cans in 15 rows:

(________ × ________) + ________ = ________

2. An ant climbs 3 feet up a pole in the morning and slides back 2 feet in the evening. The pole is 20 feet tall. How many days will it take the ant to reach the top of the pole? Explain how you can use a simpler problem to solve the problem.

____

____

____

____

What is the solution of the actual problem? ___________

3. There are 6 people at the chess club. Each person shakes hands with every other person at the club once. Find the total number of handshakes. ___________

4. Alex hiked $3\frac{1}{4}$ miles on Saturday and $5\frac{1}{2}$ miles on Sunday. Sylvia hiked $4\frac{1}{4}$ miles on Saturday and $3\frac{3}{8}$ miles on Sunday. How many more miles did Alex hike than Sylvia?

____

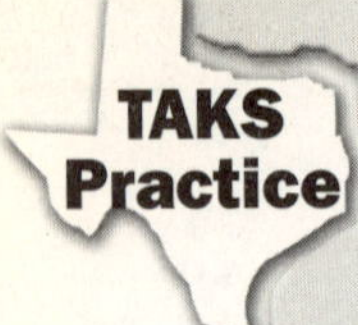

TAKS Objective 6 The student will demonstrate an understanding of the mathematical processes and tools used in problem solving.

TEKS 6.11A, 6.11B, 6.11C, 6.11D

DIRECTIONS Read each question. Then circle the letter for the correct answer.

1 The town of Summerville is hosting a soccer tournament for 22 soccer teams from the area. Each team gets eliminated after it loses. How many games need to be played to determine a winner for the tournament?

A 11

B 21

C 22

D 44

2 Nick has 8 shares each of two stocks. The first stock has a price of $3.25 per share, and the other has a price of $6.25 per share. What is the difference in the total value of the two stocks he owns?

F $8

G $24

H $26

J $50

3 Engineers are divided into groups to work on a project. There are six groups. One half of the groups have five engineers each, $\frac{1}{3}$ of the groups have six engineers each, and $\frac{1}{6}$ of the group have four engineers each. How many engineers are working on the project?

A 15

B 16

C 27

D 31

4 There are 8 students in a chemistry lab. The students work in pairs. Each student is paired once with every other student. How many different pairings are there in all?

F 28

G 21

H 16

J 6

5 A diagonal is a line segment other than a side that connects two vertices of a polygon.

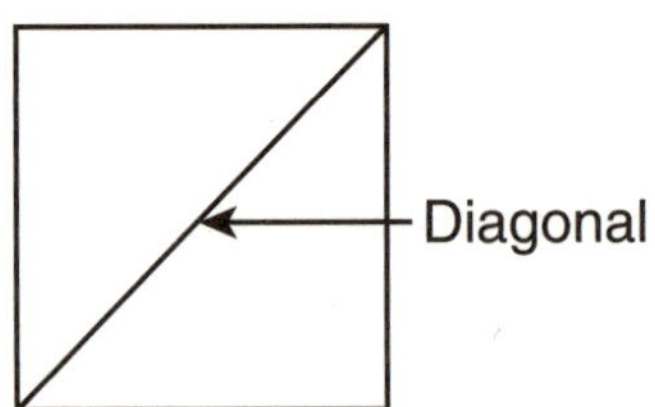

How many diagonals does an octagon (an 8-sided polygon) have?

A 5

B 12

C 20

D 24

Building Stamina®

DIRECTIONS Read each question. Then circle the letter for the correct answer. If a correct answer is <u>not here</u>, mark the letter for "Not Here."

1 In which set are all the fractions equivalent to $\frac{3}{8}$?

A $\frac{6}{16}, \frac{9}{24}, \frac{15}{18}$

B $\frac{9}{24}, \frac{15}{40}, \frac{18}{48}$

C $\frac{15}{40}, \frac{18}{24}, \frac{17}{38}$

D $\frac{21}{24}, \frac{24}{64}, \frac{27}{72}$

2 What decimal is equivalent to $\frac{13}{25}$?

Record your answer and fill in the bubbles on the grid below. Be sure to use the correct place value.

				.		
0	0	0	0		0	0
1	1	1	1		1	1
2	2	2	2		2	2
3	3	3	3		3	3
4	4	4	4		4	4
5	5	5	5		5	5
6	6	6	6		6	6
7	7	7	7		7	7
8	8	8	8		8	8
9	9	9	9		9	9

3 A caterpillar climbs up a tree 5 feet in the morning and slides back 2 feet in the evening. The tree is 20 feet tall. How many days will it take the caterpillar to reach the top of the tree?

A 18 days

B 15 days

C 12 days

D 6 days

4 Arlene served $4\frac{1}{8}$ loaves of banana bread and $3\frac{1}{4}$ loaves of cranberry bread. Each complete loaf was sliced into 8 equal slices. Each incomplete loaf was sliced to match each slice from the complete loaves. How many slices of bread did she serve in all?

F 16

G 33

H 46

J 59

5 Which model does NOT show $\frac{2}{3}$ shaded?

A

B

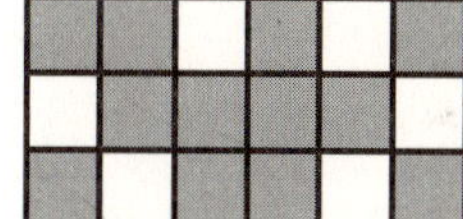

C

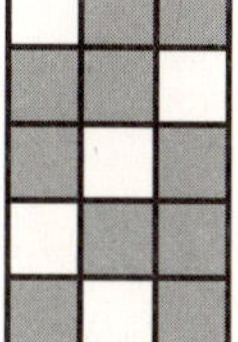

D

6 The records set in pole vaulting by students at four different schools are shown in the table below.

School	Oakmont	Chester	Central	Perry
Pole Vault Height (in feet)	$\frac{49}{3}$	$16\frac{3}{8}$	$\frac{33}{2}$	$16\frac{9}{16}$

Which school has the highest record vault?

F Oakmont

G Chester

H Central

J Perry

7 Monkey bars occupy $\frac{1}{4}$ of an obstacle course. Tires occupy $\frac{1}{3}$ of the course. A tunnel occupies $\frac{5}{12}$ of the course. How much less of the obstacle course does the tunnel occupy than the monkey bars and tires combined?

A $\frac{1}{12}$

B $\frac{1}{6}$

C $\frac{5}{12}$

D $\frac{7}{12}$

8 The sides of a triangle measure a total of 21 inches. The lengths of two of the sides are $8\frac{1}{2}$ inches and $5\frac{2}{3}$ inches. Which statement below correctly describes the length of the third side of the triangle?

F It is less than 4 inches long.

G It is between 4 and 5 inches long.

H It is greater than 6 inches long.

J It is greater than 8 inches long.

9 A scientist measures the level of ocean tides from a cliff overlooking the ocean. The low tide is $20\frac{1}{4}$ feet below the edge of the cliff. The high tide is $9\frac{1}{2}$ feet below the edge of the cliff. Which equation can you use to find how much higher the high tide is than the low tide?

A $9\frac{1}{2} + x = 20\frac{1}{4}$

B $x - 9\frac{1}{2} = 20\frac{1}{4}$

C $9\frac{1}{2} - x = 20\frac{1}{4}$

D $x = 20\frac{1}{4} + 9\frac{1}{2}$

10 A White Pine tree is $47\frac{3}{10}$ feet taller than an American Basswood, which is $7\frac{7}{10}$ feet shorter than a Northern Red Oak. If the Northern Red Oak is 119 feet tall, how tall is the White Pine?

F 64 ft

G 154 ft

H $158\frac{3}{5}$ ft

J $159\frac{3}{10}$ ft

11 A carton contains $2\frac{1}{2}$ cups of milk. You pour $1\frac{7}{8}$ cups into a bowl. How many cups of milk are left in the carton?

A $\frac{1}{4}$ cup

B $\frac{3}{8}$ cup

C $\frac{1}{2}$ cup

D $\frac{5}{8}$ cup

12 Yesterday, Henry worked from 8:45 A.M. to 1:00 P.M. He then took $\frac{1}{2}$ hour for lunch and worked until 5:00 P.M. Which expression shows the number of hours he worked yesterday?

F $4\frac{1}{4} + 3\frac{1}{2}$

G $4\frac{1}{2} + 3\frac{1}{4}$

H $4\frac{1}{2} + 3\frac{1}{3}$

J Not Here

13 Which expression has the least value?

A $5\frac{1}{4} + 2\frac{1}{4} - 2\frac{1}{8}$

B $6\frac{1}{4} + 1 - 1\frac{1}{4}$

C $8\frac{1}{3} - 1\frac{1}{2} + 1\frac{1}{3}$

D $12\frac{2}{5} - 5 + 2\frac{4}{5}$

14 You buy $\frac{2}{3}$ pound of dog biscuits at a pet store. If the scale gives a decimal weight to the nearest hundredth, what will the scale read?

Record your answer and fill in the bubbles on the grid below. Be sure to use the correct place value.

				.		
0	0	0	0		0	0
1	1	1	1		1	1
2	2	2	2		2	2
3	3	3	3		3	3
4	4	4	4		4	4
5	5	5	5		5	5
6	6	6	6		6	6
7	7	7	7		7	7
8	8	8	8		8	8
9	9	9	9		9	9

15 About $\frac{23}{25}$ of a watermelon is water. What decimal represents the portion of the watermelon that is NOT water?

A 0.92

B 0.88

C 0.80

D 0.08

16 In the set of fractions below, all fractions are equivalent.

$\frac{5}{9}, \frac{10}{18}, \frac{a}{27}, \frac{30}{b}$

What are the values of a and b?

F $a = 12, b = 36$

G $a = 15, b = 36$

H $a = 15, b = 54$

J $a = 21, b = 45$

17 The table below shows the number of students enrolled in foreign languages at Edison Middle School.

	Grade 6	Grade 7
French	18	15
Spanish	24	20
Russian	34	44

What fraction of sixth-grade students taking foreign languages takes Spanish?

A $\frac{1}{2}$

B $\frac{4}{5}$

C $\frac{9}{10}$

D $\frac{6}{19}$

18 A class of students is divided into 9 groups to work on a project. If $\frac{2}{9}$ of the groups have two students each, $\frac{1}{3}$ of the groups have three students each, and $\frac{4}{9}$ of the groups have four students each, how many students are in the class?

F 15

G 16

H 29

J 31

19 The auditorium at your school has 320 seats. If 280 of the seats are full, which of the following is NOT true?

A $\frac{56}{64}$ of the seats are full.

B $\frac{7}{8}$ of the seats are full.

C $\frac{60}{80}$ of the seats are empty.

D $\frac{1}{8}$ of the seats are empty.

20 Chuck owns 800 shares of stock in a company. When he purchased the stock, he paid $7.25 per share. The total value of Chuck's stock is now $7,200.

Which describes a method that can be used to find how much the price per share has increased?

F Multiply 800 by 7.25 and then subtract the product from 7,200.

G Divide 7,200 by 800, then subtract 7.25 from the quotient.

H Subtract 800 from 7,200 and then. multiply the difference by 7.25.

J Add 7,200 and 800 and divide the sum by 7.25.

Focus on TEKS

Lesson 21 Use Tables to Represent Relationships

TEKS 6.4A Use tables and symbols to represent and describe proportional and other relationships such as those involving conversions, arithmetic sequences (with constant range of change), perimeter and area.

TEKS 6.12A Communicate mathematical ideas using language.

TEKS 6.13A Make conjectures from patterns.

You can use tables and patterns to solve problems involving sequences. You can write an expression to describe the pattern.

A **sequence** is a set of numbers that is arranged in a pattern. Each number in a sequence is called a **term**.
An **expression** is a mathematical statement using numbers, variables, and operations. A **variable** is a letter or symbol used to represent an unknown number.

Guided Instruction

Problem

What is the value of the fifth term in this sequence? 3, 6, 9, 12, . . . What is a rule that describes how to find the value of any term in the sequence?

Make a table and look for a pattern.

Step 1 Make a table to show the terms in order.

position of terms →	1	2	3	4	5	*n*
value of terms →	3	6	9	___	___	___

Step 2 Find the pattern.

1 × ___ = 3 2 × ___ = 6 3 × ___ = 9
4 × ___ = 12 5 × ___ = ___

What is the value of the fifth term? _____

Step 3 Write a rule that shows how you found the value of the term given the position of the term.

Multiply the number in the top row of the table by _____.
Use the rule and the variable *n* to write an expression that tells how to find any term.
Multiply *n* by _____.
By placing a number next to a variable, multiplication is understood.
So the rule can be written as $3n$.

Solution

What is the value of the fifth term in the sequence? ____
What is a rule that describes how to find the value of any term in the sequence? ____

Another Example

Write an expression to describe the output in terms of input. What is the pattern?

Add _____

Write the rule as an expression in terms of *x*.

x + _____

Input (*x*)	Output (*y*)
5	9
6	10
7	11
8	12

Apply the TEKS **Write the next term in each number sequence. Explain the pattern.**

1. 16, 14, 12, 10, ____ ______________________

2. 1, 2.1, 3.2, 4.3, ____ ______________________

3.

Input	1	2	3	4	5	6	7
Output	6	12	18	24	30	36	?

____ ______________________

Draw the next term in each sequence and explain the pattern.

4.  

____

5. 

____

Solve each problem.

6. A child is building steps with these blocks: The diagram shows 5 steps she has built. If the pattern continues, how many blocks will she use to build 10 steps?

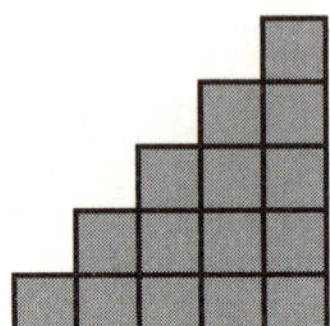

____

7. Each number in the sequence below has the same relationship to the number immediately before it.

324, 108, 36, 12, ...

What is the next number in the sequence? ______

Explain how the answer was determined.

____

____

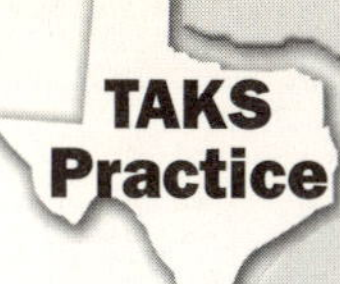

TAKS Objective 2 The student will demonstrate an understanding of patterns, relationships, and algebraic reasoning.
TEKS 6.4A

TAKS Objective 6 The student will demonstrate an understanding of the mathematical processes and tools used in problem solving.
TEKS 6.12A, 6.13A

DIRECTIONS Read each question. Then circle the letter for the correct answer.

1 Each number in the sequence below has the same relationship to the number immediately before it.

2, 4, 8, 16, ...

How can the next number in the sequence be found?

A By adding eight to the previous number

B By multiplying the previous number by 2

C By dividing the previous number by 2

D By subtracting 8 from the previous number

2 How can you find the next term in the sequence below?

5, 8, 11, 14, ...

F By adding 3

G By adding $\frac{1}{3}$

H By multiplying by 2

J By multiplying by 3

The sequence below is formed using the letters of the alphabet.

ABBCCCDDDD ...

If the pattern continues through the letter F, how many letters will be in the sequence?

A 28

B 21

C 15

D 10

4 Which expression can be used to describe n in this sequence?

Place in the Sequence	Term
1st	9
2nd	10
3rd	11
4th	12
n	...

F $3n$

G $n-3$

H $\frac{n}{8}$

J $n + 8$

This array of numbers is called *Pascal's Triangle.*

1
1 1
1 2 1
1 3 3 1
1 4 6 4 1

If the pattern continues, what is the next row of this array?

A 1 5 5 1

B 1 5 7 7 5 1

C 1 5 10 5 1

D 1 5 10 10 5 1

Focus on TEKS

Lesson 22 Write an Equation

TEKS 6.5A Formulate equations from problem situations described by linear relationships.

TEKS 6.12A Communicate mathematical ideas using language.

You can use an equation to represent a problem situation.

An **equation** is a number sentence with an equal symbol (=) that shows two expressions have the same value. Just as number sentences can describe a problem, so can an equation.

A letter or symbol, called a **variable**, is used in an equation to represent an unknown number.

Guided Instruction

Problem 1 In June 2002, the price of a first-class postage stamp increased by 3¢. This made the price 37¢. How can you write an equation that represents this situation?

Identify the unknown and use a variable to represent it in an equation.

Step 1 Which price is unknown?
The previous price of a first-class stamp is unknown.

Step 2 Let p represent the price of the previous first-class stamp, in cents. In June 2002, the price of a stamp was 3¢ more than the previous price, so the price of the new stamp can be represented by __________.

Step 3 Use the price of the previous first-class stamp to write an equation stating that $p + 3$ is equal to 37.

____

Solution What equation represents this situation? ____________________

Another Problem

Guided Instruction

Problem 2 Steve is 3 times older than Tony. Steve is 18 years old. What equation can you write to represent this situation?

Identify the unknown and use a variable to represent it in an equation.

Step 1 Whose age is unknown? __________ age is unknown.

Step 2 Let *a* represent Tony's age, in years. Since Steve is 3 times older than Tony, then Steve's age may be represented by the expression __________.

By placing a number next to a variable, multiplication is understood. So, Tony's age can be represented by 3*a*.

Step 3 Use Tony's age to write an equation stating that 3*a* is equal to 18. __________

Solution What equation represents this situation? __________

Other Examples

A. Write an equation to represent this statement. A number divided by 4 is 5.

Let *x* represent the number.

$x \div 4 = 5$

B. Write an equation to represent this situation. Steve has 5 fewer coins than Jamal. Steve has 20 coins. How many coins does Jamal have?

Let *c* represent Jamal's coins.

$c - 5 = 20$

Apply the TEKS **Match the equation to the situation.**

1. Five times a number is 20. ________ a. $y + 5 = 20$

2. A number and five make 20. ________ b. $20 - 5 = y$

3. A number divided by 5 is 20. ________ c. $5n = 20$

4. A number is five less than 20. ________ d. $x \div 5 = 20$

Write an equation to model the problem situation.

5. The bus that transports senior citizens has 16 seats more than the van that may also be used. The bus has 28 seats. How many seats are in the van? Use v to represent the number of seats in the van.

____

6. Pam weighs 6 pounds less than her friend Talisha. Pam weighs 92 pounds. How much does Talisha weigh? Use t to represent Talisha's weight.

____

7. Mrs. Kelly is 3 times taller than her daughter Lynn. Mrs. Kelly's height is 69 inches. How tall is Lynn? Use l to represent Lynn's height.

____

8. Michael said he is thinking of a number. If you divide Michael's number by 4, the result is 20. What number was Michael thinking of? Use n to represent Michael's number.

____

9. Bridgette scored 8 more points than Liz this basketball season. Bridgette scored 52 points. How many points did Liz score? Use p to represent Liz's points.

____

10. Hector has 37 coins in his coin collection. Hector has half as many coins as Jonathan has. How many coins does Jonathan have? Use j to represent the number of coins Jonathan has.

____

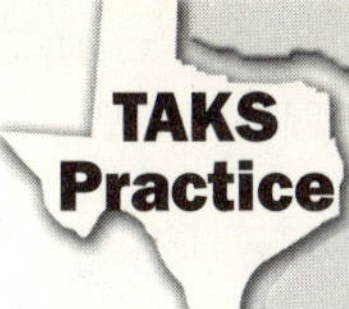

TAKS Objective 2 The student will demonstrate an understanding of patterns, relationships, and algebraic reasoning.
TEKS 6.5A

TAKS Objective 6 The student will demonstrate an understanding of the mathematical processes and tools used in problem solving.
TEKS 6.12A

DIRECTIONS Read each question. Then circle the letter for the correct answer.

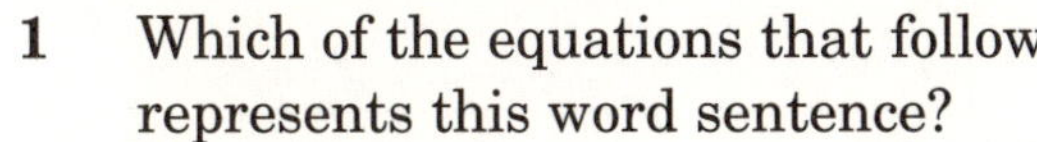

1 Which of the equations that follow represents this word sentence?

20 more than the number of plush animals, p, is 41.

A $20p = 41$

B $p = 41 + 20$

C $p + 20 = 41$

D $p - 20 = 41$

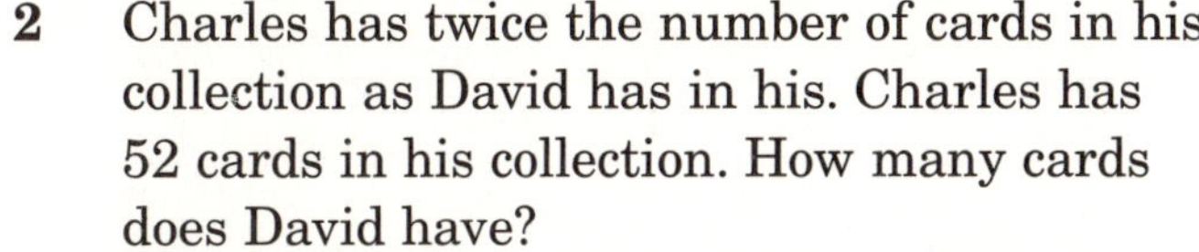

2 Charles has twice the number of cards in his collection as David has in his. Charles has 52 cards in his collection. How many cards does David have?

If n represents the number of cards in David's collection, which equation can be used to model the problem situation?

F $n + 2 = 52$

G $n = 52 \times 2$

H $2n = 52$

J $n \div 2 = 52$

3 Jose ran 6 laps at track practice on two days last week. He ran 4 laps at practice on the other two days. Which equation can be used to find l, the total number of laps he ran?

A $l = 6 \times 4$

B $l = 2(6) - 2\,(4)$

C $l = 2(6 + 4)$

D $l = (6 + 4) \div 2$

4 Ms. McCall bought 24 notebooks at a total cost of $36, excluding tax.

If p represents the price of one notebook, an equation that can be used to model this problem is $24p = 36$.

Which is an equivalent equation?

F $p = 36 \div 24$

G $p = 36 - 24$

H $p = 36 \times 24$

J $p = 36 + 24$

5 Norma is 3 inches shorter than Sara. Norma is 5 feet tall. How tall is Sara?

If h represents Sara's height, which equation can be used to model the problem situation?

A $h - 3 = 5$

B $h - 3 = 60$

C $h \div 3 = 5$

D $h \div 3 = 60$

Focus on TEKS

Lesson 23 Write a Formula

TEKS 6.4A Use tables and symbols to represent and describe proportional and other relationships such as those involving conversions, arithmetic sequences (with a constant rate of change), perimeter and area.

TEKS 6.4B Use tables of data to generate formulas for representing relationships involving perimeter, area, volume of a rectangular prism, etc.

TEKS 6.5A Formulate equations from problem situations described by linear relationships.

You can use a formula to represent a relationship.

A **formula** is an equation that states a rule or a fact.

Guided Instruction

Problem

Jason drew four different-sized rectangles on grid paper. He counted the number of units long and the number of units wide for each rectangle. He then found the area of each rectangle by counting the number of square units that filled each rectangle. He recorded the data in the table below. Write a formula that can be used to find A, the area of a rectangle, with a length of l units and a width of w units.

Length (Units)	Width (Units)	Area (Square Units)
3	6	18
5	4	20
7	5	35
8	9	72

Look for a pattern in the table. Then write the rule for the pattern as a formula.

Step 1 Find the pattern.

3 ◯ 6 = 18

5 ◯ 4 = 20

7 ◯ 5 = 35

8 ◯ 9 = 72

Step 2 Express the relationship between the area of a rectangle, its length, and its width in words. Then write the rule as a formula.

The area is equal to the __________ of the length __________ the width.

So A = __________

Solution

Write a formula that can be used to find A, the area of a rectangle, with a length of l units and a width of w units. ____________________

Apply the TEKS **Write formulas to represent the relationships shown in each table.**

This table shows the relationship between the base, height, and area of a triangle.

Triangle	Base (*b*)	Height (*h*)	Area (*A*)
A	5	8	20
B	10	12	60
C	4	9	18
D	11	4	22

1. Find the product of the base and height for each triangle.

Triangle A: $b \times h =$ ________ Triangle B: $b \times h =$ ________

Triangle C: $b \times h =$ ________ Triangle D: $b \times h =$ ________

2. How does the area of each triangle compare to the products you found in question 1? ____________________________

3. Write the formula for finding the area of a triangle. ________________

Write a formula for each.

4. Serena made this table.

Input (x)	Output (y)
8	19
14	25
25	36
34	45

What is the rule she used? ________________

Write the rule as a formula that shows how to find output (y) in terms of input (x). ________________

5. Jon's sister is younger than he is. The table shows their ages at different times. Write a formula that shows the relationship between their ages.

Formula ____________________

Jon's Age (*a*)	His Sister's Age (*s*)
7	3
9	5
12	8
15	11

6. Is there another formula you could write to show the relationship between the age of Jon and his sister in the problem above? Explain.

____

____

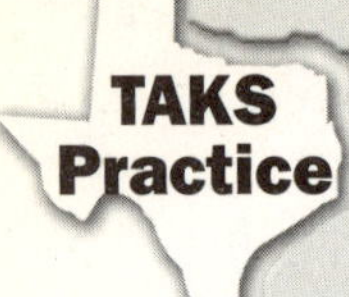

TAKS Objective 2 The student will demonstrate an understanding of patterns, relationships, and algebraic reasoning.
TEKS 6.4A, 6.4B, 6.5A

DIRECTIONS Read each question. Then circle the letter for the correct answer.

1 This table shows Kim's height, in inches, compared to Bob's height, in inches, at different times.

Kim's Height (k)	Bob's Height (b)
56	53
57	54
61	58
65.5	62.5

Let k represent Kim's height and let b represent Bob's height. Which formula shows the relationship between their heights?

A $b = k + 3$

B $k = b - 3$

C $k = b \times 3$

D $b = k - 3$

This table shows some x-values and the corresponding y-values.

x	2	4	5	7	10
y	7	13	16	22	31

Which formula shows the relationship between the variables?

F $y = 3x - 1$

G $x = 3y + 1$

H $y = 3x + 1$

J $x = 3y - 1$

This table shows the perimeter of different equilateral triangles.

Side Length (n)	Perimeter (p)
10	30
12	36
15	45
20	60

Which formula can be used to find the perimeter of an equilateral triangle with a side length of n?

A $p = n + 3$

B $p = 3n$

C $p = n^3$

D $p = 6 + n$

4 This table shows some s-values and the corresponding t-values.

s	1	2	3	4	6	12
t	12	6	4	3	2	1

Which formula shows the relationship between the variables?

F $t = s \div 12$

G $t = 12 \div s$

H $t = s + 12$

J $s = t + 12$

Focus on TEKS

Lesson 24 PROBLEM-SOLVING STRATEGY: Make a Table

TEKS 6.11B Use a problem-solving model that incorporates understanding the problem, making a plan, carrying out the plan, and evaluating the solution for reasonableness.

TEKS 6.11C Select or develop an appropriate problem-solving strategy from a variety of different types, including making a table.

Use the make-a-table strategy to help you solve the problem.
You can use the problem-solving guide on page 288 to help you.

Guided Instruction

Problem Beth's dog weighs 65 pounds. The veterinarian recommends a diet that will help the dog lose 2.5 pounds each week. How many weeks will it take for the dog to reach her goal weight of 50 pounds?

Use a table to help you find a pattern.

Understand the problem.

Look for the information you will use.

The dog weighs ______________.

The amount of weight she hopes to lose each week is ______________.

Her goal weight is ______________.

What does the problem ask you to find?

____

Make a plan.

Make a table to solve the problem. Show how much Beth's dog will weigh at the end of each week that she is on the diet.

Solve the Problem

If the dog loses 2.5 lb each week, at the end of the first week, she will weigh 65 lb − 2.5 lb, or ________ lb.

Weight	65	62.5					
Weeks	0	1	2				

What number of weeks corresponds to 50 lb? ________

How many weeks will it take Beth's dog to reach the goal? ________

Check your answer.

Think about what the total weight loss should be in 6 weeks.
$6 \times 2.5 =$ ________

Subtract total weight loss from starting weight. 65 − ________ = ________
Is the result the same as the goal weight? If yes, then 6 weeks is correct.

Apply the TEKS

Complete the table to solve each problem.

1. Jack gets an allowance of $5 a week. This week, he decided to save money according to a pattern. On Monday, he put aside 2¢. On each succeeding day, he saved twice as much as he did the day before.
How much money did he save on Sunday? ____________
What is the total amount of money he saved this week? ______________

Day	¢ saved
Monday	2
Tuesday	
Wednesday	
Thursday	
Friday	
Saturday	
Sunday	

2. A state fair will be held during the month of June. At the fair, 56 prizes will be given out: 2 on June 1, 4 on June 2, 6 on June 3, and so on.

By what day will all 56 prizes have been given out? ____________

June	Prizes Given	Sum of Prizes	Pattern for the Sums
1	2	2	2, or 1×2
2	4	$2 + 4$	6, or 2×3
3	6	$2 + 4 + 6$	12, or 3×4
4			
5			
6			
7			

What pattern do you observe for the sums?

____

____

Make a table to solve the problem.

3. A bus leaves Waco with 15 passengers. At the first stop, 5 people get off. At the second stop, 3 people get on. At the third stop, 5 people get off. At the fourth stop, 3 people get on. If this pattern continues, at which stop will the last passenger get off? ____________
What pattern do you observe about the total number of passengers at selected stops?

____

____

____

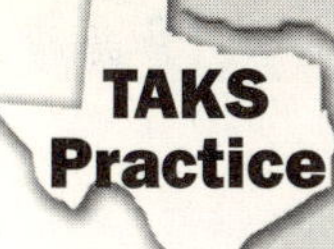

TAKS Objective 6 The student will demonstrate an understanding of the mathematical processes and tools used in problem solving.

TEKS 6.11B, 6.11C

DIRECTIONS Read each question. Then circle the letter for the correct answer.

1 A night watchman checks in at a post every $2\frac{1}{2}$ hours. Tonight, his first check-in at this post is at 10 P.M. At what time will his fourth check-in at this post be?

A 5 A.M.

B 6 A.M.

C 7 A.M.

D 8 A.M.

2 In the last 3 months, Omar saved a total of \$950. He plans to save \$250 a month for the next 3 months. If he carries out his plan, how much money, in dollars, will Omar have saved for the 6-month period?
Record your answer and fill in the bubbles on the grid below. Be sure to use the correct place value.

				.		
0	0	0	0		0	0
1	1	1	1		1	1
2	2	2	2		2	2
3	3	3	3		3	3
4	4	4	4		4	4
5	5	5	5		5	5
6	6	6	6		6	6
7	7	7	7		7	7
8	8	8	8		8	8
9	9	9	9		9	9

3 Molly wrote an *A*, then two *B*s, three *C*s, and so on. Using her pattern, what did Molly write as the 25th letter?

A E

B F

C G

D H

4 For the next 6 days, a radio show is giving free tickets to a rock concert. The tickets are given to callers according to the pattern in this table.

Day	1	2	3	4	5
Tickets	2	4	8	16	32

In all, how many tickets will be given away?

F 64

G 96

H 112

J 126

5 Jorge will do increasing numbers of situps daily, according to the pattern in this table.

Day	1	2	3	4	5
Situps	3	5	8	13	21

How many situps will he do on Day 7?

A 34

B 45

C 55

D Not Here

Building Stamina®

DIRECTIONS Read each question. Then circle the letter for the correct answer. If a correct answer is <u>not here</u>, mark the letter for "Not Here."

1 Which expression describes the nth term of the following sequence?

0, 2, 6, 12, ...

A $2(n - 1)$

B $2(n + 1)$

C $n(n + 1)$

D $n(n - 1)$

2 The expression $(2n + 1)^2$ describes a sequence, where n equals the nth term in the sequence. Which sequence shown below matches this description?

F 2, 18, 32, 50, ...

G 9, 16, 25, 36,...

H 9, 25, 49, 81,...

J 9, 25, 36, 49, ...

3 Which pattern can describe the following sequence of numbers?

2, 5, 17, 65, ...

A For each number after the first, add 3 to the previous number and multiply by 2.

B For each number after the first, multiply the previous number by 4 and subtract 3.

C For each number after the first, multiply the previous number by 3 and add 5.

D Not Here

4 Brad is a clerk at a supermarket. He decides to set up a display of cans where the top row has one can, and each row below has one more can than the row above. How many cans does Brad need to make a stack of cans 17 rows high?

F 107

G 135

H 144

J 153

5 Over the last 6 months, Janet deposited \$150 a month into her savings account. Over the next 6 months, Janet plans to deposit \$30 more each month than the previous month. If Janet sticks to her plan, how many dollars will she have deposited in her account for the year?

Record your answer and fill in the bubbles on the grid below. Be sure to use the correct place value.

				.		
0	0	0	0		0	0
1	1	1	1		1	1
2	2	2	2		2	2
3	3	3	3		3	3
4	4	4	4		4	4
5	5	5	5		5	5
6	6	6	6		6	6
7	7	7	7		7	7
8	8	8	8		8	8
9	9	9	9		9	9

6 What are the next two terms of this sequence?

4000, 2000, 1800, 900, 700....

F 350, 150

G 350, 250

H 400, 200

J 500, 300

7 If h represents the number of hours worked, which equation below can be used to represent the following word sentence?

Eight less than the number of hours worked is 27 hours.

A $h + 8 = 27$

B $h - 8 = 27$

C $27 - h = 8$

D $8 - h = 27$

8 Which equation can be used to model the following problem?

Asa owes a balance of $450 on a loan. He has 30 more equal monthly payments to make. How much is each monthly payment?

F $30m = 450$

G $30 - m = 450$

H $m \div 30 = 450$

J $450m = 30$

9 On day 1 of a contest, 6 people were selected to win a free calculator. On each day of the contest that followed, the number of people selected to win a calculator doubled from the previous day. How many people were selected on the seventh day of the contest?

A 192

B 384

C 662

D 768

10 The table below shows how the number of people who attend a dinner and the price for the dinner are related.

People	1	2	3	4	5
Cost	$15	$30	$45	$60	$75

Which equation shows how to find n, the number of people who attended dinner, if the dinner cost $330?

F $n \times 15 = 330$

G $n \times 330 = 15$

H $n \div 15 = 330$

J $n - 15 = 330$

11 The formula $A = l \times w$ shows the relationship between l and w, the length and width of a rectangle, and A, its area. Which formula shows the same relationship?

A $A = l \div w$

B $l = A \times w$

C $w = A \times l$

D $l = A \div w$

12 The formula $r = d \div t$ shows the relationship of r to d and t.

Which table of values shows this relationship?

F

d	20	30	42	72	100
r	5	6	7	8	10
t	4	5	6	9	10

G

d	5	6	7	8	10
r	4	5	6	9	10
t	20	30	42	72	100

H

d	15	25	30	35	46
r	8	9	12	15	20
t	7	16	18	20	26

J

d	2	2	3	4	4
r	2	4	4	6	9
t	4	8	12	24	36

13 Every time Karen walks 1 block north, she then walks $4\frac{1}{2}$ blocks east. Which formula below shows the relationship between n, the number of blocks Karen walks north, and e, the number of blocks she walks east?

A $e = \frac{9}{2} \times n$

B $e = n + \frac{9}{2}$

C $n = e + 4\frac{1}{2}$

D $n = 4\frac{1}{2} - e$

14 This table shows Fred's weight, in pounds, compared to Brad's weight, in pounds, at different times.

Fred's Weight (f)	Brad's Weight (b)
75	70
82	77
89	84
101	96

Let f represent Fred's weight and b represent Brad's weight. Which formula shows the relationship between their weights?

F $b = 5 - f$

G $b = f - 5$

H $f = b - 5$

J $f = b \div 5$

15 This table shows some x-values and the corresponding y-values.

x	0	3	5	8	10
y	2	8	12	18	22

Which formula shows the relationship between the variables?

A $y = x + 2$

B $y = 2x$

C $y = 2x + 1$

D $y = 2(x + 1)$

16 The table below shows the utility bills Ms. Moore paid for the first 4 months of the year.

Month	Amount
January	$150
February	$185
March	$220
April	$255

If this pattern continues, how many dollars will Ms. Moore pay for her October utility bill?

Record your answer and fill in the bubbles on the grid below. Be sure to use the correct place value.

				.		
0	0	0	0		0	0
1	1	1	1		1	1
2	2	2	2		2	2
3	3	3	3		3	3
4	4	4	4		4	4
5	5	5	5		5	5
6	6	6	6		6	6
7	7	7	7		7	7
8	8	8	8		8	8
9	9	9	9		9	9

17 How can you find the next term in the sequence below?

2, 8, 32, 128, ...

A By adding 6

B By adding 24

C By multiplying by 2

D By multiplying by 4

18 An elevator leaves the ground floor with 26 people. At the first floor 6 people get off. At the second floor, 2 people get on. At the third floor, 6 people get off. At the fourth floor, 2 people get on.

If this pattern continues, at which floor will all the people on the elevator get off?

F 6th floor

G 9th floor

H 12th floor

J Not Here

19 The table shows the number of points and the number of line segments needed to connect each pair of points, when no 3 points lie in a straight line.

Number of Points	2	3	4	5	6
Number of Line Segments	1	3	6	10	15

Based upon the pattern shown in the table, how many line segments are needed to connect 9 points, when no 3 points lie in a straight line?

A 28

B 36

C 45

D 55

Notes

Focus on TEKS

Lesson 25 Ratios

TEKS 6.3A Use ratios to describe proportional situations.
TEKS 6.3B Represent ratios with concrete models and fractions.

You can use a ratio to make comparisons.

A **ratio** is a comparison of two quantities. A ratio can compare part-to-part, part-to-whole, or whole-to-whole.

In the figure at the right, there are 6 squares.
Of these, 3 are shaded, 1 is unshaded, and 2 are striped.

The ratio of striped squares to shaded squares is 2 to 3.

The ratio of unshaded squares to all squares is 1 to 6.

Ratios can be written 3 ways.
The ratio of shaded squares to all squares is 3 to 6.

Use *to*.	3 to 6

Use a colon.	3:6

Use fraction form.	$\frac{3}{6}$

Guided Instruction

Problem

Look at the balls to the right.
What is the ratio of shaded balls to striped balls?

Write the ratio using fraction form, the word *to*, and a colon.

Write the ratio using fraction form. number of shaded circles → $\frac{\square}{\square}$ ← number of striped circles

Write the ratio using *to*. _______ to _______

Write the ratio using a colon. _______ : _______

Solution

What is the ratio of shaded circles to striped circles? ______________

Other Examples

A. What is the ratio of striped circles to all of the circles in the figure above?

number of striped circles → $\frac{\square}{\square}$ ← total number of circles or _______ to _______ or _______ : _______

B. In a class of 23 students, 15 are boys. What is the ratio of girls to boys?

number of girls → $\frac{23 - 15}{15} = \frac{\quad}{15}$ ← number of boys or _______ to _______ or _______ : _______

Apply the TEKS **Use the figure below to write each ratio.**

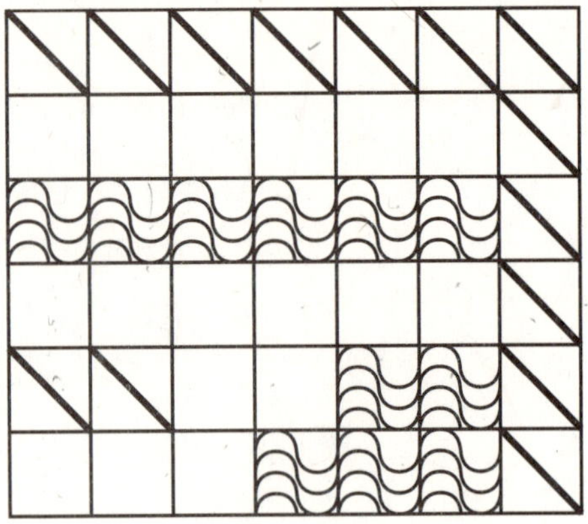

1. Number of boxes to number of boxes _______

2. Number of boxes to total number of boxes _______

3. Total number of boxes to number of boxes _______

4. Number of boxes to number of boxes + number of boxes

____

Write each ratio as a fraction.

5. 7:10 _______

6. 18 to 35 _______

7. 71:122 _______

Write each ratio.

8. 144 trees to 83 bushes

Use *to.* _______________

Use a colon. _______________

Use fraction form. _______________

9. 15 red cars to 19 blue cars

Use *to.* _______________

Use a colon. _______________

Use fraction form. _______________

Solve each problem.

10. A local animal shelter houses only cats and dogs. This week, of all the baby animals, there are 16 kittens and 7 puppies. What is the ratio of kittens to all the baby animals?

____

11. A box contains three types of fruits: apples, bananas, and pears. There are 20 pieces of fruit in all. Of these, 3 are apples and 11 are bananas. What is the ratio of pears to bananas?

____

12. During a family vacation, the ratio of sunny days to rainy days was 12 to 5. What was the ratio of rainy days to the total number of days?

____

Explain how you found your answer.

____

____

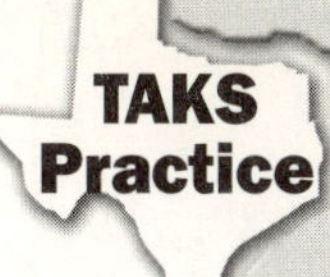

TAKS Objective 2 The student will demonstrate an understanding of patterns, relationships, and algebraic reasoning.
TEKS 6.3A, 6.3B

DIRECTIONS Read each question. Then circle the letter for the correct answer.

1 Look at the figure below.

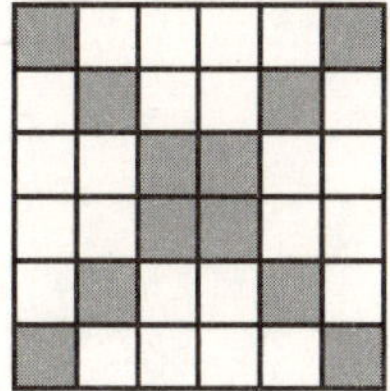

What is the ratio of shaded boxes to unshaded boxes?

A 36 to 12

B 12 to 36

C 12 to 24

D 24 to 12

2 Pages are being printed for a brochure. Four out of every 20 are in color. What is the ratio of noncolor pages to color pages?

F 20:4

G 4:16

H 16:4

J 16:20

A container holds 13 pencils, 5 black pens, and 3 blue pens. What is the ratio of pens to all writing tools?

A 8:13

B 8:21

C 3:5

D 5:21

4 What is the ratio of M's to all letters in the word MATHEMATICS?

F $\frac{2}{9}$

G $\frac{2}{11}$

H $\frac{11}{9}$

J $\frac{11}{2}$

What is the ratio of weekdays to all days in a week?

A 5 to 2

B 2 to 7

C 7 to 5

D 5 to 7

Focus on TEKS

Lesson 26 Equivalent Ratios and Ratios as Rates

TEKS 6.2C Use multiplication and division of whole numbers to solve problems involving equivalent ratios and rates.

TEKS 6.3A Use ratios to describe proportional situations.

You can use multiplication or division to find equivalent ratios.

Different ratios that have the same value are **equivalent ratios**, such as $\frac{2}{3}$ and $\frac{4}{6}$. A ratio is in **lowest terms** if the terms have no common factors other than 1. The ratio $\frac{2}{3}$ is in lowest terms because 2 and 3 have no common factors other than 1.

A ratio that compares two different kinds of quantities, such as miles and hours, is called a **rate**. A rate that is in lowest terms has a denominator of 1.

Guided Instruction

Problem Michelle traveled a distance of 110 miles in 2 hours. What was Michelle's average driving speed?

Divide to form an equivalent ratio with a denominator of 1.

Step 1 Write the rate by comparing distance to time. distance→ time→ ______

Step 2 Divide to reduce the ratio so that the denominator is 1. $\frac{110}{2} = \frac{110 \div 2}{2 \div 2} =$ ______

Step 3 Use the word *per* to express the rate. ______ miles per hour

Solution What was Michelle's average driving speed? ______________

Other Examples

A. There are 21 tulips and 14 roses in Ned's garden. What is the ratio of roses to tulips in his garden? Write the ratio in lowest terms.

number of roses → number of tulips → $\frac{14}{21} = \frac{14 \div 7}{21 \div 7} =$ ______

B. Paul can type 150 words in 3 minutes. What is Paul's average typing rate? To write the ratio for the rate, reduce the ratio so the denominator is 1.

number of words → number of minutes → $\frac{150}{3} = \frac{150 \div 3}{3 \div 3} = \frac{50}{1}$

______ words per minute

C. Express "15 miles in $\frac{1}{4}$ hour" as a unit rate. Multiply by 4 to change the ratio to a unit rate.

$\frac{15}{\frac{1}{4}} = \frac{15 \times 4}{\frac{1}{4} \times 4} = \frac{60}{1} =$ ______ miles per hour

Apply the TEKS

Find the missing term.

1. $\frac{2}{5} = \frac{\quad}{25}$

2. 5 to 9 = 50 t

4. 8: ______ = 48:24

5. $\frac{\quad}{20} = \frac{20}{80}$

Express each ratio in words as a rate in lowest terms.

7. 220 students for 11 teachers

____

8. $96 for 8 hours of work

____

9. 400 miles on 16 gallons of gas

____

10. $14.00 for 7 notepads

____

Solve each problem.

11. In 2 hours of reading, Mark counted 12 new characters. At what rate did the characters appear?

____

12. During the baseball season, Marti acted as a relief pitcher for her team. She pitched 88 strikeouts in 22 games. What was Marti's strikeout rate?

____

13. Joy's Jewels sends the same ratio of bracelet varieties every time they send a shipment to a store. The table at the right shows data for April and May shipments to Sara's Shop. How many jade bracelets should be included in the May shipment?

Bracelet Type	April	May
Turquoise	16	20
Coral	12	15
Jade	8	?

____

14. Which of the following situations represents a better salary offer? Explain why.
$550 per 40-hour week or $13.00 per hour for 40 hours

____

will demonstrate an understanding of numbers, operations, and quantitative reasoning.

.2C

student will demonstrate an understanding of patterns, relationships, and algebraic reasoning.

TEKS 6.3A

each question. Then circle correct answer.

the following is NOT equivalent ratio 3:2?

6:4

B 9:6

C 9:4

D 30:20

2 An airline manager found that during a 24-hour period, 1,440 passengers passed through one terminal. What was the rate of passenger flow?

F 60 passengers per minute

G 60 passengers per hour

H 120 passengers per minute

J 120 passengers per hour

A chemist makes a mixture of a liquid and a powder in the ratio of 6 cups of powder to 0.5 gallon of liquid. What is the rate of powder to liquid?

A 30 cups per gallon

B 24 cups per gallon

C 12 cups per gallon

D 6 cups per gallon

Michelle's Craft Shoppe sells a package of beads that has a ratio of 30 red beads to 5 green beads. If 12 red beads are added to the package, how many green beads must be added in order for the ratio of bead colors to stay the same?

F Use the same number of greens.

G Add 7 greens.

H Add 5 greens.

J Add 2 greens.

A chef finds that 0.25 teaspoon of the sugar substitute he uses equals the sweetness of 2 teaspoons of sugar. Which fraction best represents the ratio of teaspoons of sugar substitute to teaspoons of sugar?

A $\frac{0.25}{1}$

B $\frac{1}{4}$

C $\frac{1}{8}$

D $\frac{1}{16}$

Which of the following is NOT equivalent to the ratio $\frac{x}{y}$ when $x = 3$ and $y = 5$?

F $\frac{9}{25}$

G $\frac{6}{10}$

H $\frac{12}{20}$

J $\frac{15}{25}$

Focus on TEKS

Lesson 27 Proportions

TEKS 6.3A Use ratios to describe proportional situations.
TEKS 6.3C Use ratios to make predictions in proportional situations.

You can use a proportion to represent situations involving equal ratios.

A **proportion** is a sentence showing that two ratios are equivalent. The **cross products** of a proportion are found by multiplying the numbers on the diagonals of the proportion.

Two ratios form a proportion if the cross products are equivalent.

$\frac{6}{8} \times \frac{3}{4}$

Cross products: $6 \cdot 4 = 8 \cdot 3$
$24 = 24$
The ratios above form a proportion because the cross products are equal.

Guided Instruction

Problem On his computer, Kevin is working with a word processing program. In 4 minutes, he can key in 200 data items. Working at the same rate, how many data items can Kevin enter in 12 minutes?

Use a proportion to solve the problem.

Step 1 Use the same order of the ratios to write a proportion. Let *n* represent the number of data items in 12 minutes.

$\frac{\text{number of data items}}{\text{number of minutes}} = \frac{\text{number of data items}}{\text{number of minutes}}$

$\frac{200}{4} \times \frac{n}{12}$

Step 2 Use cross products.

$4 \cdot n = 200 \cdot 12$

$4n =$ ________

Step 3 Divide both sides of the equation by 4 to find the value of *n*.

$\frac{4n}{4} = \frac{2{,}400}{4}$

$n =$ ________

Solution How many data items can Kevin enter in 12 minutes? ________

Another Example

How many minutes will it take Kevin to enter 1,200 items? Write and solve a proportion. Let *m* represent the number of minutes for 1,200 data items. Use cross products.

$\frac{200}{4} = \frac{1{,}200}{m}$

$4 \cdot 1{,}200 = 200m$

$4{,}800 = 200m$

$\frac{4{,}800}{200} = m$

$24 = m$

How many minutes does it take Kevin to enter 1,200 data items? ________

Apply the TEKS **Use cross products to determine if each pair of ratios forms a proportion. Write *yes* or *no*.**

1. $\frac{4}{6} \stackrel{?}{=} \frac{10}{15}$ ________

2. $\frac{15}{10} \stackrel{?}{=} \frac{12}{8}$ ________

3. $\frac{3}{2} \stackrel{?}{=} \frac{9}{4}$ ________

Use cross products to solve each proportion.

4. $\frac{20}{6} = \frac{30}{n}$ $n =$ ________

5. $\frac{10}{x} = \frac{18}{36}$ $x =$ ________

6. $\frac{5}{20} = \frac{z}{4}$ $z =$ ________

Find the missing number in each table of values.

7. The table below shows the growth of a seedling over a period of days. If the growth rate is constant, how tall will the seedling be after 35 days?

Number of Days (since planting)	Length of Stem (centimeters)
7	3
14	6
21	9
35	

8. The table below shows the distance covered on an automobile trip. If the speed of the car is constant, how far will the car have traveled after 12 hours?

Driving Time (hours)	Distance (miles)
2	110
5	275
7	385
12	

Solve each problem.

9. Two cups of raw broccoli contain about 164 micrograms of Vitamin C. About how many micrograms of Vitamin C are contained in 6 cups of raw broccoli?

____

10. In Texas, the cities of Houston and Huntsville are 60 miles apart. The distance between these cities is represented by a line that is 3 inches long on Jorge's map. The distance between Waco and Dallas is 5 inches on Jorge's map. According to Jorge's map, what is the actual distance between Waco and Dallas?

____

11. At the local store, you can buy 6 folding chairs for $150. Explain how to write and solve a proportion to find the number of these chairs you can buy at this rate for $450.

____

____

____

____

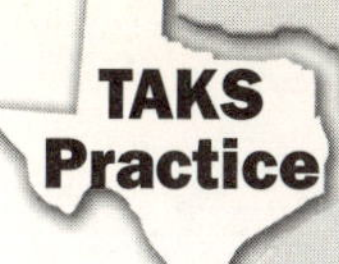

TAKS Objective 2 The student will demonstrate an understanding of patterns, relationships, and algebraic reasoning.
TEKS 6.3A, 6.3C

DIRECTIONS Read each question. Then circle the letter for the correct answer.

1 What value for x will make this proportion true?

$$\frac{x}{8} = \frac{9}{24}$$

A $x = 3$

B $x = 5$

C $x = 30$

D $x = 72$

2 Which of the following is NOT a proportion?

F 4:6 = 6:9

G 4:9 = 2:3

H 6:9 = 8:12

J 6:9 = 10:15

3 Mark bought 3 books for \$18. Which proportion can be used to find n, the number of the same books Mark can buy for \$42?

A $\frac{42}{3} = \frac{n}{18}$

B $\frac{3}{18} = \frac{42}{n}$

C $\frac{3}{n} = \frac{42}{18}$

D $\frac{3}{18} = \frac{n}{42}$

4 On a map, 1 centimeter represents a distance of 15 kilometers. How many kilometers are represented by 7 centimeters?

F 10.5 km

G 105 km

H 1,050 km

J 10,500 km

5 Ari can read 80 pages in 2 hours. If n represents the number of pages Ari can read in 5 hours, which proportion could NOT be used to find n?

A $\frac{80}{2} = \frac{n}{5}$

B $\frac{2}{80} = \frac{5}{n}$

C $\frac{80}{n} = \frac{2}{5}$

D $\frac{80}{2} = \frac{5}{n}$

6 Jill can make 6 necklaces in 2 hours. At this rate, how many necklaces can she make in 5 hours?

F 10

G 12

H 15

J 30

Focus on TEKS

Lesson 28 Percents

TEKS 6.3B Represent percents with concrete models, fractions, and decimals.

You can represent a percent as an equivalent fraction or decimal.

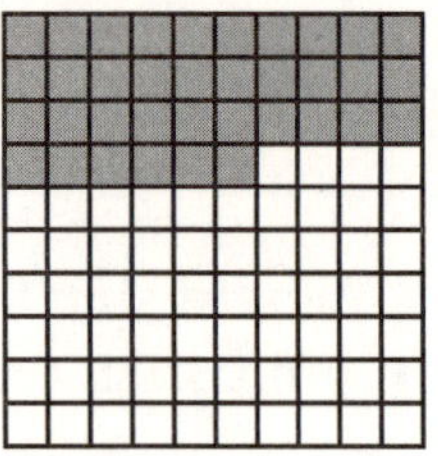

A **percent** is a ratio that compares a number to 100. Percent also means *hundredths* or *per hundred*. The symbol for percent is %. In the figure at the right, 36 out of 100 squares are shaded. This ratio may be written as a fraction, a decimal or a percent. So, 36 out of 100 may be written as $\frac{36}{100}$ or 0.36 or 36%.

Guided Instruction

Problem

Joan shaded in the grid at the right. What percent of the grid is shaded? How would you write the equivalent decimal number?

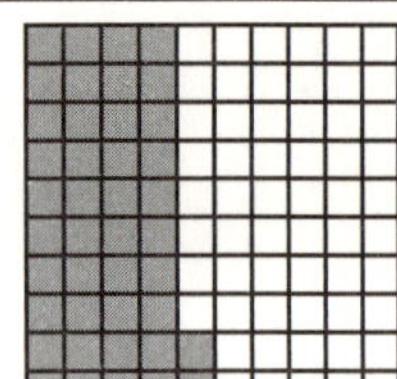

Write the number of shaded squares to all squares as a ratio, a percent, and a decimal.

Step 1 How many squares did Joan shade? __________

How many squares are in the grid? __________

Write a ratio using these numbers.

number of shaded squares → ____
total number of squares →

Step 2 $\frac{42}{100}$ means 42 out of 100.

Since the ratio has a denominator of 100, express it as a percent. $\frac{42}{100}$ = __________

Step 3 To write the percent as a decimal, move the decimal point two places to the left. 42.0% = __________

Solution

What percent of the grid is shaded? __________

How would you write the equivalent decimal number? __________

Another Example

Ken has 25 crayons. Eight are blue, 12 are red, and the rest are green. What percent of his crayons are green? Find the number of green crayons and write a ratio of the number of green crayons to the total number of crayons.

$25 - 8 - 12 = 5$

number of green crayons → 5
total number of crayons → 25

To find the percent of green crayons, find an equivalent ratio with 100 as the denominator.

$\frac{5}{25} = \frac{5 \times 4}{25 \times 4} = \frac{20}{100}$

The equivalent ratio has a denominator of 100, so change the fraction to a decimal. To express the decimal as a percent, move the decimal point two places to the right and add the percent symbol.

$\frac{20}{100}$ = 020. = 20%

Apply the TEKS **Express the ratio of shaded portions to the entire grid as a fraction, a decimal, and a percent.**

1. 

____

2. 

____

3. 

____

Write each ratio as a percent.

4. $\frac{42}{100}$ = ________

5. $\frac{125}{100}$ = ________

6. $\frac{2}{5}$ = ________

Write each ratio as a fraction in simplest form.

7. 39% = ________

8. 50% = ________

9. 60% = ________

Write each ratio as a decimal.

10. 77% = ________

11. 29% = ________

12. 150% = ________

Solve each problem.

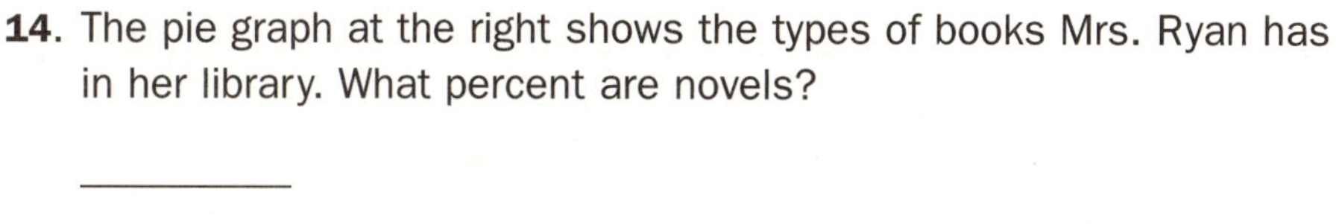

13. There are 80 marbles in a bag. Forty of these marbles are red. What percent of the marbles in the bag are red?

____

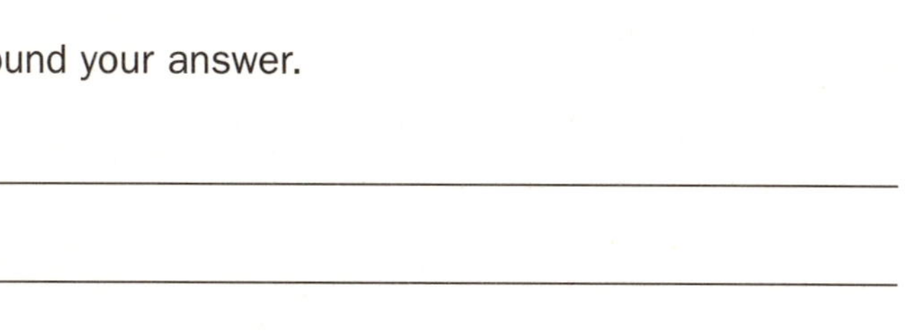

14. The pie graph at the right shows the types of books Mrs. Ryan has in her library. What percent are novels?

____

Explain how you found your answer.

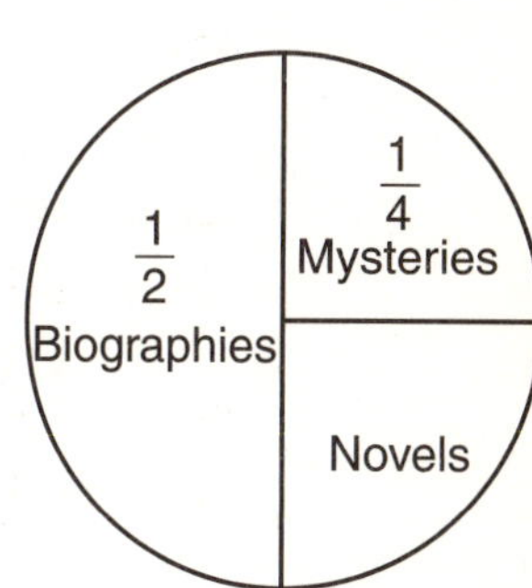

____

____

____

____

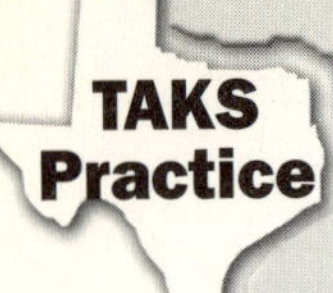

TAKS Objective 2 The student will demonstrate an understanding of patterns, relationships, and algebraic reasoning.
TEKS 6.3B

DIRECTIONS Read each question. Then circle the letter for the correct answer.

1 Which of the following is NOT equivalent to 60%?

A $\frac{60}{100}$

B $\frac{3}{5}$

C 0.60

D 0.06

2 Which of the following shaded portions does NOT represent 40% of the whole figure?

F

G

H

J

3 What percent of the figure is shaded?

A 0.30%

B 30%

C 70%

D 300%

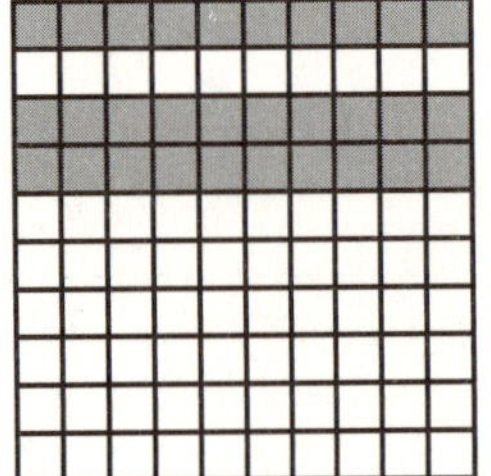

4 Which of the following statements is true?

F $\frac{1}{3} = 30\%$

G $\frac{4}{9} = 49\%$

H $\frac{3}{12} = 25\%$

J $\frac{7}{8} = 78\%$

5 Which of the following statements is NOT true?

A 7% = 0.7

B 14% = 0.14

C 100% = 1

D 140% = 1.40

6 Sammy's last math quiz consisted of 20 questions. He answered 16 questions correctly. What was his score as a percent?

F 8%

G 20%

H 80%

J 125%

Focus on TEKS

Lesson 29 PROBLEM-SOLVING STRATEGY: Guess and Check

TEKS 6.11A Identify and apply mathematics to everyday experiences, to activities in and outside of school, with other disciplines, and with other mathematical topics.

TEKS 6.11B Use a problem-solving model that incorporates understanding the problem, making a plan, carrying out the plan, and evaluating the solution for reasonableness.

TEKS 6.11C Select or develop an appropriate problem-solving strategy from a variety of different types including systematic guessing and checking.

TEKS 6.11D Select tools such as real objects, manipulatives, paper/pencil, and technology or techniques such as mental math, estimation, and number sense to solve problems.

You can use the guess-and-check strategy to help you solve problems.
You can use the problem-solving guide on page 288 to help you.

Guided Instruction

Problem

In a local village, 200 volunteers showed up for Spring Cleanup Day. The ratio of female volunteers to male volunteers was 3:2. How many females and males volunteered?

Understand the problem.

Look for the information you will use.

The total number of volunteers is _________.

The ratio of females to males is _________.

What does the problem ask you to find?

____

Make a plan.

Use the guess-and-check strategy to find two numbers that are in the ratio 3:2 and that have a sum of 200.

Solve the problem.

Make a table to show your guesses. After each guess, adjust your number choices to get closer to the correct answers.

First Guess	Second Guess	Third Guess
females 30, males 20	females 60, males 40	females 120, males 80
Check: 30:20 = _______ 30 + 20 = _______	Check: 60:40 = _______ 60 + 40 = _______	Check: 120:80 = _______ 120 + 80 = _______
30 and 20 are in the correct ratio but their sum is not 200. Try doubling the numbers.	60 and 40 are in the correct ratio but their sum is not 200. Try doubling the numbers.	120 and 80 are in the correct ratio and they have the correct sum. These numbers work!

How many females and how many males volunteered? ____________________

Check your answer.

How do you know your answer is correct?
If you divide both 120 and 80 by 40, you get the ratio 3:2.
If you add 120 and 80, you get the sum 200.

Apply the TEKS **Use the guess-and-check strategy to solve each problem.**

Work Space

1. Rosa and Eva sew lace on women's skirts. In one hour, Rosa completed 2 times as many skirts as Eva. Together, the two women completed 36 skirts. How many skirts did each woman complete?

____

2. The numbers of cans produced in one day by two companies, Atlas and Baltic, were in the ratio 8:3 and their difference was 35,000. How many cans did each company produce that day?

____

3. Avi's score on a math test was 80%. Zoe's score on a science test was also 80%. Zoe had 12 more correct answers than Avi. Together their correct answers totaled 52. How many questions were on each test?

____

4. The numerator and denominator of a certain fraction are in the ratio 4:7. The denominator of the fraction is 15 more than the numerator. What is the fraction?

____

5. At an end-of-season sale, Lisa bought a coat and a dress on sale for 50% off the original price of each. She spent a total of $150 for both items. The original price of the coat was $20 more than the original price of the dress. What was the original price of each?

____

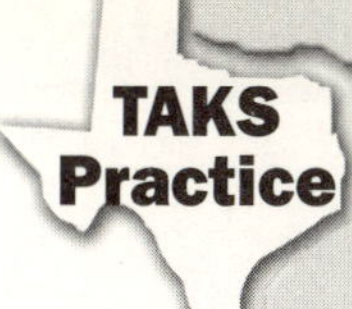

TAKS Objective 6 The student will demonstrate an understanding of the mathematical processes and tools used in problem solving.

TEKS 6.11A, 6.11B, 6.11C, 6.11D

DIRECTIONS Read each question. Then circle the letter for the correct answer.

1 Fred took a test that had 25 questions, all of equal value. Fred answered 18 questions correctly. What grade did he earn?

- **A** Between 60% and 70%
- **B** Between 70% and 80%
- **C** Between 80% and 90%
- **D** Between 90% and 100%

2 In September, Liam intended to learn 9 new words every 5 days. He met his goal, starting on September 1 and ending on the 30th. How many new words did Liam learn in September?

- **F** 44
- **G** 45
- **H** 54
- **J** 55

3 Ellen traded some bottle caps for some of Nancy's marbles. For every 3 bottle caps, Nancy gave Ellen 2 blue marbles. To begin, Nancy had 302 blue marbles. After the trade, she had 192 blue marbles. How many bottle caps had Ellen given Nancy?

- **A** 165
- **B** 110
- **C** 87
- **D** 64

4 At a farmers' market, one farmer is selling two different-sized bags of potatoes.

Which of the following statements is NOT true about these offerings?

- **F** The weight ratio is 2:10.
- **G** The larger bag is the better buy.
- **H** The cost per pound is the same.
- **J** The price ratio is 1:5.

5 Lenny is a salesman. He is paid a weekly salary of $250. In addition, Lenny gets 10% of each sale that he makes. How much would Lenny have to sell in order to earn $500 for the week?

- **A** $5,000
- **B** $4,000
- **C** $3,000
- **D** $2,500

Building Stamina®

DIRECTIONS Read each question. Then circle the letter for the correct answer. If a correct answer is not here, mark the letter for "Not Here."

Use the table below to answer Questions 1–2.

Grade	Boys	Girls
Fifth	83	68
Sixth	79	71
Seventh	72	80

1 What is the ratio of boys in the fifth grade to boys in all three grades?

A 79 to 162

B 83 to 151

C 83 to 162

D 83 to 234

2 What is the ratio of girls in the seventh grade to boys in the seventh grade?

F 9:10

G 9:19

H 10:9

J 10:19

3 Which fraction best represents the ratio of small circles to squares?

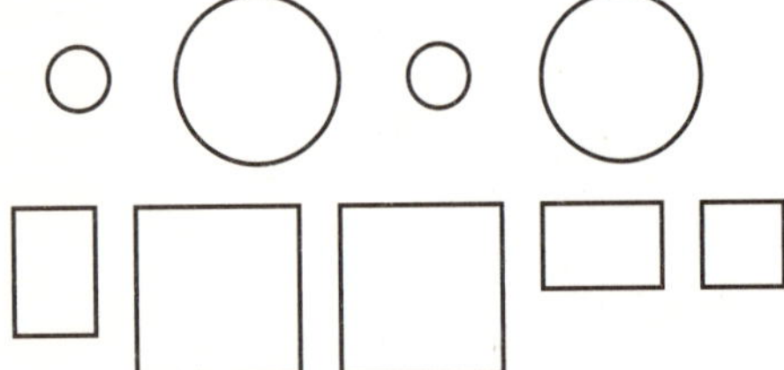

A $\frac{2}{3}$

B $\frac{2}{5}$

C $\frac{2}{9}$

D $\frac{1}{9}$

4 Erin traded some stickers for some of Mark's baseball cards. For every 5 stickers, Mark gave Erin 2 baseball cards. Mark had 560 baseball cards before he began trading. After trading, he had 528 cards. How many stickers did he receive from Erin?

Record your answer and fill in the bubbles on the grid below. Be sure to use the correct place value.

				.		
0	0	0	0		0	0
1	1	1	1		1	1
2	2	2	2		2	2
3	3	3	3		3	3
4	4	4	4		4	4
5	5	5	5		5	5
6	6	6	6		6	6
7	7	7	7		7	7
8	8	8	8		8	8
9	9	9	9		9	9

5 Andrea plans to serve orange juice for a large family brunch. She combines the orange concentrate and the water using a 2:5 ratio. How many cans of water does she combine with 10 cans of concentrate?

A 4

B 7

C 14

D 25

6 Which of the following is NOT equivalent to the ratio $x : y$, when $x = 2.1$, and $y = 2.4$?

F 21 to 24

G $\frac{4.2}{4.8}$

H 7:8

J $\frac{24}{21}$

7 Every day, Josie's Bakery bakes muffins and bagels. The ratio of muffins to bagels is always the same. The table below shows data about what Josie's Bakery baked 3 days of this week.

Day	Bagels	Muffins
Monday	250	150
Tuesday	300	180
Wednesday	?	165

How many bagels did Josie's Bakery bake on Wednesday?

Record your answer and fill in the bubbles on the grid below. Be sure to use the correct place value.

				.		
0	0	0	0		0	0
1	1	1	1		1	1
2	2	2	2		2	2
3	3	3	3		3	3
4	4	4	4		4	4
5	5	5	5		5	5
6	6	6	6		6	6
7	7	7	7		7	7
8	8	8	8		8	8
9	9	9	9		9	9

8 Which of the following is NOT a proportion?

F 1:4 = 8:2

G $\frac{4}{5} = \frac{12}{15}$

H 3 to 9 is equal to 6 to 18.

J $\frac{5}{4} = \frac{15}{12}$

9 Ben is making potato salad. The recipe calls for 5 pounds of potatoes, 8 eggs, and $1\frac{1}{2}$ cups of mayonnaise. He wants to make $\frac{1}{2}$ of the recipe. What quantities of potatoes, eggs, and mayonnaise does he need?

A Potatoes: 10 lb; eggs: 16; mayonnaise: 3 c

B Potatoes: $1\frac{1}{2}$ lb; eggs: 6; mayonnaise: $\frac{3}{4}$ c

C Potatoes: $2\frac{1}{2}$ lb; eggs: 4; mayonnaise: $\frac{3}{4}$ c

D Potatoes: $2\frac{1}{2}$ lb; eggs: 6; mayonnaise: 1 c

10 Three copies of a math textbook weigh 9 pounds. How much would 7 of the same textbook weigh?

F 3 lb

G 18 lb

H 21 lb

J 63 lb

11 Bess can do 100 jumping jacks in 4 minutes. If j represents the number of jumping jacks Bess can do in 10 minutes, which proportion can be used to find j?

A $\frac{100}{4} = \frac{10}{j}$

B $\frac{100}{4} = \frac{j}{10}$

C $\frac{100}{j} = \frac{10}{4}$

D $\frac{10}{j} = \frac{j}{100}$

12 What percent of the figure is unshaded?

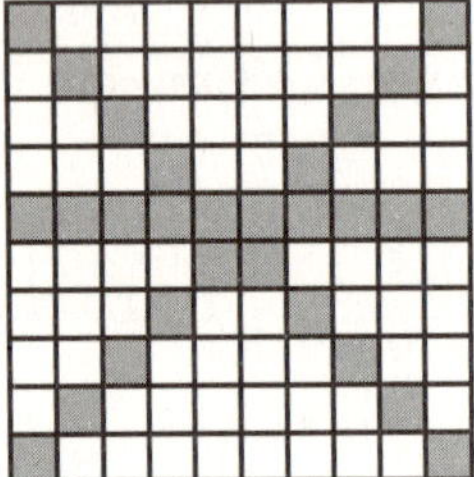

F 28%

G 38%

H 62%

J Not Here

13 Ed has 20 coins in his pocket. Twenty percent of the coins are quarters, 30% are dimes, and the rest are nickels. What is the value of the coins in Ed's pocket?

A $2.10

B $1.90

C $1.80

D $1.30

14 The numerator and denominator of a certain fraction are in the ratio of 8 to 5. The denominator is 24 less than the numerator. What is the fraction?

F $\frac{80}{56}$

G $\frac{80}{50}$

H $\frac{64}{40}$

J $\frac{40}{25}$

15 The Ames family spends $\frac{2}{5}$ of its monthly income on rent, $\frac{1}{4}$ on food, $\frac{3}{10}$ on transportation, and $\frac{1}{20}$ on entertainment. What percent of the family's monthly income is spent on food and transportation?

A 35%

B 40%

C 55%

D 65%

16 Armando bought some 37-cent stamps and some 3-cent stamps. He paid a total of $3.23. He bought a total of 17 stamps. How many 37-cent stamps did he buy?

F 9

G 8

H 5

J Not Here

17 In which figure is the ratio of unshaded boxes to shaded boxes 1 to 5?

A 

B 

C 

D 

18 Two packages have a total mass of 9.3 kilograms. One package has a mass that is 1.7 kilograms more than the other package. What is the mass of the lighter package?

F 3.5 kg

G 3.8 kg

H 4.8 kg

J 5.5 kg

19 Weston is purchasing a new car that costs $18,000. He will also pay $900 in taxes on this car. What is the tax rate, expressed as a percent?

A 50%

B 20%

C 5%

D 2%

20 Ken drove a total of 405 miles in 9 hours. What was his average rate of speed in miles per hour?

F 40.5 miles per hour

G 45 miles per hour

H 50.5 miles per hour

J 65 miles per hour

Part 1 Building Stamina®

Read each question. Then circle the letter for the correct answer. If a correct answer is not here, mark the letter for "Not Here."

1 A large park has an area of 850,000 square feet. The parking lot has an area of 120,000 square feet. What is the combined area of the park and the parking lot?

A 730,000 ft^2

B 838,000 ft^2

C 862,000 ft^2

D 970,000 ft^2

2 Which is the greatest common factor of 45 and 55?

F 5

G 7

H 11

J Not Here

3 Which fraction is NOT equivalent to 0.9?

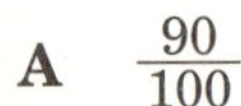

A $\frac{90}{100}$

B $\frac{45}{50}$

C $\frac{18}{20}$

D $\frac{9}{100}$

4 A sequence is formed with the following pattern:

122333444455555...

What is the 32nd term in the sequence?

Record your answer and fill in the bubbles on the grid below. Be sure to use the correct place value.

				.		
0	0	0	0		0	0
1	1	1	1		1	1
2	2	2	2		2	2
3	3	3	3		3	3
4	4	4	4		4	4
5	5	5	5		5	5
6	6	6	6		6	6
7	7	7	7		7	7
8	8	8	8		8	8
9	9	9	9		9	9

5 Which subtraction expression has the greatest difference?

A 714.53 – 88.92

B 763.56 – 654.78

C 785.85 – 66.9

D 791.32 – 76.52

6 Which pair of numbers has 80 as a common multiple?

F 2 and 15

G 3 and 6

H 4 and 7

J 5 and 16

7 In Mr. Hansen's front lawn there are 8.2 four-leaf clovers to every 1,000 clovers. Which expression shows this data as a ratio of four-leaf clovers to clovers?

A $\frac{1000}{8.2}$

B $8.2 + 1000$

C 8.2×1000

D 8.2:1000

8 During the soccer season, Carla scored 8 goals in 20 games. Which represents Carla's scoring ratio?

F $\frac{1}{20}$

G $\frac{2}{5}$

H $\frac{3}{5}$

J $\frac{8}{25}$

9 Mrs. Smith bought a new wooden television cabinet. The cabinet cost $1,824. She will pay for the cabinet over the course of 12 months. How much will she pay each month?

A $12

B $15

C $102

D $152

10 Thirty tickets were left over from a raffle. Two hundred tickets were reserved beforehand, and 75 tickets were sold at the door. If *t* represents the total number of tickets, which equation can be used to model the problem situation?

F $30 + t = 200$

G $275 - t = 30$

H $t - 30 = 200 + 75$

J $t = 275 - 30$

11 Which of the following proportions is NOT true?

A 2:3 = 4:6

B 3:5 = 9:15

C 4:1 = 8:3

D 3:4 = 12:16

12 Meg and Jordan built a wall that is 14 bricks long by 12 bricks high. They plan to paint only the brick surfaces on the front, the top, and the outer sides. How many brick surfaces will they paint?

Record your answer and fill in the bubbles on the grid below. Be sure to use the correct place value.

				.		
0	0	0	0		0	0
1	1	1	1		1	1
2	2	2	2		2	2
3	3	3	3		3	3
4	4	4	4		4	4
5	5	5	5		5	5
6	6	6	6		6	6
7	7	7	7		7	7
8	8	8	8		8	8
9	9	9	9		9	9

13 Walnut Street is 3.5 miles long. It is three blocks long. Which expression could show the lengths of the three blocks?

A 0.5 + 0.5 + 2.0
B 0.85 + 0.85 + 1.8
C 3.5 + 3.5 + 3.5
D 1.2 + 1.3 + 2.2

14 At the Dandy Candy Company, 675 sales people each sold 72 candy bars. Approximately how many candy bars were sold in all?

F 600

G 1,000

H 49,000

J 500,000

15 In a class of sixth-graders, 85 out of 340 attended a musical at the theater. What fraction of the sixth-graders attended?

A $\frac{1}{3}$

B $\frac{1}{4}$

C $\frac{1}{5}$

D $\frac{1}{6}$

16 Bonita and Nell walked 12 miles in 4 hours. How many miles did they average per hour?

F 1 mi

G 3 mi

H 6 mi

J 12 mi

17 The shallow end of the pool is $4\frac{1}{4}$ feet deep. The deep end is $12\frac{1}{2}$ feet deep. What is the difference in the depth between the deep end and the shallow end of the pool?

A 9 ft

B $8\frac{3}{4}$ ft

C $8\frac{1}{2}$ ft

D $8\frac{1}{4}$ ft

18 Which is the least common multiple of 8 and 6?

F 24

G 30

H 32

J 40

19 A floor plan is drawn so that $\frac{1}{4}$ inch on the drawing equals 2 feet of actual length. What is the ratio of distance on the drawing to actual distance?

A 1:4

B 1:2

C 1:8

D 1:1

20 Houston received $8\frac{1}{4}$ inches of rain. 1.5 inches fell before 7 A.M. and $2\frac{1}{4}$ inches fell between 7 A.M. and noon. How much rain fell after noon?

F 3.75 in.

G 4.5 in.

H 6 in.

J 6.75 in.

21 Which numbers will complete the diagram so that each row, column, and diagonal has the same sum?

8	3	4
1	5	m
6	7	n

A $m = 9, n = 3$

B $m = 8, n = 3$

C $m = 9, n = 2$

D $m = 7, n = 2$

22 Which list contains only equivalent fractions?

F $\frac{6}{8}, \frac{3}{4}, \frac{10}{14}$

G $\frac{1}{2}, \frac{4}{6}, \frac{3}{8}$

H $\frac{4}{44}, \frac{2}{11}, \frac{12}{66}$

J $\frac{1}{3}, \frac{4}{12}, \frac{6}{18}$

23 Which factor tree shows the correct prime factorization of 36?

A

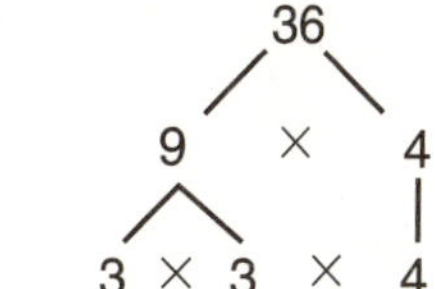

B

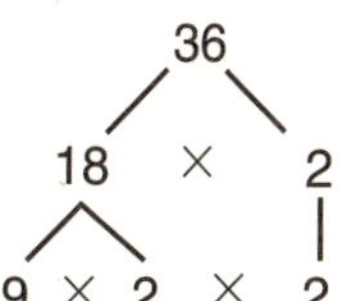

C

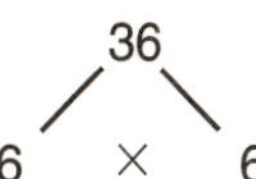

D

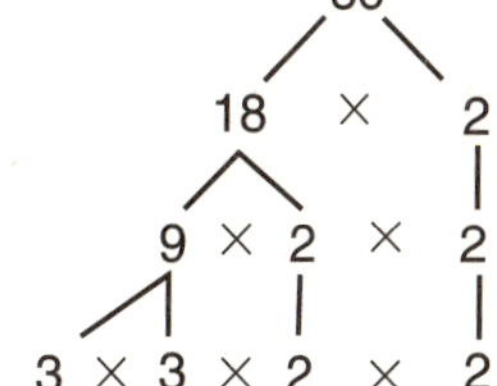

24 What is the difference between 5432.98 and 44.8?

F 243,397.5

G 5,477.78

H 5,388.18

J 121.27

25 Which is the prime factorization of 72?

A $3^3 \cdot 2^4$

B $3^3 \cdot 2^2$

C $3^2 \cdot 2^3$

D $3 \cdot 2^3$

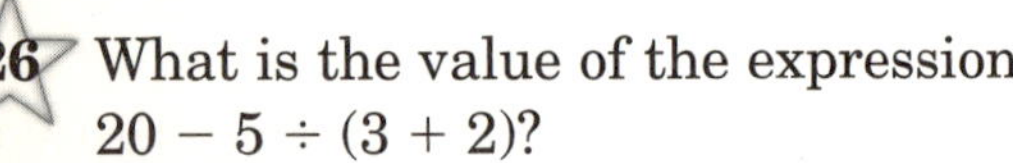

26 What is the value of the expression $20 - 5 \div (3 + 2)$?

F 3

G 5

H 7

J 19

27 Keith can type 30 words in 2 minutes. If n represents the number of words Keith can type in 25 minutes, which proportion would NOT be true?

A $\frac{25}{n} = \frac{1}{15}$

B $\frac{15}{1} = \frac{n}{25}$

C $\frac{1}{n} = \frac{15}{25}$

D $\frac{1}{15} = \frac{25}{n}$

28 At 7 A.M., when Randy looked at the thermometer, the temperature was −5°C. Which expression can be used to find the temperature at 11 A.M., when it was 8°C warmer?

F $-5 - 8$

G $5 - 8$

H $-5 + 8$

J Not Here

29 The highest score a diver can receive in a competition is 10.0. The four highest scores so far are 8.90, 8.96, 9.20, and 9.35. If Tara needs to rank within these scores, which is the minimum score she needs to stay in the competition?

A 8.88

B 8.91

C 9.21

D 9.36

30 Jodi wants to finish a 200-page book by the end of the summer. She read 10 pages the first day. If each day she reads 10 more pages than the day before, in how many days will she finish the book?

F 3 days

G 4 days

H 5 days

J 6 days

31 What percent of the figure is shaded?

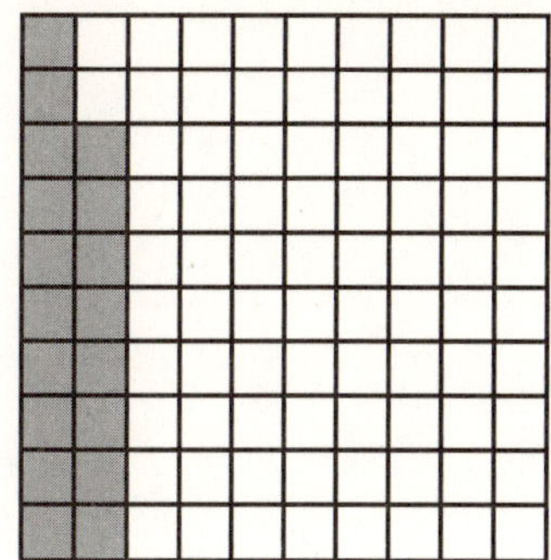

A 12%

B 18%

C 82%

D 88%

32 The table shows David's and Kelly's heights at the end of 4 consecutive years.

Year	David's Height, x (inches)	Kelly's Height, y (inches)
2000	36	44
2001	40	48
2002	42	50
2003	45	53

Which expression best represents Kelly's height in terms of David's height at the end of each year?

F $x + 8$

G $8x$

H $y + 8$

J $8y$

33 The Michael family is planning a trip across the country. The route they plan to take to the northeast is 2,235 miles. The scenic route home is 3,810 miles. Approximately how many miles will they travel in total?

A 4,000 mi

B 5,000 mi

C 6,000 mi

D 8,000 mi

34 Harrah buys 20 yards of fabric. She uses $3\frac{1}{3}$ yards to make some pillow covers and $9\frac{1}{2}$ yards to cover a chair. How many yards are left?

F $8\frac{1}{6}$ yd

G $7\frac{1}{6}$ yd

H $6\frac{2}{3}$ yd

J $5\frac{1}{3}$ yd

35 There are 396 cars in the company parking lot. Of those cars, $\frac{4}{9}$ are blue. About $\frac{1}{3}$ are black. Which of the following is true?

A About 0.3 of the cars are blue.

B About 0.4 of the cars are not blue.

C About 0.2 are either blue or black.

D About 0.2 are neither blue nor black.

36 Pedro started the month with $250 in his savings account. During the month, he withdrew $25 to purchase CDs, deposited $60 he received for mowing lawns, and withdrew $10 to go to the movies. Which expression can be used to find Pedro's savings account balance at the end of the month?

F $250 + 25 - 60 + 10$

G $250 - 25 - 60 - 10$

H $250 - 25 + 60 - 10$

J $250 - 25 + 60 + 10$

37 What is the value of the 8th term in the sequence?

Position	1	2	3	4	5	6	7	8
Value of Term	7	14	21					

A 28

B 35

C 56

D 86

38 Jorge saves $4 every three weeks. Fred saves $2 every week. Anne saves $5 twice a month. Mark saves $9 every month. At the end of 3 months, who has saved the greatest amount of money?

F Jorge

G Fred

H Anne

J Mark

39 Which of the following approximates 70.34×69.89?

A 140

B 4,900

C 8,700

D 49,000

40 A map of hiking trails for a wildlife center has a scale of 1 centimeter for every 100 meters. If Jason hikes from Swan Lake to the Waterfalls, how would he use the map to find the actual distance in meters?

F Jason would multiply the distance in centimeters between points on the map by 100 and write the units as meters.

G Jason would divide the distance in centimeters between points on the map by 100 and write the units as meters.

H Jason would add the distance in centimeters between points on the map by 100 and write the units as meters.

J Jason would subtract distance in centimeters between points on the map by 100 and write the units as meters.

41 There are 8 students in a science laboratory. Each student is paired once with every other student. How many different pairings are there in all?

A 24

B 28

C 36

D 72

42 For the school party, Lor buys a new dress for $79.95, new shoes for $33.25 and a new evening bag for $19.05. How much does she spend all together?

F $113.20

G $132.25

H $303.70

J $201.78

43 A science class is divided into 7 groups for a laboratory experiment. If $\frac{2}{7}$ of the groups have 3 students, $\frac{2}{7}$ have 4 students, and $\frac{3}{7}$ of the groups have 5 students, how many students are in the class?

A 12

B 19

C 23

D 29

44 Which quotient has a remainder of 2?

F $406 \div 7$

G $409 \div 7$

H $406 \div 14$

J $408 \div 14$

45 On an air trip overseas, Kody can take two suitcases that together weigh no more than 40 lb. Which is a possible combination of weights for his suitcases?

A 32.75; 8.25

B 28.5; 16.5

C 23.7; 27.3

D 22.65; 17.35

46 Jill lives $\frac{2}{3}$ of a mile from school. How far does she walk to and from school each day?

F $\frac{1}{3}$ mi

G $\frac{2}{3}$ mi

H $1\frac{1}{3}$ mi

J $2\frac{2}{3}$ mi

47 Marilee brought cupcakes to share with the 14 other members of her afterschool club. She brought 3 more cupcakes than she needed. Which equation could you use to find the number of cupcakes Marilee brought to the club?

A $n = 15 + 3$

B $3 + n = 15$

C $15 + n = 3$

D $n = 15 - 3$

48 Alicia saved $1 one week. If each succeeding week she saves $1 more than she did the week before, how much will she have saved by the 10th week?

F $15

G $40

H $55

J $101

49 The Texas state sales tax is 0.0825. Which equation gives the total cost *c* for an item with price *m* and the state sales tax charged on that price?

A $c = m + 0.0825$

B $c = m + 0.0825m$

C $c = m - 0.0825$

D $c = m - 0.0825m$

50 13 degrees colder than 2 degrees can be represented by which expression?

F $2 - 13$

G $13 - 2$

H $13 + 2$

J 13×2

51 Which mixed number is equal to $\frac{28}{5}$?

A $4\frac{1}{5}$

B $5\frac{3}{5}$

C $6\frac{1}{5}$

D $7\frac{3}{5}$

52 Jim runs 5 miles every 2 days and Dina runs 6 miles every 3 days. If they both go running on March 5, what is the next day that both will go running?

F March 6

G March 7

H March 9

J March 11

53 Martina's dartboard looks like this:

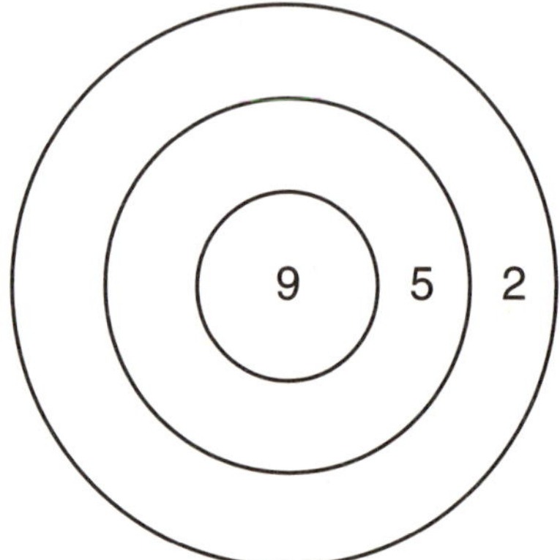

She threw 3 darts, and each hit the board. Which choice below shows a possible total score for the three throws?

A 21

B 20

C 18

D 11

54 Melanie needs at least an 83% average to receive a B. On the first three tests, she averaged 85%. What is the minimum score she must average on the last two tests to receive a B?

F 80%

G 82%

H 84%

J 85%

55 There are 26 people at the Monroe's graduation party. The hall has small square tables that seat one person on each side. How many tables do they need if they put the tables together so that all 26 guests may sit at one table?

Record your answer and fill in the bubbles on the grid below. Be sure to use the correct place value.

				.		
0	0	0	0		0	0
1	1	1	1		1	1
2	2	2	2		2	2
3	3	3	3		3	3
4	4	4	4		4	4
5	5	5	5		5	5
6	6	6	6		6	6
7	7	7	7		7	7
8	8	8	8		8	8
9	9	9	9		9	9

56 A stadium holds 43,425 spectators. There are 9 entrances to the aisles. If an equal number of spectators passed through each entrance, how many spectators would pass through each entrance?

F 3,803

G 4,825

H 43,892

J 39,0825

57 For which multiplication expression will the product be even?

A 765×755

B 721×903

C 123×675

D 982×546

58 To train for a road race, Davie rode his bicycle 55.20 miles on Monday, 58.50 miles Tuesday, and 57.40 miles on Wednesday. Which list shows the number of miles he rode in order from greatest to least?

F 57.40, 58.50, 55.20

G 57.40, 55.20, 58.50

H 55.20, 58.50, 57.40

J 58.50, 57.40, 55.20

59 Any number that has 15 as a factor also has which of these numbers as factors?

A 2 and 3

B 3 and 6

C 3 and 5

D 5 and 6

60 What is the least common multiple of 3, 5, and 10?

Record your answer and fill in the bubbles on the grid below. Be sure to use the correct place value.

				.		
0	0	0	0		0	0
1	1	1	1		1	1
2	2	2	2		2	2
3	3	3	3		3	3
4	4	4	4		4	4
5	5	5	5		5	5
6	6	6	6		6	6
7	7	7	7		7	7
8	8	8	8		8	8
9	9	9	9		9	9

61 Which two numbers have a product of 56 and a sum of 30?

A 8 and 7

B 4 and 14

C 2 and 28

D 1 and 56

62 At the supermarket, Paige buys meat for \$4.67, juice for \$2.99 and fruit for \$3.45. She hands the clerk a \$20 bill. How much change should she receive?

F \$11.11

G \$10.76

H \$8.96

J \$8.89

63 The table shows some x-values and some related y-values.

x	1	3	5	7	9
y	5	9	13	17	21

Which equation shows the relationship between the variables?

A $x = 2y + 3$

B $y = 2x - 3$

C $x = 2y - 3$

D $y = 2x + 3$

64 Which of the following is NOT true?

F The ratio 1 to 2 can be represented as 50%.

G $\frac{1}{3} = 33\frac{1}{3}\%$

H 2 out of 8 = 25%

J 1 out of 5 = 0.2%

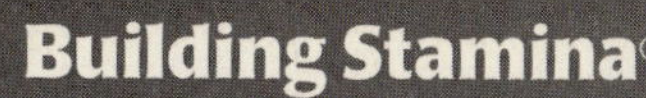

65 Jamie needs to triple a recipe, which calls for $3\frac{3}{4}$ cups of flour. How much flour will he need?

A 9 c

B $9\frac{3}{4}$ c

C $11\frac{1}{4}$ c

D $13\frac{1}{4}$ c

66 Which fraction is NOT equivalent to $\frac{5}{6}$?

F $\frac{10}{12}$

G $\frac{15}{18}$

H $\frac{20}{24}$

J $\frac{25}{35}$

67 When Kristin visited her grandparents in Norway, the exchange rate was approximately 7 kroner to the dollar. She bought a hand-knitted sweater for 2,430 kroner. About how many US dollars did she spend?

A $200

B $350

C $400

D $450

68 A fabric costs $23.75 per yard. To make curtains in the living room, Mia needs 28 yards of fabric. Which is the closest estimate to the cost of the fabric?

F $300

G $400

H $500

J $700

69 Which is another way to write $3 \times 3 \times 8 \times 8 \times 7 \times 7 \times 7$ using exponents?

A $3^2 \cdot 8^7$

B $3 \cdot 2^6 \cdot 7^3$

C $3^2 \cdot 2^6 \cdot 7^3$

D $3^2 \cdot 2^8 \cdot 7$

70 Look at the table below.

x	5	6	7	8	9
y	19	23	27	31	35

Which formula shows the relationship between the variables?

F $x = 4y + 1$

G $y = 4x - 1$

H $y = 4x + 1$

J Not Here

Part 2 Geometry, Measurement, Probability, and Statistics

Chapter 6 Geometry and Spatial Reasoning
In Chapter 6 you will study and practice:

- how to classify and measure angles;
- how to use geometric vocabulary to describe polygons;
- how to use geometric vocabulary to describe triangles;
- how to use geometric vocabulary to describe quadrilaterals;
- how to use geometric vocabulary to describe circles;
- how to locate and name points on a coordinate plane;
- how to draw the results of transformations in the coordinate plane;
- how to solve problems by looking for patterns.

★ **Building Stamina®**: This section gives you a chance to sharpen your skills with geometry and spatial reasoning, and to strengthen your test-taking abilities.

Chapter 7 Measurement
In Chapter 7 you will study and practice:

- how to solve problems involving length;
- how to solve problems involving capacity;
- how to solve problems involving weight or mass;
- how to solve problems involving temperature;
- how to solve problems involving time;
- how to solve problems by drawing a picture.

★ **Building Stamina®**: This section gives you a chance to sharpen your skills with measurement, and to strengthen your test-taking abilities.

Chapter 8 Perimeter, Area, and Volume
In Chapter 8 you will study and practice:

- how to estimate and find the perimeter;
- how to estimate and find the circumference;
- how to estimate and find the area;
- how to estimate and find the volume;
- how to identify needed information in a problem.

★ **Building Stamina®**: This section gives you a chance to sharpen your skills with perimeter, area, and volume, and to strengthen your test-taking abilities.

Part 2 Geometry, Measurement, Probability, and Statistics

Chapter 9 Probability

In Chapter 9 you will study and practice:

- how to list outcomes;
- how to construct and use tree diagrams;
- how to use experimental probability to make predictions;
- how to make an organized list to solve problems.

★ **Building Stamina®**: This section gives you a chance to sharpen your skills with probability, and to strengthen your test-taking abilities.

Chapter 10 Statistics

In Chapter 10 you will study and practice:

- how to use mean, median, mode, and range to describe data;
- how to construct and use bar graphs;
- how to construct and use line graphs;
- how to construct and use stem-and-leaf plots;
- how to construct and use circle graphs;
- how to make and use a graph to solve problems.

★ **Building Stamina®**: This section gives you a chance to sharpen your skills with statistics, and to strengthen your test-taking abilities.

Focus on TEKS

Lesson 30 Classify and Measure Angles

TEKS 6.6A Use angle measurements to classify angles as acute, obtuse, or right.
TEKS 6.8A Estimate measurements and evaluate reasonableness of results.
TEKS 6.8B Select and use appropriate tools to measure.
TEKS 6.8C Measure angles.

You can use a right angle to estimate measures of other angles.

A **ray** is part of a line. Rays have one endpoint and continue forever in one direction.

Angles are formed when two rays meet at a vertex. The symbol for angle is ∠.

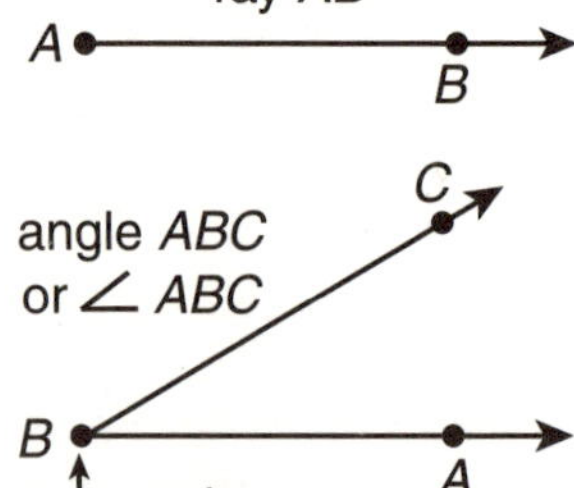

Types of Angles

A right angle is an angle that forms a square corner and measures 90 degrees.	An acute angle is an angle that measures less than 90 degrees.	An obtuse angle is an angle that measures greater than 90 and less than 180 degrees.
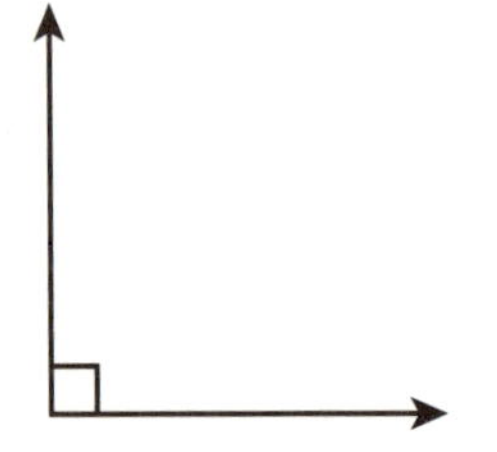	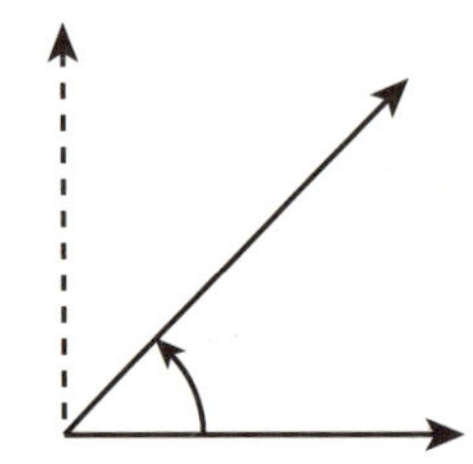	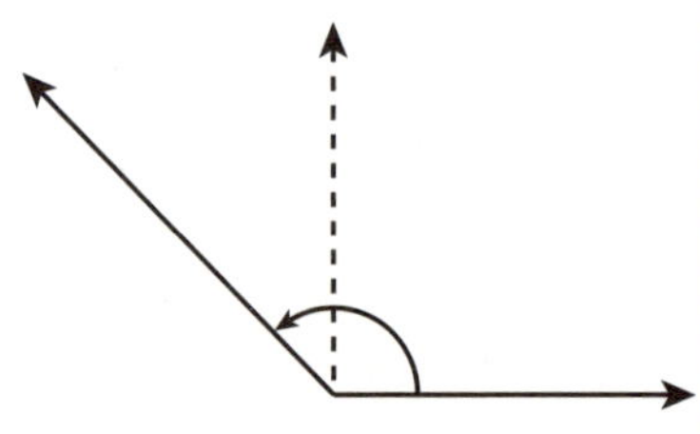

Guided Instruction

Problem 1

Michelle's teacher made a banner like the one shown for the classroom. What type of angle is at the bottom of the banner?

Decide if the angle is greater than or less than 90 degrees.

Step 1 Find the angle.

Step 2 Compare the angle to a right angle.

The angle measures ________________ a right angle.

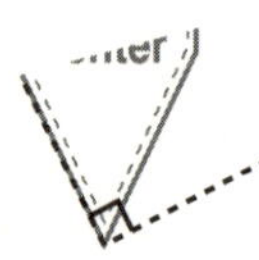

Solution What type of angle is at the bottom of the banner? ________________

Guided Instruction

Another Problem

Angles are measured as part of a circle. From its center, a circle can be divided into 360 equal parts. Each part is one **degree**, written 1°. A full circle contains 360 degrees.

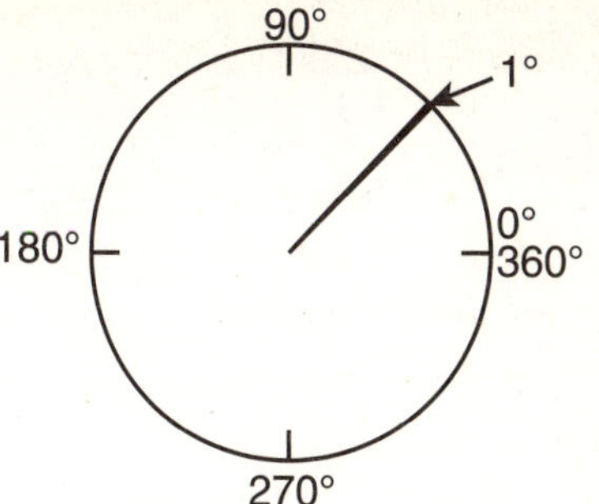

A **protractor** is an instrument used to measure angles. A protractor has two scales, each beginning at 0 degrees and ending at 180 degrees.

Problem 2 What is the measure of ∠*MNR*?

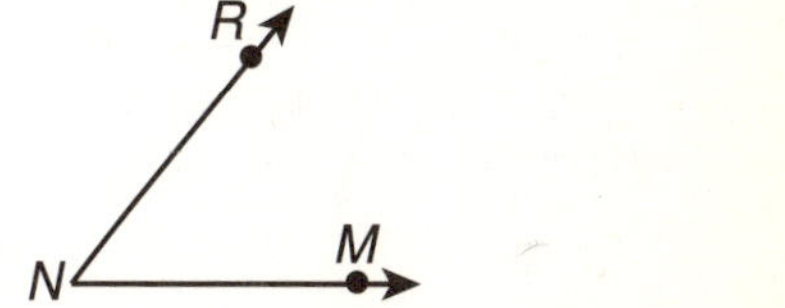

You can use a protractor to find the measure of an angle.

Step 1 Extend the sides of the angle for convenience in using the protractor. Place the center of the protractor on the vertex of the angle. Align the baseline of the protractor with one side of the angle, ray *NM*.

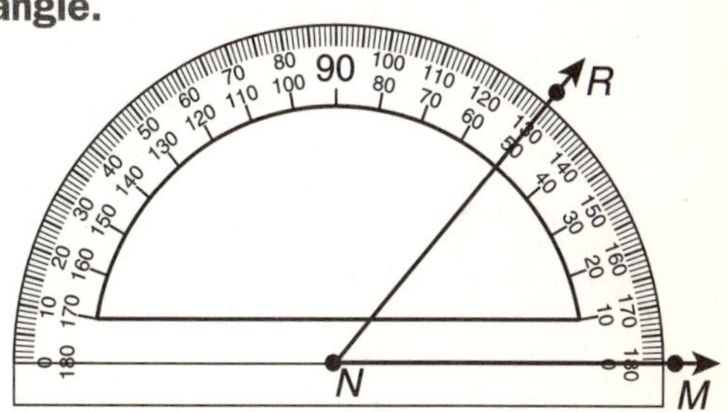

Since ray *NM* is to be aligned at 0 degrees, which scale on the protractor will you use to measure angle *MNR*, the inner scale or the outer scale? ____________________

Step 2 Where does the other side of the angle, ray *NR*, cross the inner scale?

____

What is the measure of angle *MNR*? ____________________

Step 3 Evaluate the reasonableness of your result.

Angle *MNR* is an __________ angle, and the measure of an acute angle is less than ____________________.

Solution What is the measure of angle *MNR*? ____________________

Another Example

Find the measure of obtuse angle *ZXY*.

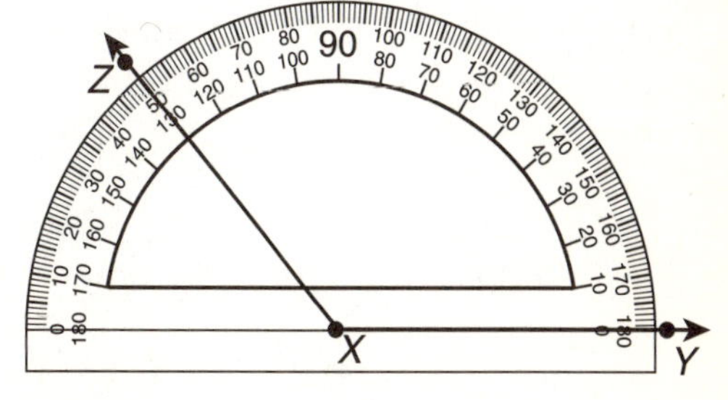

Vertex *X* of the angle is at the center of the protractor. One side of the angle, ray *XY*, is aligned with the baseline of the protractor. Ray *XY* is at 0 degrees on the inner scale of the protractor. The other side of the angle, ray *XZ*, crosses the inner scale of the protractor at 130 degrees. The measure of obtuse angle *ZXY* is 130 degrees. Since the angle is obtuse, it is reasonable that the measure is greater than 90 degrees.

Apply the TEKS

Classify each angle as *acute*, *right*, or *obtuse*.

1. 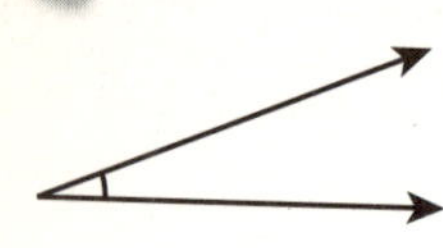

____

2. 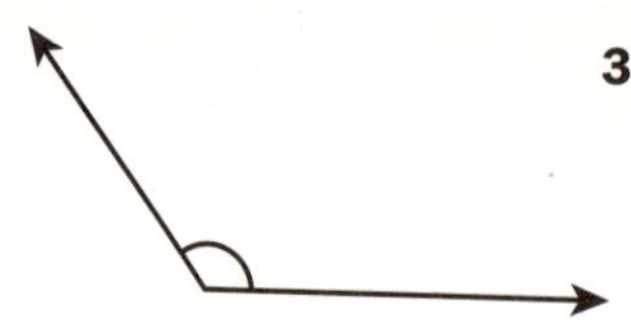

____

3. 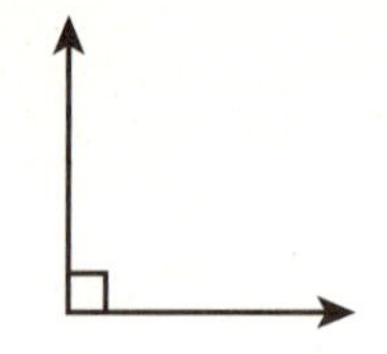

____

4. 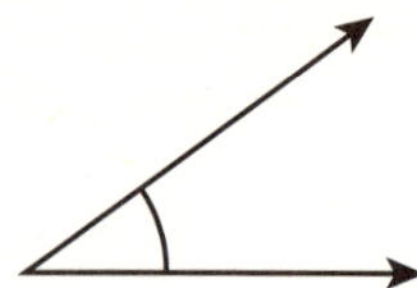

____

5. 

____

6. 

____

7. 

____

8. 

____

Use a protractor to find the measure of each angle.

9. 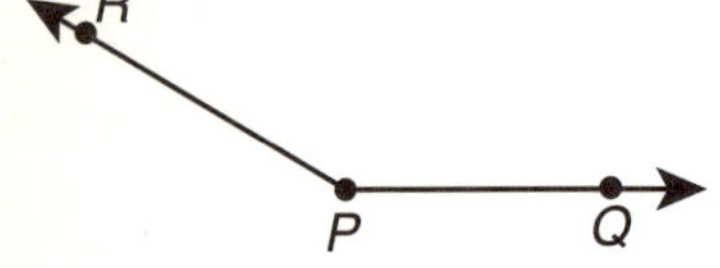

measure of angle *QPR* = ________

10. 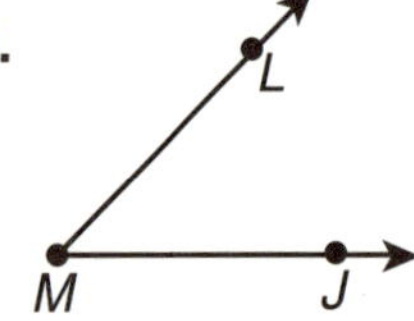

measure of angle *JML* = ________

11. 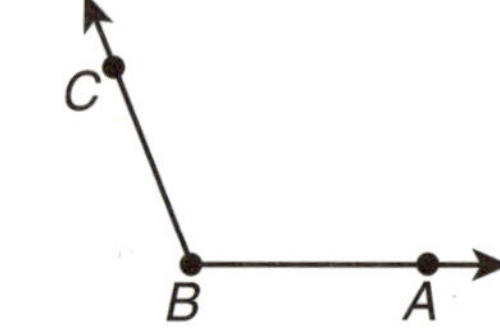

measure of angle *ABC* = ________

12. 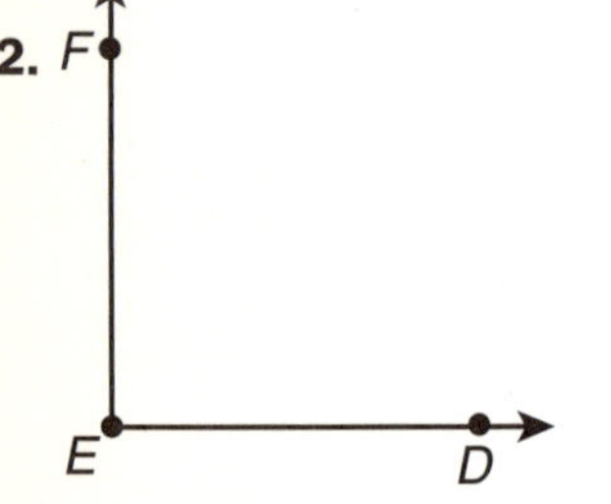

measure of angle *DEF* = ________

13. 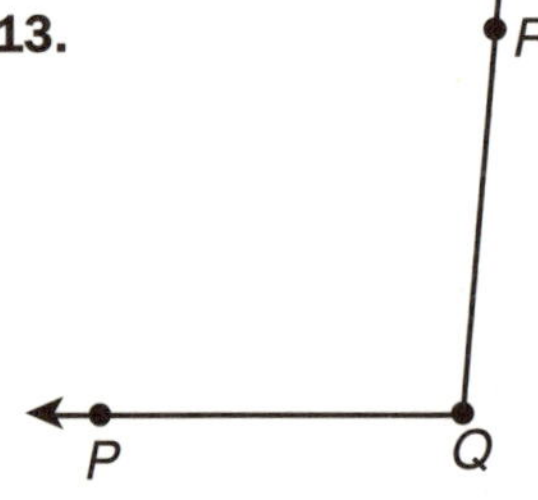

measure of angle *PQR* = ________

14. 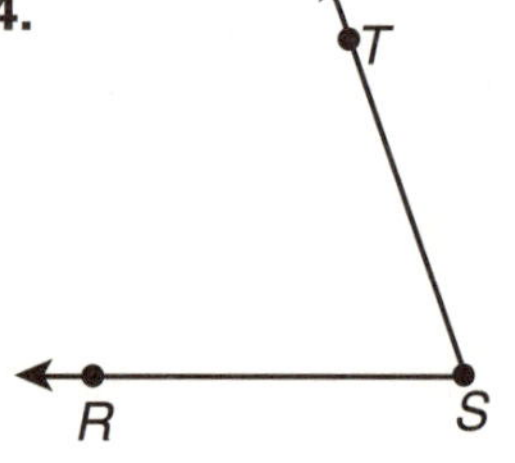

measure of angle *RST* = ________

Solve each problem.

15. A ramp is used to make wheelchair access easy. The maximum incline recommended is in the ratio 1:12. That is, for each meter in height, the ramp extends 12 meters in length. Estimate the measure of the angle that the ramp below makes with the level ground.

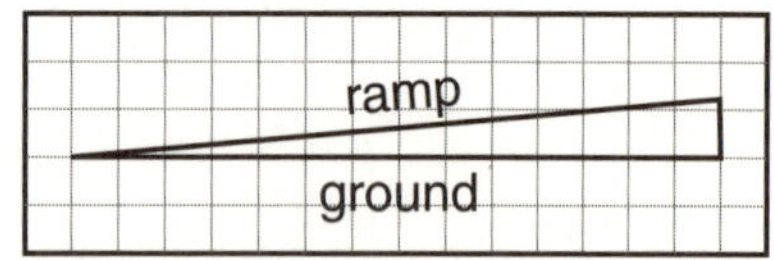

____

16. Which of the angles below is larger? ______________

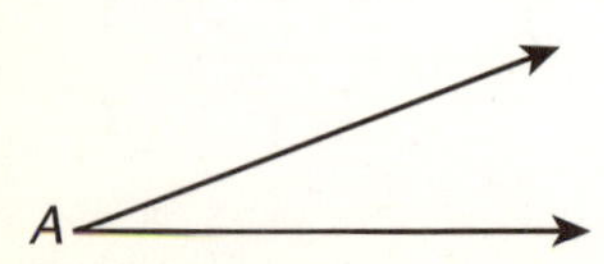

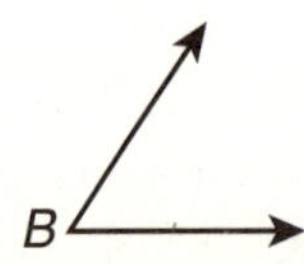

Explain your answer. ______________

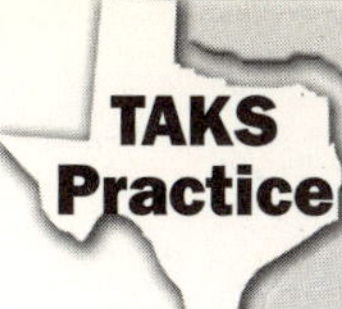

TAKS Objective 3 The student will demonstrate an understanding of geometry and spatial reasoning.
TEKS 6.6A

TAKS Objective 4 The student will demonstrate an understanding of the concepts and uses of measurement.
TEKS 6.8A, 6.8B, 6.8C

DIRECTIONS Read each question. Then circle the letter for the correct answer.

1 Which is an acute angle?

A 

B 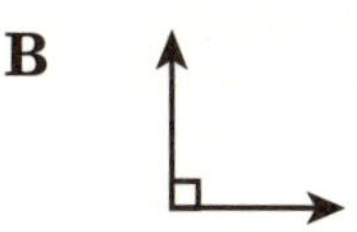

C 

D 

2 Frederick dropped toothpicks on his desk. They landed like this.

Which of these statements is true?

F No angle is formed.

G The angle formed is acute.

H The angle formed is obtuse.

J The angle formed is a right angle.

3 What is the degree measure of $\angle APC$?

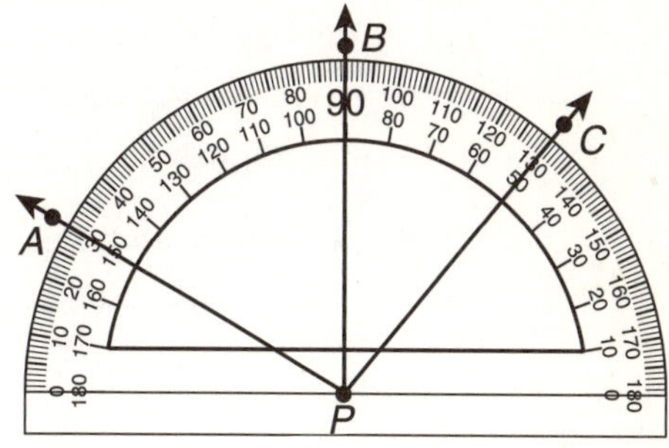

A 180°

B 100°

C 90°

D 45°

4 In the diagram below, $\angle APC$ and $\angle BPD$ are right angles. The measure of $\angle APB$ is 20 degrees.

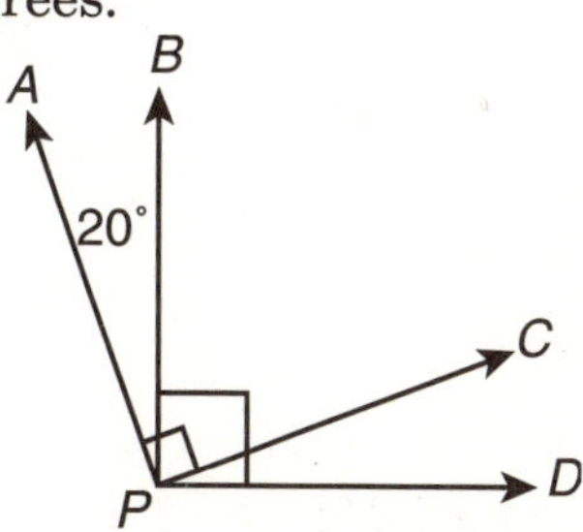

What is the measure of $\angle CPD$?

F 110°

G 90°

H 70°

J 20°

Focus on TEKS

Lesson 31 Polygons

TEKS 6.6A Use angle measurements to classify angles as acute, obtuse, or right.

TEKS 6.6B Identify relationships involving angles.

You can identify and measure angles in polygons.

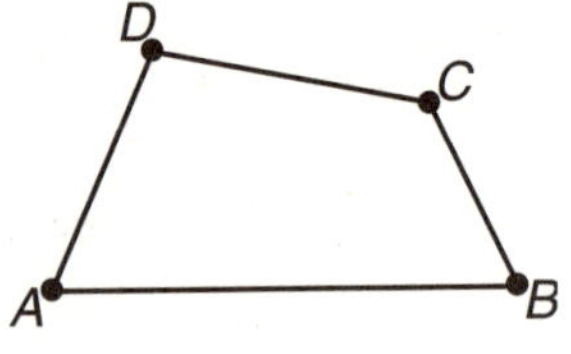

A **polygon** is a plane figure formed by joining three or more line segments. A polygon is named for the number of sides it has. Polygons have the same number of angles as sides. Polygons are named by capital letters, starting at one vertex and going in order, either clockwise or counterclockwise. A **regular polygon** is a polygon with equal sides and equal angles.

Here are some polygons:

Name of Polygon	Number of Angles	Sum of the Measure of All the Angles
Triangle	3	180°
Quadrilateral	4	360°
Pentagon	5	540°
Hexagon	6	720°
Heptagon	7	900°
Octagon	8	1080°
Nonagon	9	1260°
Decagon	10	1440°

Guided Instruction

Problem

In regular pentagon *JKLMN*, the measure of $\angle J = 108°$, the measure of $\angle K = 108°$, the measure of $\angle L = 108°$, and the measure of $\angle N = 108°$. What is the measure of $\angle M$? What is the relationship among all the angles in regular pentagon *JKLMN*?

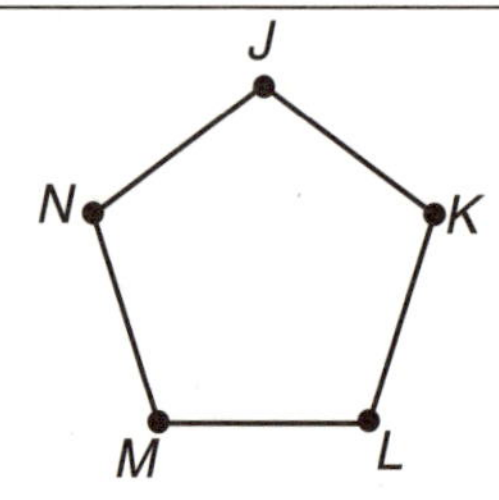

Use the fact that the sum of the measures of the angles in a pentagon is 540 degrees.

Step 1 Read $m\angle J$ as "the measure of angle *J*." Add the measures of the given angles.

$m\angle J + m\angle K + m\angle L + m\angle N = 108° + 108° + 108° + 108° =$ ________

Step 2 Subtract the total sum of the given angles from 540°.

$540° - 432° =$ ________

Solution

What is the measure of $\angle M$? ________

What is the relationship among all the angles in regular pentagon *JKLMN*?

____

Apply the TEKS **Complete each statement.**

1. The number of sides in a pentagon is __________.
2. The number of vertices in an octagon is __________.
3. The number of angles in a heptagon is __________.

Identify *x* as an *acute*, *obtuse* or *right* angle.

4. 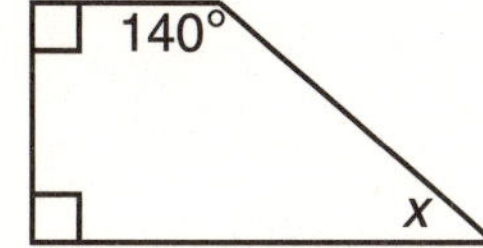

____

5. 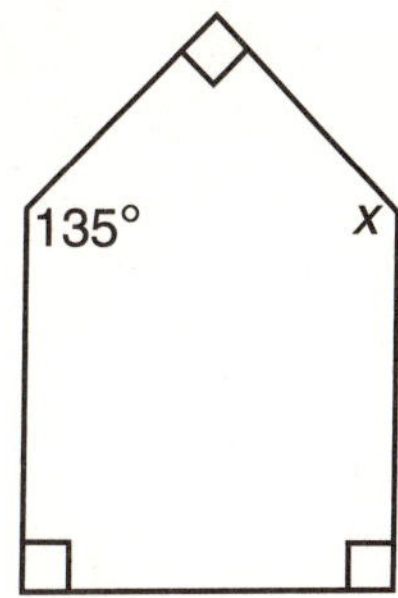

____

6. 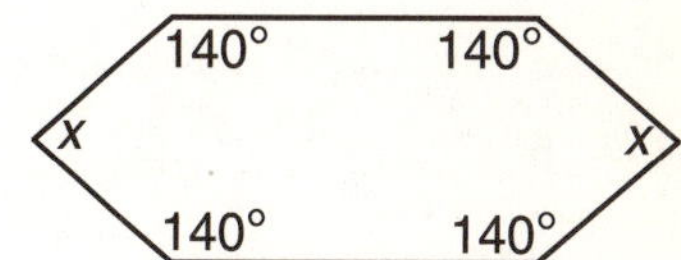

____

Use a protractor to find the measure of angle *n*.

7. 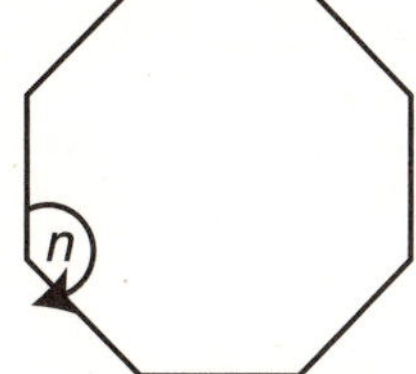

____

8. 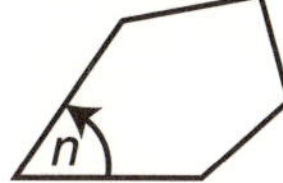

____

9. 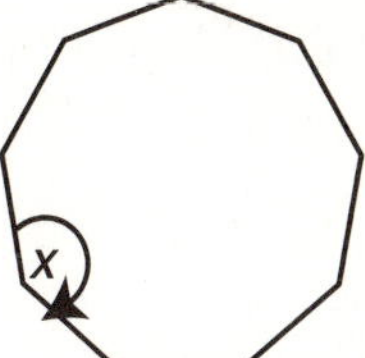

____

Solve the problem.

10. Tom has drawn a heptagon. What is the measure of angle *n* in the figure? ________

    Explain how you found your answer.

    ____

    ____

    ____

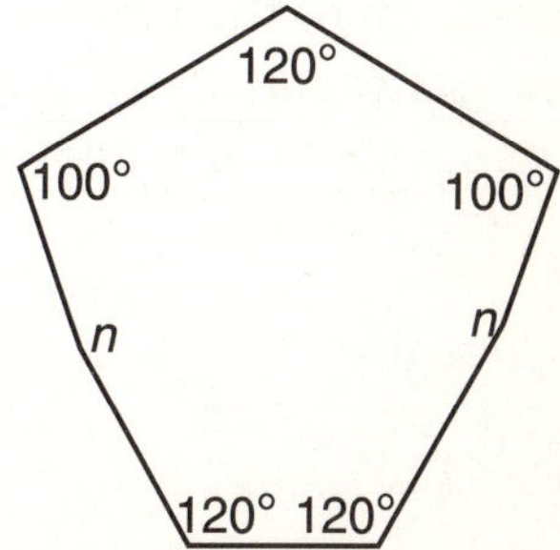

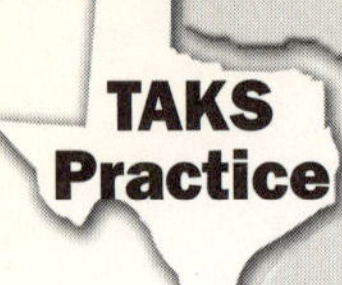

TAKS Objective 3 The student will demonstrate an understanding of geometry and spatial reasoning.
TEKS 6.6A, 6.6B

DIRECTIONS Read each question. Then circle the letter for the correct answer.

1 How many more angles are there in a decagon than there are in a heptagon?

A 10

B 7

C 5

D 3

Use the pentagon below to answer Questions 2–3.

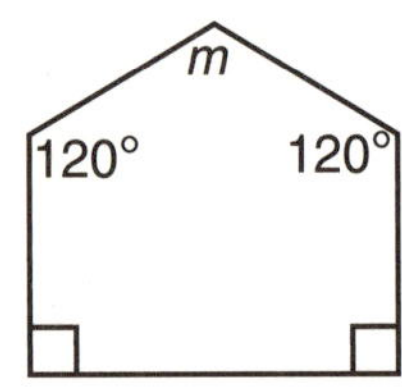

2 What kind of angle is angle *m* in the pentagon shown above?

F Acute

G Right

H Obtuse

J Straight

3 The sum of the measures of the angles in the pentagon above is 540 degrees. Which is the measure of angle *m*?

A 30°

B 60°

C 120°

D 180°

4 Which of these quadrilaterals is a regular polygon?

F 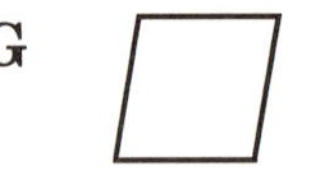

G 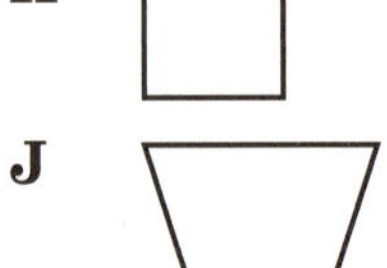

H

J

5 What is the best description for the STOP sign used in traffic control?

A Octagon

B Equilateral octagon

C Equiangular octagon

D Regular octagon

Focus on TEKS

Lesson 32 Triangles

TEKS 6.6B Identify relationships involving angles in triangles.

You can solve problems involving triangles.

Triangles can be named by the lengths of their sides.

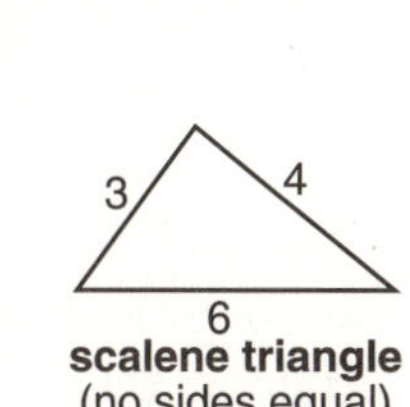 **scalene triangle** (no sides equal)	8, 8, 4 **isosceles triangle** (2 equal sides)	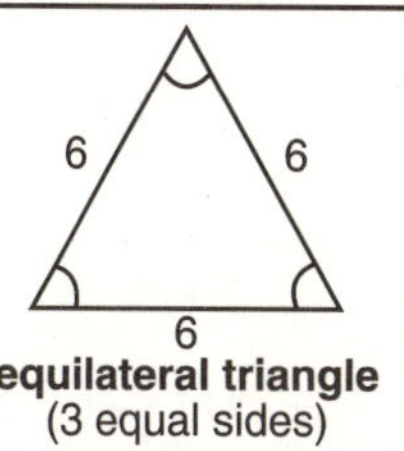 **equilateral triangle** (3 equal sides)

Triangles can be named by the sizes of their angles.

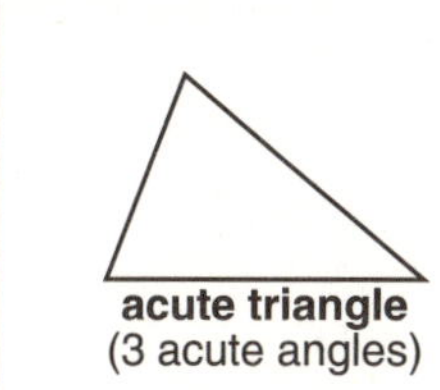 **acute triangle** (3 acute angles)	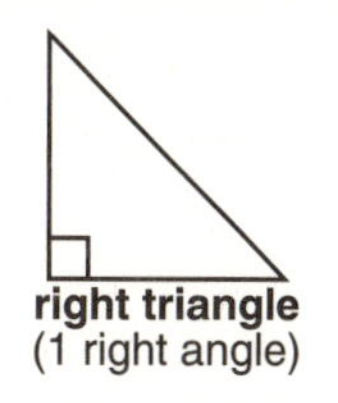 **right triangle** (1 right angle)	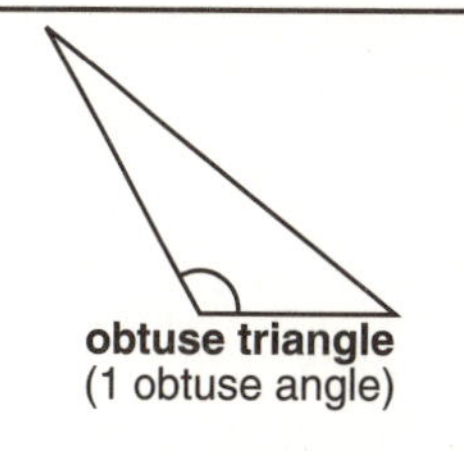 **obtuse triangle** (1 obtuse angle)

In any triangle, the sum of the measures of the three angles is 180 degrees.
In triangle XYZ, $m\angle X + m\angle Y + m\angle Z = 180°$.

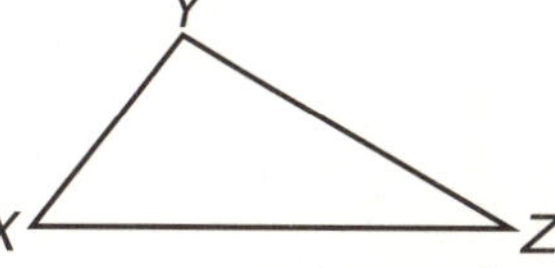

Guided Instruction

Problem 1

In triangle ABC, $m\angle A$ is 50 and $m\angle B$ is 70°. What is $m\angle C$? Is the triangle an acute, right, or obtuse triangle?

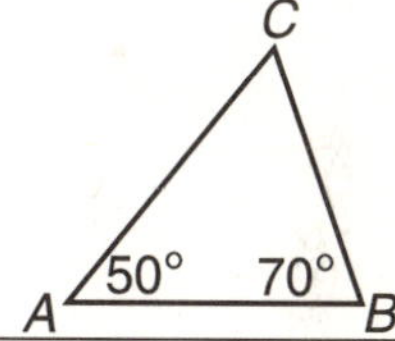

Use what you know about the sum of the measures of the angles in a triangle.

Step 1 Add the measures of the two given angles.

$m\angle A =$ _______ $m\angle B =$ _______ $m\angle A + m\angle B =$ _______

Step 2 Subtract the sum of the measures of the two angles from the sum of the measures of the three angles.

$m\angle A + m\angle B + m\angle C =$ _______

$m\angle A + m\angle B =$ _______

So, $m\angle C$ is _______.

Solution

What is $m\angle C$? _______
Is the triangle an acute, right, or obtuse triangle? Explain.

____

____

Guided Instruction

Another Problem

Isosceles Triangle

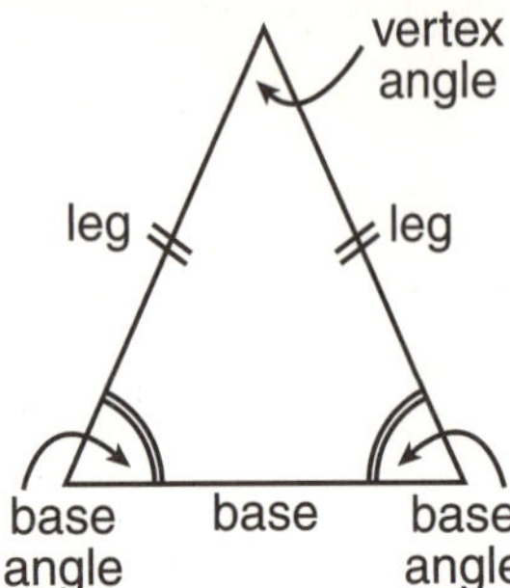

The base angles of an isosceles triangle are equal in measure.

Equilateral Triangle

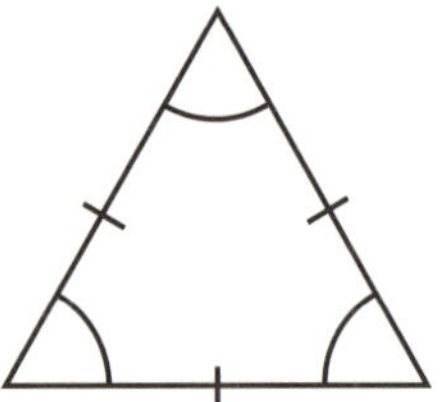

An equilateral triangle is also equiangular, with all three angles equal in measure.

Problem 2

Segment *AB* is the base of isosceles triangle *ABC*. The measure of vertex angle *C* is 80 degrees.

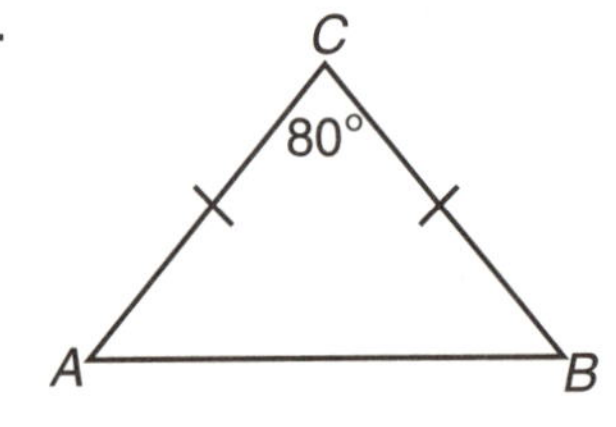

What is m$\angle A$?

What is m$\angle B$?

Step 1 Subtract the measure of the vertex angle from the total sum.
The sum of the measures of the three angles of any triangle is _______.

m$\angle C$ = _______

The number of degrees that remain for m$\angle A$ + m$\angle B$ is _______.

Step 2 Use the property of the base angles of an isosceles triangle.

What is true about the measures of the base angles of an isosceles triangle?

____

Since m$\angle A$ + m$\angle B$ = 100° and since m$\angle A$ = m$\angle B$, then:

m$\angle A$ is _______ and m$\angle B$ is _______.

Solution

What is the m$\angle A$? ________

What is the m$\angle B$? ________

Apply the TEKS **Classify each triangle as *scalene, equilateral,* or *isosceles.***

1. 

____

2. 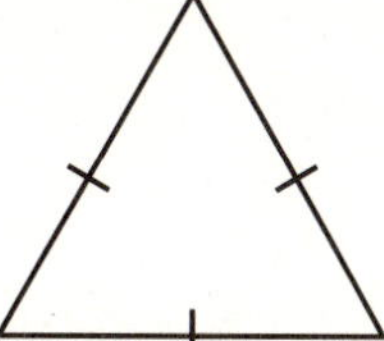

____

3. 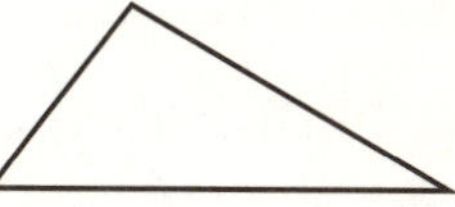

____

Classify each triangle as *obtuse, right,* or *acute.*

4. 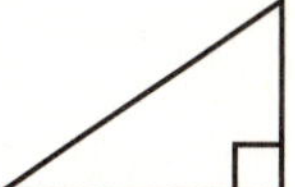

____

5. 

____

6. 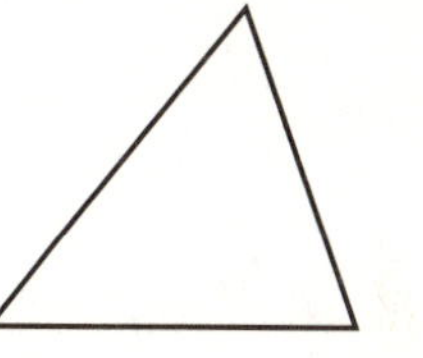

____

Complete each statement.

7. The sum of the measures of the three angles of any triangle is __________.
8. The base angles of an isosceles triangle are ______________ in measure.
9. A triangle with three angles equal in measure is called ______________.

Solve each problem.

10. In triangle *XYZ*, the measure of $\angle X$ is 30 degrees. The m$\angle Z$ is twice the m$\angle Y$.

    What is the m$\angle Y$? __________ What is the m$\angle Z$? __________

11. In right triangle *ABC*, the right angle is $\angle C$. The measure of $\angle A$ is 20 degrees.

    What is the measure of $\angle B$? __________

12. What is the measure of each angle of any equilateral triangle?
    Explain your answer.

____

____

____

____

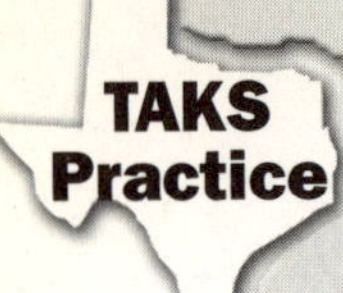

TAKS Objective 3 The student will demonstrate an understanding of geometry and spatial reasoning.
TEKS 6.6B

DIRECTIONS Read each question. Then circle the letter for the correct answer.

1 Which type of triangle does NOT have any angles equal in measure?

A Scalene triangle

B Isosceles triangle

C Equilateral triangle

D Equiangular triangle

2 The measure of angle A and the measure of angle B in the isosceles triangle shown below is 35 degrees. What is the measure of angle C?

C

A B

F 35°

G 70°

H 110°

J 180°

3 The drawing below shows a right triangle.

What is the measure of a?

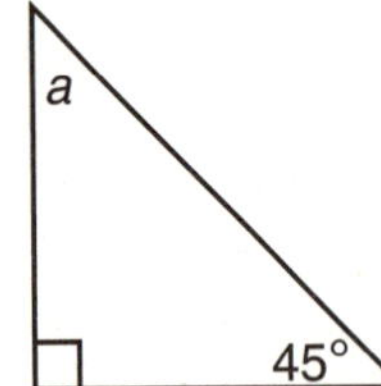

Record your answer and fill in the bubbles on the grid below. Be sure to use the correct place value.

				.		
0	0	0	0		0	0
1	1	1	1		1	1
2	2	2	2		2	2
3	3	3	3		3	3
4	4	4	4		4	4
5	5	5	5		5	5
6	6	6	6		6	6
7	7	7	7		7	7
8	8	8	8		8	8
9	9	9	9		9	9

4 Which is an equilateral triangle?

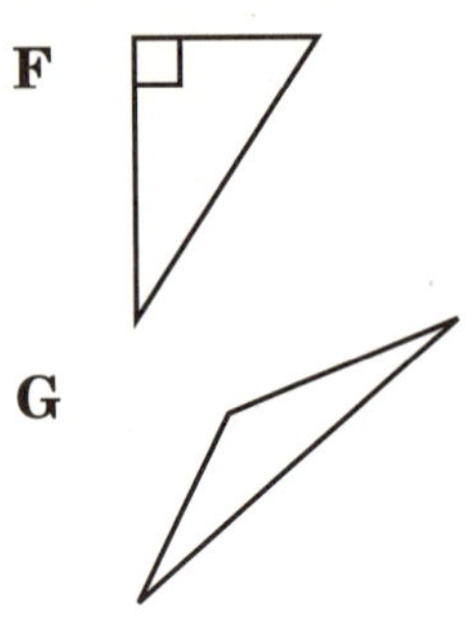

F

G

H

J
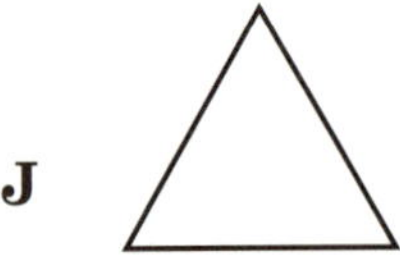

5 The measures of the three angles of a certain triangle are in the ratio 3:2:1. What are the degree measures of these angles?

A 180°, 120°, 60°

B 90°, 60°, 30°

C 45°, 30°, 15°

D 30°, 20°, 10°

6 If the measure of one angle of a triangle is equal to the sum of the measures of the other two angles, what type must this triangle be?

F An acute triangle

G A right triangle

H An obtuse triangle

J An equilateral triangle

Focus on TEKS

Lesson 33 Quadrilaterals

TEKS 6.6B Identify relationships involving angles in quadrilaterals.

You can solve problems involving the measures of the angles of a quadrilateral.

A **diagonal** is a line segment that joins two vertices of a polygon, but is not a side of the polygon.

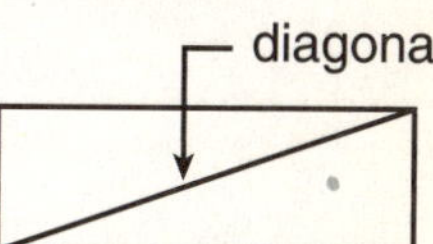

A **quadrilateral** is a polygon with four sides and four angles. In any quadrilateral, the sum of the measures of the four angles is 360 degrees.

These are some examples of quadrilaterals:

A **trapezoid** is a quadrilateral with exactly one pair of parallel sides.

An **isosceles trapezoid** has one pair of parallel sides called bases. Base angles have the same measure. The nonparallel sides are called legs and are equal in length.

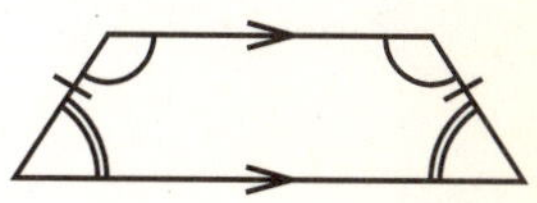

A **parallelogram** has opposite sides that are parallel and the same length. Opposite angles are congruent. A diagonal separates a parallelogram into two congruent triangles. The sum of consecutive angles is 180 degrees. In parallelogram $ABCD$: $m\angle A = m\angle C$ and $m\angle B = m\angle D$.

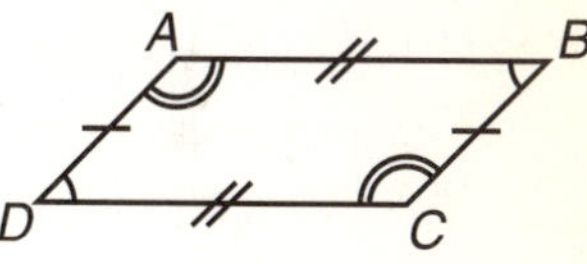

A **rectangle** is a parallelogram with four right angles. A diagonal separates a rectangle into two congruent triangles.

A **rhombus** is a parallelogram with four equal sides. A diagonal separates a rhombus into two congruent triangles.

A **square** is a rectangle with four equal sides. A diagonal separates a square into two congruent right triangles.

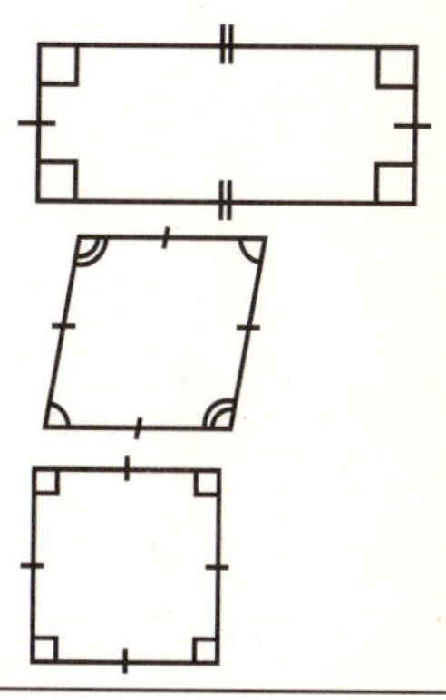

Guided Instruction

Problem 1

In parallelogram $JKLM$, the measure of $\angle J = 50°$, the measure of $\angle K = 130°$, and the measure of $\angle L = 50°$. What is the measure of $\angle M$? What is the relationship between $m\angle K$ and $m\angle M$?

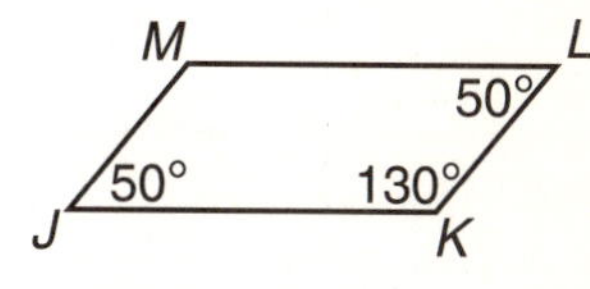

Use the fact that the sum of the measures of the four angles in a quadrilateral is 360 degrees.

Step 1 Add the measures of the given angles.

$m\angle J + m\angle K + m\angle L = 50° + 130° + 50° =$ ________

Step 2 Subtract the sum of the given angles from 360°.

$360° - 230° =$ ________

Solution

What is the measure of $\angle M$? ________

What is the relationship between $m\angle K$ and $m\angle M$? ________

Guided Instruction

Another Problem

When a line **bisects** an angle, it divides that angle into 2 angles that are congruent. In a rhombus, the diagonals are perpendicular and bisect the opposite angles of the rhombus.

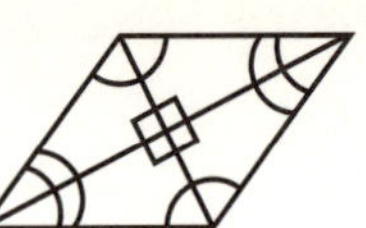

Problem 2

In rhombus *ABCD*, diagonal *AC* is drawn.
The measure of $\angle DAB$ is 60 degrees.

What is the measure of the following angles?
$\angle DAC$, $\angle CAB$, $\angle DCA$, $\angle BCA$, $\angle ADC$, $\angle ABC$?

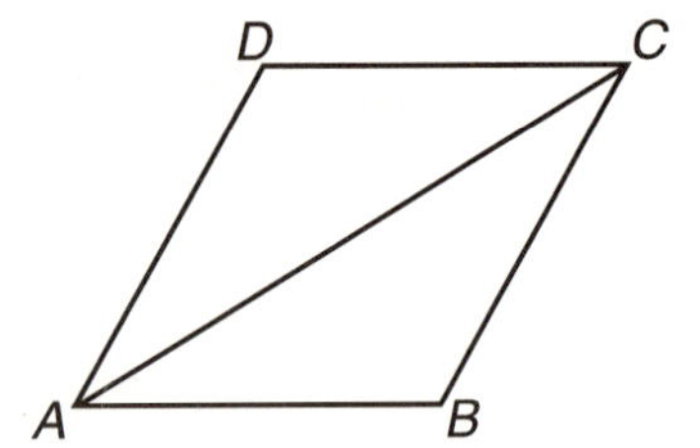

Use the facts about the angles of a triangle, a rhombus, and a parallelogram.

Step 1 A diagonal of a rhombus bisects the angles through which it is drawn.

Since diagonal *AC* bisects $\angle DAB$ and $m\angle DAB = 60°$, then

$m\angle DAC =$ ______ and $m\angle CAB =$ ______.

Step 2 Opposite angles of a rhombus are equal in measure.

Since $m\angle DAB = 60°$, then $m\angle DCB =$ ______.

Since diagonal *AC* also bisects $\angle DCB$ and $m\angle DCB = 60°$,

then $m\angle DCA =$ ______ and $m\angle BCA =$ ______.

Step 3 The sum of the measures of consecutive angles of a parallelogram is 180°.

Since $m\angle DAB = 60°$, then $m\angle ADC =$ ______ and $m\angle ABC =$ ______.

Solution

What is the measure of the following angles?

$m\angle DAC =$______, $m\angle CAB =$______, $m\angle DCA =$______, $m\angle BCA =$______,

$m\angle ADC =$______, $m\angle ABC =$______

Apply the TEKS **Find the measures of the indicated angles of each quadrilateral.**

1. Quadrilateral *ABCD*

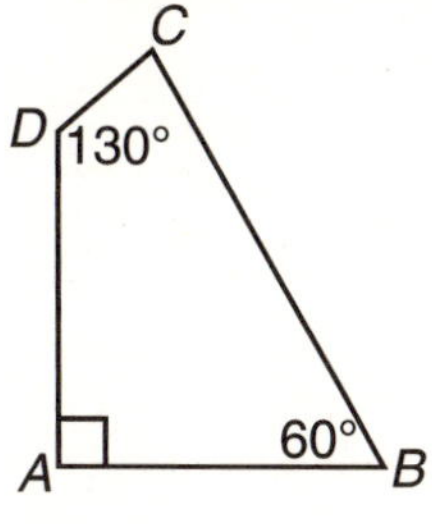

m∠*A* = ______

m∠*C* = ______

2. Trapezoid *JKLM*

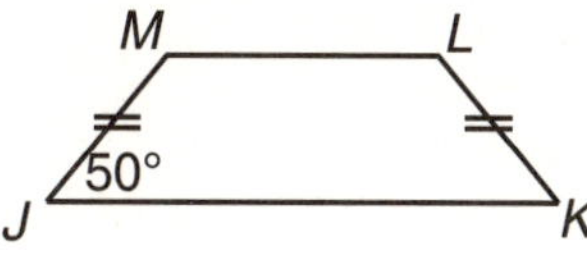

m∠*K* = ______

m∠*L* = ______

m∠*M* = ______

3. Parallelogram *RSTU*

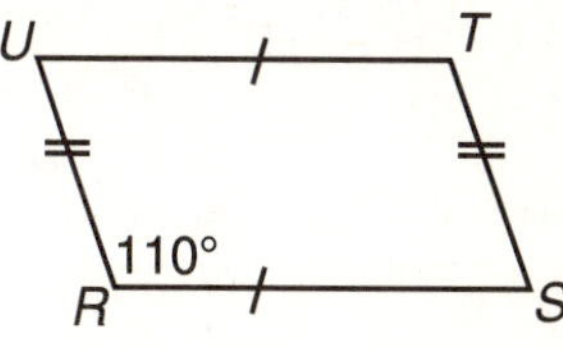

m∠*S* = ______

m∠*T* = ______

m∠*U* = ______

The diagram shows the relationships among the various types of quadrilaterals. For example, all quadrilaterals are polygons. Tell if each statement is true or false.

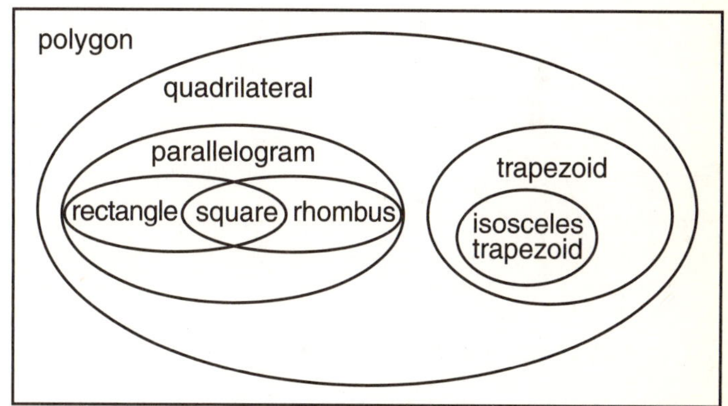

4. All rectangles are parallelograms. __________

5. All squares are rhombuses. __________

6. All rectangles are squares. __________

7. All trapezoids are isosceles. __________

Solve the problem.

8. Ms. Frank told her class that a good definition includes the least amount of information possible. She asked for a good definition of a rectangle. Rob said that you can define a rectangle as a parallelogram with a right angle. Larry said that you have to tell that a rectangle has four right angles. So Larry's definition is that a rectangle is a parallelogram with four right angles. Mike said that a rectangle can be defined as a quadrilateral with 2 pairs of parallel sides and four right angles. With which boy's definition do you agree? Explain.

____

____

____

____

____

____

____

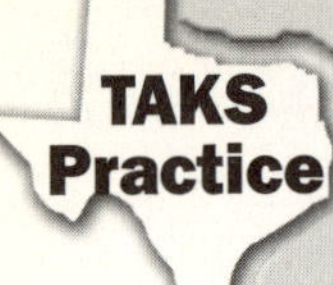

TAKS Objective 3 The student will demonstrate an understanding of geometry and spatial reasoning.
TEKS 6.6B

DIRECTIONS Read each question. Then circle the letter for the correct answer.

1 In which types of quadrilaterals are there always four right angles?

A Parallelograms and rhombuses

B Parallelograms and rectangles

C Rectangles and rhombuses

D Rectangles and squares

2 Rhombus *WXYZ* is shown below.

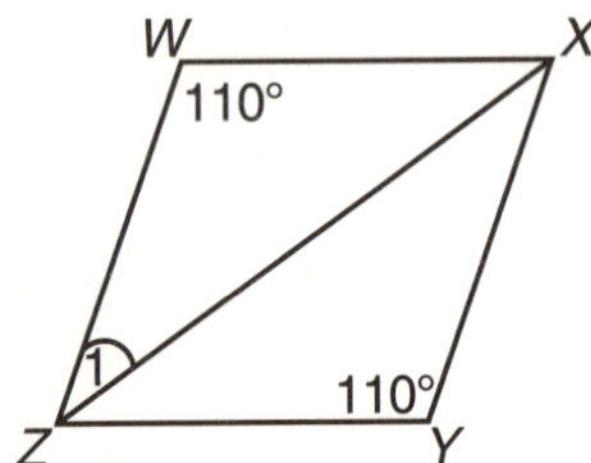

What is the measure of ∠1?

F 35°

G 70°

H 110°

J Not Here

3 Which is NOT always true in a parallelogram?

A The sum of the measures of the four angles is 360°.

B Opposite angles are equal in measure.

C A diagonal bisects the opposite angles through which it is drawn.

D The sum of the measures of two consecutive angles is 180°.

4 A square and an equilateral triangle have a vertex in common.

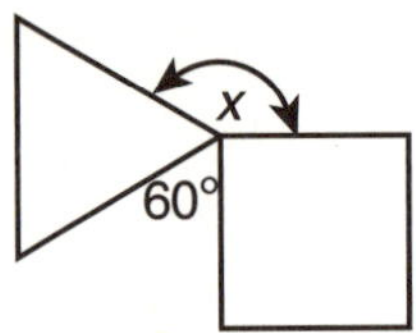

What is the measure of angle x?

F 250°

G 150°

H 125°

J 110°

5 In rhombus *ABCD*, diagonals *AC* and *BD* intersect at point *P*. The measure of ∠*ADC* is 120°.

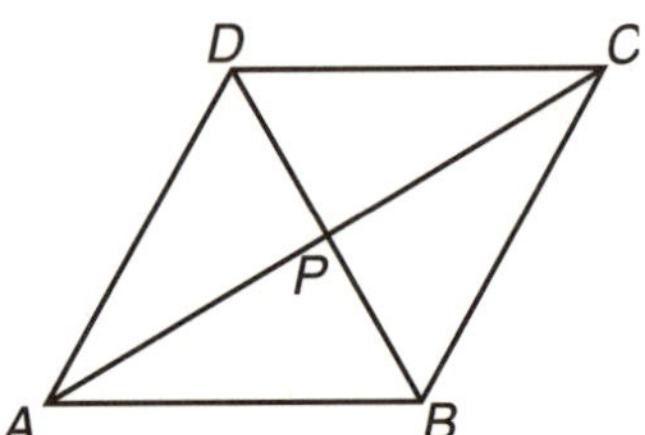

What is the measure of ∠*DPC*?

A 120°

B 90°

C 60°

D 30°

Focus on TEKS

Lesson 34 Circles

TEKS 6.6C Describe the relationship between radius, diameter, and circumference of a circle.

Investigate the relationship between the radius, diameter, and circumference of a circle.

A **circle** is a closed figure having all points the same distance from the center point. A **center point** is a point in the middle of a circle that is the same distance from all points on the circle. **Circumference** is the distance around a circle. A **diameter** is a line segment that passes through the center of the circle and has endpoints on the circle. A **radius** is a line segment that connects the center and an endpoint on the circle. A **chord** is a line segment whose endpoints are on the circle. There are 360 degrees in a circle.

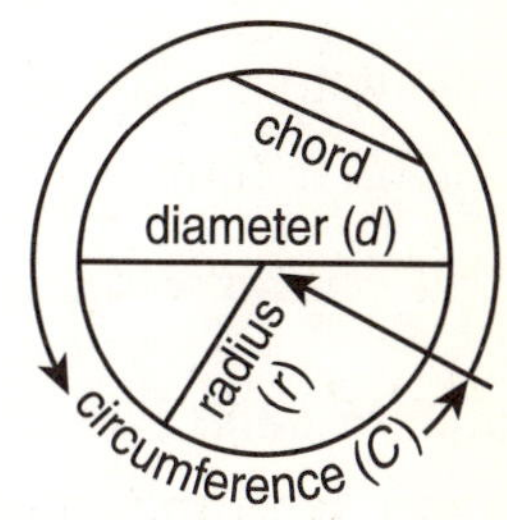

Guided Instruction

Problem

What is the relationship between the length of the diameter and the circumference of the circle below? What is the relationship between the length of the radius and the length of the diameter?

Use string to help you understand the parts of a circle.

Step 1 Look at the circle at the right. Cut a piece of string the length of the diameter. Make sure that the diameter goes through the center of the circle. Use the string to measure the circumference of the circle. About how many times will the diameter string fit around the circle? _______

The circumference of the circle is about _______ times the length of the diameter.

Step 2 Cut the string representing the diameter in half. Is it the same size as the radius of the circle? _______

Step 3 Look at the radius of the circle. What part of the diameter string does it represent? _________

Solution

What is the relationship between the diameter and the circumference?

____

What is the relationship between the length of the radius and the length of the diameter?

____

Apply the TEKS

Name the indicated part shown in this circle.

1. center ____________________
2. radius ____________________
3. diameter ____________________
4. chord ____________________

A C P D B

Complete each statement.

5. A segment that connects two points on a circle is called a ____________________.
6. A chord that passes through the center of a circle is called a ____________________.
7. The number of degrees in a circle is ____________________.

Solve each problem.

8. What is the relationship between the measure of the diameter of a circle and the measure of the radius of that circle?

____

9. Draw a circle. Label the center *O*. Draw diameter *AOB*. From point *A*, draw a chord to any place on the circle (other than to point *B*). Use *D* to label the other point where your chord touches the circle. Now draw chord *BD*.

Use a protractor to find the measure of $\angle ADB$. __________

Repeat the steps in the same circle but use a different point *D*.

Use a protractor to find the measure of your new $\angle ADB$. __________

Repeat the steps to form a third such angle. What do you notice about the triangles you have drawn?

____

Generalize your result. An angle formed by two chords drawn from the ends of a diameter of a circle and meeting at a point on the circle is a ____________________.

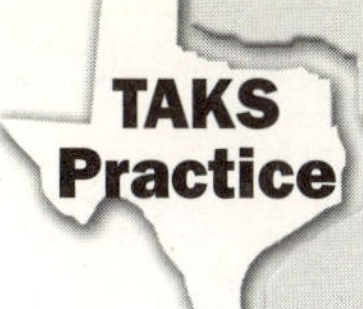

TAKS Objective 3 The student will demonstrate an understanding of geometry and spatial reasoning.
TEKS 6.6C

DIRECTIONS Read each question. Then circle the letter for the correct answer.

Use the diagram below to answer questions 1–2.

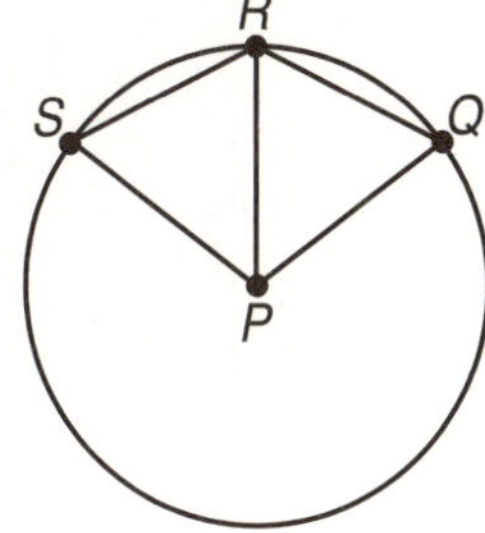

1 Which line segment is a radius of the circle?

A $\overline{SR}$

B $\overline{RQ}$

C $\overline{PQ}$

D Not Here

2 What is the center point of the circle?

F Point P

G Point Q

H Point R

J Point S

3 The diameter of a circle is 90 yards.

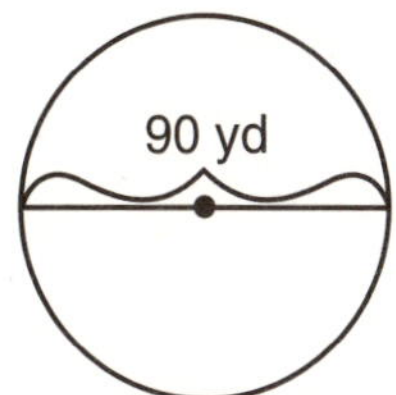

What is the measure of the radius?

A 180 yd

B 135 yd

C 45 yd

D 30 yd

4 Which measurement of a circle is twice its radius?

F Circumference

G Perimeter

H Diameter

J Not Here

5 The distance around a circle is —

A Radius

B Circumference

C Chord

D Diameter

6 The Smiths' volleyball net stretches 12 feet end-to-end across the diameter of their circular pool. How does the circumference compare to the diameter of the pool?

F The diameter is about $\frac{1}{2}$ the circumference.

G The diameter is about 3 times the circumference.

H The circumference is about $\frac{1}{3}$ the diameter.

J The circumference is about 3 times the diameter.

Focus on TEKS **Lesson 35** **The Coordinate Plane**

TEKS 6.7A Locate and name points on a coordinate plane using ordered pairs of non-negative rational numbers.

You can use ordered pairs to locate and name points on a coordinate plane.

A **coordinate plane** is a plane formed by two perpendicular number lines in which every point is assigned an ordered pair of numbers. The horizontal number line is called the ***x*-axis**; the vertical number line is called the ***y*-axis**. The x-axis and the y-axis intersect at a point called the **origin** (0, 0). **Coordinates** are ordered pairs of numbers that describe the location of a point with reference to the x- and y-axes. The first number in an ordered pair is the x-coordinate. The second number is the y-coordinate.

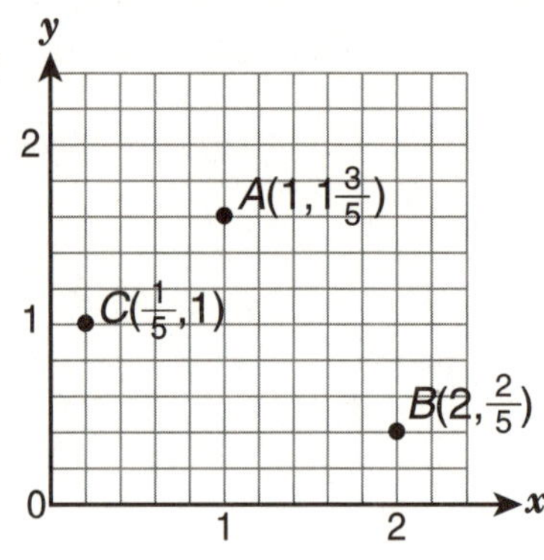

Guided Instruction

Problem 1

What ordered pair names the location of point C on triangle ABC?
What ordered pair names the location of point B on triangle ABC?

Use what you know about naming the locations of points on coordinate planes.

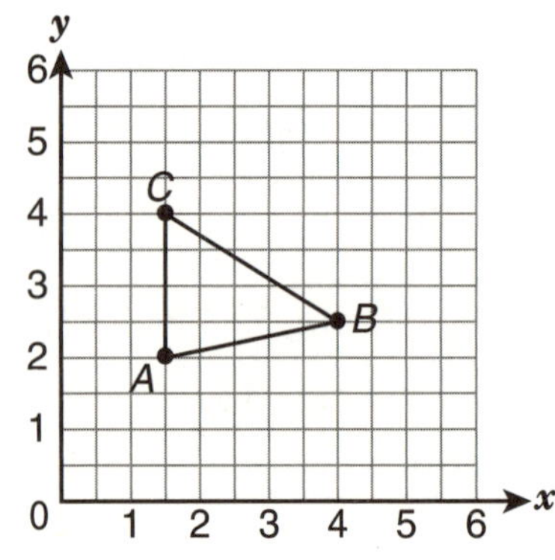

Step 1 The x- and y-axes on this coordinate plane are in intervals of $\frac{1}{2}$. To locate point C on the plane, start at the origin (0, 0) and move right along the x-axis counting by halves, $\frac{3}{2}$ units; then move up 4 units. Use lowest terms to name the coordinates of point C.

____

Step 2 To locate point B on the plane, start at the origin (0, 0) and move right along the x-axis _______ units; then move up _______ units. Use lowest terms to name the coordinates of point B.

____

Solution

What ordered pair names the location of point C on triangle ABC?

____

What ordered pair names the location of point B on triangle ABC?

____

Guided Instruction

Another Problem

Problem 2

For rectangle *ABCD*, three of the vertices are *A*(1.25, 2), *C*(3.5, 1) and *D*(1.25, 1). What are the coordinates of vertex *B*?

You can locate coordinates on a coordinate plane.

The *x*- and *y*-axes on this coordinate plane are in intervals of 0.25.
To locate the coordinates of vertex *B* on the grid, start at the origin (0, 0) and move right along the *x*-axis counting by 0.25 to ________ units; then move up ________ units.

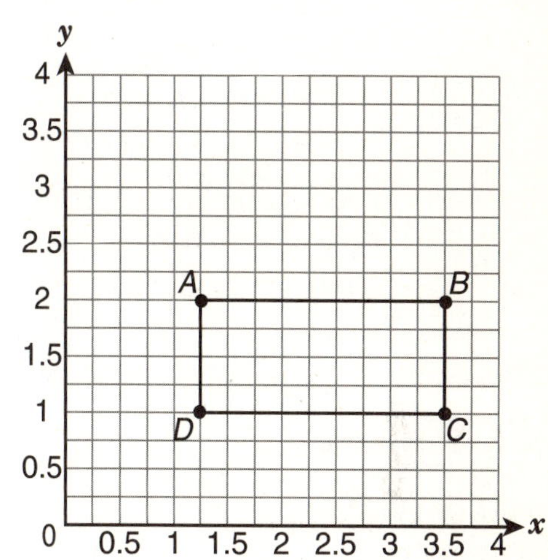

Solution

What are the coordinates of vertex B? ______________

Another Example

You can locate and name points on a coordinate plane.

The *x*- and *y*-axes on this coordinate plane are in intervals of thirds.

Locate $P(0, 2\frac{1}{3})$.

Point *P* is on the vertical axis.

Locate $Q(2\frac{1}{3}, 0)$.

Point *Q* is on the horizontal axis.

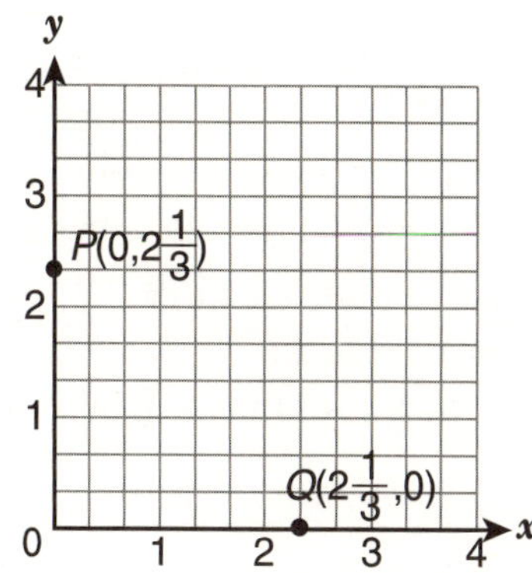

Apply the TEKS **Write the coordinates of the indicated points.**

1. point M ____________
2. point N ____________
3. point O ____________
4. point P ____________
5. point Q ____________
6. point R ____________

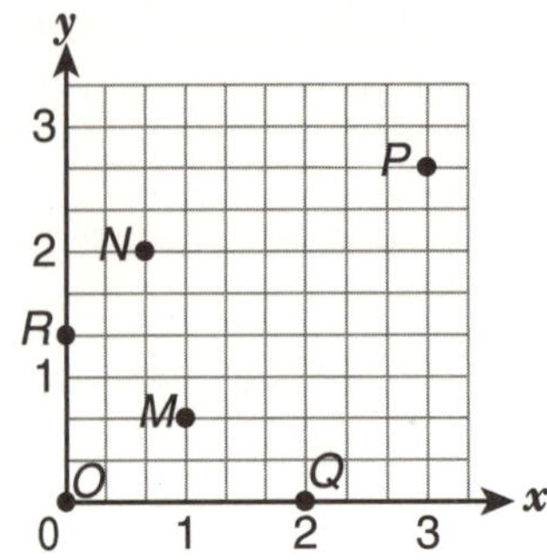

Give the name of the point for each ordered pair.

7. $(1.5, 2\frac{1}{2})$ point ______
8. (3, 1.5) point ______
9. $(3\frac{1}{2}, 0)$ point ______
10. (0, 0) point ______
11. (2.5, 3) point ______
12. (0, 2.5) point ______

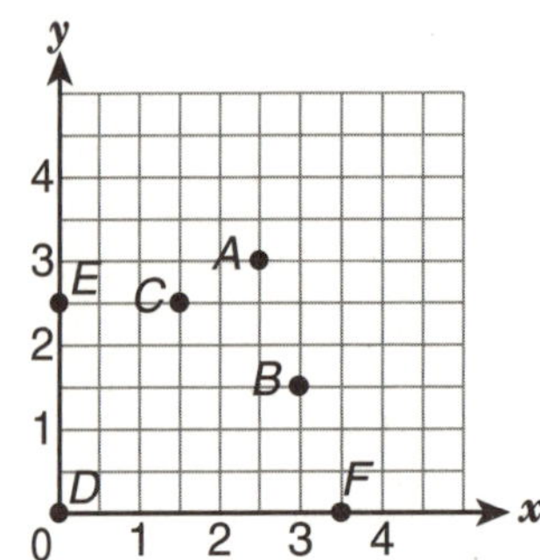

Solve each problem.

13. Kris and Pat are playing a game where each player throws small balls at a target. The balls stick to the target, and players score points depending on where the balls stick to the target. The points earned for each section are shown on the target. If the ball does not stick to the target, the player receives no points. Kris threw 3 balls which hit the target at (2, 2), $(3, \frac{2}{3})$, and $(\frac{2}{3}, 2)$. Pat threw 3 balls which hit the target at $(1\frac{1}{3}, 2)$, $(3\frac{1}{3}, 3)$, and $(2, 2\frac{2}{3})$. How many points did each player receive?

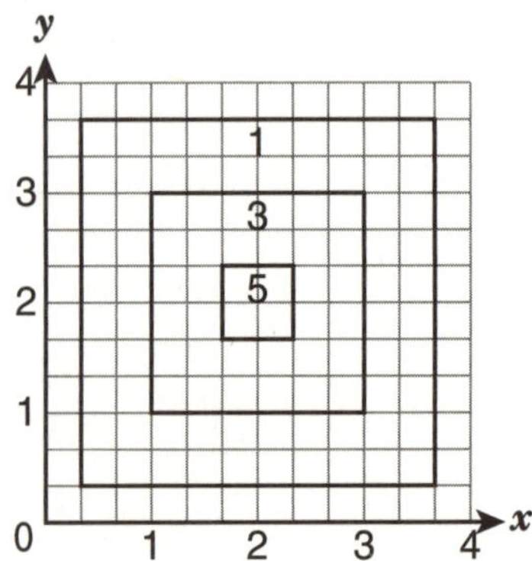

____

14. Explain the difference between the coordinates $(3\frac{3}{4}, 7)$ and $(7, 3\frac{3}{4})$.

____

____

____

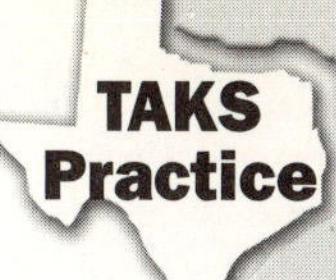

TAKS Objective 3 The student will demonstrate an understanding of geometry and spatial reasoning.
TEKS 6.7A

DIRECTIONS Read each question. Then circle the letter for the correct answer.

Use the coordinate grid below to answer Questions 1–3.

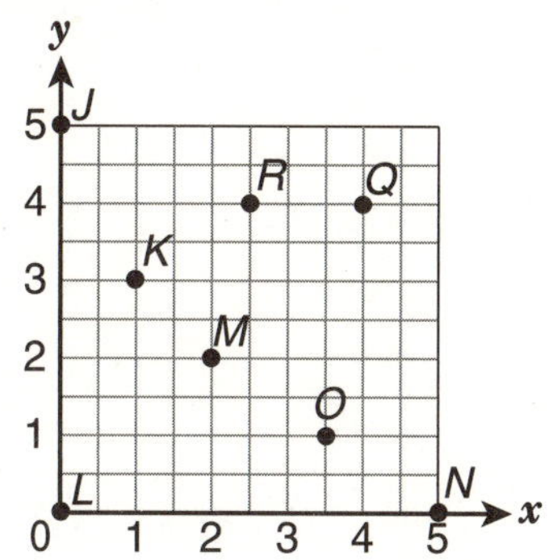

1 Which point has coordinates $(3\frac{1}{2}, 1)$?

- **A** Point *J*
- **B** Point *M*
- **C** Point *N*
- **D** Point *O*

2 Which point is on both the horizontal axis and the vertical axis?

- **F** Point *J*
- **G** Point *L*
- **H** Point *N*
- **J** Not Here

3 Which coordinate pair represents point *R*?

- **A** $(2\frac{1}{2}, 4)$
- **B** $(4, 2\frac{1}{2})$
- **C** $(2, 4\frac{1}{2})$
- **D** $(4\frac{1}{2}, 2)$

Use the coordinate grid below to answer Questions 4 and 5.

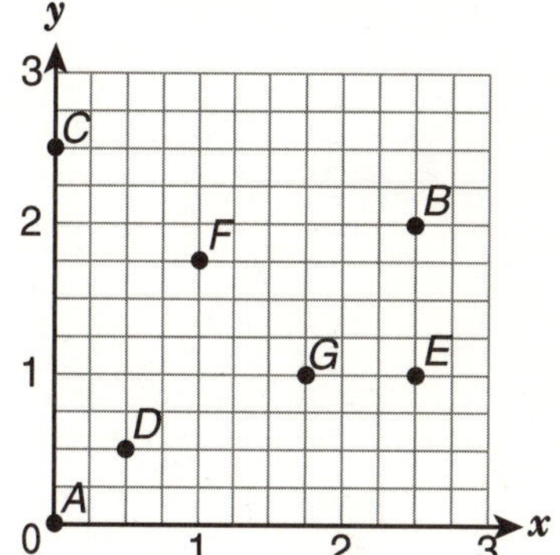

4 Which point corresponds to the coordinate pair (2.5, 2)?

- **F** Point *A*
- **G** Point *B*
- **H** Point D
- **J** Point *E*

5 Which coordinate pair represents point *F*?

- **A** (0, 0)
- **B** $(0.5, \frac{1}{2})$
- **C** $(1, 1\frac{3}{4})$
- **D** $(1\frac{3}{4}, 1)$

Focus on TEKS

Lesson 36 PROBLEM-SOLVING STRATEGY: Look for a Pattern

TEKS 6.11A Identify and apply mathematics to everyday experiences.

TEKS 6.11B Use a problem-solving model that incorporates understanding the problem, making a plan, carrying out the plan, and evaluating the solution for reasonableness.

TEKS 6.11C Select or develop an appropriate problem-solving strategy.

You can look for a pattern to help you solve problems. Use the problem-solving guide on page 288 to help you.

Guided Instruction

Problem

The numbers 1, 5, 12, 22, ... are called *pentagonal numbers*.

1st	2nd	3rd	4th
			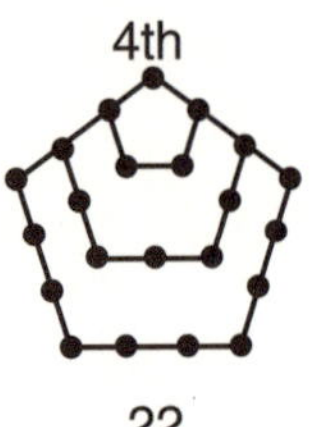
1	5	12	22

What is the 5th pentagonal number?

You can find the next number in this sequence by looking for patterns.

Understand the problem.

What does the problem ask you to find?

____

Make a plan.

Look for a pattern in the way the pentagons are arranged.

Solve the problem.

How many pentagons are in the:

1st pentagonal number? _______ 2nd pentagonal number? _______

3rd pentagonal number? _______ 4th pentagonal number? _______

How many pentagons will be in the 5th pentagonal number? _______

Draw the 5th pentagonal number.

What is the 5th pentagonal number? _______

Check your answer.

Use this pattern: $1 = 1$

$1 + 4 = 5$

$1 + 4 + 7 = 12$

$1 + 4 + 7 + 10 = 22$

$1 + 4 + 7 + 10 +$ _____ $=$ _____

Apply the TEKS **Look for patterns to solve each problem.**

1.

Figure 1

Figure 2

Figure 3

Figure 1 relates to Figure 2 in the same way that Figure 3 relates to which of the following figures?

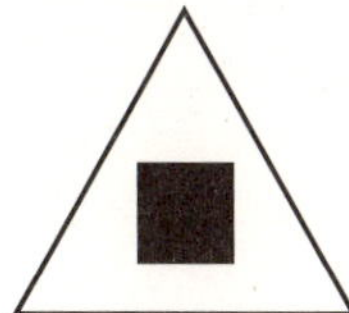
Figure A

Figure B

Figure C

____

2. In Question 1, how did you know which figure to choose?

____

____

____

3. Using other polygons, draw a set of figures that relate in the same way.

Solve each problem.

4. The figures on the right are composed of small squares like this: □.

If the pattern continues, how many small squares will be in the next figure of the sequence?

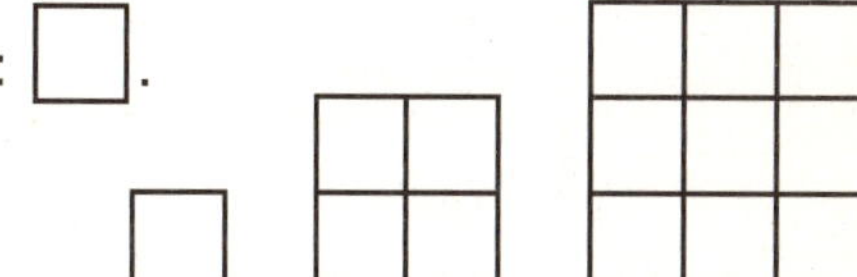

____

5. Write a numerical sequence for the geometric pattern shown in Question 4. Include the first 8 terms of the sequence.

____

6. The numbers 1, 6, 15, 28, ... are called hexagonal numbers. What is a rule for the geometric models shown?

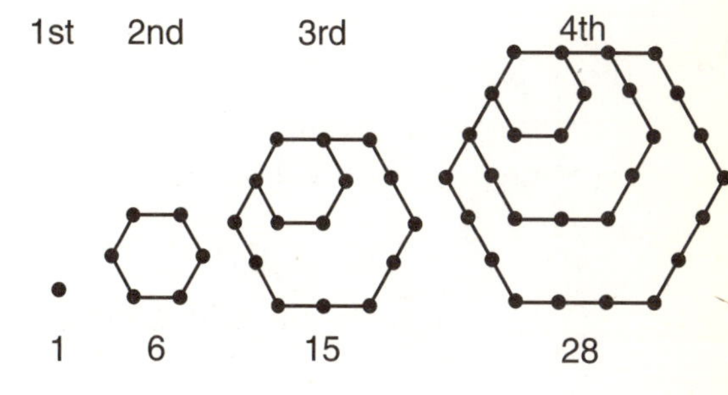

____

____

____

7. Use this pattern to write the 5th hexagonal number.

1 = 1 1 + 5 = 6 1 + 5 + 9 = 15 1 + 5 + 9 + 13 = 28 1 + 5 + 9 + 13 + ____ = ____

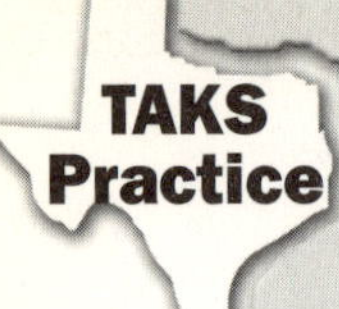

TAKS Objective 6 The student will demonstrate an understanding of the mathematical processes and tools used in problem solving.

TEKS 6.11A, 6.11B, 6.11C

DIRECTIONS Read each question. Then circle the letter for the correct answer.

1 Figure 1 relates to Figure 2 in the same way that Figure 3 relates to which of the following figures?

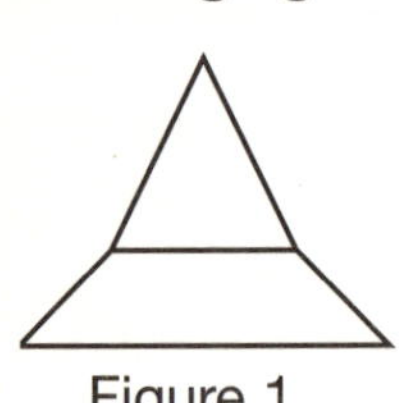

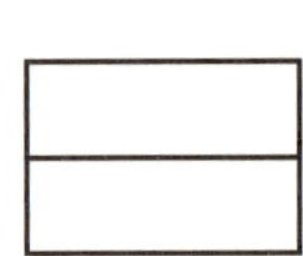

Figure 1 Figure 2 Figure 3

A 

B 

C

D 

2 If the pattern in the sequence below is continued, what fractional part of the next figure will be shaded?

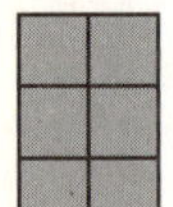 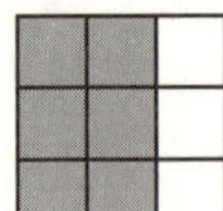 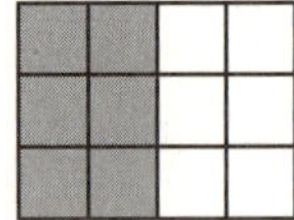 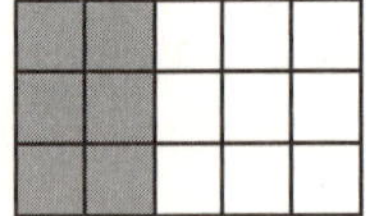

F $\frac{1}{2}$

G $\frac{1}{3}$

H $\frac{1}{4}$

J $\frac{1}{5}$

3 If the pattern in the sequence below is continued, how many squares will be in the 6th term?

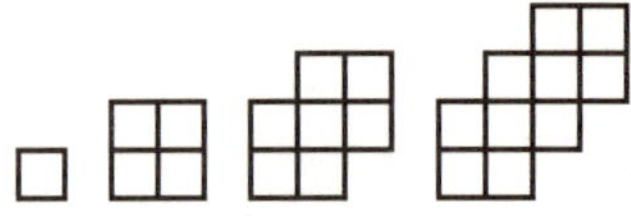

A 22

B 19

C 16

D 13

4 Look at the pattern in the visual sequence below.

Which of the following decimals shows a similar pattern?

F 0.131313 …

G 0.333333 …

H 0.123123123 …

J 0.123412341234 …

DIRECTIONS Read each question. Then circle the letter for the correct answer. If a correct answer is <u>not here</u>, mark the letter for "Not Here."

1 Angle *KLM* is shown below.

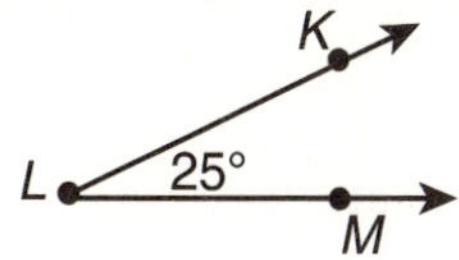

What type of angle is angle *KLM*?

A Acute

B Right

C Obtuse

D Straight

2 ∠*MNO* is an obtuse angle. Suppose it is divided into 2 angles that are equal in measure. What types of angles are possible?

F Acute angles

G Right angles

H Obtuse angles

J Straight angles

3 Which line segment is a radius of the circle?

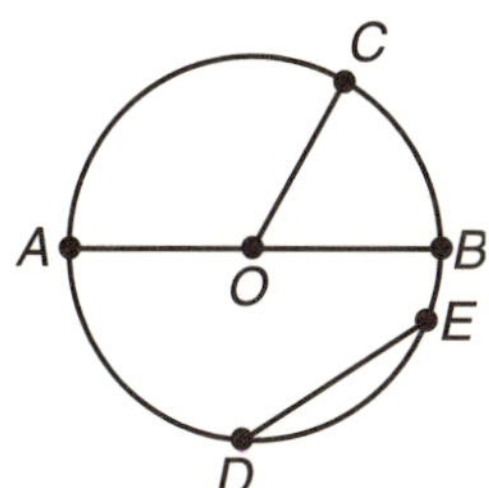

A *AB*

B *OC*

C *DE*

D Not Here

4 Line segments *CD* and *DE* are perpendicular. Line segment *CD* is twice as long as line segment *DE*.

Which of the following statements is true?

F ∠*DEC* is a right angle.

G ∠*ECD* is a right angle.

H ∠*CDE* is a right angle.

J ∠*CED* is an obtuse angle.

5 Which methods described below can you use to find the measure of ∠*KMJ*?

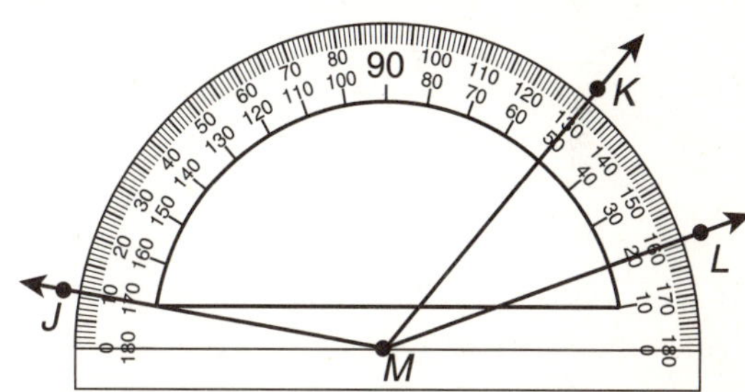

Method 1: Read where $\overrightarrow{MJ}$ and $\overrightarrow{MK}$ both cross the outer scale. Then subtract 10° from 130°.

Method 2: Read where $\overrightarrow{MJ}$ and $\overrightarrow{MK}$ both cross the inner scale. Then subtract 50° from 170°.

A Method 1 only

B Method 2 only

C Both methods

D Neither method

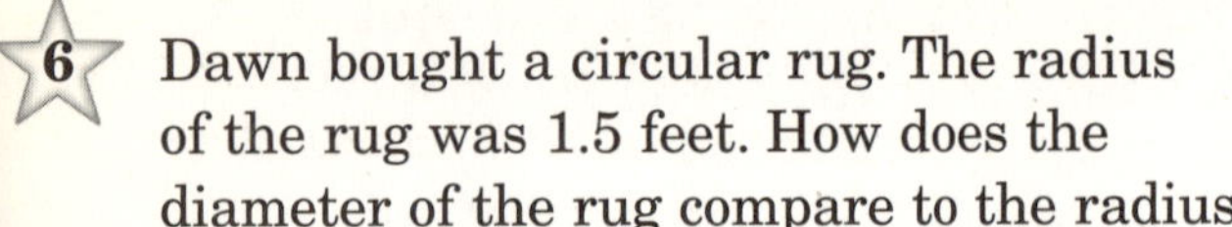

6 Dawn bought a circular rug. The radius of the rug was 1.5 feet. How does the diameter of the rug compare to the radius?

F The diameter of the rug is twice the radius.

G The diameter of the rug is half the radius.

H The radius is twice the circumference.

J Not Here

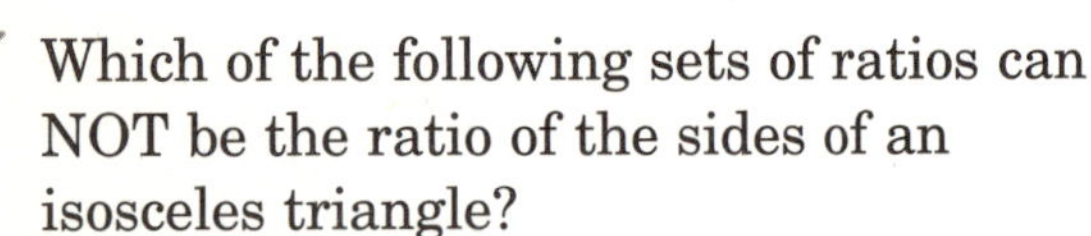

7 Which of the following sets of ratios can NOT be the ratio of the sides of an isosceles triangle?

A 4:4:5

B 4:5:6

C 5:3:3

D 8:7:8

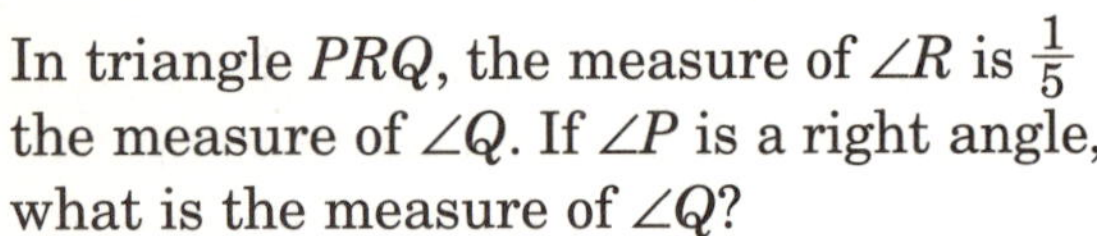

8 In triangle PRQ, the measure of $\angle R$ is $\frac{1}{5}$ the measure of $\angle Q$. If $\angle P$ is a right angle, what is the measure of $\angle Q$?

F 15°

G 25°

H 45°

J 75°

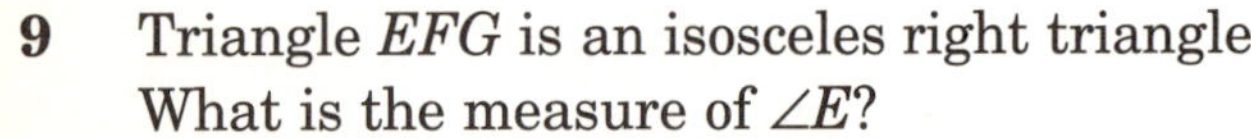

9 Triangle EFG is an isosceles right triangle. What is the measure of $\angle E$?

A 25°

B 45°

C 60°

D Not Here

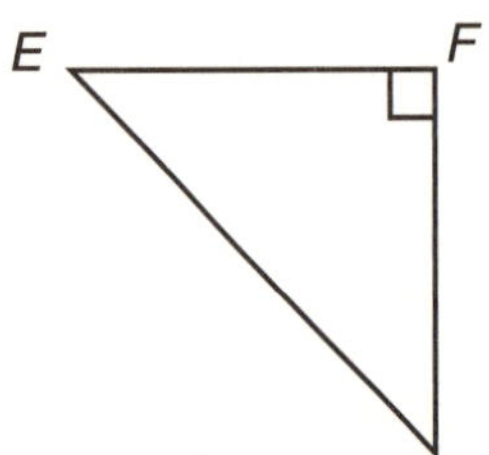

10 Jane described the triangle she drew as follows: "Side AB is 3 cm long. Side BC is 3 cm long. Side CA is 3 cm long." Which of the following statements must be true about the triangle Jane drew?

F Angle A is a right angle.

G The measure of angle B is 45°.

H The measure of each angle in triangle ABC is 60°.

J The measure of angle A is greater than the measure of angle B.

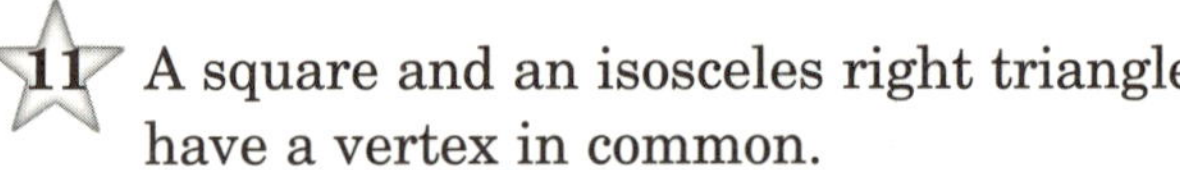

11 A square and an isosceles right triangle have a vertex in common.

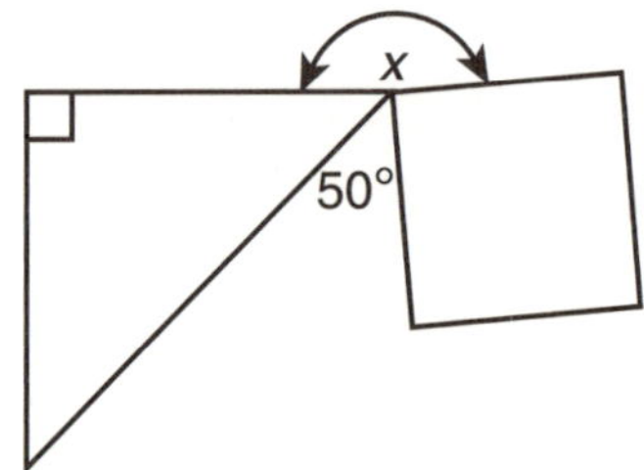

What is the measure of angle x?

Record your answer and fill in the bubbles on the grid below. Be sure to use the correct place value.

				.		
0	0	0	0		0	0
1	1	1	1		1	1
2	2	2	2		2	2
3	3	3	3		3	3
4	4	4	4		4	4
5	5	5	5		5	5
6	6	6	6		6	6
7	7	7	7		7	7
8	8	8	8		8	8
9	9	9	9		9	9

12 Which statement below is NOT true about an isosceles trapezoid?

F For each base, the measures of the base angles are equal.

G Its legs are sometimes not equal in measure.

H It has one pair of parallel sides.

J It has two base angles that are obtuse angles.

13 Two quadrilaterals are shown below.

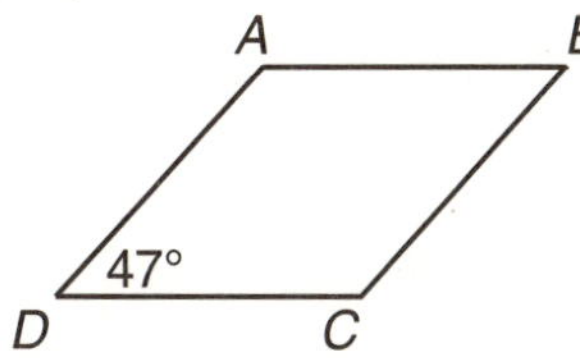

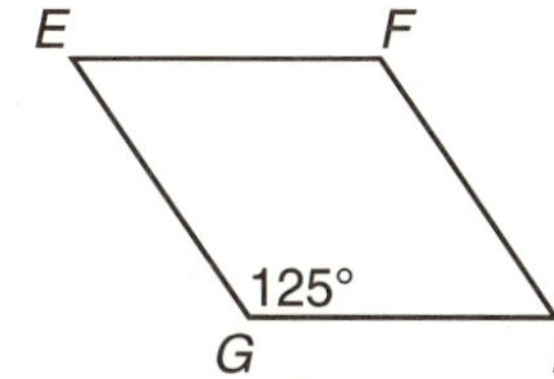

Which statement is NOT true?

A The measure of $\angle A$ is less than the measure of $\angle F$.

B The measure of $\angle B$ is equal to the measure of $\angle D$.

C The measure of $\angle E$ is equal to 55°.

D The measure of $\angle H$ is greater than the measure of $\angle B$.

14 The sum of the measures of the angles in pentagon *ABCDE* shown below is 540 degrees. What is the measure of angle *BCD*?

F 8°

G 98°

H 188°

J 360°

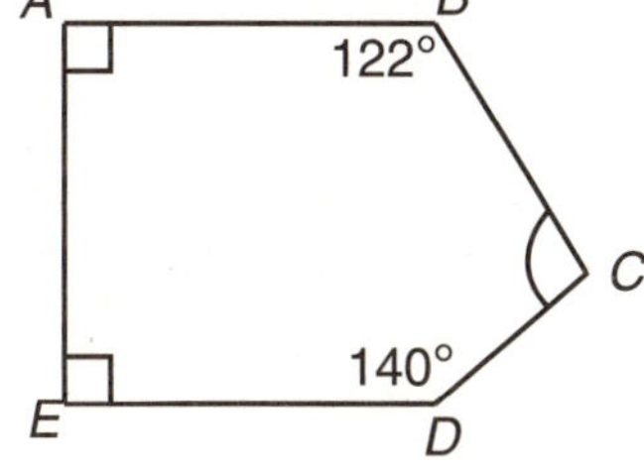

15 The length of diameter *MP* is 5 cm. Which expression shows how to find the length of *NS*?

A 2×5

B $2 \div 5$

C $5 \div 2$

D Not Here

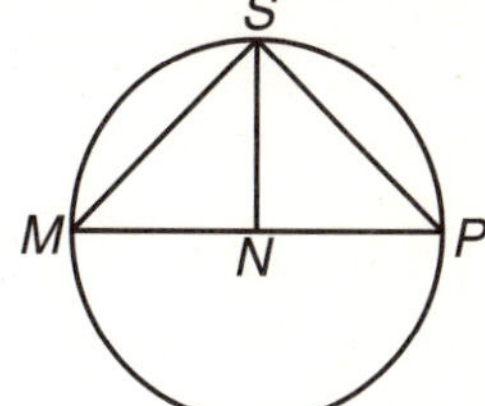

16 What are the coordinates of point *G*?

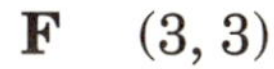

F (3, 3)

G (3, 4.5)

H (4.5, 3)

J (4, 4)

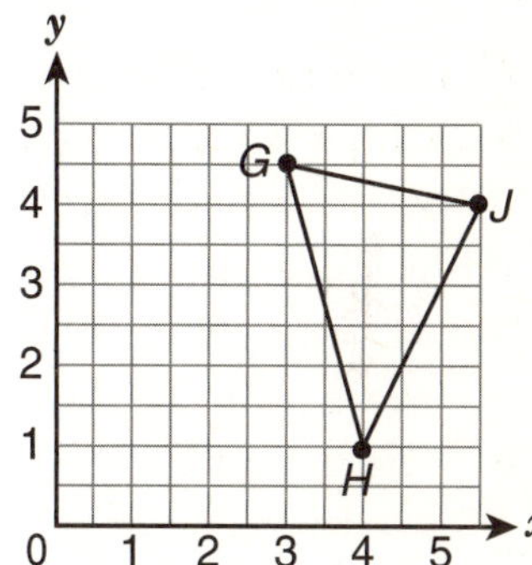

17 The first four triangular numbers are the number of dots in the patterns shown below.

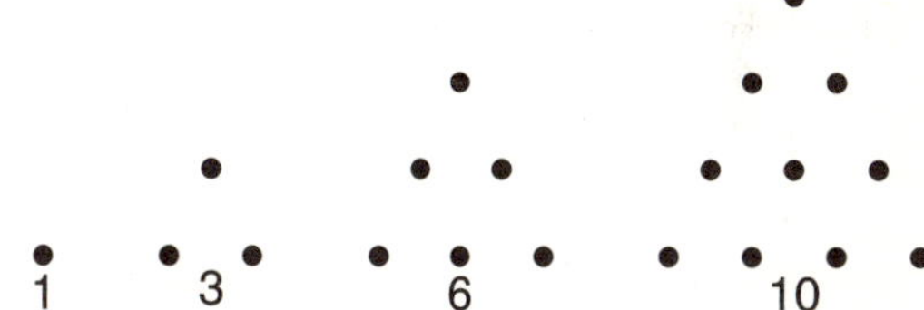

What would be the eighth triangular number?

Record your answer and fill in the bubbles on the grid below. Be sure to use the correct place value.

				.		
0	0	0	0		0	0
1	1	1	1		1	1
2	2	2	2		2	2
3	3	3	3		3	3
4	4	4	4		4	4
5	5	5	5		5	5
6	6	6	6		6	6
7	7	7	7		7	7
8	8	8	8		8	8
9	9	9	9		9	9

18 The diagram below shows the first five arrows in a sequence of arrows.

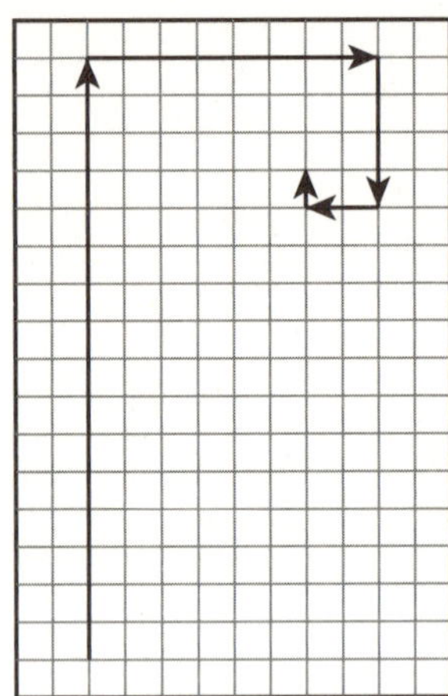

What will be the direction and length of the next arrow in this sequence?

F Up 1 unit

G Right $\frac{1}{2}$ unit

H Left $\frac{1}{2}$ unit

J Down 2 units

19 If the sequence of geometric shapes is continued, what shape will be the seventh term in this sequence?

A Heptagon

B Octagon

C Nonagon

D Decagon

20 What is the measure of angle *MAR* to the nearest degree?

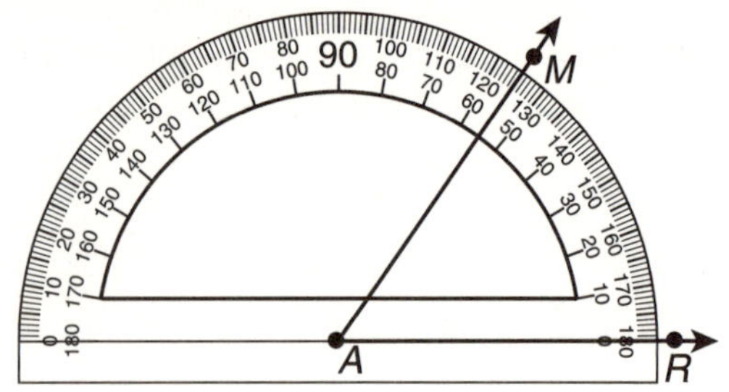

F 135°

G 125°

H 65°

J 55°

21 Which coordinate pair represents point *A*?

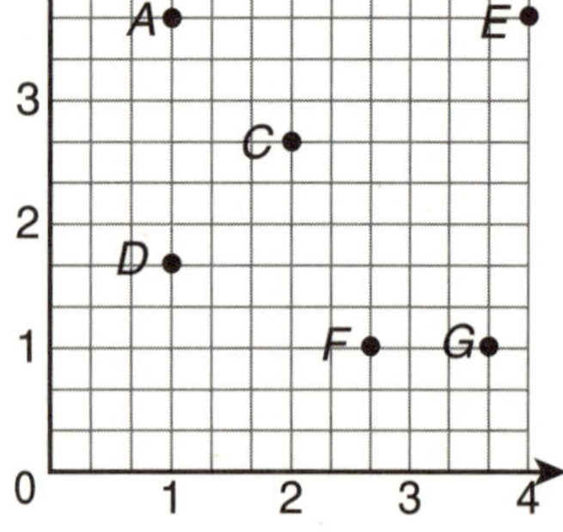

A $(4, 3\frac{2}{3})$

B $(3\frac{2}{3}, 1)$

C $(1, 3\frac{2}{3})$

D $(1, 1\frac{2}{3})$

22 Which is an acute angle?

F

G

H

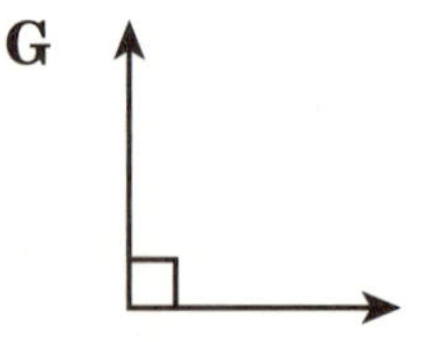

J

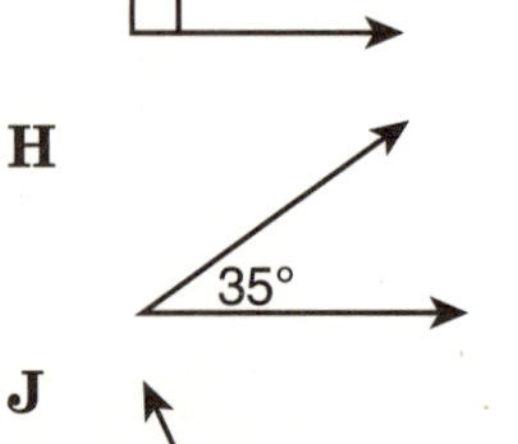
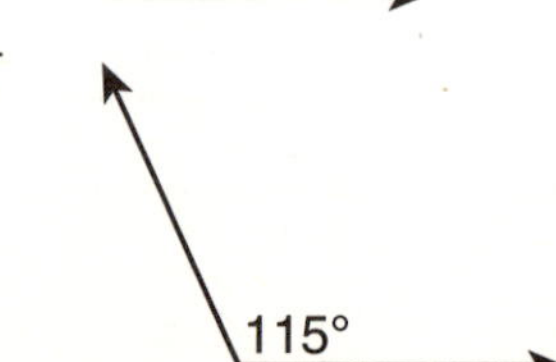

Focus on TEKS

Lesson 37 Solve Problems Involving Length

TEKS 6.8A Estimate measurements (including circumference) and evaluate reasonableness of results.

TEKS 6.8B Select and use appropriate units, tools, or formulas to measure and solve problems involving length (including perimeter), area, time, temperature, volume, and weight.

TEKS 6.8D Convert measures within the same measurement system based on relationships between units.

You can use customary or metric units to measure length.

Length

Metric	Customary
1 kilometer (km) = 1,000 meters (m) 1 meter = 100 centimeters (cm) 1 centimeter = 10 millimeters (mm)	1 mile (mi) = 1,760 yards (yd) 1 mile = 5,280 feet (ft) 1 yard = 3 feet 1 foot = 12 inches (in.)

Guided Instruction

Problem 1

Alex wants to swim at least 3 km each week. He plans to swim 450 m, 5 days a week. Will he meet his goal? Explain.

When you change from a larger unit to a smaller unit, multiply.

Step 1 Alex's goal is to swim at least 3 km each week. Convert 3 km into meters.

When converting kilometers into meters, you are changing from a larger unit to a smaller unit.

Therefore, you need to ____________.

1 km = 1,000 m

3 km = 3 × __________ = __________ m

Step 2 Find the number of meters Alex will swim in a week.

Alex swims __________ m in 1 day.

In 5 days, he will swim 5 × __________ = __________ m.

Step 3 Compare the goal to the distance, he plans to swim using the same unit of length.

Compare 3,000 to 2,250.

3,000 ◯ 2,250

Solution

Will Alex meet his goal of swimming 3 kilometers a week if he swims 450 m 5 days a week? __________

He will swim a total of __________m each week, which is ____________ his goal of swimming __________ each week.

Guided Instruction

Another Problem

Problem 2

The Boulder Creek Middle School student council is making awards for a track meet. Each award is a medallion on 22 in. of ribbon. The student council needs to make 18 awards. How many yards of ribbon do they need to make the awards?

When you change from a smaller unit to a larger unit, divide.

Step 1 Find the total number of inches of ribbon that is needed. There are 18 awards. Each award uses 22 in. of ribbon.

$18 \times 22 =$ __________ in.

Step 2 Convert from inches to feet. When converting inches into feet, you are changing from a smaller unit to a larger unit.

Therefore, you need to __________.

12 in. = 1 ft

$396 \div 12 =$ __________ ft

Step 3 Convert from feet to yards.

3 ft = 1 yard

$33 \div 3 =$ __________ yd

Step 4 Check your answer to see if the solution is reasonable. A yard of ribbon is 3 ft.

$3 \text{ ft} = 3 \times 12 = 36 \text{ in.}$

Eighteen awards are needed. Each award uses 22 in. of ribbon, which is less than 1 yd of ribbon. So the solution should be less than 18 yd.

The solution is reasonable since __________ yd is less than 18 yd.

Solution

How many yards of ribbon are needed for the 18 awards?

____

Another Example

Use your ruler to measure the length of the line segment below in inches.

The line is about __________ inches long.

Apply the TEKS **Use the table on page 157 to answer each question.**

1. About how many centimeters long is the line segment at the right? ____________

   ____

2. About how many inches long is the ribbon at the right?

   ____

3. A stack of 3 quarters is 5 mm high. How many centimeters tall is a stack of 30 quarters? ____________

4. Ellen has two pieces of muslin. One piece measures 74 in. The other piece measures 82 in. How many feet of muslin does she have in all?

   ____

5. Ken rode his bike 4.5 km on Monday. He rode 6.2 km on Tuesday and 4.8 km on Wednesday. How many more meters did Ken ride on Tuesday than he rode on Monday? ____________

6. Mrs. Rodriguez is making costumes for a folklorico dance recital. She uses 15 in. of lace on each costume. How many yards of lace does she need for 60 costumes? ____________

7. The distance from Frank's house to Jane's house is 830 yd greater than the distance from Ellie's house to Jane's house. If the distance from Ellie's house to Jane's house is exactly 1 mi, what is the distance in feet from Frank's house to Jane's house? ____________

Use the table below to answer Questions 8–9.

Plant	Height After 1 Week	Height After 6 Weeks
A	6 mm	5 cm
B	8 mm	45 mm
C	7 mm	65 mm
D	1 cm	7 cm

8. What is the difference in height between the tallest plant and the shortest plant after 1 week? ____________

9. After 6 weeks, how many centimeters would Plant D have to grow to be 1 meter tall?

   ____

10. A statue is 62 in. in height. When it is shipped in a box, it will have padding that is 4 inches thick on each end. Will the statue fit into a box that is 2 yards in height? Explain your answer. ____________

    ____

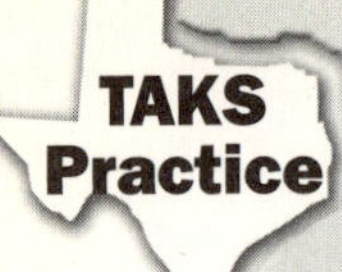

TAKS Objective 4 The student will demonstrate an understanding of the concepts and uses of measurement.
TEKS 6.8A, 6.8B, 6.8D

DIRECTIONS Read each question. Then circle the letter for the correct answer.

1 The highest point in Texas is Guadalupe Peak. It is 8,749 feet. About how many miles high is Guadalupe Peak?

A Less than 1 mi

B About 1 mi

C Between 1 and 2 mi

D More than 2 mi

2 Phil has a calculator that he keeps in his pocket. Which could be the length of the calculator?

F 11 mm

G 11 cm

H 11 m

J 11 km

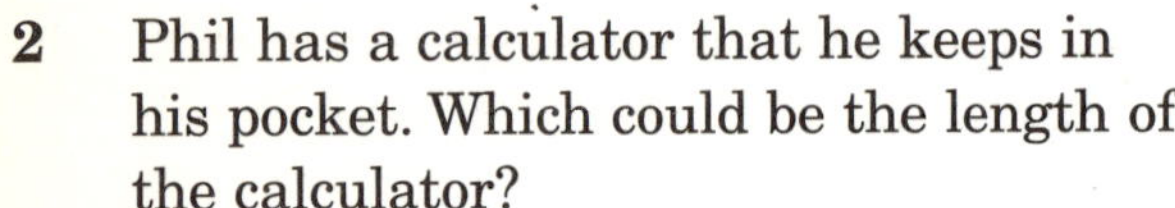

3 Pablo wants to run a marathon which is just over 26 miles. He estimates that he covers about 1 yard with each step. Which gives the best estimate of the number of steps Pablo will need to take to complete the marathon?

A Less than 20,000 steps

B Between 40,000 and 50,000 steps

C Between 100,000 and 200,000 steps

D More than 400,000 steps

4 Marco's father is 4 centimeters short of being 2 meters tall. How many centimeters tall is he?

F 196 cm

G 104 cm

H 24 cm

J 6 cm

5 Use your ruler to measure the length of the pencil below in centimeters.

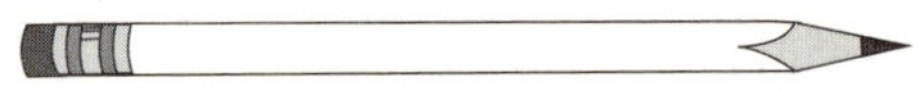

Which best represents the length of the pencil?

A About 4 cm

B About 5 cm

C About 6 cm

D About 7 cm

6 Ruben is preparing a display of photographs. He uses 18 inches of wire to hang each framed photograph. He has a 25-foot roll of wire. How many photographs can he hang with that roll of wire?

F 6

G 9

H 16

J 35

Focus on TEKS

Lesson 38 Solve Problems Involving Capacity

TEKS 6.8A Estimate measurements (including circumference) and evaluate reasonableness of results.

TEKS 6.8B Select and use appropriate units, tools, or formulas to measure and to solve problems involving length (including perimeter), area, time, temperature, volume, and weight.

TEKS 6.8D Convert measures within the same measurement system based on relationships between units.

You can use customary or metric units to measure capacity.

Capacity

Metric	Customary
1 liter (L) = 1000 milliliters (mL)	1 gallon (gal) = 4 quarts (qt) 1 gallon = 128 ounces (oz) 1 quart = 2 pints (pt) 1 pint = 2 cups (c) 1 cup = 8 ounces

Guided Instruction

Problem 1

There are 15 students in a science class. Each student will need 125 mL of pond water. There are 2 L of pond water in the science kit. How many milliliters of pond water will be left over?

Multiply to convert from a larger unit of capacity to a smaller unit.

Step 1 Find the number of mL of pond water that the class will use. Multiply the number of students times the amount of pond water each student needs.

15 × 125 mL = __________ mL

Step 2 Find the number of milliliters supplied in the science kit.

Convert 2 L to milliliters.

1 L = 1,000 mL

2 × 1,000 __________ mL

Step 3 Find the difference between the numbers of milliliters of pond water that the class will use and the amount supplied in the kit.

2,000 − 1,875 = __________ mL

Solution

How many milliliters of pond water will be left over? __________

Guided Instruction

Another Problem

Problem 2

Janice served apple juice at a party. She bought quart bottles of apple juice and poured the contents into a bowl that had a 160-oz capacity. The contents filled the bowl exactly. How many cups of juice can be served? How many quart bottles did she buy?

Divide to convert from a smaller unit of capacity to a larger unit.

Step 1 Find the number of cups of apple juice served.

Convert from ounces to cups.

1 c = __________ oz

160 ÷ 8 = __________ c

Step 2 Find the number of quarts of apple juice bought.

Convert from cups to pints.

1 pt = 2 c

20 ÷ 2 = __________ pt

Convert from pints to quarts.

1 qt = 2 pt

10 ÷ 2 = __________ qt

Step 3 Check that your answer is reasonable.

Convert the number of ounces of juice served to quarts. There are 32 oz in one quart.

160 ÷ 32 = __________qt

Does this amount match the number of quarts of juice bought as found in Step 2? __________

Since the amount bought and the amount served are equivalent, the answers are reasonable.

Solution

How many cups of apple juice can be served? __________

How many quart bottles did Janice buy? __________

Apply the TEKS **Use the table on page 161 to answer each question.**

1. Evie is making blackberry jelly. She has a gallon of jelly mixture to pour into pint jars. How many jars can she fill? ________________

2. A recipe for cream of broccoli soup calls for 1 pint of cream and a quart of milk. To reduce the fat, Mrs. Gomez plans to use all milk. How many cups of milk should she use in the recipe?

   ____

3. An aquarium holds 15,000 mL of water. Another aquarium holds 3.46 L more. How many liters of water does the second aquarium hold? ________________

4. Raphael drinks a half-liter of water 6 times a day. How many milliliters of water does he drink during a 7-day week?

   ____

5. Mr. Frederick waters each tomato plant with a quart of water every day. How many gallons of water does he use to water 6 tomato plants during the month of June? ________________

Use the table to answer Questions 6–8.

Recipe for Fruit Punch

Amount	Ingredient
3 qt	apple cider
3 c	cranberry juice
1 pt	ginger ale
1 oz	lemon juice

6. What is the total number of ounces of punch that the recipe makes? __________

7. Using this recipe, how many quart bottles can be completely filled with fruit punch? ________________

8. What amount of punch will be left over? __________

9. An orphaned baby armadillo weighing 2 ounces is fed formula 6 times a day. Each feeding is about 3 mL of formula. If there are 5 baby armadillos being fed, about how many days will 1 L of formula last? Explain how you found your answer.

   ____

   ____

   ____

   ____

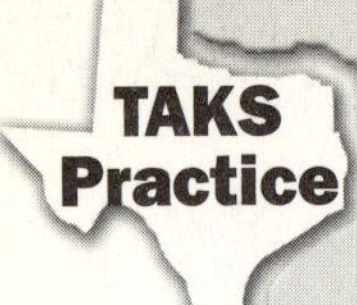

TAKS Objective 4 The student will demonstrate an understanding of the concepts and uses of measurement.
TEKS 6.8A, 6.8B, 6.8D

DIRECTIONS Read each question. Then circle the letter for the correct answer.

1 Mr. Wilson uses 320 ounces of oil when he changes the oil in his car and his wife's car. He uses the same amount of oil in each car. How many quarts of oil does each car require?

A 2 qt

B 5 qt

C 10 qt

D 32 qt

2 Natalie takes a juice box in her lunch. The juice box holds about 6.75 ounces. About how many juice boxes does it take to make a half-gallon of juice?

F 6

G 10

H 16

J 20

3 Mrs. Hernandez makes a gallon of chili for the school PTA International Food Festival. Each serving is a cup and sells for $1.25. How much money will the PTA make if all the chili is sold?

A $8.00

B $10.00

C $17.50

D $20.00

4 Felicia gives her dog medication morning and evening. She gives the dog 5 milliliters of medicine for each 10 pounds of the dog's weight. Her dog weighs 40 pounds. How much medication does she give the dog each day?

F 0.02 L

G 40 mL

H 0.2 L

J 2 L

5 A punch bowl holds 3 quarts of punch. Each punch cup holds 5 ounces. How many punch cups can be filled if the punch bowl is full?

A 10

B 12

C 15

D 19

6 Ricardo donates blood to the local blood bank once every 3 months. His goal is to become a member of the 10-Gallon Club by giving a total of 10 gallons of blood over a period of years. Each time he gives blood, he donates 1 pint of blood. How long will it take him to meet his goal?

F 5 yr

G 10 yr

H 20 yr

J 25 yr

Focus on TEKS

Lesson 39 Solve Problems Involving Weight or Mass

TEKS 6.4A Use tables and symbols to represent and describe relationships involving conversions.

TEKS 6.8A Estimate measurements (including circumference) and evaluate reasonableness of results.

TEKS 6.8B Select and use appropriate units, tools, or formulas to measure and to solve problems involving length (including perimeter), area, time, temperature, volume, and weight.

TEKS 6.8D Convert measures within the same measurement system based on relationships between units.

You can use customary or metric units to measure weight or mass.

Mass and Weight

Metric	Customary
1 kilogram (kg) = 1,000 grams (g)	1 ton (T) = 2,000 pounds (lb)
1 gram = 1,000 milligrams (mg)	1 pound = 16 ounces (oz)

Guided Instruction

Problem 1

A truck weighs $2\frac{1}{2}$ tons and carries its maximum load of 4,000 pounds. A bridge has a sign stating that the weight limit of the bridge is 10,000 pounds. Explain if it is safe for the truck to use the bridge.

Multiply to convert from a larger unit of weight to a smaller unit.

Step 1 Find the weight of truck in pounds.

1 T = ______________ lb

$2\frac{1}{2}$ T = $2\frac{1}{2} \times 2{,}000 = 2{,}000 + 2{,}000 + 1{,}000 =$ ______________ lb

Step 2 Find the total weight of the truck and its maximum load.

5,000 + 4,000 = ______________ lb

Step 3 Compare the total weight of the truck, including its maximum load, with the weight limit of the bridge.

If the total weight of the truck and its maximum load is less than the weight limit of the bridge, it will be safe for the truck to use the bridge.

9,000 ◯ 10,000

Solution

Is it safe for the truck to use the bridge? Explain.

____

____

____

Guided Instruction

Another Problem

Problem 2

Kim recorded all the fruits and juice that she consumed yesterday. What was her intake of Vitamin C from the fruits and juice equal to? How many more milligrams of Vitamin C should she have consumed in order to consume 1 gram?

Food	Vitamin C Content
8 ounces of orange juice	97 mg
10 cherries	5 mg
1 apple	8 mg
3 apricots	11 mg

Find the exact answers and check your answers for reasonableness.

Step 1 Add to find the total number of milligrams.

97 + 5 + 8 + 11 = __________ mg

Step 2 Subtract to find how much more Vitamin C she needed to equal 1 gram.

1 g = 1,000 mg

1,000 − __________ = __________ mg

Step 3 Estimate to check if the answer is reasonable.

Round 121 to the nearest hundred.

121 rounds to __________.

1,000 − __________ = __________ mg

Compare the estimate to the exact answer.

879 is close to 900, so the answer is reasonable.

Solution

What was her intake of Vitiman C from the fruits and juice equal to? __________
How many more milligrams of Vitiman C should she have consumed in order to consume 1 gram? __________

Apply the TEKS **Use the chart on page 165 to answer each question.**

1. In Texas, blue catfish are a popular variety for fried fish. A blue catfish can weigh up to 40 pound. What is that weight in ounces? ___________

2. A rock has a mass of 3,520 grams. What is the mass of the rock in kilograms? ___________

3. Many types of cacti grow in Texas. A 50-foot saguaro cactus weighs $7\frac{3}{4}$ ton. What is the weight in pounds of the saguaro cactus? ___________

4. A horse has a mass of 587 kilograms. A cow has a mass of 592 kilograms. How many grams greater is the mass of the cow than the mass of the horse?

____

Use the table to answer Questions 5–6.

5. Mr. Woodward has a package that weighs 13 ounces. What is the cost of mailing the package using Express Mail?

____

6. Mrs. Hammond has two packages to mail. One package weighs 4 pounds The other package weighs 2 pounds 7 ounces. What is the total cost of mailing the two packages using Express Mail? ___________

Express Mail Rates

Weight	Rate
Up to 8 oz	$13.65
Over 8 oz up to 2 lb	$17.85
Over 2 lb up to 3 lb	$21.05
Over 3 lb up to 4 lb	$24.20
Over 4 lb up to 5 lb	$27.30

Use the table to answer Questions 7–8.

7. About how many apricots are in a kilogram of fresh apricots?

____

8. Mrs. Costa dehydrated 1 kilograms of figs. What was the mass of the figs in kilograms after dehydrating? Explain your answer.Z

____

____

____

Mass of Fruits Before and After Dehydrating

Fruit	Mass Before Dehydrating	Mass After Dehydrating
1 fig	50 g	19 g
$\frac{1}{2}$ cup grapes	128 g	31 g
10 apple slices	280 g	64 g
3 apricots	106 g	21 g

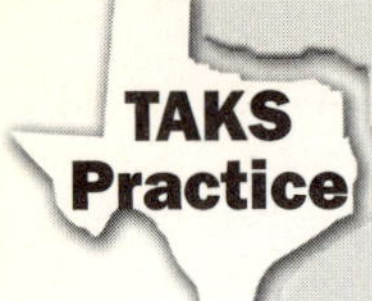

TAKS Objective 2 The student will demonstrate an understanding of patterns, relationships, and algebraic reasoning.
TEKS 6.4A

TAKS Objective 4 The student will demonstrate an understanding of the concepts and uses of measurement.
TEKS 6.8A, 6.8B, 6.8D

DIRECTIONS Read each question. Then circle the letter for the correct answer.

1 When Alice's pet Chihuahua, Toby, was 10 weeks old, it weighed 19 ounces. Now it is full-grown and weighs 3 pounds. About how much weight did Toby gain?

A About 10 oz

B About 1 lb

C About 2 lb

D About 3 lb

A carpenter bought 1 pound 10 ounces of 8-penny nails and 2 pounds 7 ounces of drywall screws. What was the total weight of the purchases?

F 1 lb 3 oz

G 3 lb 11 oz

H 4 lb

J 4 lb 1 oz

Mrs. Watson plans to serve 6-ounce portions of shrimp for dinner. How many 6-ounce portions can she make from 3 pounds of shrimp?

A 2

B 5

C 8

D 18

Use the table to answer Questions 4–5.

Animal	Average Mass of Body	Average Mass of Brain
Horse	521 kilograms	655 grams
Cat	3,300 grams	25 grams
Rhesus monkey	6,800 grams	179 grams
African elephant	6,654 kilograms	6 kilograms

What is the difference in grams between the mass of an elephant's brain and the mass of a horse's brain?

Record your answer and fill in the bubbles on the grid below. Be sure to use the correct place value.

				.		
0	0	0	0		0	0
1	1	1	1		1	1
2	2	2	2		2	2
3	3	3	3		3	3
4	4	4	4		4	4
5	5	5	5		5	5
6	6	6	6		6	6
7	7	7	7		7	7
8	8	8	8		8	8
9	9	9	9		9	9

About how many times greater is a rhesus monkey's body mass and brain than a cat's body mass and brain?

A Double the body mass and double the brain mass

B Half the body mass and 7 times the brain mass

C Three times the body mass and 4 times the brain mass

D Double the body mass and 7 times the brain mass

Focus on TEKS

Lesson 40 Solve Problems Involving Temperature

TEKS 6.4A Use tables and symbols to represent and describe relationships involving conversions.

TEKS 6.8A Estimate measurements (including circumference) and evaluate reasonableness of results.

TEKS 6.8B Select and use appropriate units, tools, or formulas to measure and to solve problems involving length (including perimeter), area, time, temperature, volume, and weight.

You can use customary or metric units to measure temperature.

Fahrenheit (°F) is the customary unit for measuring temperature.

Celsius (°C) is the metric unit for measuring temperature.

Guided Instruction

Problem

The thermometer shows the temperature at 6:00 A.M. The temperature rises 9 degrees by 8 A.M. What is the temperature in degrees Celsius at 8 A.M.?

Use the thermometer to find the temperature.

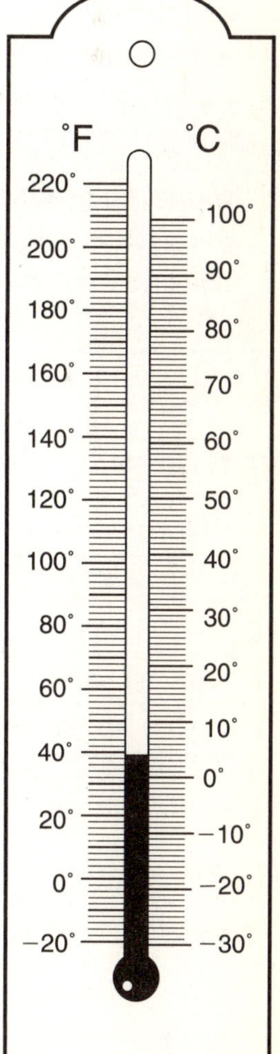

Step 1 Read the temperature on the Celsius scale of the thermometer to determine the 6:00 A.M. temperature.

On the Celsius scale, each tick mark stands for 1 degree.

How many tick marks above 0°C is the temperature?

____

What is the temperature at 6:00 A.M.? ________°C

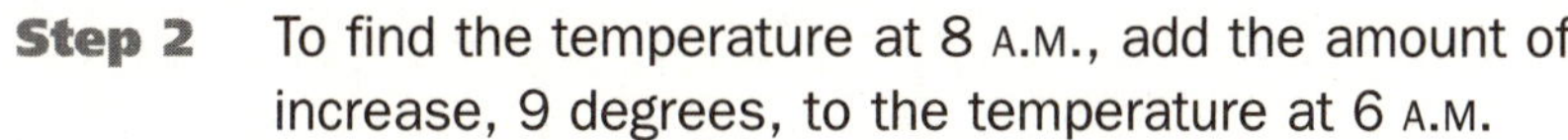

Step 2 To find the temperature at 8 A.M., add the amount of increase, 9 degrees, to the temperature at 6 A.M.

$4 + 9 =$ ________

Write the temperature, using the correct unit of measure.

The temperature is ________.

Solution

What was the temperature at 8 A.M.? ________

Apply the TEKS **Write the temperatures shown on each thermometer in Fahrenheit and Celsius.**

1.

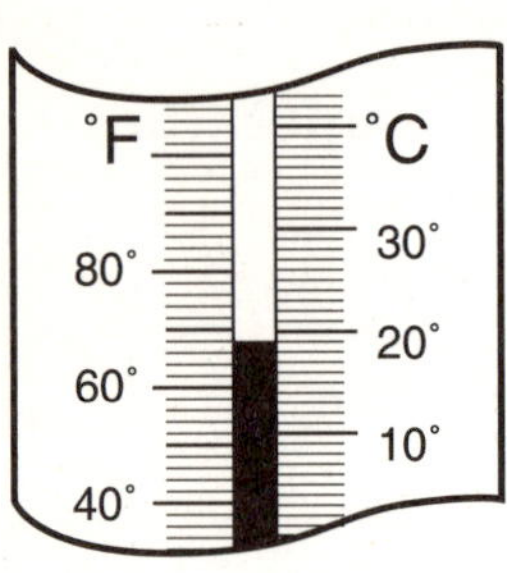

____

2.

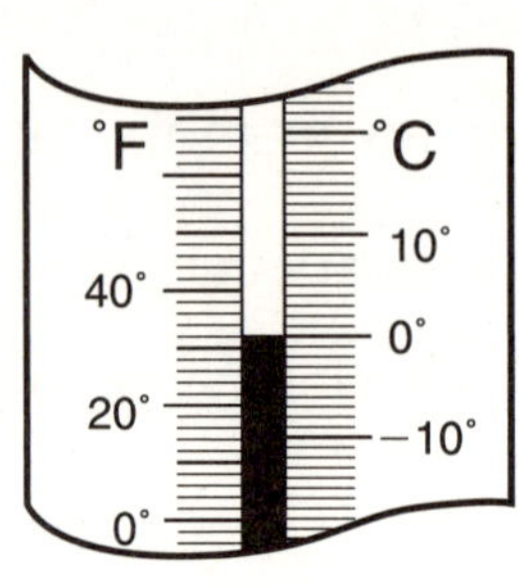

____

3.

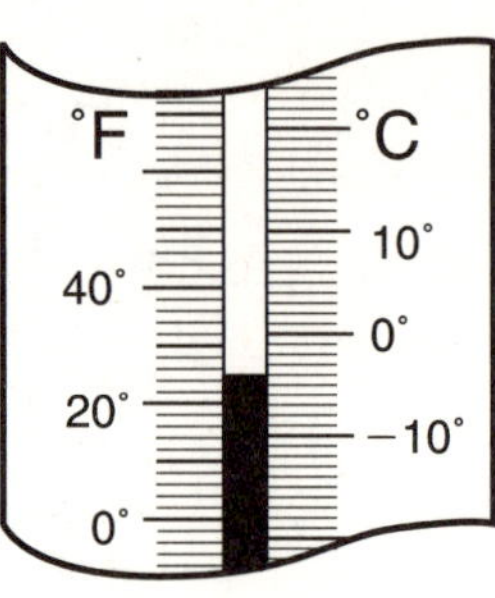

____

4. The thermometer at the right shows the low temperature for a day in May in Austin. The high temperature that day was 18°F warmer than the low temperature. What was the high temperature in degrees Fahrenheit? __________

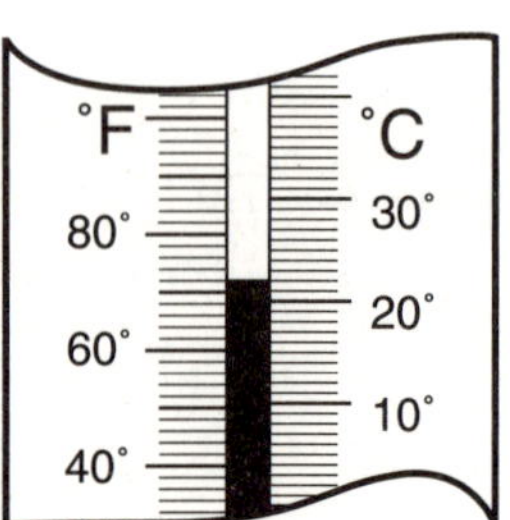

5. Normal body temperature is 98.6°F. Ruth has a fever, and her temperature is 101.4°F. How many degrees above normal is her temperature?

____

Use the table to answer Questions 6–7.

Normal Body Temperatures for Animals

Animal	Temperature
Dog	38.8°C
Cat	38.6°C
Rabbit	39.5°C
Sheep	39.1°C

6. Lydia takes her dog Brandy to the veterinarian. The vet takes Brandy's temperature. The vet tells Lydia that Brandy's temperature is 1.5°C above normal. What is Brandy's temperature? ____________

7. Which animal's normal body temperature is 2.5°C higher than a human's normal body temperature of 37°C? ____________

8. Pepper plants do not grow well when temperatures drop below 59°F. Yesterday the high temperature was 75°F. During the night, the temperature dropped 19 degrees. Was it cold enough to affect the pepper plants? Explain your answer. ______________________________________

____

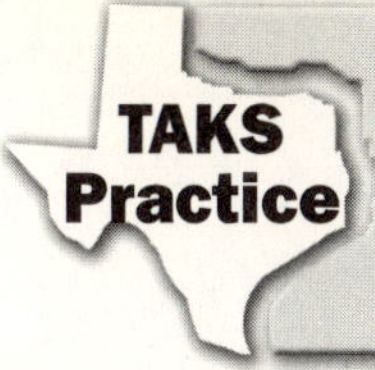

TAKS Objective 2 The student will demonstrate an understanding of patterns, relationships, and algebraic reasoning.
TEKS 6.4A

TAKS Objective 4 The student will demonstrate an understanding of the concepts and uses of measurement.
TEKS 6.8A, 6.8B

DIRECTIONS Read each question. Then circle the letter for the correct answer.

1 The thermometer shows the average high temperature in Dallas in August.

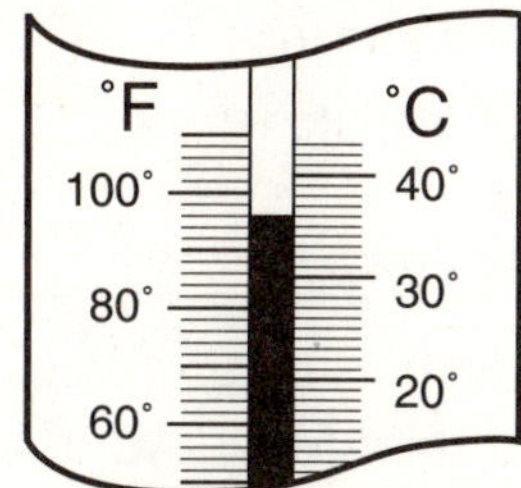

The record high temperature in Texas occurred on August 12, 1936 in Seymour. The temperature was 13 degrees Celsius warmer than the average high temperature in Dallas in August. What was the record high temperature?

A 23°C

B 49°C

C 99°C

D 109°C

2 Tomato plants stop developing fruit when nighttime temperatures are above 86°F or below 55°F. Which would NOT be a good situation for tomato plants?

F High of 76°F with a drop of 19 degrees during the night

G High of 82°F with a drop of 10 degrees during the night

H High of 70°F with a drop of 9 degrees during the night

J High of 88°F with a drop of 34 degrees during the night

3 The temperature outside Mindy's house was 36.6°C. At the same time, the temperature of the water in the swimming pool was 9.3 degrees cooler. What is the best estimate of the temperature of the water in the swimming pool?

A Between 40°C and 45°C

B Between 30°C and 35°C

C Between 25°C and 30°C

D Between 20°C and 25°C

4 A recipe for fudge calls for cooking a mixture of sugar, salt, chocolate, and corn syrup to 236°F and then cooling it to 110°F without stirring. What is the change in temperature?

F 126°F

G 136°F

H 226°F

J 346°F

5 Tiffany recorded the following temperatures at noon for a week.

Mon	Tues	Wed	Thurs	Fri
27°C	26°C	22°C	21°C	24°C

What was the average temperature at noon for the 5 days?

A 22°C

B 23°C

C 24°C

D 25°C

Focus on TEKS

Lesson 41 Solve Problems Involving Time

TEKS 6.8A Estimate measurements (including circumference) and evaluate reasonableness of results.

TEKS 6.8B Select and use appropriate units, tools, or formulas to measure and to solve problems involving length (including perimeter), area, time, temperature, volume, and weight.

TEKS 6.8D Convert measures within the same measurement system based on relationships between units.

You can solve problems involving units of time.

Time	
1 year (yr) = 12 months (mo)	1 week = 7 days
1 year = 52 weeks (wk)	1 day = 24 hours (h)
1 year = 365 days (d)	1 hour = 60 minutes (min)
1 minute = 60 seconds (s)	

Guided Instruction

Problem

Mr. Robertson has been going to the same barber for 15 years. He faithfully gets his hair cut on the first and third Mondays of each month. How many haircuts did he get from his barber in 15 years?

You can solve the problem by converting between different units of time.

Step 1 Find the number of hair cuts in 1 year.
How many haircuts does Mr. Robertson get each month? ________

1 year = ________ months

So in 1 year, Mr. Robertson gets ________ haircuts.

Step 2 Find the number of haircuts in 15 years.
Multiply the number of haircuts in 1 year by 15.

15 × 24 = ________

Step 3 Check that your answer is reasonable.
Estimate the number of haircuts by rounding to the nearest ten.

15 rounds to 20. 24 rounds to 20.

20 × 20 = 400

The exact answer of ________ haircuts is close to the estimate of ________ haircuts. So the answer is reasonable.

Solution

How many haircuts did Mr. Robertson get from his barber in 15 years?

____

Other Examples

A. 40 h = ? s
1 h = 60 min
40 h = 40 × 60 = 2,400 min
1 min = 60 s
2,400 min = 2,400 × 60, or 144,000 s

So 40 h = ________ s

B. 170 d = ? wk ? d
1 wk = 7 d
170 ÷ 7 = 24 R 2

So 170 d = ________ wk ________ d

Apply the TEKS **Solve each problem.**

1. Kathryn Sullivan was the first American woman to walk in space. She spent $3\frac{1}{2}$ hours outside the Challenger on October 11, 1984. For how many minutes was she walking in space? ____________________

2. Ellie practices the piano for 45 minutes a day. If she starts keeping track of her practice time on July 1, on which day will she have logged a total of at least 10 hours of practice? ____________________

3. Freddie works at a pet-grooming salon on Saturday mornings. It takes him 45 minutes to groom a dog. He earns $9.50 for each dog that he grooms. What is the maximum amount of money he can earn in 6 hours? ____________________

4. A roller coaster ride at the fair lasts about 3 minutes. It takes at least 2 minutes to reload the roller coaster cars. About how many times can the roller coaster be run from 4:00 P.M. to 10:00 P.M.?

   ____

5. Marco's watch loses 1 sec every hour. How many days will it take for the watch to be 10 minutes slow? ____________________

6. The South Pole has no sunshine for 182 days each year. How many weeks without sunshine is that?____________________

Use the table to answer Questions 7–8.

CD Track	Time (Minutes: Seconds)
1. As Long	4:27
2. Flight of the Falcon	5:49
3. Spring Dance	6:11
4. Great Ocean	3:22
5. One Bird	3:22

7. How long does it take to listen to the first 2 tracks on the CD? Write your answer in minutes and seconds ____________________________

8. About how long does it take to listen to all 5 tracks of the CD?

   ____

9. Mrs. Murton needs to bake 20 trays of cookies for a bake sale. Two trays fit into the oven at one time, and it takes 12 minutes to bake the cookies. If she starts baking at 10:30 A.M., will she be done by noon? Explain how you know.

   ____

   ____

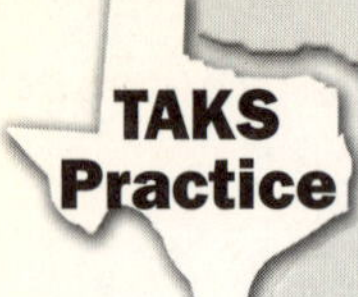

TAKS Objective 4 The student will demonstrate an understanding of the concepts and uses of measurement.
TEKS 6.8A, 6.8B, 6.8D

DIRECTIONS Read each question. Then circle the letter for the correct answer.

1 A photographer is taking time-lapse photos of a rose as it blooms. The camera automatically takes a picture once every 2 hours. How many photos will be taken in a week?

A 12

B 84

C 168

D 336

2 A receptionist answers the phone about 13 times each hour. If she works a 40-hour week, about how many times does she answer the phone in a year?

F Between 400 and 500 times

G Between 1000 and 2000 times

H Between 5000 and 10,000 times

J Between 20,000 and 30,000 times

3 A copy machine can make a copy every 2 seconds. About how long will it take to make 700 copies?

A 11 min

B 23 min

C 30 min

D 42 min

4 Mrs. Edwards turned her crock-pot on at 6:30 A.M. She turned it off at 4:10 P.M. How many minutes was the crock-pot on?

Record your answer and fill in the bubbles on the grid below. Be sure to use the correct place value.

				.		
0	0	0	0		0	0
1	1	1	1		1	1
2	2	2	2		2	2
3	3	3	3		3	3
4	4	4	4		4	4
5	5	5	5		5	5
6	6	6	6		6	6
7	7	7	7		7	7
8	8	8	8		8	8
9	9	9	9		9	9

5 A Web site averages 221 hits a day. About how many hits does it get in a year?

A Between 600 and 900

B Between 6,000 and 9,000

C Between 60,000 and 90,000

D Between 600,000 and 900,000

Focus on TEKS

Lesson 42 PROBLEM-SOLVING STRATEGY: Draw a Picture

TEKS 6.11A Identify and apply mathematics to everyday experiences, to activities in and outside of school, with other disciplines, and with other mathematical topics.

TEKS 6.11B Use a problem-solving model that incorporates understanding the problem, making a plan, carrying out the plan, and evaluating the solution for reasonableness.

TEKS 6.11C Select or develop an appropriate problem-solving strategy from a variety of different types, including drawing a picture.

TEKS 6.11D Select tools such as real objects, manipulatives, paper/pencil, and technology or techniques such as mental math, estimation, and number sense to solve problems.

You can draw a picture to help you solve a problem. Use the problem-solving guide on page 288 to help you.

Guided Instruction

Problem

Hayden is decorating a cake for his great-grandmother's 90th birthday. The cake is a rectangular sheet cake that measures 14 inches by 10 inches. In the center of the cake, Hayden plans to place two large numerals, a 9 and a 0. Then, 1 inch from the edges of the cake, he plans to place birthday candles spaced 2 inches apart. How many birthday candles does he need?

Understand the problem.

You know where the birthday candles go on the cake. What do you need to find?

____

Make a plan.

Draw a picture to show where the birthday candles will go.

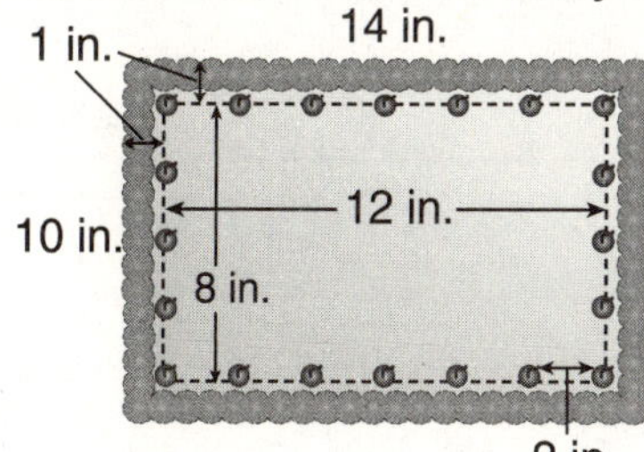

Solve the problem.

Use the picture to solve the problem.

What are the dimensions of the rectangle formed by the candles Hayden placed 1 in. from the edge of the cake?

__________ in. by __________ in.

Count to find the number of birthday candles in all.

How many candles are needed in all to run across the top and bottom sides of the rectangle? ________

How many more candles are needed to fill the sides? ________

How many birthday candles are there in all? ________

Check your answer.

Look at your picture. Make sure the candles are placed as the problem said they should be: 1 inch from the edges and 2 inches apart. Count the candles clockwise, starting at one edge.

There are ________ birthday candles needed for the cake.

Apply the TEKS **Draw a picture to solve each problem.**

Workspace

1. Carl, Brock, Tanner, and Nick need to line up by height from shortest to tallest. Carl is taller than Brock, but shorter than Nick. Nick is not the tallest. How should they line up to be in order from shortest to tallest?

____

2. Melvin hung a 38-centimeter-wide painting in the center of a wall. He left 26 centimeters on each side of the painting. How many meters wide is the wall?

____

3. Mrs. Lopez is planting a flower garden that is 6 feet by 5 feet. Each plant will have 1 square foot of growing space. The edge of the flower garden will be all red mums, and the inside will alternate a pink mum and a white mum. How many of each color of mum does she need?

____

4. Leanne placed a 10-foot-long shelf along a 22-foot-long wall. The distance from the left end of the shelf to the left end of the wall is 3 times the distance from the right end of the shelf to the right end of the wall. How far is the left end of the shelf from the left end of the wall? ____________

5. A 12-yard fence has a post at each end and posts every foot across. How many posts does the fence have?

____

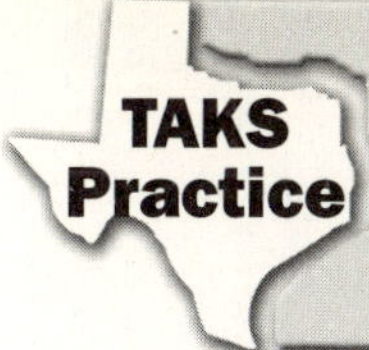

TAKS Objective 6 The student will demonstrate an understanding of the mathematical processes and tools used in problem solving.

TEKS 6.11A, 6.11B, 6.11C, 6.11D

DIRECTIONS Read each question. Then circle the letter for the correct answer.

1 Michael is helping set up tables for a PTA luncheon. All the tables are square and seat only one person on each of four sides. Mr. Brock wants Michael to set up one long table at the front that seats 12 people. How many of the square tables need to be pushed together to make a long table that seats 12?

A 3

B 4

C 5

D 6

2 James, Barry, Susan, and Pat competed in a charity road race. James finished 25 meters behind Susan. Susan finished 30 meters ahead of Barry. Barry was 10 meters behind Pat. Which statement below is true?

F Barry finished 10 m behind James.

G Pat finished 500 cm ahead of James.

H James finished last in the race.

J Pat finished 5 m behind Susan.

3 The towns of Hopewell, Briarwood, Turner, and Casey lie along a straight road in the order given. The distance from Hopewell to Casey is 150 miles. The distance from Briarwood to Casey is twice the distance from Hopewell to Briarwood. The distance from Turner to Casey is 35 miles. What is the distance from Briarwood to Turner?

A 65 mi

B 100 mi

C 115 mi

D 185 mi

4 Reggie leaves his house in the morning and walks 3 blocks north to the home of his friend Alan. Together, he and Alan walk 6 blocks east to a park. After playing for 45 minutes, they walk 1 block south and 2 blocks west to buy ice cream cones. After eating the ice cream, Reggie and Alan go their separate ways.

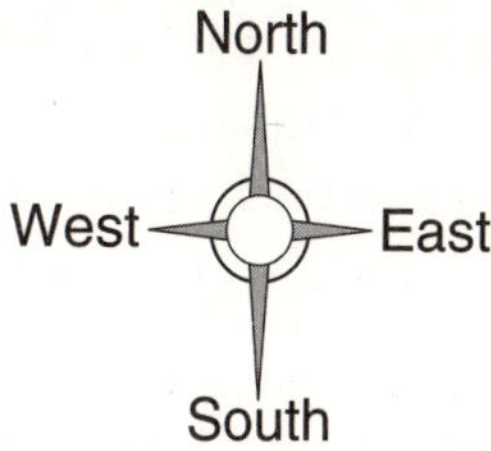

What is the least number of blocks Reggie needs to walk in order to get back to his house?

F 2

G 6

H 12

J 15

5 A goat pen is 26 meters by 20 meters. There is a post for the fence at each corner of the pen and a post every meter. There is a gate that is 2 meters wide in the middle of one of the 26-meter sides. The gate has a post at each side. How many posts are used to make the fence for the goat pen?

A 56

B 72

C 91

D 93

Building Stamina®

Read each question. Then circle the letter for the correct answer. If a correct answer is not here, mark the letter for "Not Here."

Use the table below to answer Questions 1–2.

Days to Maturity for Plants
Started from Seeds or Transplant

Plant	Days to Maturity
Honeydew melon	110-125 (from seed)
Watermelon	75 (from seed)
Beefsteak tomato	80-90 (from transplant)
Cherry tomato	65 (from transplant)

1 Paco plants honeydew melon seeds and watermelon seeds on the same day. About how much sooner will he be eating watermelon than honeydew melon?

A About 2 wk

B About 5 wk

C About 4 mo

D About 6 mo

2 Fran wants to grow tomato plants from seed. The package says it takes about 10 days for the seeds to sprout and then another 2 months for the plant to have ripe tomatoes. About how many weeks does it take from planting tomato seeds until you have ripe tomatoes?

F About 7 wk

G About 10 wk

H About 12 wk

J About 23 wk

3 Rudy is 4 feet 11 inches tall. His brother Jimmy is 6 feet 1 inch tall. How many more inches does Rudy need to grow to be the same height as his brother?

A 9 in.

B 11 in.

C 13 in.

D Not Here

4 Toby is training for a 10-kilometer race. He trains on the track at a gym. A lap around the track is 450 meters. Toby runs 8 laps on Monday, Wednesday, and Friday. On Tuesday, Thursday, and Saturday, he runs 6 laps. Then on Sunday he rests. How many kilometers does Toby run in a week?

F 18.9 km

G 10.8 km

H 6.3 km

J 0.89 km

5 Half of a red grapefruit has 158 milligrams of potassium. About how many red grapefruits does it take to have a gram of potassium?

A About 30

B About 9

C About 3

D About $\frac{1}{3}$

6 Misty is working part-time at a garden nursery. She has 10 gallons of potting soil. She fills quart planters with the potting soil. How many quart planters can she fill?

F 4

G 40

H 80

J Not Here

7 Susan is comparing the cost of buying distilled water with distilling it at home. She learns that it will cost $0.05 in electricity to distill a quart of water at home and $1.20 to buy a gallon of distilled water. The distiller itself costs $250. How many gallons of water would she have to distill before the distiller would pay for itself?

Record your answer and fill in the bubbles on the grid below. Be sure to use the correct place value.

				.		
0	0	0	0		0	0
1	1	1	1		1	1
2	2	2	2		2	2
3	3	3	3		3	3
4	4	4	4		4	4
5	5	5	5		5	5
6	6	6	6		6	6
7	7	7	7		7	7
8	8	8	8		8	8
9	9	9	9		9	9

8 Alice wants to know how much money she spends on milk in a month. She estimates that her family consumes 6 cups of milk a day. She buys milk in $\frac{1}{2}$-gallon containers that cost $1.89 each. About how much does she spend on milk in a month?

F Between $40 and $45

G Between $30 and $35

H Between $20 and $25

J Between $10 and $15

9 Patty is gluing 1-inch tiles onto a 1-foot square of wood to make a hotplate for her mother. She starts on the outside edge and works her way in toward the center. The outer edge of the hotplate has all blue tiles. The inside tiles will all be white except for the 4 center tiles that will also be blue. How many blue tiles does she need for the project?

A 38

B 48

C 52

D 56

10 A computer consultant charges his client $75 an hour and $20 for every 15 minutes over an hour, including his travel time. If he leaves his house at 8:30 A.M. and returns at 1:15 P.M., what does he charge his client?

F $405

G $360

H $285

J $260

Use the table below to answer Questions 11–12.

Book Catalog Shipping Charges

Weight	Shipping Costs
less than 16 oz	$4.25
16 oz to less than 2 lb 8 oz	$5.50
2 lb 8 oz to less than 5 lb	$7.25
5 lb to less than 10 lb	$8.50

11 Michelle weighs an order of books to send out. The total weight of the order is 73 ounces. What is the cost of the shipping?

A $4.25

B $5.50

C $7.25

D $8.50

12 Mrs. Winston, the librarian, places an order from a catalog. She orders 3 copies of a book that costs $6.00. The catalog lists the shipping weight of the book as 12 ounces. What is the total cost of the 3 books, including shipping? Assume that the 3 copies are sent in one box.

F $25.25

G $23.50

H $22.25

J $11.50

13 Mark lives 2 miles from school. His teacher gave him the following information and asked him how many furlongs he lives from school.

1 furlong = 220 yards

How many furlongs are in 2 miles?

A 8 furlongs

B 12 furlongs

C 16 furlongs

D 48 furlongs

14 Sarah placed an 8-foot-long shelf along a 20-foot-long wall. The distance from the left end of the shelf to the left end of the wall is $\frac{1}{2}$ the distance from the right end of the shelf to the right end of the wall. How far is the left end of the shelf from the left end of the wall?

F 16 ft

G 12 ft

H 8 ft

J 4 ft

15 A landscape contractor orders 5 tons of imported river rock. The rock costs $2 a pound delivered. What is the cost of the order?

A $100,000

B $20,000

C $10,000

D $2000

Use the graph below to answer Questions 16–17.

High and Low Temperatures for 5 Days in Abilene, TX

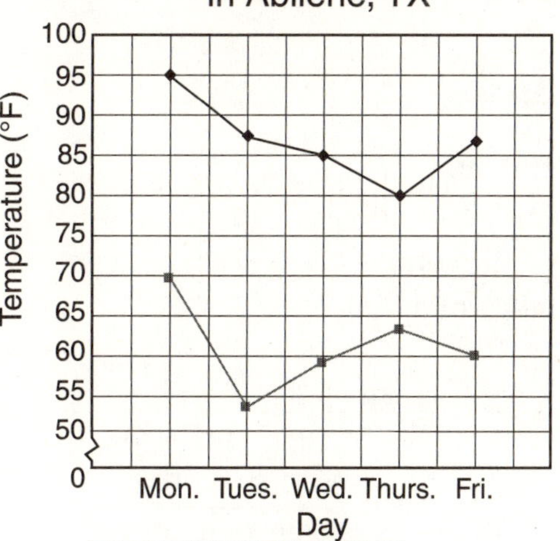

High Temperatures
Low Temperatures

16 What was the difference between the high and low temperatures on Wednesday?

F 144°F

G 35°F

H 26°F

J 26°C

17 What was the average low temperature for the 5 days?

A 87°F

B 71°F

C 67°F

D 61°F

18 Which statement below is true?

F 1,000 kg = 10,000 mg

G 0.86 L < 840 mL

H 5,020 g > 5.1 kg

J 8 km = 800,000 cm

19 Which number makes the sentence true?
5 yards 2 feet 3 inches = ? inches

Record your answer and fill in the bubbles on the grid below. Be sure to use the correct place value.

				.		
0	0	0	0		0	0
1	1	1	1		1	1
2	2	2	2		2	2
3	3	3	3		3	3
4	4	4	4		4	4
5	5	5	5		5	5
6	6	6	6		6	6
7	7	7	7		7	7
8	8	8	8		8	8
9	9	9	9		9	9

20 Texas carpenter ants eat and digest wood. They will travel up to 350 feet from their nest when searching for food. Which of the following is possible food for the carpenter ants?

F A stack of firewood 3,000 in. from the nest

G A garage 150 yd from the nest

H A playhouse $\frac{1}{2}$ mi from the nest

J A patio deck 100 yd and 70 ft from the nest

21 Ed, Mike, Cathy, and Liu competed in a race. Ed finished 6 meters behind Cathy. Cathy finished 12 meters ahead of Liu. Which fact below do you need to know in order to determine how far Mike finished behind Cathy?

A Liu finished 6 m behind Ed.

B Liu finished 1,200 cm behind Cathy.

C Liu finished last in the race.

D Liu finished 8 m behind Mike.

Focus on TEKS

Lesson 43 Estimate and Find Perimeter

TEKS 6.4A Use tables and symbols to represent and describe proportional and other relationships such as those involving conversions, arithmetic sequences (with a constant rate of change), perimeter and area.

TEKS 6.4B Use tables of data to generate formulas representing relationships involving perimeter, area, volume of a rectangular prism, etc.

TEKS 6.8A Estimate measurements (including circumference) and evaluate reasonableness of results.

TEKS 6.8B Select and use appropriate units, tools, or formulas to measure and to solve problems involving length (including perimeter).

You can estimate and find perimeter to solve problems.

Perimeter is the distance around a figure. Perimeter can be measured in standard units such as the inch, foot, yard, and mile. It can also be measured in metric units such as the millimeter, centimeter, meter, and kilometer. To find the perimeter of a figure, add the lengths of its sides.

Guided Instruction

Problem Alex bought a bulletin board to hang in his room. What is the perimeter of his bulletin board?

Side Measures of Bulletin Board

Side	Measure
Side 1	36 in.
Side 2	24 in.
Side 3	36 in.
Side 4	24 in.

Write a formula to find the perimeter of the bulletin board.

Step 1 The length of the bulletin board is 36 inches.

What is the width of the bulletin board? ______________

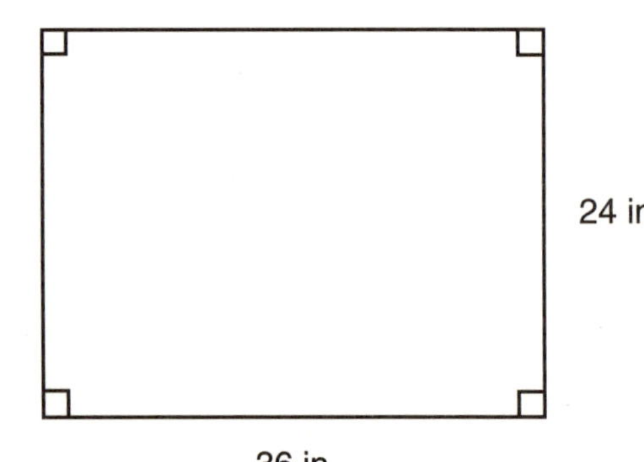

Step 2 Use the length and width to write a formula.

$P =$ _______ $\times$ length $+$ _______ $\times$ width

OR

$P = 2(\text{length} + \text{width})$

Step 3 Substitute the values into your formula and solve for P.

$P = 2 \times$ _______ $+ 2 \times$ _______

$P = 72 + 48$

$P =$ _______

OR

$P = 2(\text{length} + \text{width})$

$P = 2($_______ $+$ _______$)$

$P = 2(60)$

$P =$ _______

Solution What is the perimeter of his bulletin board? ______________

Apply the TEKS **Estimate the perimeter of each figure to the nearest whole number.**

1. Polygon

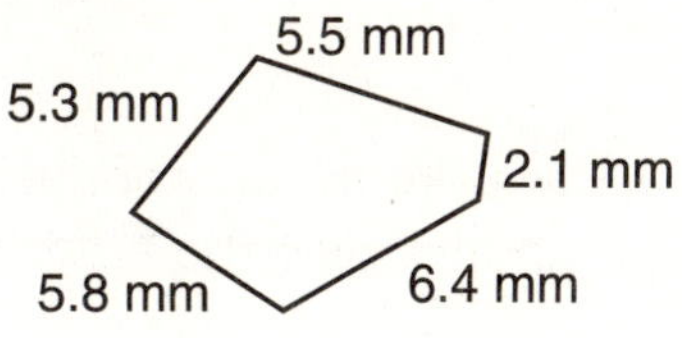

____

2. Rectangle

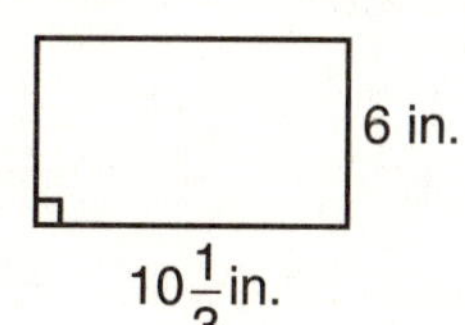

____

3. Square

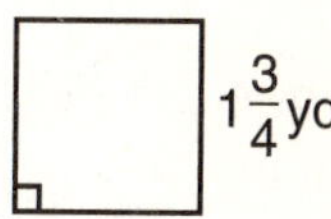

____

Find the perimeter of each.

4. Rectangle
$l = 18$ mm
$w = 6$ mm

$P =$ _______________

5. Rectangle
$l = 10$ in.
$w = 8$ in.

$P =$ _______________

6. Square
$s = 9$ m

$P =$ _______________

7. Square
$s = 3$ ft

$P =$ _______________

Use a centimeter ruler to measure the perimeter of each figure.

8.

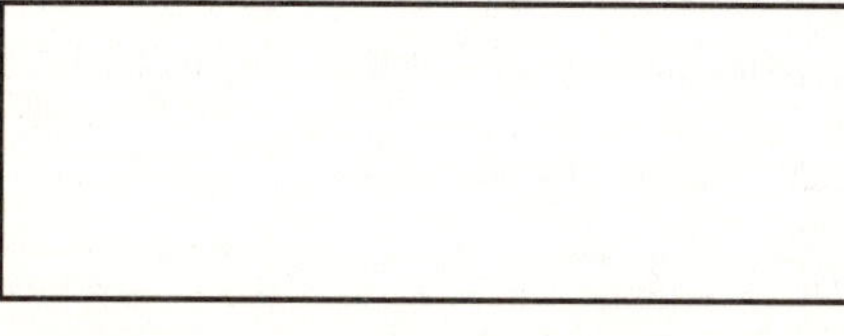

perimeter: _______________

9.

perimeter: _______________

Solve each problem.

10. Julio wants to put a string of lights along the top rectangular edge of his room, where the wall meets the ceiling. The rectangular edge measures 8 ft by 9 ft. What is the shortest string of lights Julio can use? _______________

11. Martina fenced off a space in her backyard for her new puppy. The perimeter of the rectangular space is 6 meters. If two opposite sides are each 2 meters long, what are the lengths of each of the other two sides? _______________

12. Ms. Ramos wants to put a fringe on the edge of a square-shaped pillow that measures 14 inches on each side. She allows an extra 2 inches of fringe on each side for overlap. How many inches of fringe should Ms. Ramos buy? _______________

13. Ralph's garden is shown in the drawing to the right. What are the measures of the two missing sides if the perimeter of the garden is 28 ft? _______________

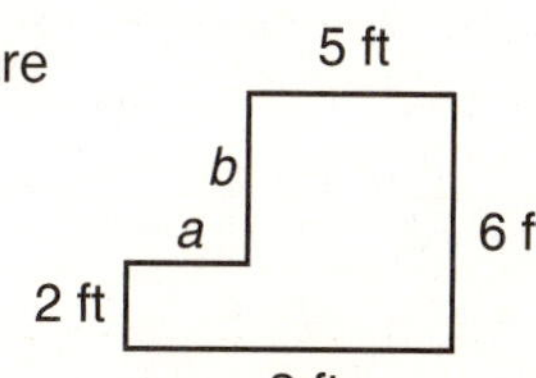

Explain how you solved the problem.

____

____

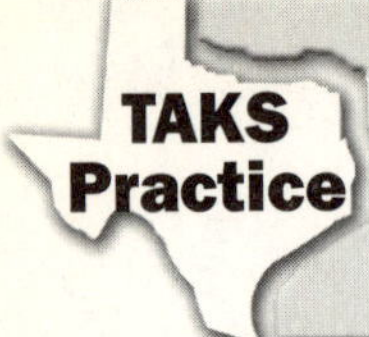

TAKS Objective 2 The student will demonstrate an understanding of patterns, relationships, and algebraic reasoning.
TEKS 6.4A, 6.4B
TAKS Objective 4 The student will demonstrate an understanding of the concepts and uses of measurement.
TEKS 6.8A, 6.8B

DIRECTIONS Read each question. Then circle the letter for the correct answer.

1 Which is the best estimate of the perimeter of the figure?

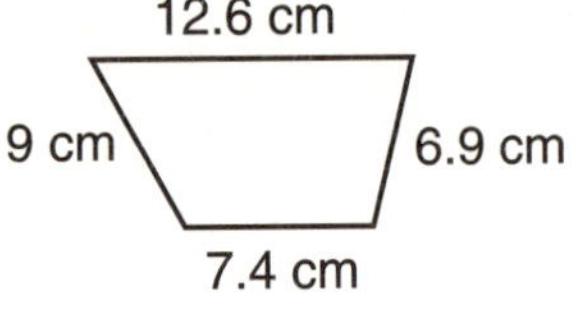

A 17 cm

B 28 cm

C 36 cm

D 45 cm

2 The perimeter of a square is 144 meters. What is the length of a side of this square?

F 12 m

G 24 m

H 32 m

J 36 m

3 The length of a rectangle is half as long as its width. The perimeter is 27 yards. What are the length and width of the rectangle?

A $l = 12$ yd, $w = 6$ yd

B $l = 9$ yd, $w = 4$ yd

C $l = 9$ yd, $w = 4\frac{1}{2}$ yd

D $l = 36$ yd, $w = 18$ yd

4 The table below shows the perimeters of some equilateral triangles and the lengths of their sides.

Perimeters of Equilateral Triangles

Perimeter (units)	Length of a Side (units)
12	4
15	5
21	7
24	8

Which equation below shows the relationship between the length of a side and the perimeter of an equilateral triangle?

F $l = P + 3$

G $l = P - 3$

H $l = P \div 3$

J $l = 3 \times P$

5 Mrs. Wong wants to put trimming around a square-shaped picture frame that measures 15 inches on each side. She bought 2 yards of trimming. How much more trimming did she buy than she needed?

A 12 in.

B 36 in.

C 58 in.

D 60 in.

Focus on TEKS

Lesson 44 Estimate and Find Circumference

TEKS 6.6C Describe the relationship between radius, diameter, and circumference of a circle.

TEKS 6.8A Estimate measurements (including circumference) and evaluate reasonableness of results.

TEKS 6.8B Select and use appropriate formulas to solve problems.

When you find the circumference of a circle, you are finding the perimeter of the circle.

Circumference is the distance around a circle.

A **radius** is a line segment that connects the center of a circle and an endpoint on the circle.

A **diameter** is a line segment that passes through the center of a circle and has both endpoints on the circle. The length of a diameter is twice the length of a radius.

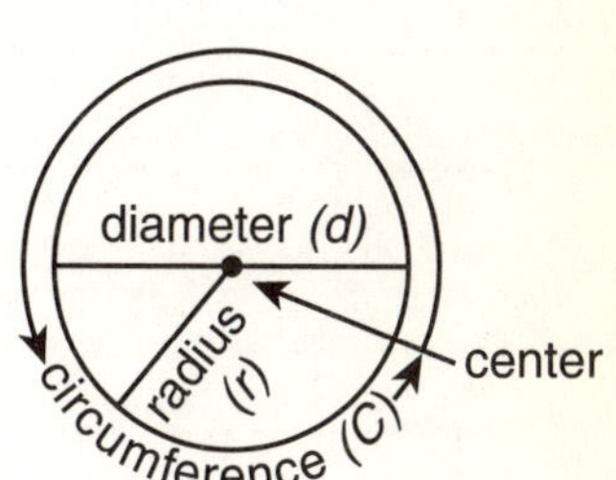

The ratio of the circumference of any circle to its diameter ($\frac{C}{d}$) is always the same. This ratio is known as **pi** (π). For any circle, the ratio π is about $\frac{22}{7}$, or 3.14. The formula for finding the circumference of a circle: Circumference (C) = πd or $C = 2\pi r$.

Guided Instruction

Problem

Adrian bought a circular rug for his room. It has a radius of $3\frac{1}{2}$ feet. About how long is the circumference of the rug?

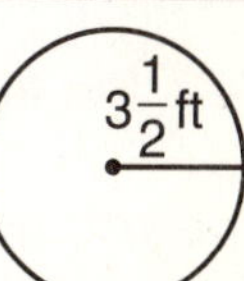

Use the formula and estimate, using 3 as an approximation for π.

Step 1 Since you are given the radius, use the formula $C = 2\pi r$.

Step 2 Substitute 3 for π and $r = 4$ into the formula and solve for C. Use the symbol $\approx$ for "is approximately equal to."

$C \approx 2 \times 3 \times 4$

$C \approx$ ________

Solution About how long is the circumference of the rug? ____________

Other Examples

A. About how long is the diameter of a pool with a circumference of 45 feet. Use 3 as an approximation of π.

Use $d = \frac{C}{\pi}$. $\quad d = \frac{C}{\pi}$

Substitute. $C = 45$ and use $\pi \approx 3$. $\quad d \approx \frac{45}{3}$

Solve for d. $\quad d \approx 15$

The diameter is about 15 feet.

B. About how long is the radius of a circular sign with a circumference of 24 centimeters. Use 3 as an approximation of π.

Use $r = \frac{C}{2\pi}$. $\quad r = \frac{C}{2\pi}$

Substitute. $C = 24$ and use $\pi \approx 3$. $\quad r \approx \frac{24}{6}$

Solve for r. $\quad r \approx 4$

The radius is about 4 centimeters.

Apply the TEKS **Estimate the circumference. Use 3 as an approximation of π.**

1. 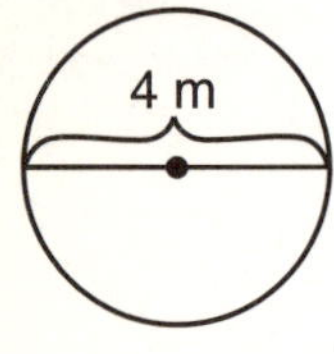

2. 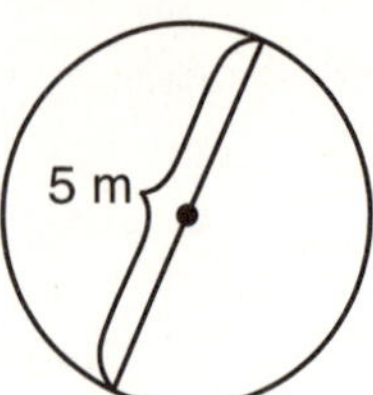

3. 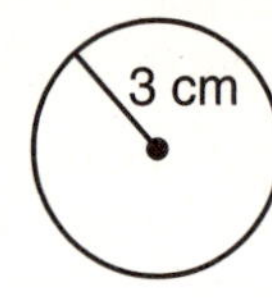

________________ ________________ ________________

4. $d = 2$ km **5.** $d = 7$ m **6.** $r = 1$ m **7.** $r = 4$ cm

________________ ________________ ________________ ________________

Estimate the length of the diameter. Use 3 as an approximation of π.

8. $C = 42$ ft **9.** $C = 60$ m **10.** $C = 75$ in.

________________ ________________ ________________

Estimate the length of the radius. Use 3 as an approximation of π.

11. $C = 132$ m **12.** $C = 90$ in. **13.** $C = 228$ cm **14.** $C = 324$ mm

________________ ________________ ________________ ________________

Solve each problem.

15. Jerry has a vinyl record that has a 20-centimeter diameter.
About how long is the circumference of the record? ________________

16. Mrs. Kane has a circular birdbath in her yard.
The birdbath has a radius of 14 centimeters.
About how long is the circumference of the birdbath? ________________

17. A circular table measures about 9 meter around its edge.
About how long is its diameter? ________________

18. A bakery cake has a circumference of 44 inches.
Will it fit into a 10-inch-by-10-inch box? ________________

Explain how you solved the problem.

____

____

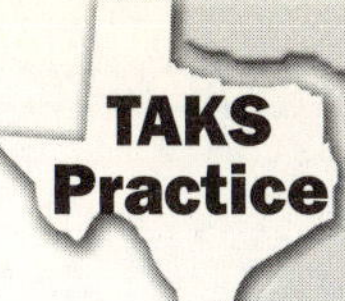

TAKS Objective 3 The student will demonstrate an understanding of geometry and spatial reasoning.
TEKS 6.6C

TAKS Objective 4 The student will demonstrate an understanding of the concepts and uses of measurement.
TEKS 6.8A, 6.8B

DIRECTIONS Read each question. Then circle the letter for the correct answer.

1 Which is the best estimate for the circumference of the circle below?

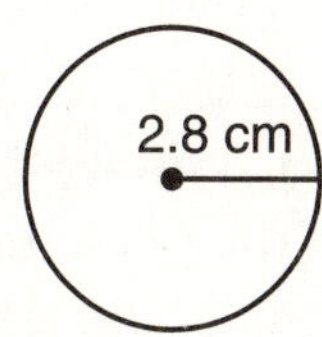

A About 6 cm

B About 9 cm

C About 12 cm

D About 18 cm

2 The circumference of a circle is 66 inches. Find the approximate length of the circle's radius.

F $3\frac{1}{2}$ in.

G 11 in.

H 14 in.

J 21 in.

3 The circumference of a circle that has a radius of 7 centimeters is approximately the same as the perimeter of a square. About how long is one side of the square?

A 5 cm

B 9 cm

C 11 cm

D 22 cm

4 Jack has two plates. One plate has a diameter of 20 centimeters. The other plate has a radius of 12 centimeters. How much greater is the circumference of the larger plate than the circumference of the smaller plate?

Which expression below can be used to solve the problem?

F $24 - \pi$

G $(24 - 20)\pi$

H $20\pi - 12$

J $(20 - 12)\pi$

5 It takes Kevin 5 minutes to jog once around a circular track that has a diameter of 400 meters. About how many meters per minute is Kevin jogging?

A About 250 meters per minute

B About 350 meters per minute

C About 420 meters per minute

D About 500 meters per minute

Focus on TEKS

Lesson 45 Estimate and Find Area

TEKS 6.4A Use tables and symbols to represent and describe relationships involving area.
TEKS 6.4B Use tables of data to generate formulas representing relationships involving area.
TEKS 6.8A Estimate measurements and evaluate reasonableness of results.
TEKS 6.8B Select and use appropriate units, tools, or formulas to measure and to solve problems involving area.

You can use formulas to find the area of some figures.

Area is the number of square units used to cover a region. Area can be measured in standard or metric square units such as the square inch (in.^{2}) or square centimeter (cm^2).

Rectangle	**Square**	**Parallelogram**
Area (A) = length × width $A = l \times w$	Area (A) = side × side $A = s \times s = s^2$	Area (A) = base × height $A = b \times h$

Triangle	**Trapezoid**
Area (A) = $\frac{\text{base} \times \text{height}}{2}$ $A = \frac{b \times h}{2}$	Area (A) = $\frac{1}{2}$ (sum of the bases) × height $A = \frac{(b_1 + b_2)h}{2}$

Guided Instruction

Problem Alex bought a bulletin board to hang in his room. What is the area of the bulletin board?

Side Measures of Bulletin Board

Side 1	36 in.
Side 2	24 in.

Find the area of the bulletin board.

Step 1 The length of the bulletin board is 36 inches.

What is the width of the bulletin board? ____________

Step 2 Use the length and width to write a formula.

Area = length × width

Step 3 Substitute the values into your formula and solve for A.

$A = lw$

$A =$ ________ × ________

$A =$ ________

Solution What is the area of the bulletin board? ____________

Apply the TEKS **Find the area of each figure.**

1. 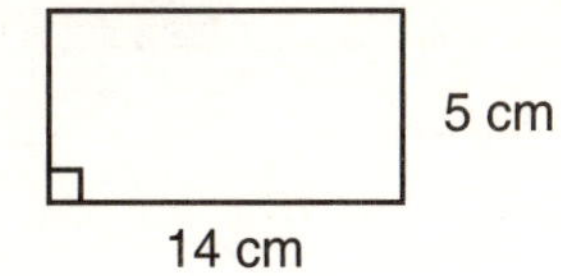

$A =$ ______

2. 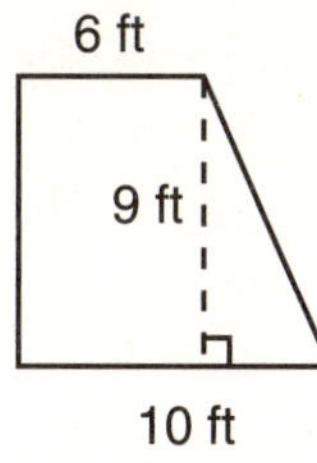

$A =$ ______

3. 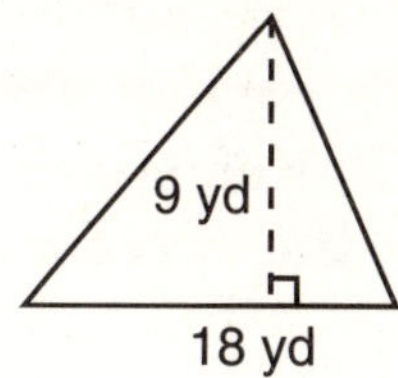

$A =$ ______

Use a centimeter ruler to measure the dimensions. Then find the area of each figure.

4. 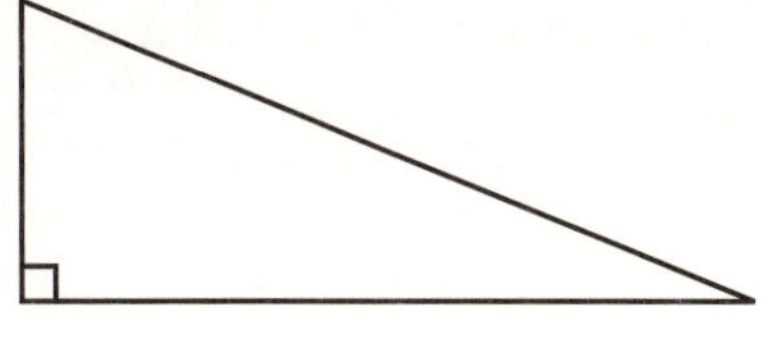

$A =$ ______

5. 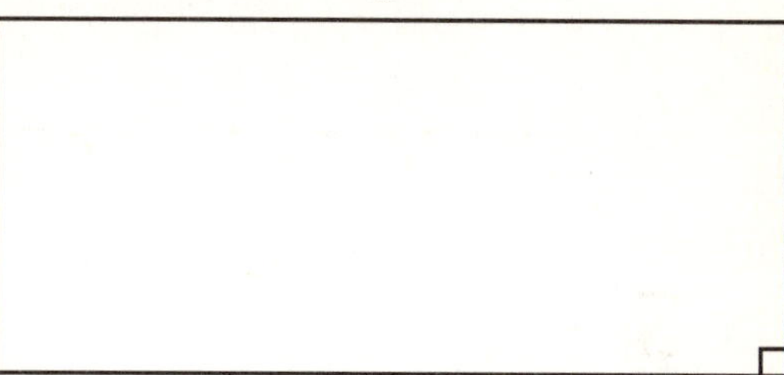

$A =$ ______

Estimate the area to the nearest whole number.

6. trapezoid
$b_1 = 3.2$ m
$b_2 = 6.8$ m
$h = 4.5$ m
$A =$ ______

7. triangle
$b = 25.2$ cm
$h = 19.8$ cm
$A =$ ______

8. square
$s = 18\frac{1}{3}$ ft
$A =$ ______

9. parallelogram
$b = 6\frac{1}{2}$ yd
$h = 2\frac{1}{3}$ yd
$A =$ ______

Solve each problem.

10. A triangular banner has a base of 20 centimeters and a height that is twice the length of the base. What is the area of the banner? ______

11. Franklin bought two photographs. One photograph was 14 inches by 16 inches. The second photograph was a square photograph that had an area 103 square inches less than the first photo. What was the size of the square photograph? ______

12. Which has the greatest area: a triangle with a base of 17 centimeters and a height of 20 centimeters, a parallelogram with a base of 15 centimeters and a height of 11 centimeters, or a rectangle with a length of 0.18 meter and a width of 0.06 meter? ______

13. A city's building code requires a building to be at least 30 feet long or 30 feet wide. John plans to build a house that meets the city building code. The base of his one-floor home will have an area of 1,680 square feet. The width of his home will exceed the building code minimum by 5 feet. What will be the length of John's home? Explain how you solved the problem.

______

______

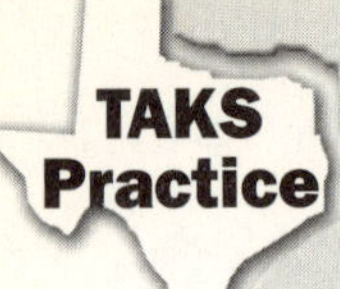

TAKS Objective 2 The student will demonstrate an understanding of patterns, relationships, and algebraic reasoning.
TEKS 6.4A, 6.4B

TAKS Objective 4 The student will demonstrate an understanding of the concepts and uses of measurement.
TEKS 6.8A, 6.8B

DIRECTIONS Read each question. Then circle the letter for the correct answer.

1 Which is the best estimate for the area of the trapezoid?

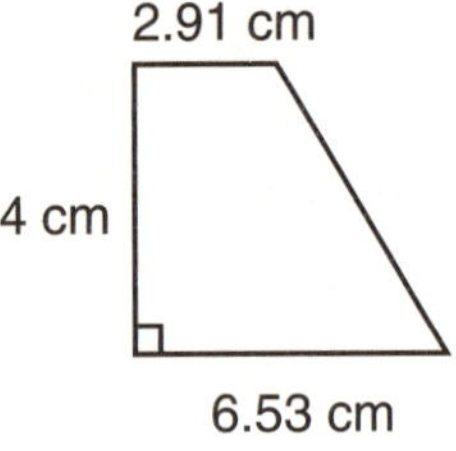

A 13 cm^2

B 16 cm^2

C 20 cm^2

D 26 cm^2

2 The table below shows the areas of some circles. Next to each area is the length of the radius of the circle.

Areas of Circles

Area (square units)	Length of Radius (units)
4π	2
9π	3
25π	5
49π	7
	r

Which formula below shows the relationship between the length of a radius and the area of the circle?

F $A = \pi r^2$

G $A = 2\pi r$

H $A = \pi r$

J $A = \pi r + 2$

3 The area of a square is 85 square meters. Which best describes the length of a side of the square?

A It is less than 7 m long.

B It is between 7 m and 8 m long.

C It is between 8 m and 9 m long.

D Not Here

4 A rectangle has an area of 48 square yards and a side that measures 6 yards. What are the lengths of the other sides in yards?

F 6, 6, 5

G 6, 7, 7

H 6, 8, 8

J Not Here

5 Mr. Levin bought a square rug that measures 8 feet on each side. He laid down the rug on a rectangular floor. The length of the floor is 6 feet longer than the side of the rug and the width is $10\frac{1}{2}$ feet wider. How much of the floor is NOT covered by the rug?

A 64 ft^2

B 195 ft^2

C 259 ft^2

D 323 ft^2

Focus on TEKS

Lesson 46 Estimate and Find Volume

TEKS 6.4B Use tables of data to generate formulas representing relationships involving volume of a rectangular prism.
TEKS 6.8A Estimate measurements.
TEKS 6.8B Select and use appropriate formulas to solve problems involving volume.
TEKS 6.13A Make conjectures from patterns or sets of examples and nonexamples.
TEKS 6.13B Validate his/her conclusions using mathematical properties and relationships.

To find the volume of a 3-dimensional object, you can count the number of cubic units in the figure.

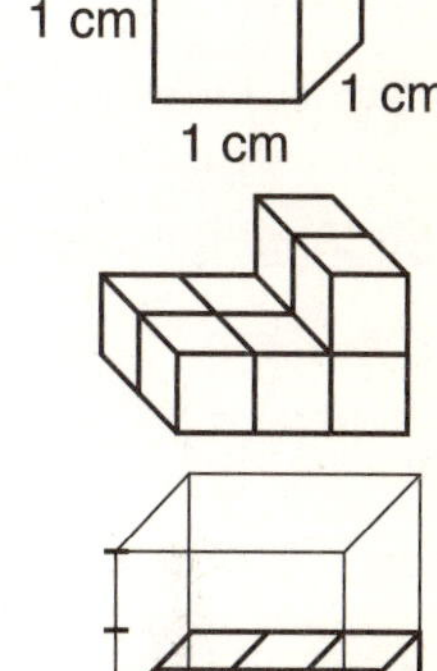

Volume is the number of cubic units a container can hold. Volume can be measured in cubic units, such as cubic centimeters (cm^3) or cubic inches ($in.^3$). A cubic centimeter is shown at the right.

To find the volume of a space figure, you can count the number of cubic units in the figure. The volume of the figure shown at the right is 8 cubic units.

To find the volume of a rectangular prism, find the number of unit cubes that will fit in one layer. Then multiply by the number of layers. This results in the formula: Volume (V) = $l \times w \times h$ or lwh

To find the volume of a cube, you can use this formula:

Volume (V) = $s \times s \times s$ or s^3

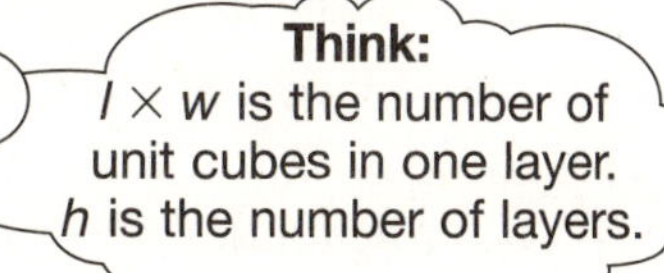

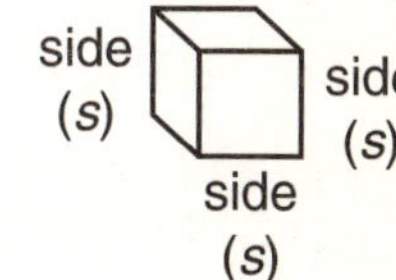

Guided Instruction

Problem

Jamie built a rectangular prism with cubes. He recorded the number of cubes he used in the table below. What is the volume of the prism?

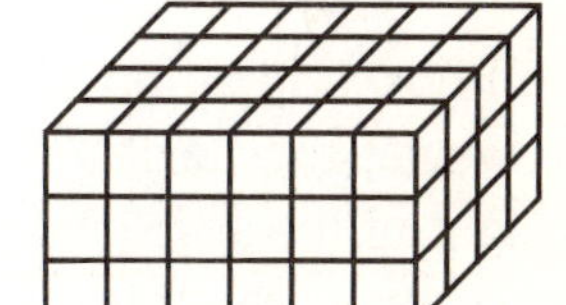

Number of Blocks

Layer	Length	Width
1	6	4
2	6	4
3	6	4

Find the volume of the prism.

Step 1 Multiply the length and width of layer 1 to find the number of units used in one layer. length ______ × width ______ = ______

Step 2 Multiply the number of units in one layer by the number of layers. $3 \times 24 =$ ______

Solution What is the volume of Jamie's rectangular prism? ____________

Apply the TEKS **Find the volume of each figure.**

1. 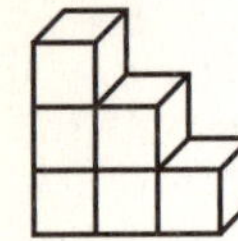

$V =$ ______

2. 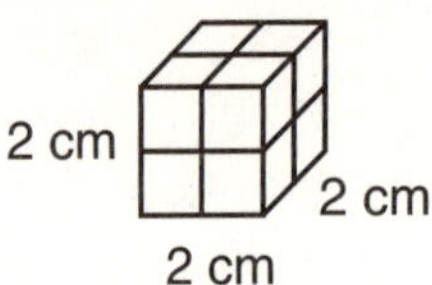

$V =$ ______

3. 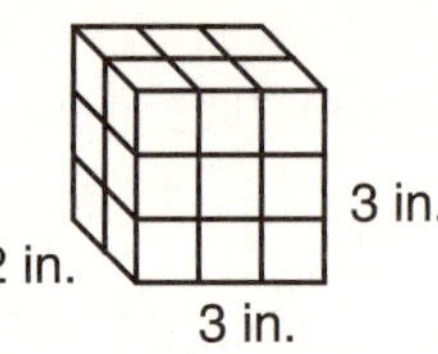

$V =$ ______

Find the volume of each.

4. rectangular prism

$l = 7$ cm

$w = 3$ cm

$h = 5$ cm

$V =$ ______

5. rectangular prism

$l = 9$ yd

$w = 3$ yd

$h = 2$ yd

$V =$ ______

6. cube

$s = 3$ cm

$V =$ ______

7. cube

$s = 16$ in

$V =$ ______

Solve each problem.

8. A toy chest is shaped like a rectangular prism. It measures 2 feet by 2 feet by 1 foot. What is the volume of the toy chest? ______

9. Mary paints boxes to sell at craft fairs. The boxes are in the shape of a cube measuring 6 inches on each side. What is the volume of each box? ______

10. Two boxes each have a length of 5 inches and a width of 3 inches. However, the height of the second box is 8 inches taller than the height of the first box. If the height of the first box is 2 inches, how many more cubic inches of space does the second box contain? ______

11. Vin has a brown carton that measures 1 meter × 4 meters × 2 meters, a white carton that measures 1 meter × 1 meter × 2 meters, and a gray carton measures 2 meters × 2 meters × 1 meter. Order the cartons from least to greatest volume.

______

12. About how many cubic inches would fit inside the container shown at the right? Explain how you found your answer.

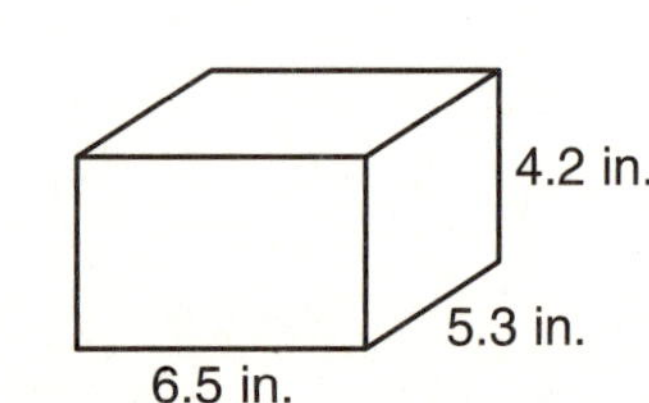

______

______

______

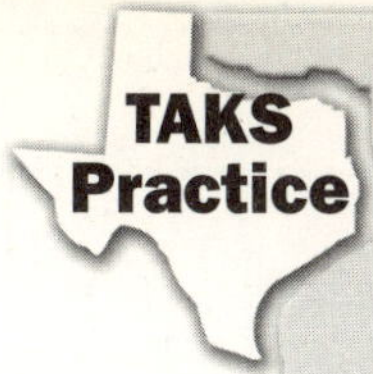

TAKS Objective 2 The student will demonstrate an understanding of patterns, relationships, and algebraic reasoning.
TEKS 6.4B

TAKS Objective 4 The student will demonstrate an understanding of the concepts and uses of measurements.
TEKS 6.8B

TAKS Objective 6 The student will demonstrate an understanding of the mathematical processes and tools used in problem solving.
TEKS 6.13A, 6.13B

DIRECTIONS Read each question. Then circle the letter for the correct answer.

1 The length, width, height, and volume of some boxes are shown below.

Length (units)	Width (units)	Height (units)	Volume (cubic units)
2	3	1	6
2	3	2	12
2	3	3	18
2	3	4	24

What happens when the height increases by one unit and the length and width remain the same?

A The volume remains the same.

B The volume increases by the number of cubic units in the first layer.

C The volume decreases by the number of cubic units in the first layer.

D The volume decreases by 6 cubic units.

2 Which is a true statement about the three boxes?

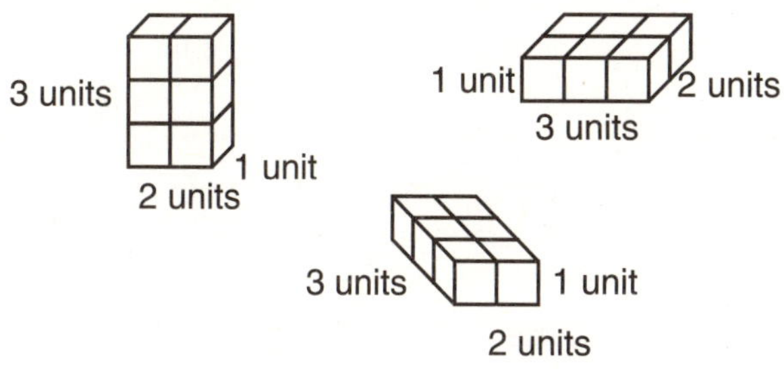

F The boxes have the same volume.

G The boxes have the same height.

H The shortest box has the least volume.

J The tallest box has the greatest volume.

3 A box can hold 4 rows of 5 cubes in its first layer. Which expression shows the number of cubes the box can hold in n layers?

A $(4 \times 5) + n$

B $4n + 5n$

C $4 \times 5 \times n$

D $n - (4 \times 5)$

4 The table below shows the dimensions of some boxes and their volumes.

Length (units)	Width (units)	Height (units)	Volume (cubic units)
2	2	2	8
3	3	3	27
5	5	5	125
10	10	10	1,000
n	n	n	?

Which formula below shows the relationship between n and the volume of the box?

F $V = n^2 + n$

G $V = n^3$

H $V = 3 + n$

J $V = 3n$

5 A box with a height of 2 centimeters has a volume of 24 cubic centimeters. The length of the box is 3 times longer than its width. What is the length of the box?

A 3 cm

B 4 cm

C 6 cm

D 9 cm

Focus on TEKS Lesson 47 PROBLEM-SOLVING STRATEGY: Identify Needed Information

TEKS 6.11A Identify and apply mathematics to everyday experiences.

TEKS 6.11B Use a problem-solving model that incorporates understanding the problem, making a plan, carrying out the plan, and evaluating the solution for reasonableness.

TEKS 6.11C Select or develop an appropriate problem-solving strategy.

Some problems may not contain enough information to solve them. Others may contain more information than you need. Before solving a problem, you need to identify what information is needed. Use the problem-solving guide on page 288 to help you.

Guided Instruction

Problem Find the perimeter and area of this trapezoid.

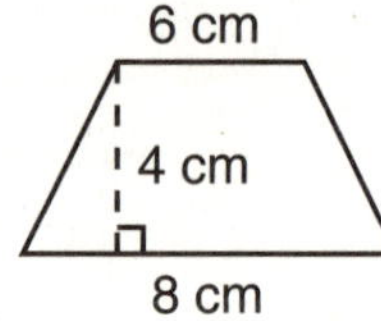

Understand the problem.

What do you know?

____

What are you trying to find?

____

Make a plan.

To find the perimeter, add the lengths of the sides.

To find the area, use the formula $A = \frac{(b_1 + b_2)h}{2}$.

Solve the problem.

What information do you need to know to find the perimeter of the trapezoid?

____

Why isn't it possible to find the perimeter of the trapezoid? Explain.

____

To find the area of the trapezoid, what values do you need to know?

____

Since all of these values are given, substitute the values for b_1, b_2, and h in the formula and solve for A.

$$A = \frac{(b_1 + b_2)h}{2}$$

$$A = \frac{(6 + 8)4}{2} = \_\_\_\_\_\_$$

The area of the trapezoid is _______ cm^2.

Check your answer.

A parallelogram with base of 8 cm and a height of 4 cm would have an area slightly greater than the trapezoid. Its area = 8 × 4, or 32 cm, which is slightly greater than 28 cm. So the answer is reasonable.

Apply the TEKS

Solve each problem. If there is not enough information, write what information is needed to solve the problem.
The drawings below represent five different garden designs. Use the drawings to solve the Problems 1–4.

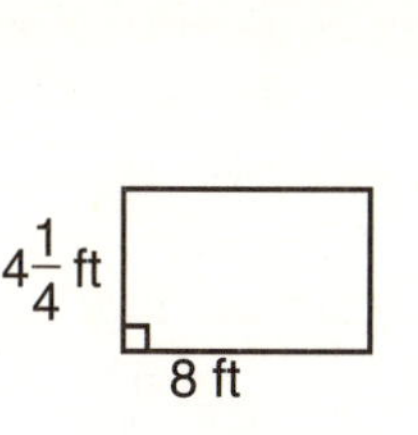

Design A

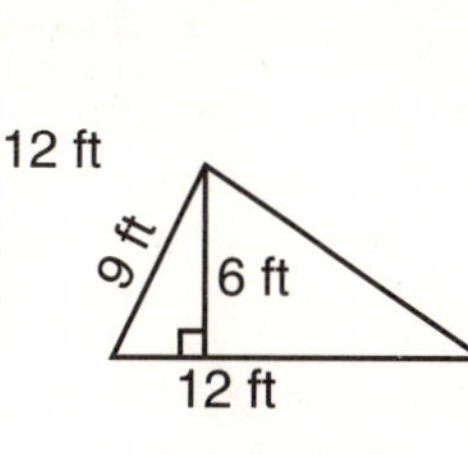

Design B

Design C

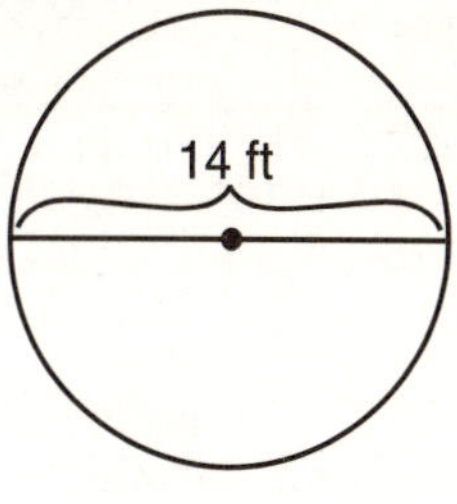

Design D

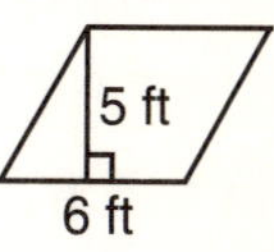

Design E

1. How many square feet greater is the area of design B than the area of design A? ____________

2. How many square feet less is the area of design A than the area of design C? ____________

3. Which design has the greater perimeter: design A or design C?

____

____

4. Which is greater, the perimeter of design B or the circumference of design D? Use 3 as an approximation of π. ____________

About how many feet greater? ____________

Use the information below to answer Problems 5–6.

The drawing below represents two boxes used for storing small gardening tools. The boxes are not drawn to scale.

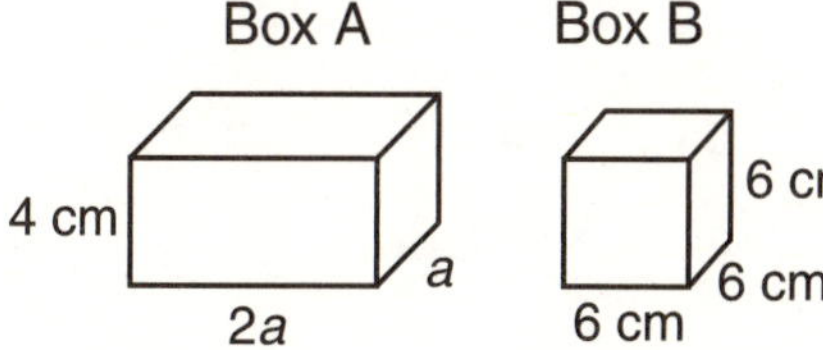

5. Which has a greater volume, Box A or Box B, if $a = 2$ cm? ____________
How many cubic centimeters greater is the volume of Box B? ____________

6. Which has a greater volume, Box A or Box B, if $a = 3$ cm?

____

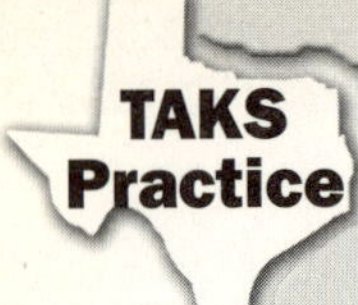

TAKS Objective 6 The student will demonstrate an understanding of the mathematical processes and tools used in problem solving.

TEKS 6.11A, 6.11B, 6.11C

DIRECTIONS Read each question. Then circle the letter for the correct answer.

1 To find how much border is needed to decorate a rectangular-shaped pillow, Keisha found the length of one of the sides of the pillow. The side measures 20 centimeters. What is the perimeter of the pillow?

What information is needed to solve the problem?

A The height of the pillow

B The width of the pillow

C The thickness of the pillow

D Not Here

For which triangle(s) described below, is there enough information to find both the area and the perimeter.

Triangle A is an equilateral triangle. One side is 6 centimeters. It has a height of 4 centimeters.

Triangle B is an obtuse scalene triangle. One side is 3 centimeters. Another side is 4 centimeters.

Triangle C is an isosceles triangle that has sides that are 2 inches, 4 inches, and 4 inches long.

F Triangle *A*

G Triangles *A* and *B*

H Triangles *A* and *C*

J Triangle *C*

Joe has a rectangular box whose base has a length of 8 inches and a width of 6 inches.

Which problem can NOT be solved using this information?

A What is the perimeter of the base of the box?

B What is the area of the base of the box?

C What is the volume of the box?

D Not Here

Mrs. Lee started a vegetable garden in her backyard. She drew the following diagram.

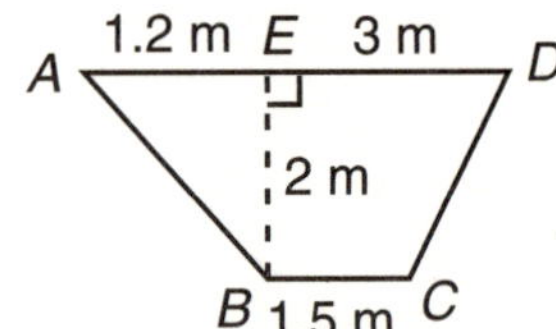

Which of the following measurements can she find by using the information given in her diagram?

F The perimeter of triangle *ABE*

G The perimeter of trapezoid *BCDE*

H The area of triangle *ABE*

J Not Here

Building Stamina®

DIRECTIONS Read each question. Then circle the letter for the correct answer. If a correct answer is not here, mark the letter for "Not Here."

1 The rectangle below has an area of 100 square feet. What is the value of a?

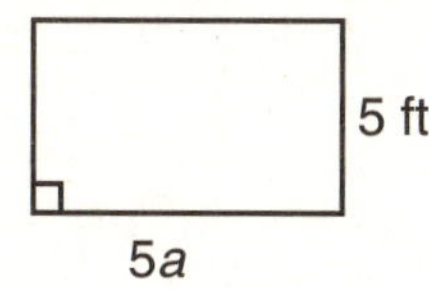

A 4 ft

B 5 ft

C 20 ft

D 50 ft

2 Which is the best estimate for the area of the trapezoid?

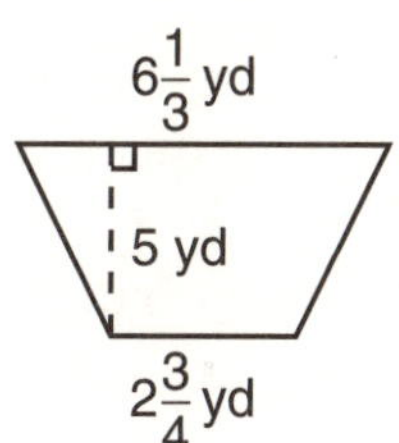

F 11 yd^2

G 15 yd^2

H 23 yd^2

J 45 yd^2

3 The area of a parallelogram is 80 square meters. Its base is 3.8 meters. Which best describes the height of the parallelogram?

A It is less than 10 m long.

B It is between 10 m and 15 m long.

C It is between 15 m and 20 m long.

D It is between 20 and 25 m long.

4 The table below shows the lengths, widths, and perimeters of some rectangles.

Length (l) (units)	Width (w) (units)	Perimeter (P) (units)
4	3	14
8	2	20
7	5	24
4	9	26

Which formula below shows the relationship of the perimeter (P) to the length (l) and width (w)?

F $l = 2 \times P \times w$

G $l = \frac{P}{2} - w$

H $l = w + 2P$

J $P = 2 + (l + w)$

5 About how many more inches is the circumference of the circle than the perimeter of the quadrilateral?

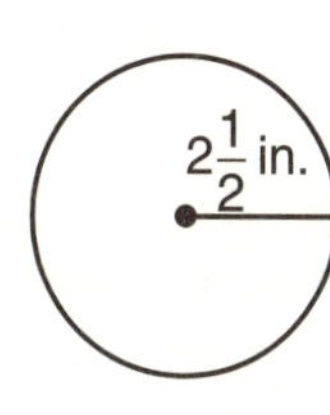

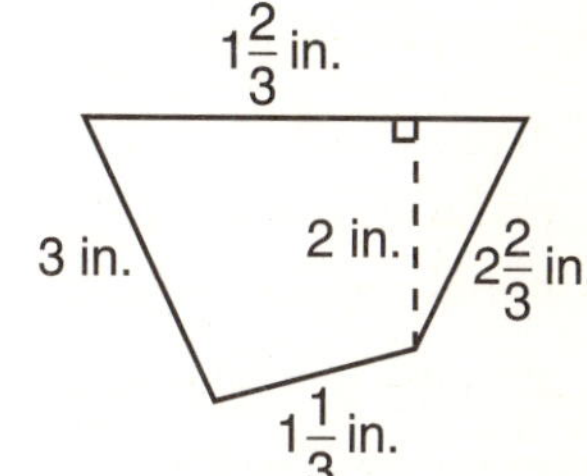

A 1 in.

B 2 in.

C 3 in.

D 6 in.

Use the figures described below to answer Questions 6–7.

Figure A is an equilateral triangle. One side is 5 centimeters.

Figure B is a trapezoid. One base is 0.8 meter long, and the other base is 0.33 meter longer. Its height is 0.8 meter.

Figure C is a square. One side is 18 inches long.

6 For which figure(s) is there enough information to find the perimeter?

F None of the figures

G Figures *A* and *B*

H Figures *A* and *C*

J All of the figures

7 For which figure(s) is there enough information to find the area?

A Figures *A* and *B*

B Figures *B* and *C*

C Figures *A* and *C*

D All of the figures

8 Yolanda looks at the drawing of a shape. She multiplies the length of the base by the height, and then divides the product by 2. Based on her calculations, which statement below is true?

F The shape is triangular, and she has calculated its area.

G The shape is like that of a trapezoid, and she has calculated its area.

H The shape is rectangular, and she has calculated its perimeter.

J The shape is circular, and she has calculated its circumference.

Use the diagrams below for Questions 9–11.

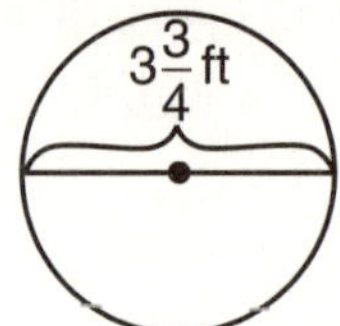

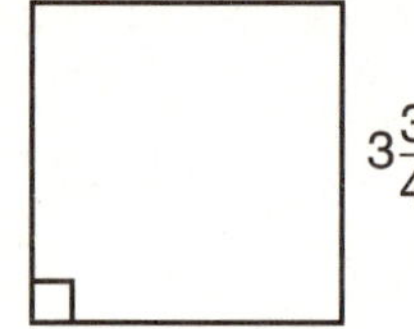

The drawings above represent the tablecloths Margot is thinking about buying. She plans to sew a decorative fringe on each tablecloth.

9 About how much fringe will Margot have to sew on the round tablecloth?

A 7 ft

B 8 ft

C 9 ft

D 12 ft

10 About how much fringe will Margot have to sew on the square tablecloth?

F 10 ft

G 12 ft

H 16 ft

J Not Here

11 Which statement about the areas of the two tablecloths is true?

A The round tablecloth has the greater area.

B The square tablecloth has the greater area.

C The square tablecloth and the round tablecloth have equal areas.

D More information is needed to find the area of the square tablecloth.

12 A triangle has a base of 18 millimeters. What is the area of the triangle in square millimeters if its base is three times as long as its height?

Record your answer and fill in the bubbles on the grid below. Be sure to use the correct place value.

				.		
0	0	0	0		0	0
1	1	1	1		1	1
2	2	2	2		2	2
3	3	3	3		3	3
4	4	4	4		4	4
5	5	5	5		5	5
6	6	6	6		6	6
7	7	7	7		7	7
8	8	8	8		8	8
9	9	9	9		9	9

13 How many more cubic centimeters is the volume of the rectangular prism than the volume of the cube?

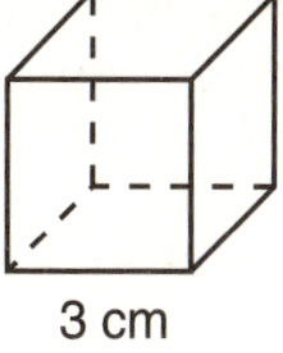

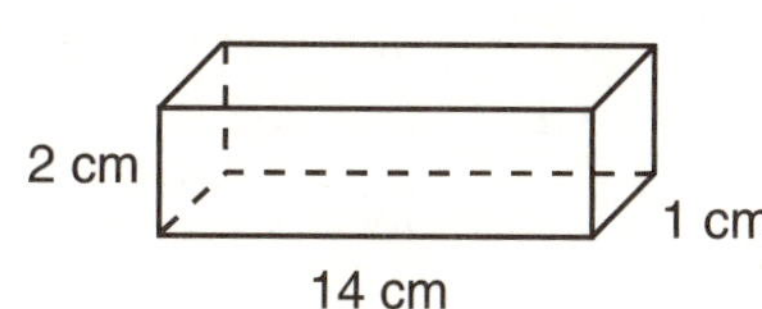

A 1 cm^3

B 10 cm^3

C 19 cm^3

D 22 cm^3

14 Mr. Tyler wants to put fencing around the square patch of flowerbed that he prepared. One side of the patch measures $2\frac{5}{8}$ yards. How much fencing does Mr. Tyler need for the flowerbed?

F About 3 yd

G About 6 yd

H About 12 ft

J About 36 ft

15 A box has a volume of 48 cubic centimeters. Its width measures 4 centimeters. Its length is 3 times as long as the height. What are the length (l) and height (h) of the box?

A $l = 2$ cm, $h = 6$ cm

B $l = 9$ cm, $h = 3$ cm

C $l = 6$ cm, $h = 2$ cm

D $l = 12$ cm, $h = 4$ cm

16 For which figures below can you use the formula $V = s^3$ to find the volume?

Figure 1	**Figure 2**	**Figure 3**	**Figure 4**
$l = 3$ yd	$l = 1\frac{1}{2}$ yd	$l = \frac{4}{2}$ yd	$l = 1\frac{1}{2}$ yd
$w = 3$ yd	$w = \frac{3}{2}$ yd	$w = \frac{6}{3}$ yd	$w = 1\frac{1}{4}$ yd
$h = 2$ yd	$h = \frac{3}{2}$ yd	$h = \frac{8}{4}$ yd	$h = \frac{4}{3}$ yd

F Figures 1 and 2

G Figures 2 and 3

H Figures 2 and 4

J Figures 3 and 4

17 Mr. Ruiz wants to put strips of molding around the ceilings of his living room and dining room. The ceiling of the living room is shaped like a rectangle. Its length is 12 feet. The ceiling of the dining room is shaped like a square. The length of one of its sides is 10 feet.

Living Room

12 ft

Dining Room

10 ft

What information do you need to find how many feet of molding Mr. Ruiz needs for the two rooms?

A The width of the living room

B The height of the living room

C The length of the dining room

D The height of the dining room

18 Ms. Lewis designed a circular walkway in front of her house. The diameter of the walkway is about 6 feet long. How does the diameter of the walkway compare to its circumference?

F The diameter is about $\frac{1}{2}$ as large as the circumference.

G The diameter is about $\frac{1}{3}$ as large as the circumference.

H The diameter is about twice as large as the circumference.

J The diameter is about 3 times as large as the circumference.

19 The length, width, height, and volume of some boxes are shown below.

Length (units)	Width (units)	Height (units)	Volume (cubic units)
2	3	1	6
2	3	2	12
2	3	4	24
2	3	8	48

What happens to the volume of the box when the height is doubled while the length and width remain the same?

A The volume remains the same.

B The volume increases by 6.

C The volume doubles.

D The volume triples.

20 Jennifer cuts out a trapezoid shape from a sheet of paper that measures 11 inches by 14 inches. The bases of the trapezoid measure 3 inches and 5 inches. The height measures 4 inches. How many square inches of paper is left?

Record your answer and fill in the bubbles on the grid below. Be sure to use the correct place value.

				.		
0	0	0	0		0	0
1	1	1	1		1	1
2	2	2	2		2	2
3	3	3	3		3	3
4	4	4	4		4	4
5	5	5	5		5	5
6	6	6	6		6	6
7	7	7	7		7	7
8	8	8	8		8	8
9	9	9	9		9	9

Focus on TEKS Lesson 48 Listing Outcomes

TEKS 6.9A Construct sample spaces using lists.

You can solve some problems by using lists to find all possible outcomes.

A **sample space** is a list of all possible outcomes for an event.
A **fair game** is a game in which all the players have the same chance of winning.

Guided Instruction

Problem

Sharon and Rose are playing a game. Each turn consists of one toss of a fair coin and one toss of a cube, numbered from 1 to 6.
What is the sample space for one turn of the game? How many possible outcomes are there?

Construct a sample space.

Step 1 List all of the possible outcomes for one turn of the game. The possible outcomes for tossing the coin are ____________________.
The possible outcomes for tossing the number cube are ______________________.

Step 2 Combine the outcome Heads with each possible outcome for tossing the number cube. The outcome "a head and the number one" can be written as Heads, 1.

Complete the list of possible outcomes with Heads and a number.

Step 3 Combine the outcome Tails with each possible outcome for tossing the number cube. Complete the list of possible outcomes with Tails and a number.

Possible Coin Outcomes	Possible Number Cube Outcomes
Heads	1
Tails	1

Step 4 Count all possible outcomes in the sample space. __________

Solution

What is the sample space for one turn of the game?

____

____

How many possible outcomes are there? ____________

Another Example

Andrea, Ben, and Chris are playing a game. How many ways can they be paired in groups of two? Let A, B, and C represent Andrea, Ben, and Chris. Make a list of all the possible outcomes. Then cross out any group that is a duplicate of another.

A, B A, C ~~B, A~~ B, C ~~C, A~~ ~~C, B~~

How many groups remain? _________

How many ways can they be paired in groups of two? _________

Apply the TEKS **Use the items to the right to answer Problems 1–3.**

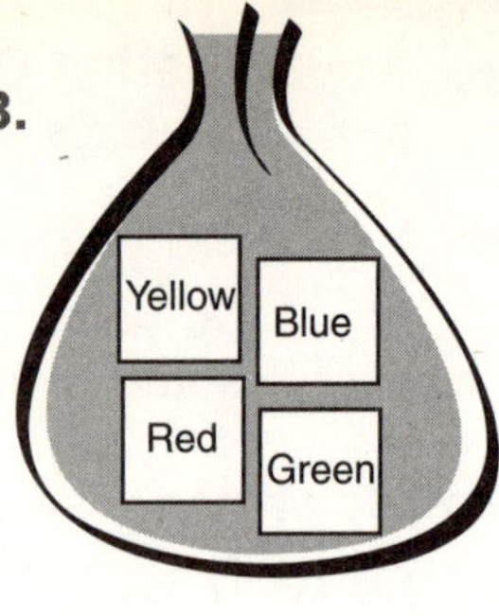

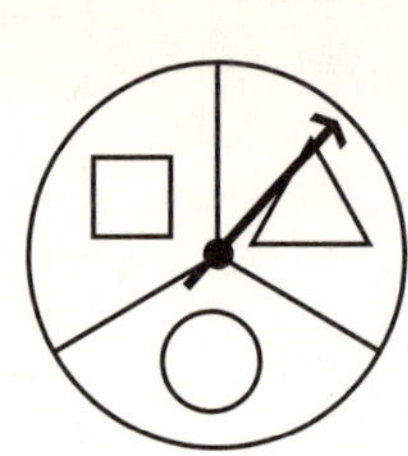

1. What is the sample space if you draw one tile from the bag?

____

2. What is the sample space for spinning the spinner one time?

____

3. List the sample space for spinning the spinner one time and drawing a tile from the bag.

____

____

List all the possible outcomes for each situation. Then find the number of possible outcomes.

4. Choose 2 different letters from the word GARDEN.

____

____

5. Four friends—Amos, Betty, Carlos, and Diego—want one photograph taken of each possible pair of friends. Use A, B, C, and D, and list all the possible pairs that should be photographed.

____

Solve each problem.

6. In a computer game, each player must choose a car or a truck to drive. Each vehicle can be black or red. What is the sample space for choosing a vehicle?

____

How many different vehicles can a player choose? ________________

7. For her vacation, Lanie packed the items in the chart at the right. What is the sample space for Lanie's pants-shirt outfits?

____

____

____

How many different pants-shirt outfits will Lanie have to wear on her vacation? ________________

Clothes to Pack
blue jeans
khaki pants
red T-shirt
blue T-shirt
white T-shirt
black T-shirt

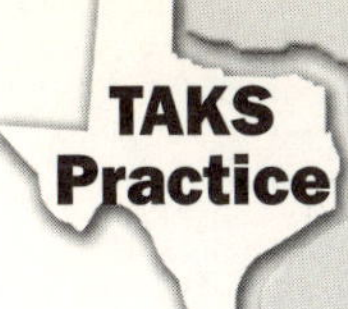

TAKS Objective 5 The student will demonstrate an understanding of probability and statistics.
TEKS 6.9A

DIRECTIONS Read each question. Then circle the letter for the correct answer.

1 Mike listed the *First Spinner*, *Second Spinner* outcomes for spinning these two spinners as: A, 1; A, 2; B, 1; B, 2; B, 3.

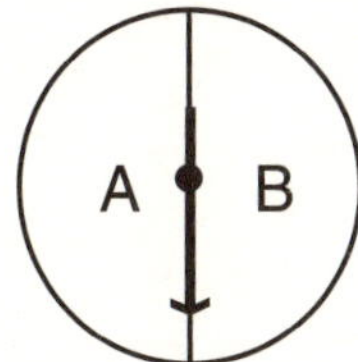

Which of the following is also a possible outcome?

A A, A

B A, 3

C B, 5

D Not Here

2 Chocolate cakes and spice cakes are sold at Jan's Bakery. For each cake, you can choose chocolate, vanilla, or butterscotch icing. Which of the following is NOT a possible cake-icing outcome for sale?

F Vanilla cake with butterscotch icing

G Spice cake with butterscotch icing

H Chocolate cake with chocolate icing

J Spice cake with vanilla icing

3 The list below shows the possible outcomes for pizza toppings and sizes.

Large ⟶ Sausage
Large ⟶ Pepperoni
Large ⟶ Onions
Small ⟶ Sausage
Small ⟶ Pepperoni

Which possible outcome is missing from this list?

A Large pizza with pepperoni

B Small pizza with onions

C Large pizza with onions

D Small pizza with pepperoni

4 Which is NOT a possible outcome if you spin these three spinners?

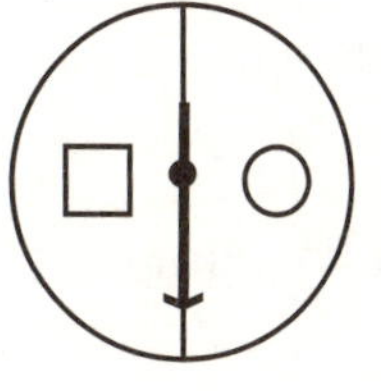

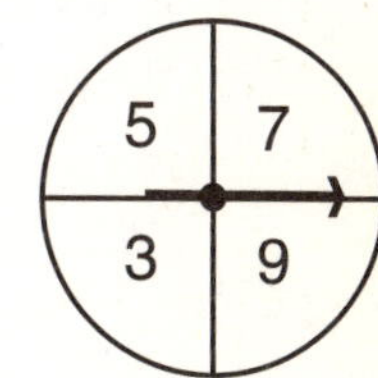

F □, C, 7

G ○, A, 5

H □, C, 4

J ○, T, 9

Focus on TEKS

Lesson 49 Tree Diagrams

TEKS 6.9A Construct sample spaces using tree diagrams.

You can use a tree diagram to show sample spaces.

A **sample space** is a list of all possible outcomes for an event.

Guided Instruction

Problem

Tamara and Stan are playing a game in which they flip a fair coin and spin this spinner each time it is their turn. What is the sample space for one turn of the game? How many possible outcomes are there?

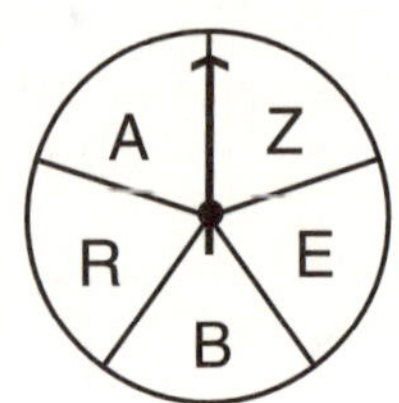

Make a tree diagram.

Step 1 Find the possible outcomes for one turn in the game. What are the possible outcomes for flipping a coin?

____

What are the possible outcomes for spinning the spinner?

____

Step 2 Draw a tree to combine Heads with all of the possible outcomes for spinning the spinner.

Step 3 Draw a tree to match Tails with all of the possible outcomes for spinning the spinner.

Step 4 Each final branch of the tree represents one possible outcome, so count the number of branches to find the sample space.

Tree Diagram

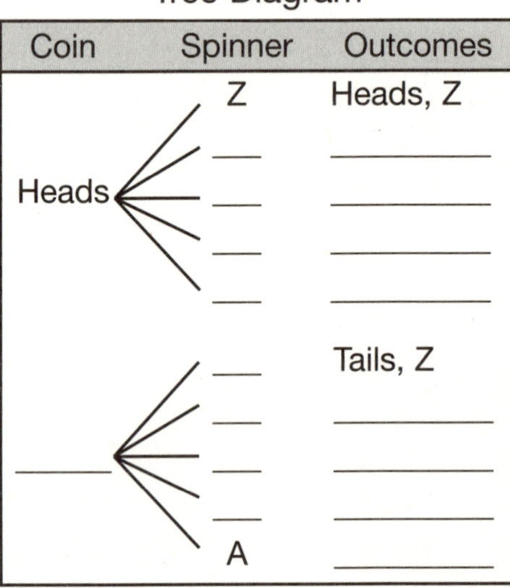

Solution

What is the sample space for one turn of the game?

____

____

How many possible outcomes are there? ____________

Apply the TEKS

Use the items below to answer Problems 1–4.

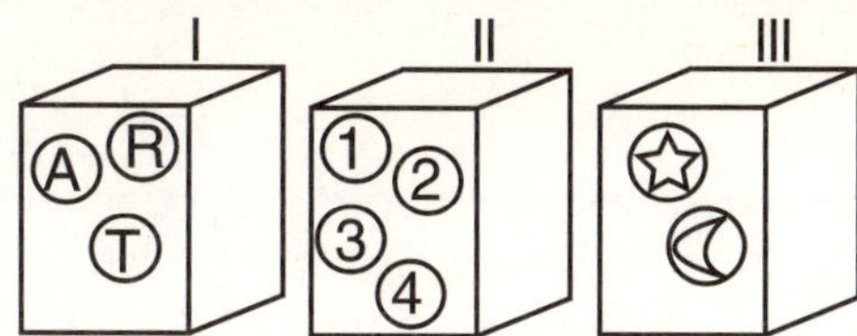

1. Draw a tree diagram to show all the possible outcomes for drawing a ball from box I and a ball from box II.

2. How many possible outcomes are there for drawing a ball from boxes I and II?

   ____

3. Draw a tree diagram to show all the possible outcomes for drawing a ball from boxes II and III.

4. How many possible outcomes are there for drawing a ball from boxes II and III?

   ____

5. The Snack Shack prepares chicken or tuna on white, wheat, or rye bread. Draw a tree diagram to show the possible outcomes. How many different sandwiches are possible?

   ____

Solve the problem.

6. How can you use mathematics to find the number of possible outcomes for two or more events?

   ____

   Explain your answer.

   ____

   ____

   ____

   ____

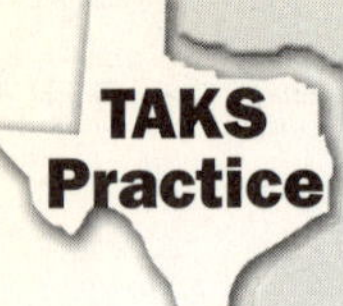

TAKS Objective 5 The student will demonstrate an understanding of probability and statistics.
TEKS 6.9A

DIRECTIONS Read each question. Then circle the letter for the correct answer.

Use the pictures below to answer Questions 1–2.

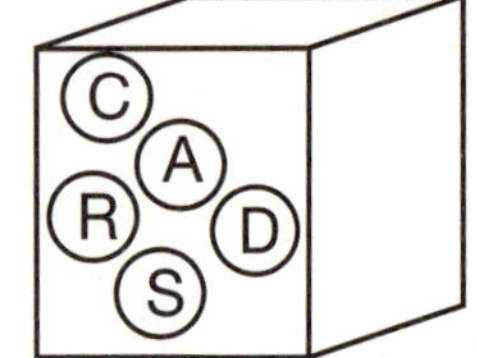

1 Which shows the correct tree diagram for tossing a coin and spinning the spinner?

A

B

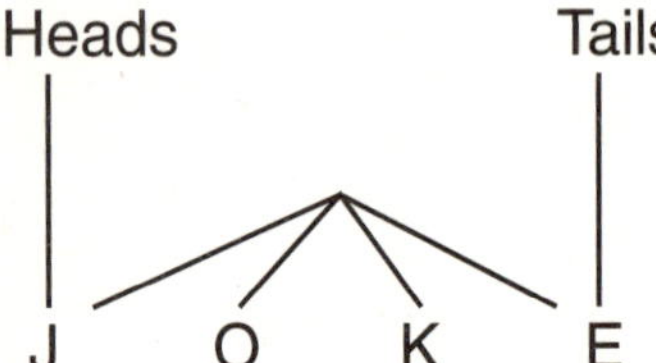

C

D

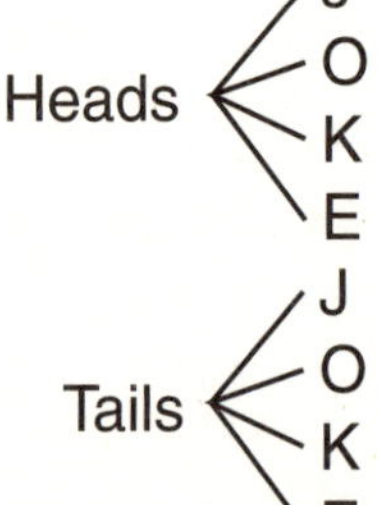

2 A partial sample space for drawing a tile and spinning the spinner is shown below.

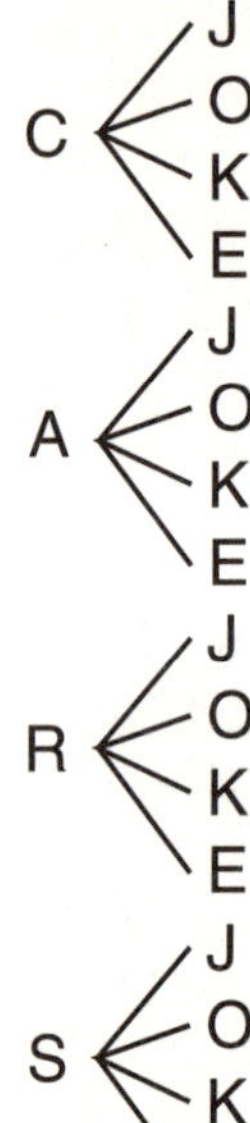

Which is the missing section?

F

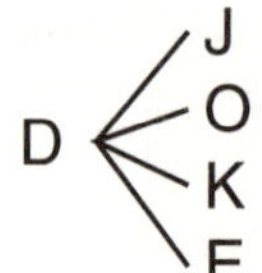

H

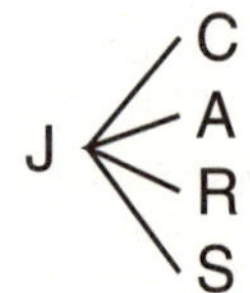

G

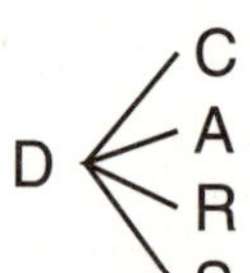

J

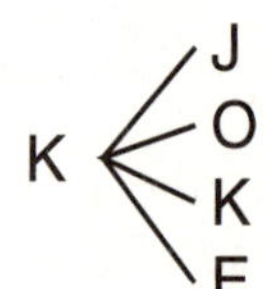

3 Which is NOT an outcome for tossing four coins?

A H,H,H,H

B H,T,H, T

C T, T, T, H

D Not Here

Focus on TEKS

Lesson 50 Theoretical Probability

TEKS 6.9B Find the probabilities of a simple event and its complement and describe the relationship between the two.

You can find the probability of a simple event.

Theoretical probability is a ratio of how likely it is that an event will happen based on all the possible outcomes.

$P(E) = \frac{\text{number of favorable outcomes}}{\text{number of possible outcomes}}$ Read $P(E)$ as "the probability of event E."

A **certain event** has a probability of 1 and will always occur. An **impossible event** has a probability of 0 and will never occur. If $P(E)$ is the probability of an event occurring, the probability that the event will not occur is $1 - P(E)$.

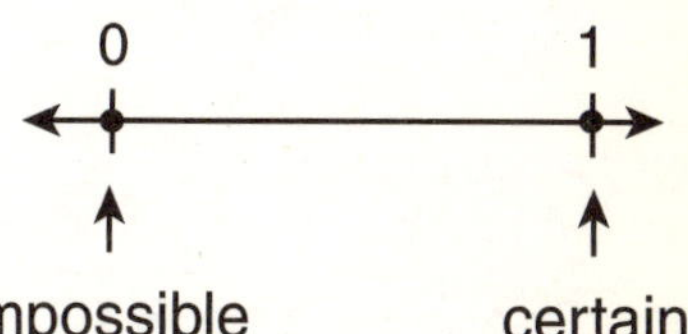

Guided Instruction

Problem 1 If Mason draws a green cube from a bag, he wins a prize. There are 5 red cubes, 8 green cubes, and 7 yellow cubes in a bag. What is the probability that Mason will win a prize?

Find P(green).

Step 1 Find the number of possible outcomes.
What is the total number of cubes in the bag? ____________

Step 2 Find the number of favorable outcomes.

What is the number of green cubes in the bag? ____________

Step 3 Write a fraction. Simplify the fraction if possible.

P(green) = ______________________

Solution What is the probability that Mason will win a prize? _______

Another Problem

Problem 2 What is the probability that Mason will NOT draw a green cube?

Find P(not green).

Step 1 Use the probability that Mason will draw a green cube.

P(green) = _________

Step 2 Subtract the probability that Mason will draw a green cube from 1.

$1 - \frac{2}{5} =$ _________

So, *P*(not green) = _________

Solution What is the probability that Mason will NOT draw a green cube? ________

Apply the TEKS

Use the spinner at the right to find the probability for each event.

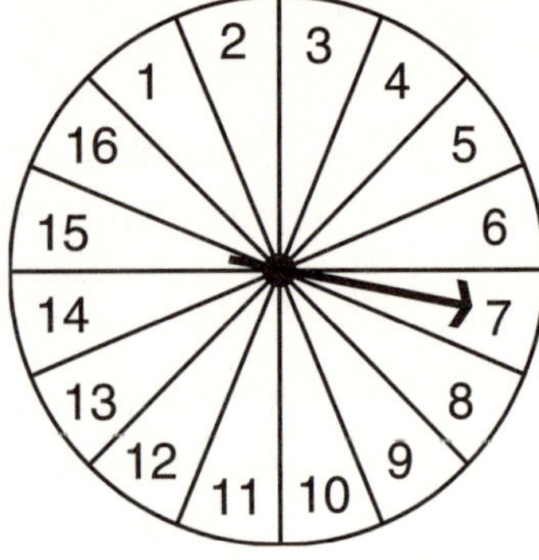

1. $P(6)$ _________
2. $P(\text{not } 6)$ _________
3. $P(\text{even number})$ _________
4. $P(\text{multiple of } 3)$ _________
5. $P(\text{not a multiple of } 3)$ _________
6. $P(\text{divisible by } 4)$ _________
7. $P(\text{not divisible by } 4)$ _________
8. $P(24)$ _________
9. $P(\text{less than } 10)$ _________

Solve each problem.

10. If Jason tosses a cube numbered from 1 to 6, what is the probability that he will NOT toss a 3?

____

11. What is the probability that Jason will toss a number less than 7?

____

12. A box contains 25 cubes. If you select one cube, the probability of choosing a red cube is $\frac{6}{25}$. How many of the cubes in the box are red?

____

How many of the cubes in the box are not red? _________

13. A bag has 20 balls numbered from 1 to 20. If you guess the number of the ball you draw from the bag, you win a prize. What is the probability that you will NOT win a prize?

____

14. If Keri draws a card from a stack, the probability that it will be a 10 is $\frac{4}{13}$. What is the probability that the card will NOT be a 10?

____

Explain your reasoning.

____

____

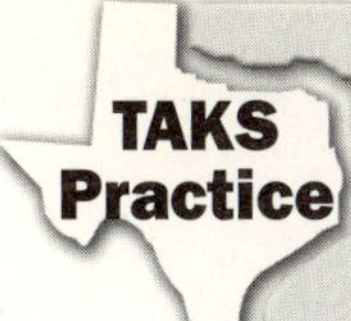

TAKS Objective 5 The student will demonstrate an understanding of probability and statistics.
TEKS 6.9B

DIRECTIONS Read each question. Then circle the letter for the correct answer.

Use the cards below to answer Questions 1–6.

9	3	5	9
7	4	6	5
9	2	6	9

1 What is the probability of NOT drawing a 6?

A $\frac{1}{6}$

B $\frac{2}{3}$

C $\frac{5}{6}$

D 1

2 Which has a greater probability than drawing a 5?

F Drawing a 9

G Drawing a 6

H Drawing a 4

J Drawing a 1

3 What is the probability of drawing a number less than 2?

A 1

B $\frac{11}{12}$

C $\frac{10}{11}$

D 0

4 What is the difference between the probability of drawing a 5 and the probability of drawing a 2?

F 1

G $\frac{1}{2}$

H $\frac{1}{11}$

J $\frac{1}{12}$

5 If you draw a 9 and then draw another card without replacing the 9, what is the probability that you will draw a 4?

A $\frac{1}{12}$

B $\frac{1}{11}$

C $\frac{1}{9}$

D $\frac{1}{4}$

6 What is $P(9)$?

F 1

G $\frac{2}{3}$

H $\frac{1}{3}$

J 0

Focus on TEKS

Lesson 51 Experimental Probability

TEKS 6.3C Use ratios to make predictions in proportional situations.

TEKS 6.9B Find the probabilities of a simple event and its complement and describe the relationship between the two.

You can use experimental data to determine probability and make predictions.

Experimental probability is a ratio based on experimental data that is found by repeating the experiment several times.

$$P(E) = \frac{\text{number of times an event happens}}{\text{number of times the experiment is done}}$$

Guided Instruction

Problem 1

Jason did an experiment to test his corn seeds' ability to germinate. Of the 100 corn seeds Jason planted, 88 sprouted. What is the experimental probability that Jason's corn seeds will sprout?

Use the probability formula.

Step 1 Find the total number of events.
How many corn seeds did Jason plant? ___________

Step 2 Find the number of favorable events.
How many seeds sprouted? ___________

Step 3 Write the fraction for $\frac{\text{favorable events}}{\text{total events}}$.
What fraction describes $\frac{\text{sprouted seeds}}{\text{total seeds}}$? ___________

Solution

What is the probability that Jason's corn seeds will sprout?

____

Another Problem

Problem 2

Suppose Jason plants 2,000 of the same corn seeds. Predict how many will sprout.

Write and solve a proportion.

Step 1 Use the experimental probability to write a proportion.

$$\frac{88 \leftarrow \text{sprouted seeds}}{100 \leftarrow \text{total seeds}} = \frac{s \leftarrow \text{sprouted seeds}}{2{,}000 \leftarrow \text{total seeds}}$$

Step 2 Solve the proportion.

$100s = 88 \times 2{,}000$

$100s = 176{,}000$

$s =$ _______________

Solution

Predict the number of seeds Jason can expect to sprout if he plants 2,000 seeds. ___________

Apply the TEKS **Use the results of the experiments to answer each problem.**

Experiment: Draw a card from the bag. Record the shape. Replace the card.	
Dan's Results	Jan's Results
Shape Tally	Shape Tally
□ 𝍸 I	□ IIII
○ III	○ IIII
△ I	△ III
♡ II	♡ I

1. What is Dan's experimental probability of drawing a triangle?

____

2. What is Dan's experimental probability of NOT drawing a square?

____

3. What is Jan's experimental probability of NOT drawing a square?

____

4. There are 48 cards in the bag. Use Dan's results to predict how many of the cards are circles.

____

5. Use Jan's results to predict how many of the cards in the bag are circles.

____

6. Why are Jan's results not the same as Dan's results?

____

____

7. Combine the results of Dan's experiment and Jan's experiment. Use the results to predict the number of circles in the bag._________

8. Which shape do you predict is on the fewest cards? ___________

9. Suppose that 23 of the 48 cards in the bag are squares. If you do the experiment 48 times, do you think you are likely to get exactly 23 squares? Why or why not?

____

____

10. Suppose Dan and Jan did the experiment 300 times. Do you think they are more likely or less likely to accurately predict the number of each shape in the bag? ____________ Explain your reasoning.

____

____

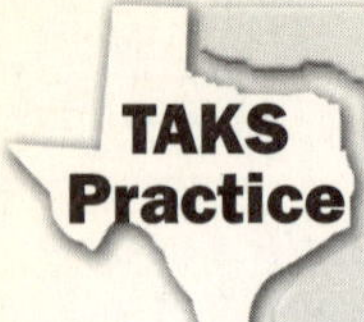

TAKS Objective 2 The student will demonstrate an understanding of patterns, relationships, and algebraic reasoning.
TEKS 6.3C

TAKS Objective 5 The student will demonstrate an understanding of probability and statistics.
TEKS 6.9B

DIRECTIONS Read each question. Then circle the letter for the correct answer.

1 Gloria hit 38 out of 50 balls at batting practice. Which is the best prediction of the number of balls she will hit out of 300 balls?

A 72

B 154

C 228

D 280

2 The table below shows Greg's experimental results for spinning a spinner 100 times.

A	B	C
48	12	40

Which spinner did Greg most likely spin?

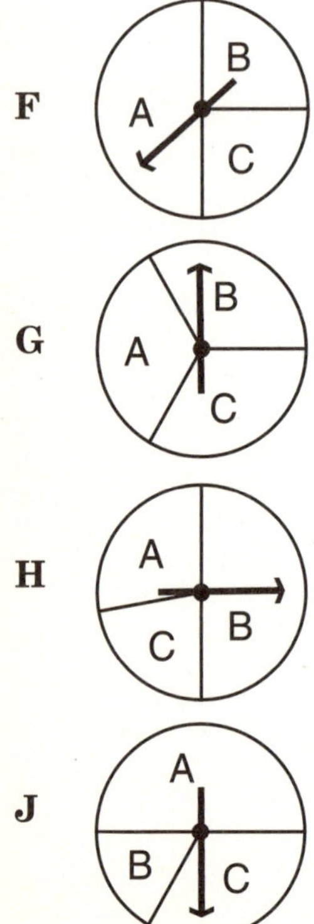

Jessica measured the heights of some pine trees she planted last year. The table below shows the results.

Number of Trees	Height (in inches)
2	$10\frac{1}{2}$
3	13
4	$15\frac{1}{4}$
5	$11\frac{3}{4}$

Which is most likely true of the next tree she measures?

A It will be 14 inches tall.

B It will be less than 15 inches tall.

C It will be less than 11 inches tall.

D It will be exactly 13 inches tall.

Sarah tossed a number cube numbered 1 to 6 one hundred times. Her chart shows that a 3 came up 15 times. Based on her experiment, predict how many times she would toss a 3 if she tossed the cube 10,000 times.

Record your answer and fill in the bubbles on the grid below. Be sure to use the correct place value.

				.		
0	0	0	0		0	0
1	1	1	1		1	1
2	2	2	2		2	2
3	3	3	3		3	3
4	4	4	4		4	4
5	5	5	5		5	5
6	6	6	6		6	6
7	7	7	7		7	7
8	8	8	8		8	8
9	9	9	9		9	9

Focus on TEKS

Lesson 52 PROBLEM-SOLVING STRATEGY: Make an Organized List

TEKS 6.11A Identify and apply mathematics to everyday experiences, to activities in and outside of school, with other disciplines, and with other mathematical topics.

TEKS 6.11B Use a problem-solving model.

TEKS 6.11C Select or develop an appropriate problem-solving strategy.

TEKS 6.11D Select tools such as real objects, manipulatives, paper/pencil, and techniques such as mental math, estimation, and number sense to solve problems.

You can make an organized list to help you solve problems.
Use the problem-solving guide on page 288 to help you.

Guided Instruction

Problem

Jake's Nursery has red, white, and pink geraniums in 4-inch, 6-inch, and 8-inch pots. How many different size and color combinations does Jake's Nursery carry?

Understand the problem.

What are you trying to find? ________________________________

____

Make a plan.

You can make an organized list of the possible combinations of colors and pot sizes. Then count the number of combinations.

Solve the problem.

List all of the possible combinations of pots and red geraniums:

____

List all of the possible combinations of pots and white geraniums:

____

List all of the possible combinations of pots and pink geraniums:

____

How many possible combinations are there? ________

Check your answer.

Multiply the number of color choices by the number of pot-size choices.

Color choices × Pot-size choices = Possible combinations

3 × 3 = ________

Apply the TEKS **Make an organized list to solve each problem.**

1. Hannah has red, yellow, and green scarves. She has black, white, and brown gloves. What are the different scarf, glove combinations Hannah can make? ______________________

____

____

2. Use the list shown to the right. What are the possible soup, sandwich, drink combinations?
Write P for split pea, N for chicken noodle, T for tuna, C for cheese, H for ham, M for milk, and J for juice.

Soups	Sandwiches	Drinks
Split Pea	Tuna	Milk
Chicken Noodle	Cheese	Juice
	Ham	

____

____

3. How many different 4-digit numbers can you make with the numbers 2, 4, 6, and 8?

____

____

____

4. School sweatshirts come in gray (G), red (R), blue (B), and white (W). If Brent buys three different-color sweatshirts, what are the possible color combinations? Note that gray, red, blue is the same as red, blue, gray or blue, gray, red. ______________________

5. What are all of the possible ways to multiply two whole numbers to get a product of 36? Treat $a \times b$ and $b \times a$ as two different expressions.

____

____

6. If you toss three coins, what are the possible outcomes?

____

7. If you toss three coins, which outcome is most likely, three coins that are all heads or all tails, or two of one type and one of the other?

____

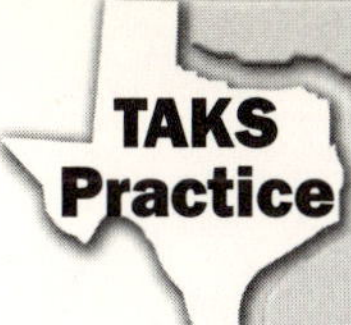

TAKS Objective 6 The student will demonstrate an understanding of the mathematical processes and tools used in problem solving.

TEKS 6.11A, 6.11B, 6.11C, 6.11D

DIRECTIONS Read each question. Then circle the letter for the correct answer.

1 Karen has a dog, a cat, a rabbit, and a gerbil. She has blue, red, green, and yellow ribbons. How many different combinations of one ribbon on one pet can Karen make?

A 4

B 8

C 16

D 32

2 Dinner at David's Diner comes with a choice of 2 different soups, 3 different salads, and 3 different types of potato. How many different combinations are there?

F 24

G 18

H 12

J 8

3 Each of 5 friends, Andy, Barbara, Carlos, Dotty, and Eileen, hugged each other goodbye. How many hugs was that in all?

A 5

B 10

C 20

D 24

4 If Mandy tosses 4 coins, which of the following outcomes is most likely?

F Four heads

G One tail and three heads

H Two heads and two tails

J Three tails and one head

5 Austin tossed two cubes each numbered from one to six. How many different sums are possible?

A 6

B 11

C 12

D 36

6 John's model train has four cars, an engine, a flat car, a box car, and a passenger car. In how many different ways can John arrange the cars if the engine is always first?

F 24

G 12

H 6

J 4

Building Stamina®

Read each question. Then circle the letter for the correct answer. If a correct answer is not here, mark the letter for "Not Here."

1 The probability that Audrey will visit her grandmother this weekend is $\frac{3}{5}$. What is the probability that she will NOT visit her grandmother this weekend?

A 1

B $\frac{2}{3}$

C $\frac{3}{5}$

D $\frac{2}{5}$

2 For her turn at a game, Dee spun these spinners one time.

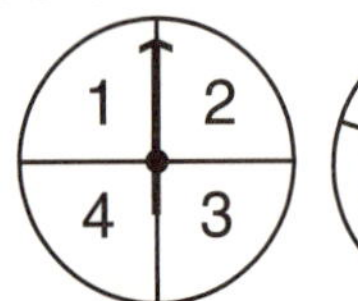

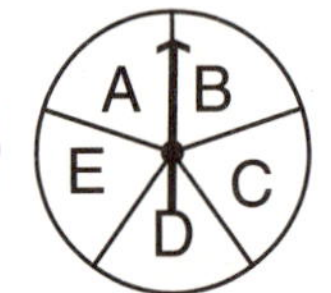

Which shows all the possible outcomes for her spin?

F

All Possible Outcomes			
1,A	2,A	3,A	4,A
1,B	2,B	3,B	4,B
1,E	2,E	3,E	4,E

G

All Possible Outcomes			
1,A	2,A	3,A	4,A
1,1	2,2	3,3	4,4
1,E	2,E	3,E	4,E

H

All Possible Outcomes			
1,A	2,A	3,A	4,A
1,B	2,B	3,B	4,B
1,C	2,C	3,C	4,C
1,D	2,D	3,D	4,D
1,E	2,E	3,E	4,E

J Not Here

3 A bag contains 3 white marbles, 4 black marbles, 6 striped marbles, 8 yellow marbles, and 3 red marbles. If Ismael draws a marble at random, what is the probability that he will draw a striped marble?

A $\frac{1}{8}$

B $\frac{1}{6}$

C $\frac{1}{4}$

D $\frac{1}{3}$

4 What is the probability of NOT picking a consonant from this bag?

F $\frac{1}{12}$

G $\frac{1}{3}$

H $\frac{2}{3}$

J Not Here

5 A spinner has only odd numbers. What is the probability that you will NOT spin an odd number?

A 0

B $\frac{1}{4}$

C $\frac{1}{3}$

D 1

6 If you toss a cube numbered from 1 to 6, which has the greatest probability?

F Tossing a number less than 10

G Tossing an odd number

H Tossing a multiple of 2

J Tossing a 6

7 Ron made 16 out of 25 baskets from the foul line. Using this data, predict the number of baskets he will make from the foul line if he shoots 200 times?

A 64

B 72

C 92

D 128

8 Which experiment is this tree diagram for?

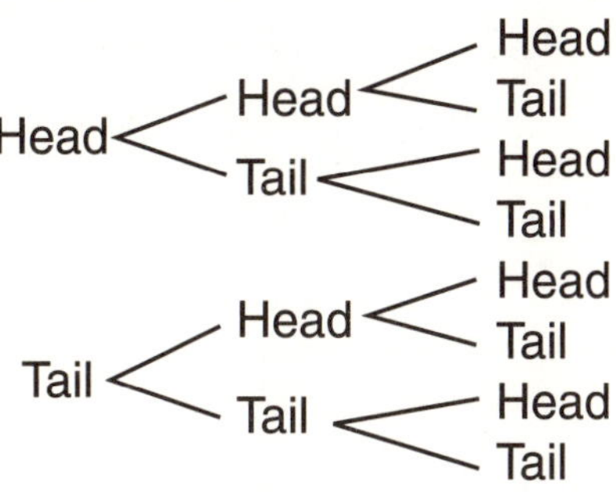

F Tossing 2 pennies

G Tossing 3 dimes

H Tossing 4 quarters

J Tossing a penny and a dime

9 Suppose you draw one of these cards. What is the probability that it will NOT be an S?

S U C C E S S

A $\frac{4}{7}$

B $\frac{3}{5}$

C $\frac{1}{2}$

D $\frac{3}{8}$

10 Five friends are going to the movies. How many different ways can they sit in a row if Amy is in the middle?

F 24

G 16

H 15

J 5

11 An inspector in a factory found 3 out of 150 shirts were defective. About how many out of 30,000 shirts will be defective?

Record your answer and fill in the bubbles on the grid below. Be sure to use the correct place value.

				.		
0	0	0	0		0	0
1	1	1	1		1	1
2	2	2	2		2	2
3	3	3	3		3	3
4	4	4	4		4	4
5	5	5	5		5	5
6	6	6	6		6	6
7	7	7	7		7	7
8	8	8	8		8	8
9	9	9	9		9	9

12 Joan counted the number of eggs in some chickens' nests.

<table>
<tr><th>Nest</th><th>Number of Eggs</th></tr>
<tr><td>1</td><td>||||</td></tr>
<tr><td>2</td><td>~~||||~~ |||</td></tr>
<tr><td>3</td><td>||||</td></tr>
<tr><td>4</td><td>|||</td></tr>
</table>

Using her data, what is the probability that the next nest will have 4 eggs?

F $\frac{1}{8}$

G $\frac{1}{4}$

H $\frac{1}{2}$

J $\frac{3}{4}$

13 Sam has 2 red, 1 green, 3 blue, and 2 black pens in his desk. What is the probability that he will draw out 2 black pens?

A $\frac{1}{2}$

B $\frac{1}{4}$

C $\frac{1}{5}$

D $\frac{1}{8}$

14 A bag contains blue and green tiles. If you pick a tile without looking, $P(\text{blue}) = \frac{4}{16}$. What is $P(\text{green})$?

F $\frac{1}{16}$

G $\frac{1}{2}$

H $\frac{3}{4}$

J Not Here

15 There are 10 balls numbered 0 through 9 in a bag. If you draw a ball from the bag and then draw another ball without replacing the first ball, which outcome is NOT possible?

A 9, 9

B 9, 3

C 8, 5

D 0, 9

16 A partial sample space for spinning each spinner below once is shown.

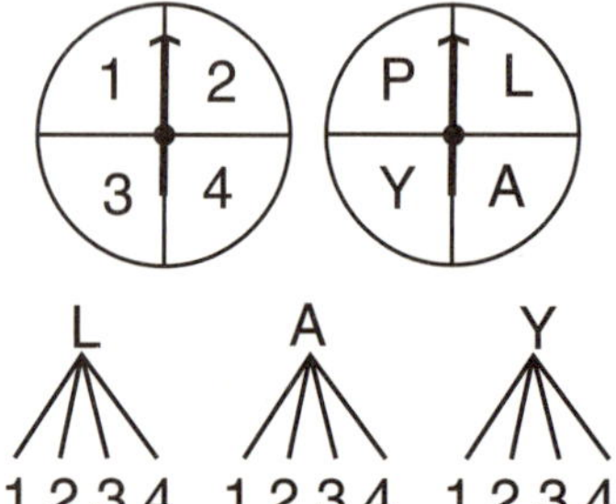

L: 1 2 3 4 A: 1 2 3 4 Y: 1 2 3 4

Which is the missing part of the tree diagram for spinning these two spinners?

F P: 1 2 3 4

G P: P L A Y

H 1: P L A Y

J 1: 1 2 3 4

17 Which lists all of the possible outcomes for spinning the three spinners?

A M,7; M,3; M,5; K,7; K,3; K,5; 7,C; 7,D; 3,C; 3,D; 5,C; 5,D

B M,K,7; M,K,3; M,K,5; 7,C,D; 3,C,D; 5,C,D

C M,7,C; M,7,D; M,5,C; M,5,D; M,3,C; M,3,D; K,7,C; K,7,D; K,5,C; K,5,D; K,3,C; K,3,D

D Not Here

18 Darius is thinking of a whole number between and including 1 and 20. What is the probability that he is thinking of an even, two digit number?

F $\frac{1}{4}$

G $\frac{3}{10}$

H $\frac{11}{20}$

J $\frac{1}{2}$

Use the tree diagram below to answer Questions 19–20.

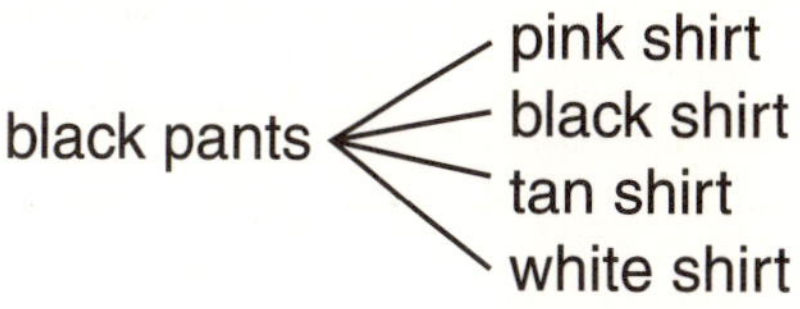

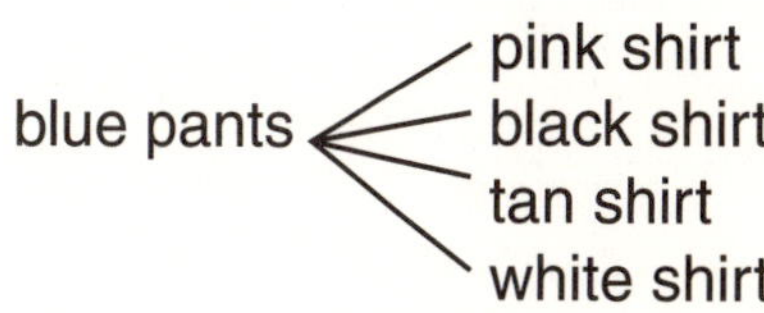

19 How many possible combinations of pants and shirts does Grace have to choose from?

A 4

B 5

C 6

D 8

20 What is the probability that Grace will choose blue pants and a pink shirt?

F $\frac{1}{2}$

G $\frac{1}{4}$

H $\frac{1}{5}$

J $\frac{1}{8}$

Notes

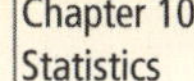

Focus on TEKS

Lesson 53 Mean, Median, Mode, and Range

TEKS 6.10B Identify mean, median, mode, and range of a set of data.

You can use mean, median, mode, and range to describe a set of data.

The **mean** is the sum of the data items divided by the number of addends, or data items. The mean is also called the average.

The **median** is the middle number or the average of the two middle numbers in a set of data arranged in numerical order.

The **mode** is the number that occurs most often in a data set. The data set may have no mode, one mode, or more than one mode.

The **range** is the difference between the greatest and least numbers in a set of data.

Guided Instruction

Problem 1

Students in Mrs. Harper's Advanced Mathematics class received these test scores: 82, 90, 87, 93, 85, 78, 90, 94, 84. What is the mean or average test score of this data set? Suppose an absent student scored 97 on the make-up test. How does the additional test score affect the mean?

Step 1 Find sum of the numbers.

78 + 82 + 84 + 85 + 87 + 90 + 90 + 93 + 94 = ___________

Step 2 Divide the sum by the number of addends or data items.

783 ÷ _________ = _________

Step 3 Find the new mean when the extra score is added.

78 + 82 + 84 + 85 + 87 + 90 + 90 + 93 + 94 + 97 = ___________

___________ ÷ 10 = ___________

Step 4 Compare the new mean to the original mean.

Did the mean increase, decrease, or remain the same? ___________

Solution

What is the mean of the original data set? ___________

How does the additional test score of 97 affect the mean?

____

Guided Instruction

Another Problem

Problem 2

The Dalmations entered at the Dog Show had the following heights in inches: 19.6, 23.5, 21.4, 22.5, 20.2, 20.8, 22.5, 20.8, 22.8, 19.7, and 22.5. What is the range of the heights? What is the mode of the heights? What is the median of the heights?

Use numerical order to help find the range, mode, and median of the data set.

Step 1 Arrange the data items in numerical order.

19.6, 19.7, 20.2, 20.8, 20.8, 21.4, 22.5, 22.5, 22.5, 22.8, 23.5

Step 2 Identify the least number and the greatest number.

least: __________ greatest: __________

Step 3 Subtract the least number from the greatest number.

The difference is the range.

__________ − __________ = __________ in.

Step 4 Find the number that is listed the greatest number of times.

This is the mode.

__________ is listed 3 times.

Step 5 Find the middle number or the average of the two middle numbers. This is the median.

The median is __________.

Solution

The range of the data set is __________, the mode of the data set is __________, and the median of the data set is __________.

Other Examples

Some data sets have no mode or more than one mode.

No Mode

In the following data set, no number is listed more than one time. So this data set does not have a mode.

145, 206, 219, 312, 347, 402

Multiple Modes

In the following data set, more than one number is listed the greatest number of times. The data set has more than one mode.

2.4, 2.4, 2.5, 2.6, 2.7, 2.7, 2.9, 3.0

The numbers 2.4 and 2.6 are each listed two times.

So 2.4 and 2.6 are the modes of this data set.

Apply the TEKS **Find the mean, median, mode(s), and range of each data set. Indicate when a data set has no mode.**

1. 13 18 14 12 15 14 19

mean: ____________ median: ____________ mode(s): ____________ range: ____________

2. 8.2 7.7 8.3 8.0 8.6 7.8

mean: ____________ median: ____________ mode(s): ____________ range: ____________

3. 77 77 77 84 77 77 77

mean: ____________ median: ____________ mode(s): ____________ range: ____________

4. 14 12 19 15 12 22 20 14

mean: ____________ median: ____________ mode(s): ____________ range: ____________

5. 4 9 8 12 3 17 15 9 10 5 7

mean: ____________ median: ____________ mode(s): ____________ range: ____________

6. 58 71 93 84 52 67 66 91 89 70 84

mean: ____________ median: ____________ mode(s): ____________ range: ____________

7. 6.7 7.0 7.2 6.5 7.4 6.9 7.7 7.7 7.4 8.6 7.7 7.4 6.7

mean: ____________ median: ____________ mode(s): ____________ range: ____________

Use the table to answer Problems 8–12.

At the county fair, the judges recorded the weights in pounds of the giant pumpkins.

Weights of Pumpkins		
257	259	249
267	247	249
263	260	253

8. What is the mean weight of the giant pumpkins? ____________

9. What is the median weight of the giant pumpkins? ____________

10. What is the mode weight? ____________

11. What is the range of the weights? ____________

12. Describe how the additional entry of a pumpkin weighing 276 pounds will affect the original mean, median, mode, and range? ____________________________

____

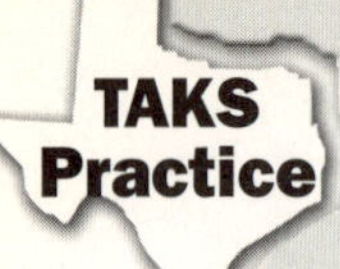

TAKS Objective 5 The student will demonstrate an understanding of probability and statistics.
TEKS 6.10B

DIRECTIONS Read each question. Then circle the letter for the correct answer.

1 What is the mean of the data set?

5	6	6	5	4	4	6
4	6	5	6	4	4	5

A 4

B 5

C 6

D Not Here

2 Which data set has a median of 16, a mode of 16, and a range of 16?

F 13, 17, 19, 12, 15, 29

G 20, 28, 14, 12, 16, 22, 16

H 14, 20, 12, 16, 22, 14, 28

J 16, 21, 13, 23, 17, 16

3 Which number could be added to the data set to produce a median of 87?

95	89	74	82	79
97	73	85	90	?

A Any number less than 73

B Any number less than 85

C Any number greater than 85

D Any number greater than or equal to 89

4 Which number, when added to the data set, will NOT change the mean?

107	119	158	106	131
102	102	135	?	

F 102

G 113

H 120

J Any number greater than 120

5 Which number could be eliminated from the data set without changing the median, mode, or range?

220	224	226	237	235
217	222	224	224	

A 217

B 224

C 237

D Not Here

Focus on TEKS

Lesson 54 Make Bar Graphs

TEKS 6.10D Solve problems by collecting, organizing, displaying, and interpreting data.

You can display data in a bar graph to compare numbers and solve problems.

A **bar graph** shows numerical data and is used to compare data. Bar graphs can have vertical or horizontal bars.

Guided Instruction

Problem

A survey of all sixth-grade students at one school showed that 18 students had no pets, 19 students had 1 pet, 9 students had 2 pets, 8 students had 3 pets, 3 students had 4 pets, 1 student had 5 pets, and 2 students had more than 5 pets. How many more students had 1 pet than had 4 pets?

Use a bar graph to display and compare the data.

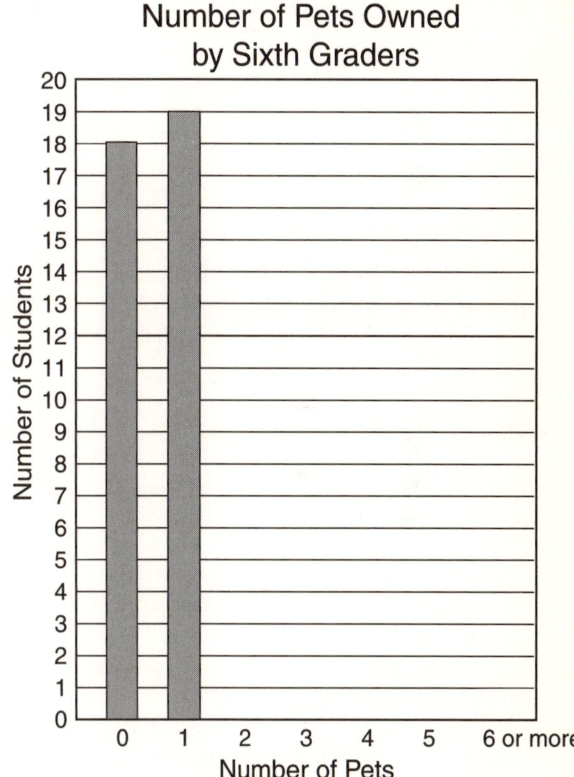

Step 1 Draw the axes of the graph and label each axis.

Step 2 Enter the information from the problem by drawing bars. Each bar shows the number of students who have the indicated number of pets.

Step 3 Read the graph to find the number of students who have 1 pet and the number of students who have 4 pets.

Step 4 Subtract. $19 - 3 =$ __________

Solution How many more students had 1 pet than had 4 pets? __________

Another Example

How many students have 2 or more pets?

Read the information from the graph and add.

$9 + 8 + 3 + 1 + 2 =$ __________

How many students have 2 or more pets? __________

Apply the TEKS **Use the graph to answer Problems 1–3.**

1. What is the approximate circulation of the Houston daily newspaper?

2. About how many fewer papers are sold in Austin than in Dallas?

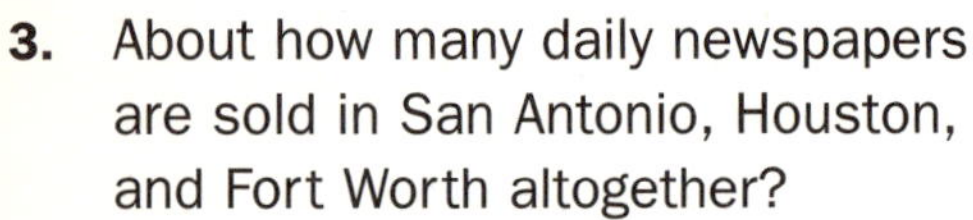

3. About how many daily newspapers are sold in San Antonio, Houston, and Fort Worth altogether?

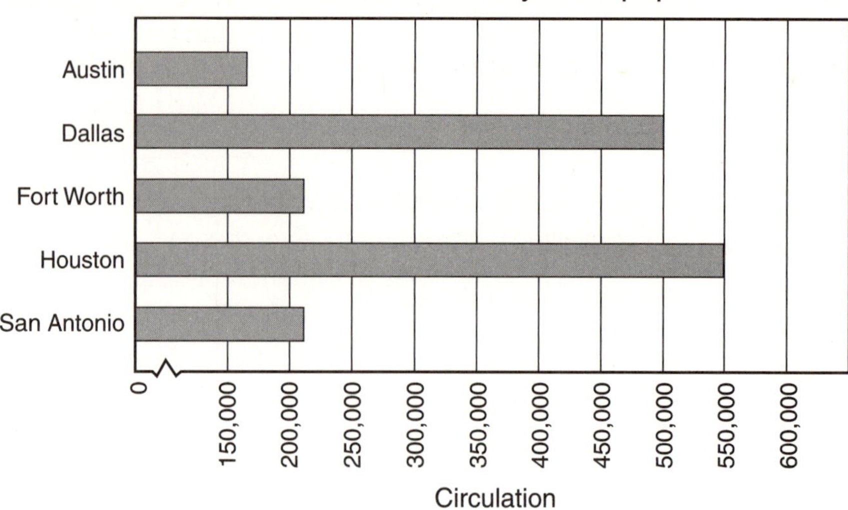

4. Use the information in the table to the right to make a vertical bar graph.

5. What is the range of the points scored by the Cowboys in their eight Super Bowl appearances?

6. What is the mode of the Cowboys' Super Bowl scores?

7. What is the median of the Cowboys' Super Bowl winning scores?

Describe how to find the median using the bar graph.

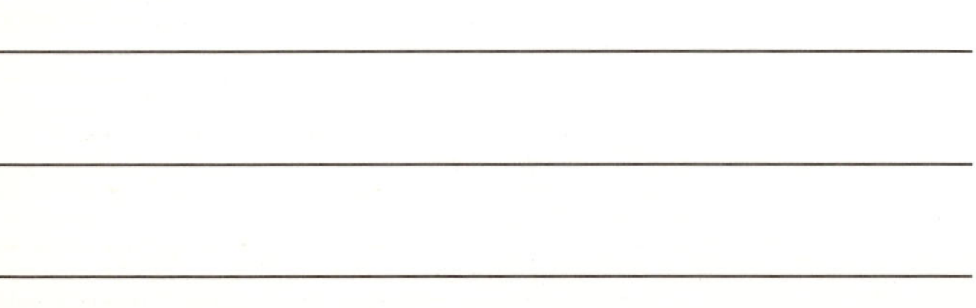

Points Scored by Dallas Cowboys in Super Bowls

Year	Score	Year	Score
1971	13	1979	31
1972	24*	1993	52*
1976	17	1994	30*
1978	27*	1996	27*

* = winning score

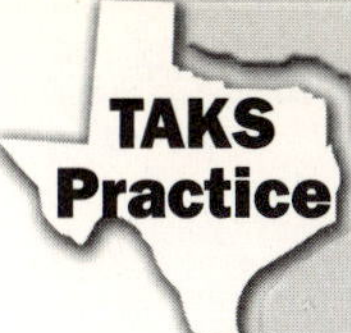

TAKS Objective 5 The student will demonstrate an understanding of probability and statistics.
TEKS 6.10D

DIRECTIONS Read each question. Then circle the letter for the correct answer.

Use the graph below to answer Questions 1–3.

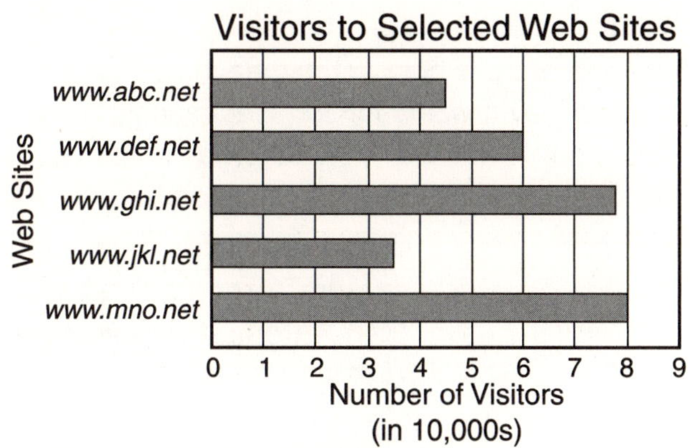

1 The web site *www.ghi.net* had about how many visitors?

A 7.75

B 7,750

C 77,500

D 7,750,000

2 Which Web site had about sixty thousand visitors?

F *www.abc.net*

G *www.def.net*

H *www.jkl.net*

J *www.mno.net*

3 About how many more visitors did *www.mno.net* have than *www.def.net*?

A 2

B 2,000

C 20,000

D 200,000

4 The sixth grade students in Mr. Dean's class made a bar graph to show how many of them visited national points of interest last summer.

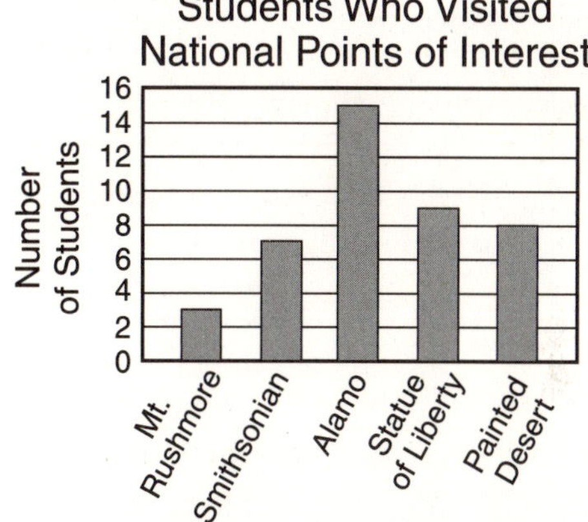

Which table shows the same data as the bar graph?

F

Site	Number of Students
Mt. Rushmore	3
Smithsonian	7
Alamo	15
Statue of Liberty	9
Painted Desert	8

G

Site	Number of Students
Mt. Rushmore	3
Painted Desert	8
Alamo	15
Statue of Liberty	8

H

Site	Number of Students
Statue of Liberty	8
Alamo	17
Mt. Rushmore	3
Smithsonian	7
Painted Desert	12

J Not Here

Focus on TEKS

Lesson 55 Make Line Graphs

TEKS 6.10D Solve problems by collecting, organizing, displaying, and interpreting data.

You can display data in a line graph to show changes in the data, to show trends, and to solve problems.

A **line graph** is used primarily to show how one item of data changes over time. Coordinate points are plotted and then joined by a line.

Guided Instruction

Problem

Jevan kept a record of the high temperature in San Antonio each day for a week. On Monday it was 74°F, on Tuesday it was 77°F, on Wednesday it was 81°F, on Thursday it was 79°F, on Friday it was 80°F, on Saturday it was 82°F, and on Sunday it was 86°F. What trend is shown by these temperatures?

Use a line graph to make a visual representation of the temperatures.

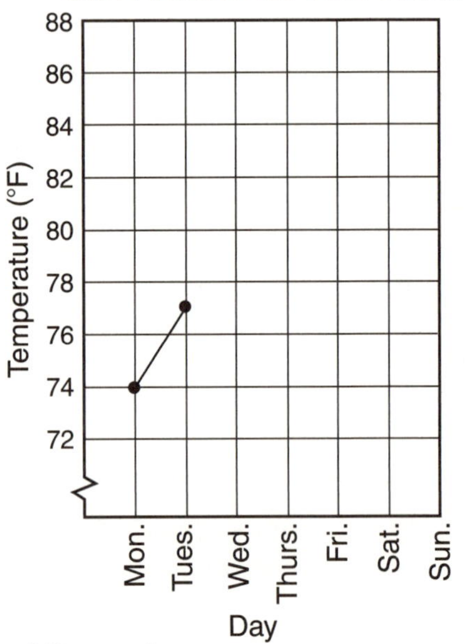

Step 1 Draw the axes of the graph and label each axis.

Step 2 Plot the points as ordered pairs (day, temperature).

Step 3 Connect the points. Look at the shape of the line formed. A line going up indicates rising temperatures. A line going down indicates falling temperatures.

The line ______________ from Monday to Wednesday.

The line ______________ from Wednesday to Thursday.

The line then continues to ________ for the rest of the week.

Solution In general, the temperatures ______________ throughout the week.

Another Example

What is the difference between the lowest temperature and the highest temperature for the week?

Find the lowest and highest temperatures. Then subtract.

Lowest temperature: __________ Highest temperature: __________

86° − 74° = __________

The difference between the highest and lowest temperatures is __________ .

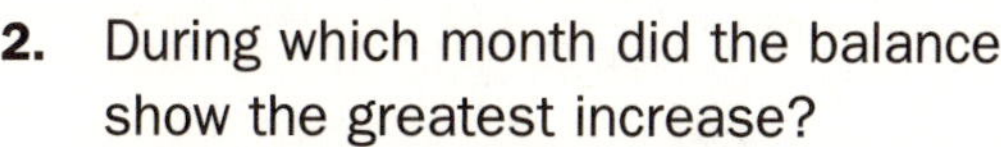

Use the graph to answer Problems 1–4.

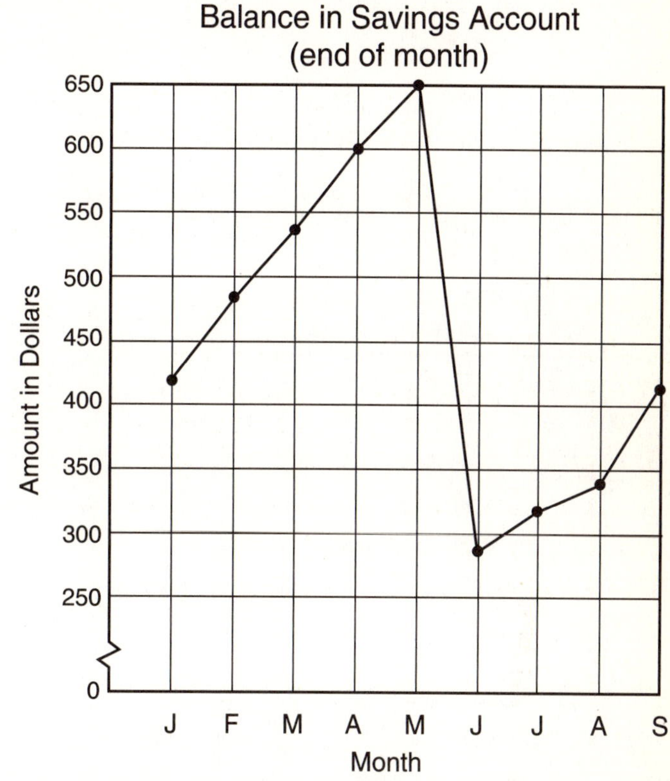

1. During which month did the balance show the greatest decrease?

____

2. During which month did the balance show the greatest increase?

____

3. During which month(s) was the balance between \$450 and \$550?

____

4. What was the approximate average monthly change in the balance of the account from the end of January through the end of April?

____

5. Brendan is diabetic and must test his glucose level several times each day. Use the information in the table to make a line graph.

Brendan's Morning Glucose Readings

Day	Mon	Tues	Wed	Thurs	Fri	Sat	Sun
Reading	145	160	140	155	110	130	115

6. Many consider normal glucose levels to be between 80 and 120. For which days was Brendan's morning glucose level in the normal range?

____

What is the range of the morning glucose readings?

____

What is the median of the morning glucose readings for this week? _______________

Explain how to find this data on the line graph.

____

____

____

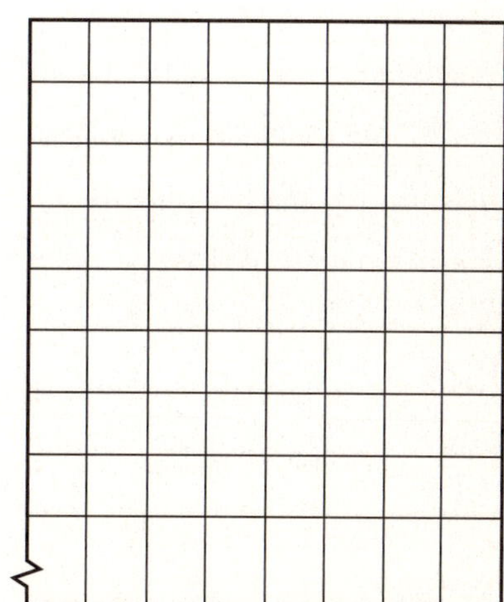

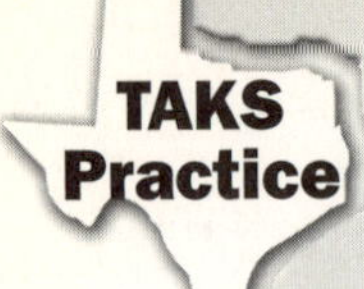

TAKS Objective 5 The student will demonstrate an understanding of probability and statistics.
TEKS 6.10D

DIRECTIONS Read each question. Then circle the letter for the correct answer.

Use the line graph below to answer Questions 1–2.

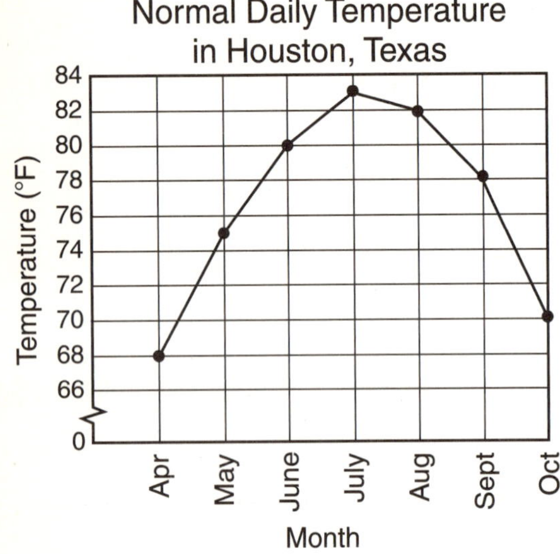

1 During which month did the normal daily temperature show the greatest increase from the previous month?

A May

B June

C July

D August

2 In which month is the average daily temperature greater than 75 degrees and less than 80 degrees?

F April

G July

H August

J September

Toni wants to graph a set of data that has a range of 80. In order to keep the graph a reasonable size and still be readable, what is the best choice for the scale?

A By 1s

B By 8s

C By 20s

D By 40s

Which table accurately shows the information in the graph below?

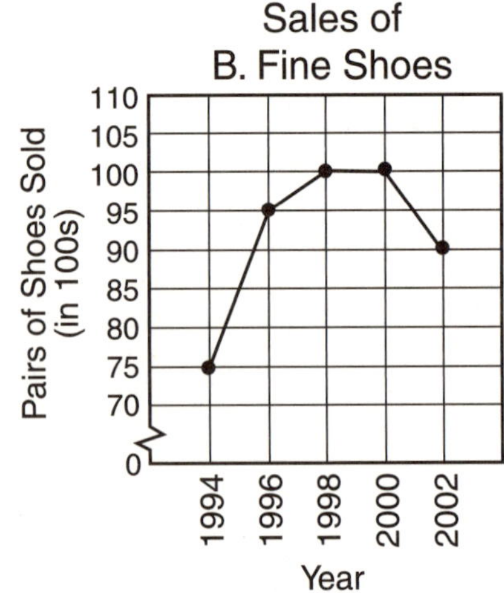

F

1994	7,500
1996	9,500
1998	10,000
2000	10,000
2002	9,000

H

1994	750
1996	950
1998	1,000
2000	1,000
2002	900

G

1994	75
1996	95
1998	100
2000	100
2002	90

J

1994	75,000
1996	95,000
1998	100,000
2000	100,000
2002	90,000

Focus on TEKS

Lesson 56 Make Stem-and-Leaf Plots

TEKS 6.10D Solve problems by collecting, organizing, displaying, and interpreting data.

You can organize and display data in a stem-and-leaf plot.

A **stem-and-leaf plot** displays data items in order by place value. The leaf shows each data item's last digit on the right. The stem shows the digits to the left of the leaf.

Guided Instruction

Problem

Texas League football teams scored the following points in their games last year: 24, 11, 35, 7, 14, 21, 28, 14, 31, 21, 12, 19, 21, 28, and 38. Use a stem-and-leaf plot to find the median, mode, and range of the scores.

Use place values to make a stem-and-leaf plot.

Step 1 Use the tens as the stems and the ones as the leaves. Write the stems from least to greatest at the left. Use 0 as the stem for one-digit numbers. Then write the leaves for each stem in numerical order from least to greatest at the right.

Stem	Leaf
0	7
1	1 2 4 4 9
2	____________
3	____________

Step 2 Find the median.
There is a total of 15 numbers shown on the stem-and-leaf plot.
The median is the middle or __________ number, which is ________.

Step 3 Find the mode.
Which leaf occurs most often for one stem? ______________________
The mode is ________.

Step 4 Find the range.
Subtract the smallest stem with its smallest leaf from the largest stem with its largest leaf. 38 − ______ = ______

The range is ________.

Solution

The median and the mode of the scores is ________.
The range is ________.

Another Example

You can also display this information on a line plot.
A **line plot** shows where data clusters and where there are gaps.
Every X on the number line represents one data point.

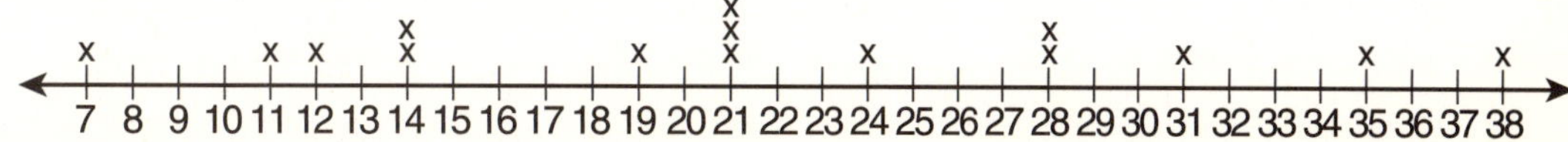

Apply the TEKS

Use the stem-and-leaf plot below to answer Problems 1–4.

1. List the numbers shown in the stem-and-leaf plot.

____

____

____

Stem	Leaf
8	3 7 8
9	0 4 4 4
10	9
12	1 2 3 3 9
13	0 2 4 5 8 9

2. What is the median of the data set? ____________

3. What is the mode of the data set? ____________

4. What is the range of the data set? ____________

5. Complete the stem-and-leaf plot below using the information in the table.

Land Area of Selected Counties in Texas (in square miles)

County	Area	County	Area	County	Area
Borden	899	Crosby	900	Carson	923
Baylor	871	Bastrop	888	Freestone	877
Castro	898	Eastland	926	Dawson	902
Callahan	899	Bell	880	Armstrong	914
Fannin	891	Cameron	906	Archer	910

6. What is the median of the areas of the counties? ____________

7. How many counties have more than 910 square miles of area? ____________

List these areas. ____________________

Stem	Leaf

8. Add the following counties to the stem-and-leaf plot: Coke (area: 899 sq mi), Collingsworth (area: 919 sq mi), Hamilton (area: 908 sq mi), and Lubbock (area: 927 sq mi),

How do these additional counties affect the the median and the mode?

____

____

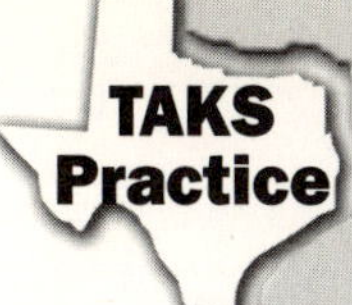

TAKS Objective 5 The student will demonstrate an understanding of probability and statistics.
TEKS 6.10D

DIRECTIONS Read each question. Then circle the letter for the correct answer.

Use the stem-and-leaf plot to answer Questions 1–3.

Stem	Leaf
1	2 5 6 8 8 9
2	1 2 3 5 7 7 9
3	0 2 4 5 8
4	0 2 3

1 A leaf of 2 and a stem of 5 represents which number?

A 55

B 52

C 25

D 22

2 The mode or modes of the data set shown in the stem-and-leaf plot have which digit or digits as stems?

F 1 and 3

G 2 and 3

H 3 and 4

J 1 and 2

3 Which number is NOT shown in the stem-and-leaf plot?

A 19

B 27

C 36

D 40

4 Which stem-and-leaf plot accurately shows this data set of golf scores?

92	84	70	85	73
67	85	79	80	91
87	78	81	77	68

F

Stem	Leaf
6	7 8
7	0 3 7 8 9
8	0 1 4 5 5 7
9	1 2

G

Stem	Leaf
6	67 68
7	70 73 77 78 79
8	80 81 84 85 85 87
9	91 92

H

Stem	Leaf
6	7 8
7	0 3 7 8 9
8	0 1 4 5 7
9	1 2

J

Stem	Leaf
6	7 8
7	3 7 8 9
8	1 4 5 5 7
9	1 2

Focus on TEKS

Lesson 57 Make Circle Graphs

TEKS 6.10C Sketch circle graphs to display data.

TEKS 6.10D Solve problems by collecting, organizing, displaying, and interpreting data.

You can make a circle graph to show the parts of a whole.

A **circle graph** shows the parts of a whole and how those parts relate to the whole and to each other.

Guided Instruction

Problem

Two hundred people were surveyed about their favorite movie. The results of the survey are shown in the table. Make a circle graph of this information.

Movie	Number of People
To the Rescue	25
Hard to Spot	100
The Mulligans	50
Chimps on Skates	25

Use fractions to find the size of each part of the circle.

Step 1 What fraction of the people surveyed chose *Hard to Spot* as their favorite movie? Write the fraction in lowest terms. So $\frac{1}{2}$ of the circle graph represents the people surveyed who chose Hard to Spot. $\frac{100}{200} = \frac{1}{2}$

Step 2 What fraction of the people surveyed chose *The Mulligans* as their favorite movie? Write the fraction in simplest form. Add this to your circle graph. $\frac{50}{200} =$ ____________

Step 3 What fraction chose *To the Rescue* as their favorite movie? Write the fraction in simplest form. $\frac{25}{200} =$ ____________

Step 4 Since the same number of people chose *Chimps on Skates* as chose *To the Rescue*, the same sized part of the circle, $\frac{1}{8}$, will represent the fraction of people who chose *Chimps on Skates*.

Step 5 Give your circle graph a title.

Solution

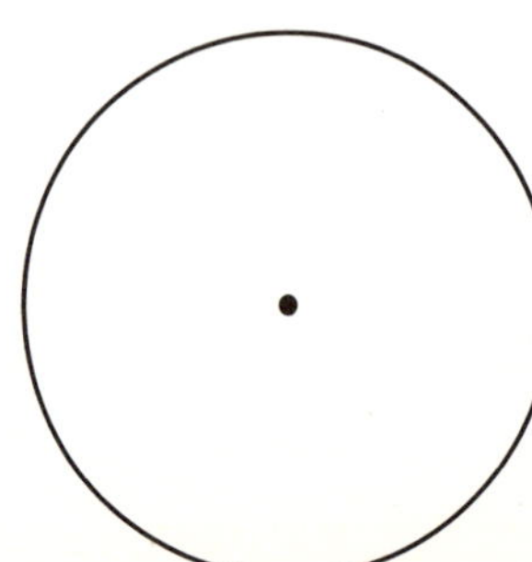

Apply the TEKS **Use the circle graph below to answer Problems 1–4.**

1. What percent of the budget is spent on transportation?

____

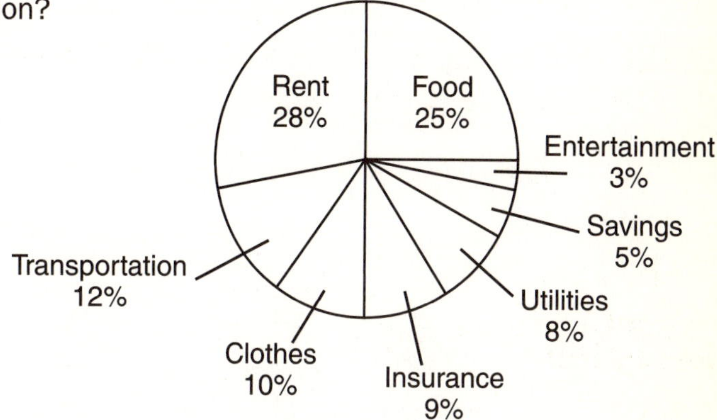

2. Which expenses represent less than $\frac{1}{10}$ of the budget?

____

____

3. Which expense represents the greatest amount of the budget? _______________

4. If the total budget is $3,000, how much would be spent on food? _______________

Use the information below to make a circle graph. Use the circle graph you make to answer Problems 5–6.

Four hundred people were asked who their favorite scientist is. The results are in the table to the right.

Survey of 400 People: Favorite Scientists

Scientist	Number of People Responding
Alexander G. Bell	120
George W. Carver	100
Thomas A. Edison	100
Albert Einstein	40
Marie Curie	40

5. Which scientists are represented by one quarter of the circle?

____

6. Find the difference between Bell's fraction of the votes and Einstein's? __________

Explain your answer.

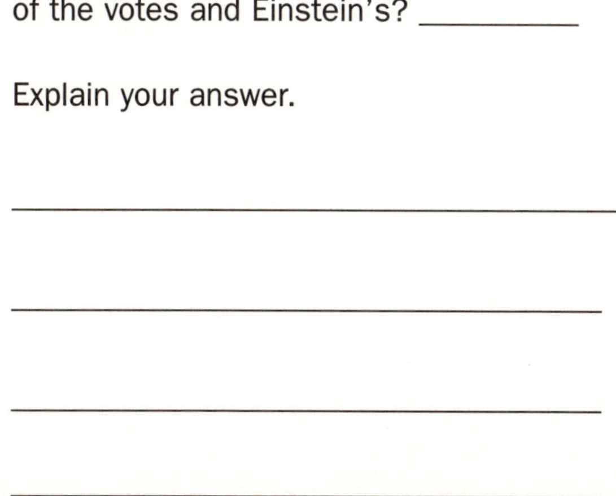

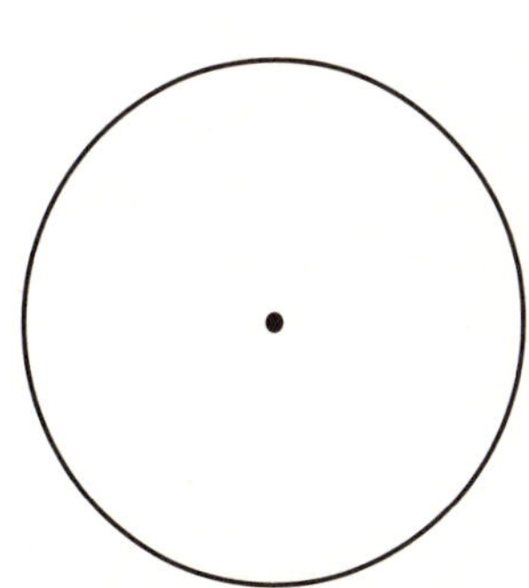

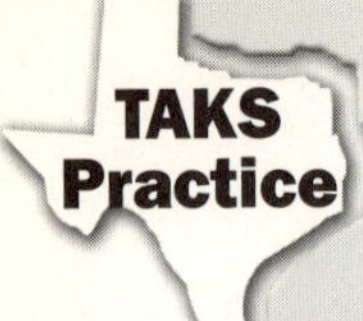

TAKS Objective 5 The student will demonstrate an understanding of probability and statistics.
TEKS 6.10C, 6.10D

DIRECTIONS Read each question. Then circle the letter for the correct answer.

Use the circle graph below to answer Questions 1–3.

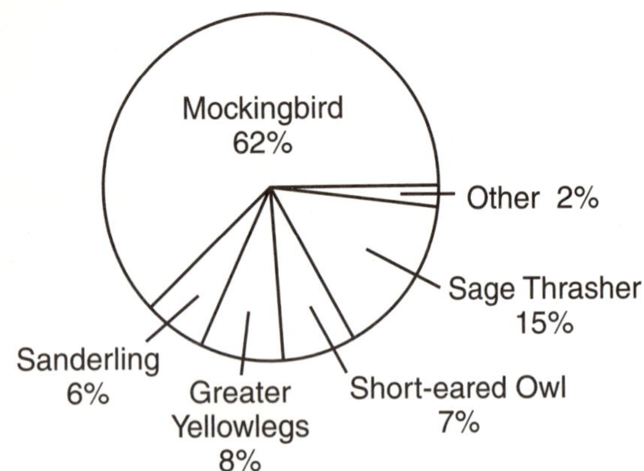

1 Which bird received the second most votes for Texas state bird?

A sanderling

B greater yellowlegs

C short-eared owl

D sage thrasher

2 If a total of 1,000 people voted for the state bird, about how many voted for the Greater Yellowlegs?

Record your answer and fill in the bubbles on the grid below. Be sure to use the correct place value.

				.		
0	0	0	0		0	0
1	1	1	1		1	1
2	2	2	2		2	2
3	3	3	3		3	3
4	4	4	4		4	4
5	5	5	5		5	5
6	6	6	6		6	6
7	7	7	7		7	7
8	8	8	8		8	8
9	9	9	9		9	9

If 20,000 people voted for the state bird, about how many more people voted for the mockingbird than voted for the short-eared owl?

A 55

B 1,400

C 11,000

D 19,800

The total sales of personal computers for four companies was $60,000 in October. The table below shows the sales of these companies.

Company	Sales
Zipp	$10,000
PDQ	$15,000
Flash	$20,000
Quick	$15,000

Which circle graph accurately shows this information?

F

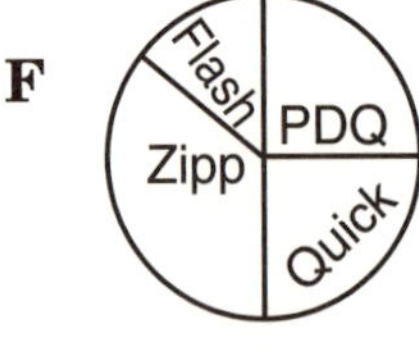

H

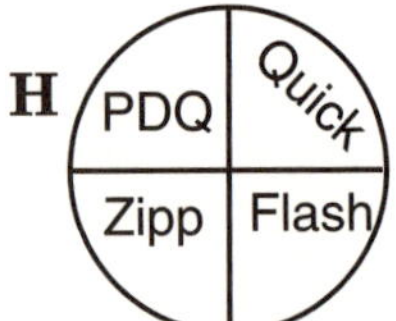

G

Quick
Flash
PDQ
Zipp

J

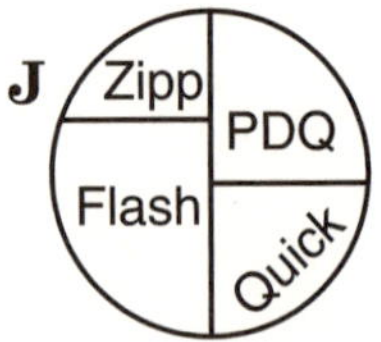

Focus on TEKS

Lesson 58 Compare Graphs

TEKS 6.10A Select and use an appropriate representation for presenting and displaying different graphical representations of the same data including line plot, line graph, bar graph, and stem and leaf plot.

TEKS 6.12B Evaluate the effectiveness of different representations to communicate ideas.

You can choose which kind of graph is most appropriate for each set of data.

A bar graph or double-bar graph compares groups of data.

A line graph or double-line graph shows changes over time.

A stem-and-leaf plot shows data in order by place value.

A circle graph shows parts of a whole.

A line plot shows where data clusters and where there are gaps.

Guided Instruction

Problem 1

Barry kept track of his puppy's weight every month. The data table shows the weights he recorded. Decide what kind of graph would best represent the data and draw the graph.

Age (in months)	Weight (in pounds)
1	5
2	11
3	14
4	19
5	24

Use the kind of graph that best represents the data.

Step 1 Analyze the data to determine what the graph should show. Does the data show a comparison of groups of data, a change over time, data in order by place value, or parts of a whole?

The data shows a ______________________________.

Step 2 Which kind of graph best represents the data in the table?

____

Step 3 In the space below, draw the graph. Label each axis, number, or section as needed to complete the graph. Title the graph.

Solution What kind of graph best represents the data? ______________________________

Another Problem

Guided Instruction

Problem 2

A survey was taken in which people were asked how many cups of coffee they drank each day. The table below shows the results of this survey. The company conducting the survey wants to graphically see which number is most common. Which type(s) of graph should they use?

3, 1, 2, 2, 3, 2, 1, 3, 2, 0
2, 2, 3, 5, 2, 2, 1, 1, 3, 5

Use the kind of graph that best represents the data.

Step 1 Analyze the data.

Does the data change over time? __________

So a line graph is not the best way to display the data.

Does the data involve ordering numbers by place value? __________

So ________________________is not the best way to display the data.

Is the purpose of displaying the data to compare parts to a whole? __________

So __________________ is not the best way to display the data.

Which two graphs make comparing the number of cups of coffee easy to see visually? ____________________________________

Step 2 In the space below, draw and title each graph. Label each axis, number, or section as needed to complete the graphs.

Solution

Which type(s) of graph best represent the data?

____

Apply the TEKS **Tell what kind of graph would best represent the data for each situation.**

1. Compare the number of different makes of cars sold in March.

____

2. Compare the percentages of different kinds of cars driven by all the members of the car club.

____

3. Order the horsepower ratings of different makes of cars.

____

4. Show any changes in the cost of a certain model car over the last 10 years.

____

5. Show the percentages of the money spent on caring for your car.

____

Tell which graph is more effective in displaying the data in each situation and explain your reasons.

6.

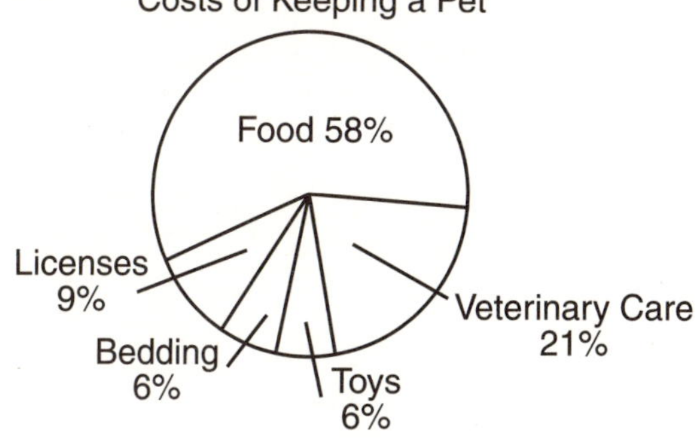

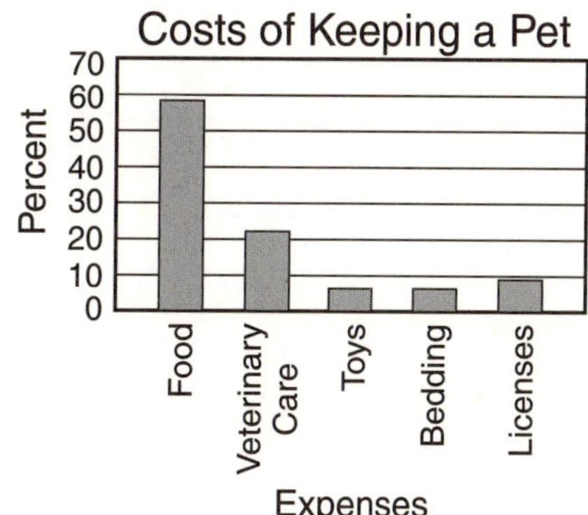

____

____

7.

Stem	Leaf
5	0
10	0 5
40	0
60	0
90	0

Key: 10|0 = 100

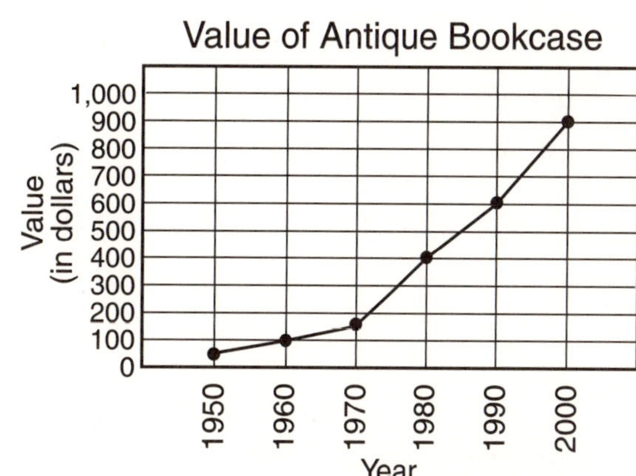

____

____

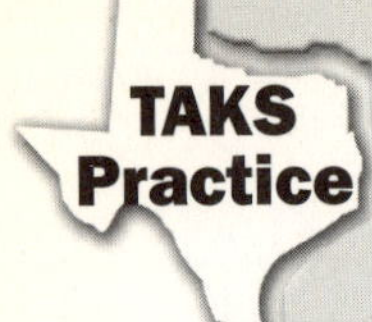

TAKS Objective 5 The student will demonstrate an understanding of probability and statistics.
TEKS 6.10A
TEKS 6.12B

DIRECTIONS Read each question. Then circle the letter for the correct answer.

1 Which phrase best describes the purpose of a stem-and-leaf plot?

A Compares groups of data

B Shows data in order by place value

C Shows parts of a whole

D Shows changes over time

2 You have collected data about the average wing span and height of five different birds. Which is the best type of graph to use to display this data?

F Double-line graph

G Circle graph

H Stem-and-leaf plot

J Double-bar graph

3 One hundred people are surveyed about their favorite pizza topping. Which two kinds of graphs could show the data equally well?

A Line graph and bar graph

B Line graph and stem-and-leaf plot

C Bar graph and circle graph

D Stem-and-leaf plot and circle graph

4 Which graph best represents the data?

F Monthly cost of Medical Insurance (Adult Female)

Stem	Leaf
4	0 2
5	5
6	0
10	0
21	5
30	0

G

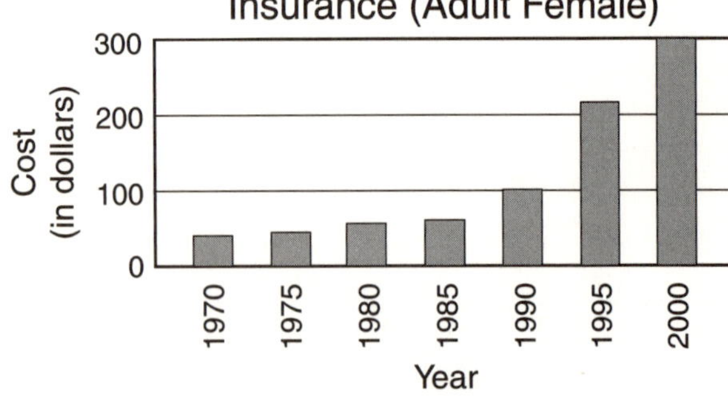

H

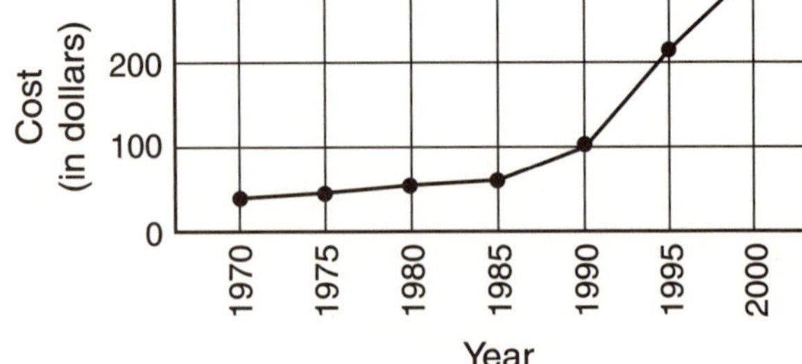

J

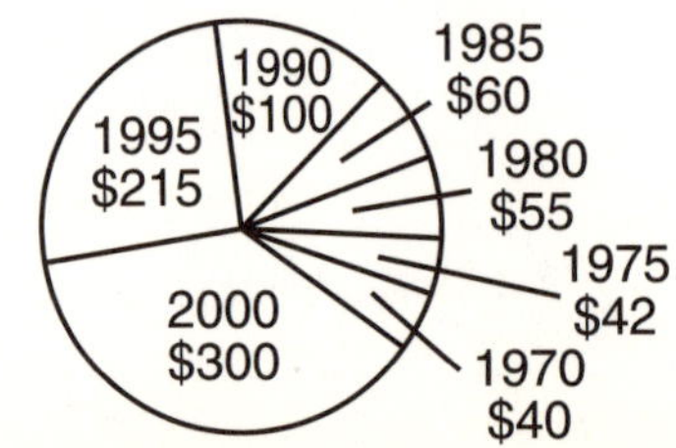

Focus on TEKS

Lesson 59 PROBLEM-SOLVING STRATEGY: Interpret Graphs

TEKS 6.11A Identify and apply mathematics to everyday experiences, to activities in and outside of school, with other disciplines, and with other mathematical topics.

TEKS 6.11B Use a problem-solving model that incorporates understanding the problem, making a plan, carrying out the plan, and evaluating the solution for reasonableness.

TEKS 6.11C Select or develop an appropriate problem-solving strategy from a variety of different types to solve a problem.

TEKS 6.11D Select tools such as real objects, manipulatives, paper/pencil, and technology or techniques such as mental math, estimation, and number sense to solve problems.

You can interpret graphs to solve problems. You can use the problem-solving guide on page 288 to help you.

Guided Instruction

Problem

The graph at the right shows the population of Holtsville over the last few years. What does the graph tell you about how the population is changing?

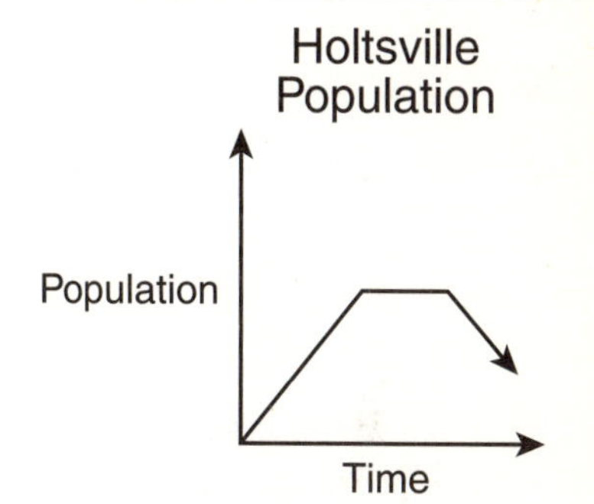

Understand the problem.

What are you given?

____

____

What are you trying to find? ______________________________

Make a plan.

Look at the shape of the line as it relates the two variables named on the axes.

In the first few years, the line went up. This indicates that Holtsville's population ________________ during these years.

As time passed, the line then flattened out. This indicates that Holtsville's population ____________________ during this time.

Then during the latter years, the line started to go down. This indicates that Holtsville's population ________________ over the past few years.

Solve the problem.

The graph shows that at first Holtsville's population ________________, then over a period of time ____________________ , and recently has begun to ________________ .

Check your answer.

As you tell the story of the graph, check that it matches what is displayed.

Apply the TEKS **Describe the trend shown by each graph.**

1. 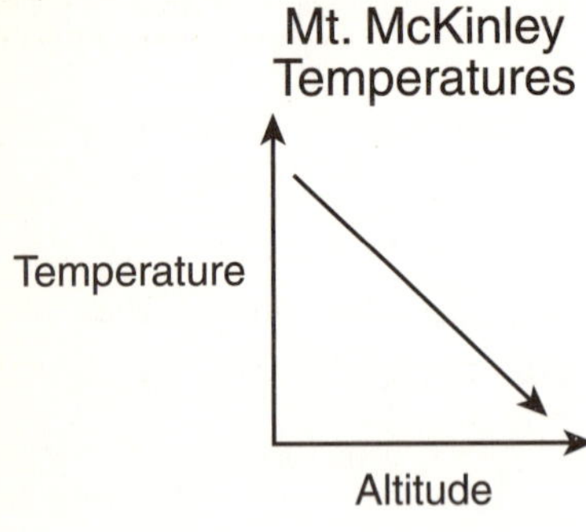

2. 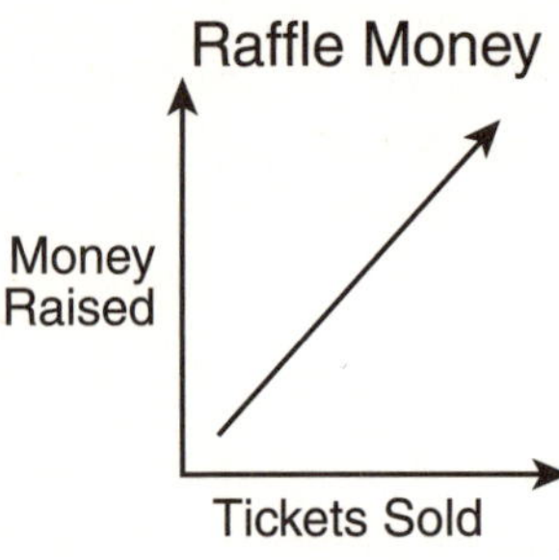

3. 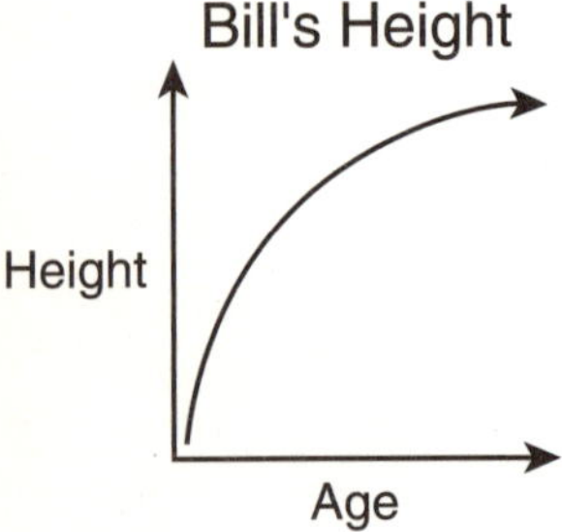

4. 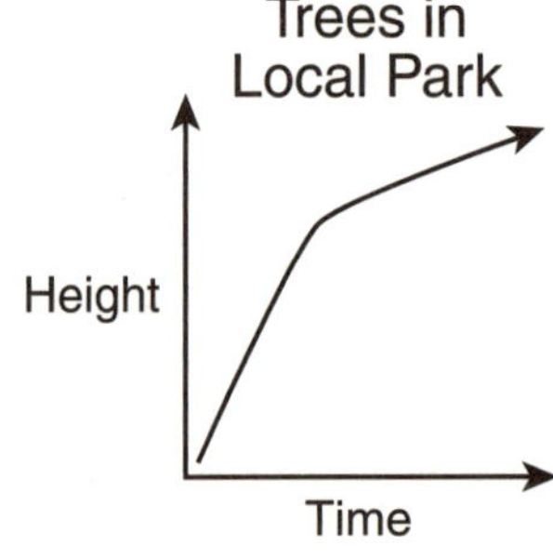

Draw a graph that shows each general trend.

5. The number of traffic accidents increases as the speed limit increases.

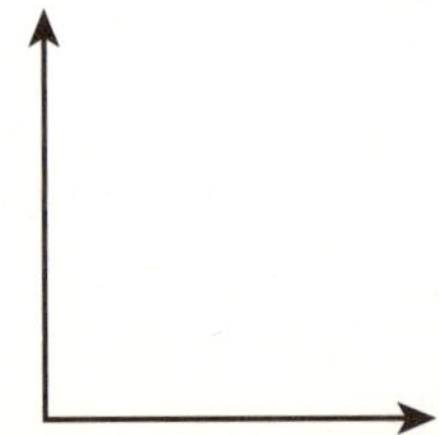

6. Over time, the number of visitors to the museum decreases, then holds steady, and then increases.

TAKS Objective 6 The student will demonstrate an understanding of the mathematical processes and tools used in problem solving.

TEKS 6.11A, 6.11B, 6.11C, 6.11D

DIRECTIONS Read each question. Then circle the letter for the correct answer.

Use the graph below to answer Questions 1–2.

1 Which statement best describes the data shown by the graph?

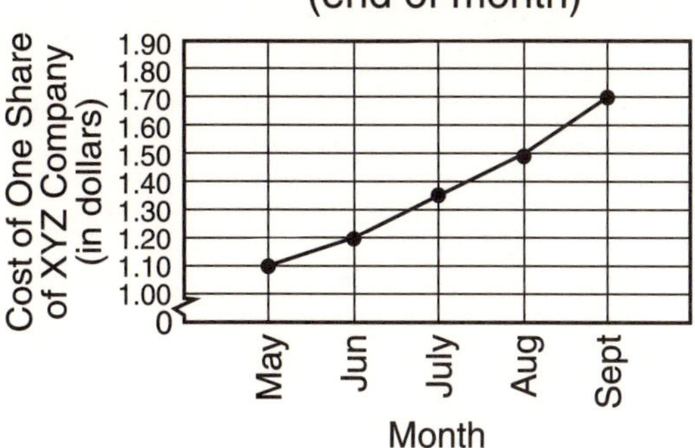

A The value of the stock is increasing.

B The value of the stock shows little or no change.

C The value of the stock is decreasing.

D No conclusion can be determined.

2 Based upon the graph, which is the best prediction of the value of XYZ stock in October?

F \$1.50

G \$1.60

H \$1.90

J \$2.50

3 Which graph best represents the following statement? "Sales of cellular phones increased for several years and then leveled off to show little change."

A

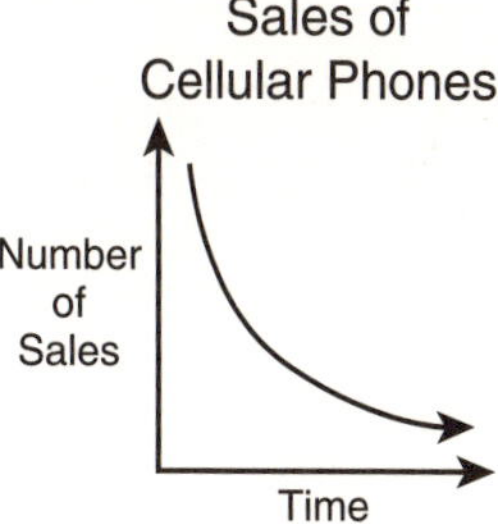

B

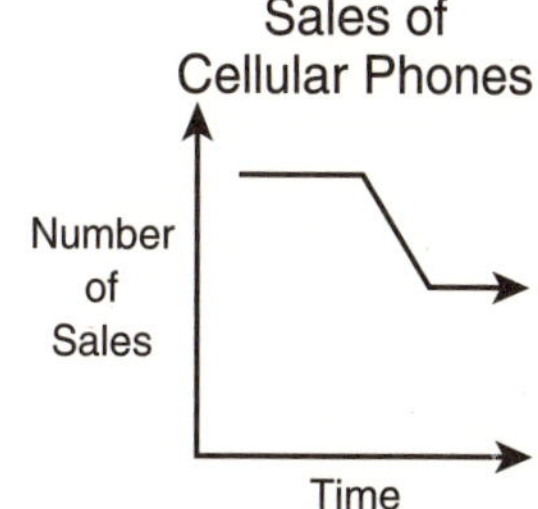

C

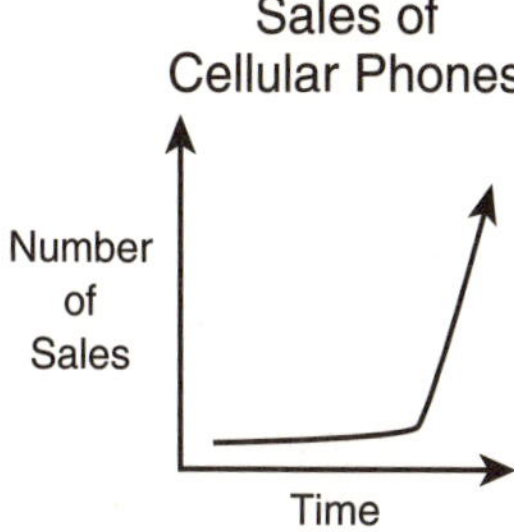

D

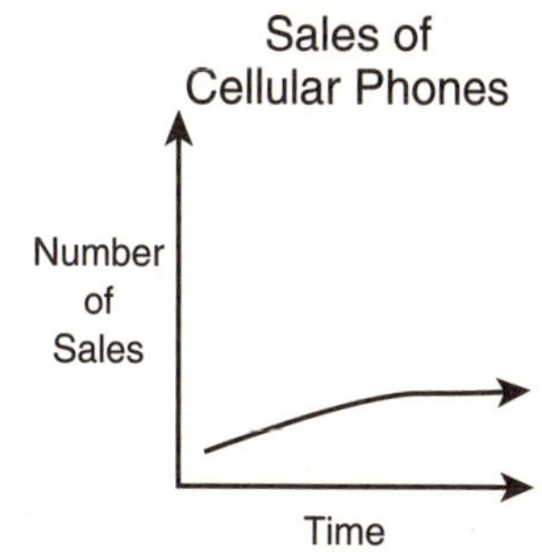

Building Stamina®

DIRECTIONS Read each question. Then circle the letter for the correct answer. If a correct answer is <u>not</u> <u>here</u>, mark the letter for "Not Here."

Use the data list below to answer Questions 1–2.

Birth Weights for
Labrador Puppies in Ounces

7	6	8	8	6
7	8	12	9	

1 Suppose the weight of 5 oz is added to the data set. Which statement below is true?

A The median does not change.

B The mode changes.

C The range changes.

D There is no change in the median, mode, or range.

2 Which three values, if added to the set of data, will change both the mode and the median?

F 6, 6, and 6

G 6, 7, and 8

H 7, 8, and 9

J 7, 11, and 12

3 Which data set has a mean of 20, a median of 20, a mode of 20, and a range of 20?

A 23, 20, 29, 42, 25, 20

B 20, 28, 14, 12, 20, 22, 20

C 20, 12, 19, 20, 32, 18, 16

D 14, 20, 20, 32, 12, 20, 22

Use the test scores below to answer Questions 4-6.

I

55	85	90	80
45	90	100	

II

70	75	80	80
95	90	90	

III

70	80	90	75
65	95	100	

IV

85	60	60	75
80	70	70	

4 Which set of test scores has the greatest median score?

F I

G II

H III

J IV

5 Which set of test scores has no mode?

A I

B II

C III

D IV

6 Which set of test scores has the least range?

F I

G II

H III

J IV

Use the graph below to answer Questions 7–9.

Populations of Five Counties in Texas
Using 2000 Census Data

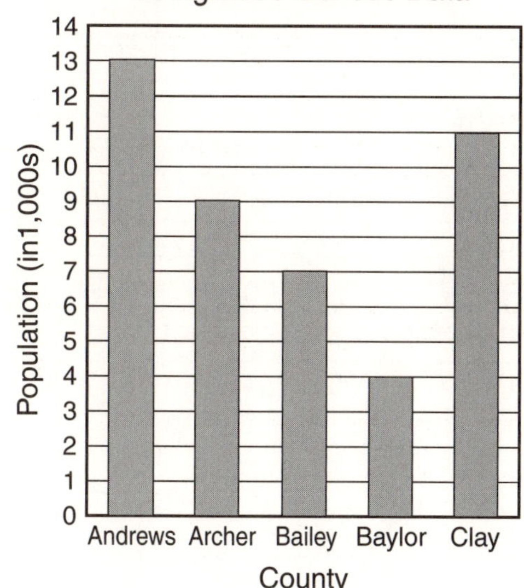

7 Approximately how many more people lived in Archer County than in Baylor County, Texas in 2000?

Record your answer and fill in the bubbles on the grid below. Be sure to use the correct place value.

8 Which counties have populations greater than 10,000?

F Andrews and Clay

G Archer and Clay

H Archer, Bailey, and Clay

J Andrews and Archer

9 James added a bar to the graph to represent the population of Carson County in 2000. He drew a bar that was taller than Baylor County and shorter than Bailey County. Which of the populations listed below is the population of Carson County?

A 3,876

B 6,516

C 7,423

D 8,280

10 Marla's allowance is $100 a month. She earns another $25 a month walking a neighbor's dog. The table shows how she plans to budget her monthly income.

Category	Amount
Savings	$36.00
School lunches	$18.00
Entertainment	$48.00
School supplies	$15.00
Other	$8.00

What kind of graph would best represent the data in the table?

F Line graph

G Circle graph

H Stem-and-leaf plot

J Bar graph

11 For which situation would a line graph best represent the data?

A The number of students attending Desert Sands Middle School over the last 5 years

B The number of students in each grade this year

C The PTA budget for the year

D A comparison of the numbers of students riding the bus, walking, and being driven to school in a car

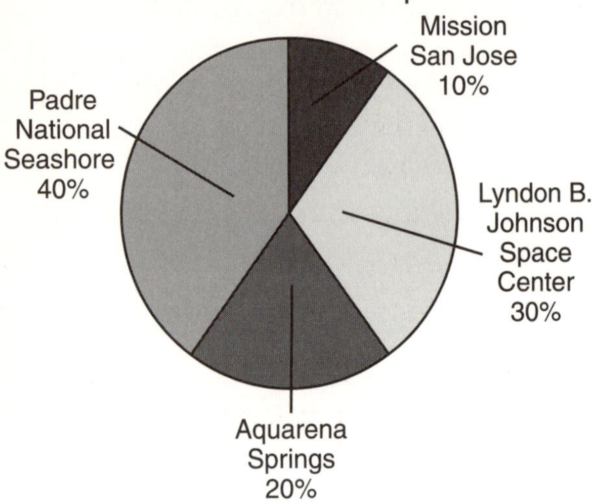

12 Which table accurately shows the information in the circle graph?

F

Location	Number of votes
Mission San Jose	9
Lyndon B. Johnson Space Center	27
Aquarena Springs	18
Padre Island National Seashore	36

G

Location	Number of votes
Mission San Jose	18
Lyndon B. Johnson Space Center	27
Aquarena Springs	9
Padre Island National Seashore	36

H

Location	Number of votes
Mission San Jose	36
Lyndon B. Johnson Space Center	27
Aquarena Springs	9
Padre Island National Seashore	18

J

Location	Number of votes
Mission San Jose	9
Lyndon B. Johnson Space Center	36
Aquarena Springs	18
Padre Island National Seashore	27

Use the graph below to answer Questions 13–15.

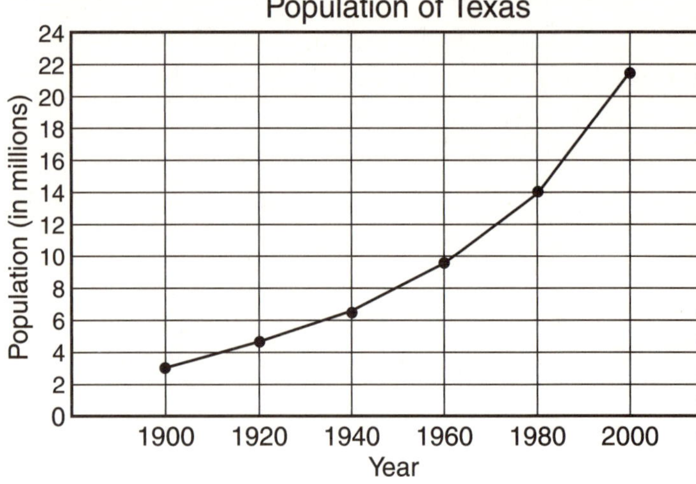

13 During which 20-year period did the population exceed 10 million?

A 1900–1920

B 1920–1940

C 1940–1960

D Not Here

14 Which statement below best describes the trend shown by the graph?

F The population has been decreasing.

G There is no change in the population.

H The population has been increasing at an accelerated rate.

J The population has been increasing at a steady rate.

15 Which is the best prediction of the population of Texas in 2010?

A Between 20 and 25 million

B Between 25 and 35 million

C Between 35 and 45 million

D Greater than 50 million

Use the stem-and-leaf plot below for Questions 16–17.

Student Scores
on a Geography Test

Stem	Leaf
2	6
3	2 2 7 8 9 9
4	2 2 5 5 6 6 8 9
5	3 6 6 6 6 7 8 9
6	0

16 What was the range of scores on the geography test?

F 23

G 34

H 44

J 60

17 What was the median of scores on the geography test?

Record your answer and fill in the bubbles on the grid below. Be sure to use the correct place value.

				.		
0	0	0	0		0	0
1	1	1	1		1	1
2	2	2	2		2	2
3	3	3	3		3	3
4	4	4	4		4	4
5	5	5	5		5	5
6	6	6	6		6	6
7	7	7	7		7	7
8	8	8	8		8	8
9	9	9	9		9	9

18 Erin collected the data shown below about blood type for a science report.

Type of Blood	Percent of Americans
O	43%
A	40%
B	12%
AB	5%

Then she made the circle graph shown below using the collected data found in the table.

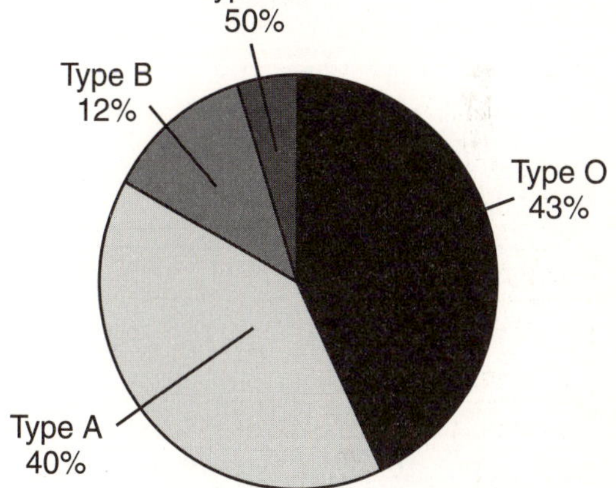

Which best describes the error that she made in her circle graph?

F Used an incorrect percent for Type A

G Mixed up the percents for Type B and Type AB.

H Mixed up the percents for Type O and Type A

J Mislabeled the percent for Type AB

Part 2 Building Stamina®

Read each question. Then circle the letter for the correct answer. If a correct answer is not here, mark the letter for "Not Here."

1 Jason cuts a pecan pie into 6 pieces as shown below. He serves himself the biggest piece.

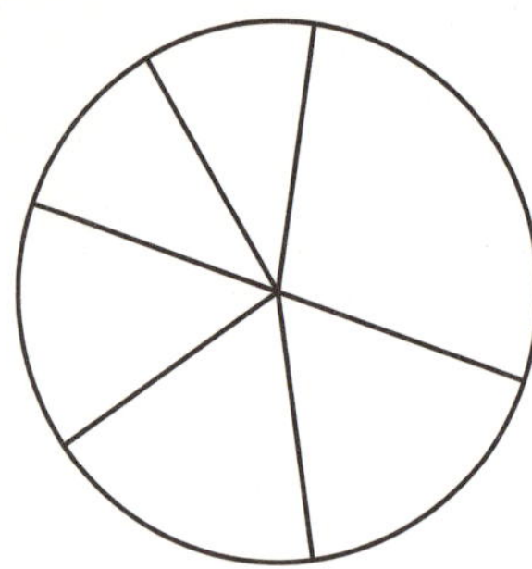

What type of angle does Jason's slice of pie have?

A Acute

B Right

C Obtuse

D Straight

2 Ellen's pet goldfish, Archie, weighs 78 grams. Her dog, Silver, weighs 10.45 kilograms. How much more does Silver weigh than Archie?

F 372 g

G 5,528 g

H 9,528 g

J 10,372 g

3 The angle below is a —

A acute angle

B obtuse angle

C right angle

D straight angle

4 Which is the measure of angle *EBD*?

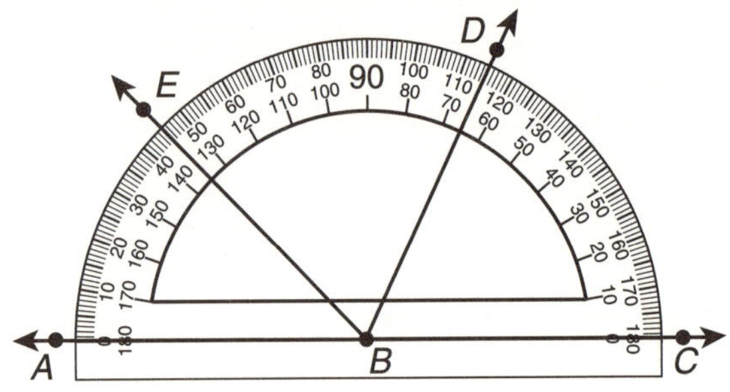

F 65°

G 70°

H 145°

J 180°

5 A public garden has a rectangular flowerbed that has a perimeter of 38 feet. If the width of the bed is 6 feet, what is the length?

A 6 ft

B 13 ft

C 19 ft

D 32 ft

6 Frank's swimming pool has a radius of 12 feet. How does the radius compare to the diameter?

F The diameter is $\frac{1}{2}$ the radius.

G The diameter is twice the radius.

H The diameter is three times the radius.

J Not Here

Use the information below to answer Questions 7–8.

The sixth graders at Oak Grove Middle School are choosing a class color and mascot from those shown in the table below.

Color Choices	Mascot Choices
Gold	Tiger
Blue	Eagle
Maroon	

7 Which tree diagram shows all possible combinations of class color and mascot?

A

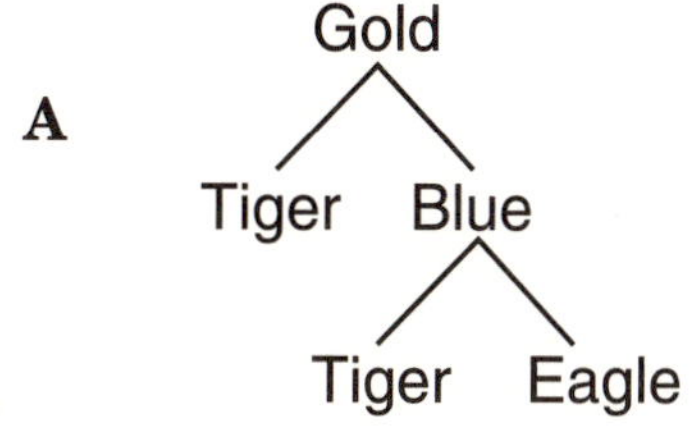

B

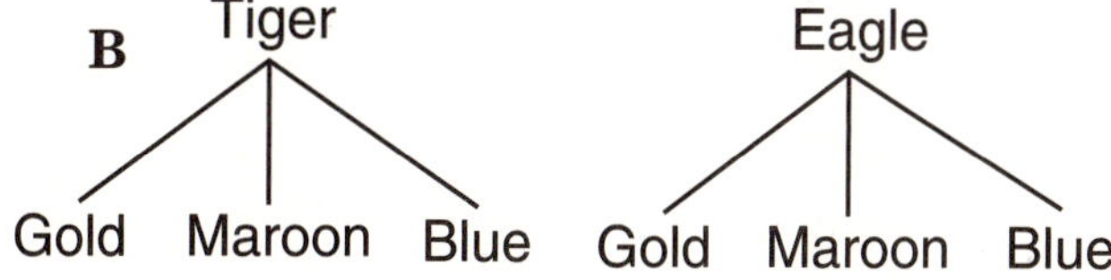

C

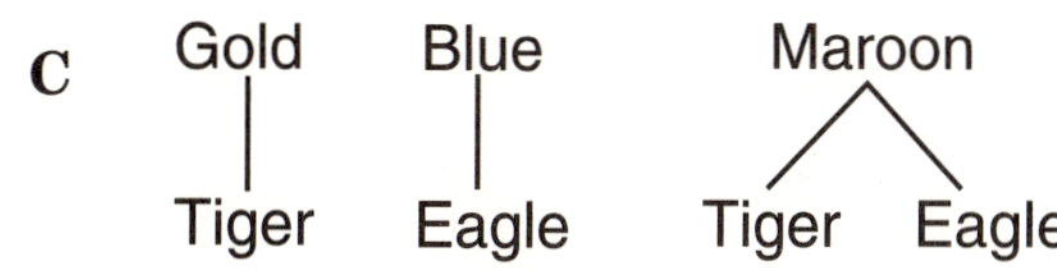

D

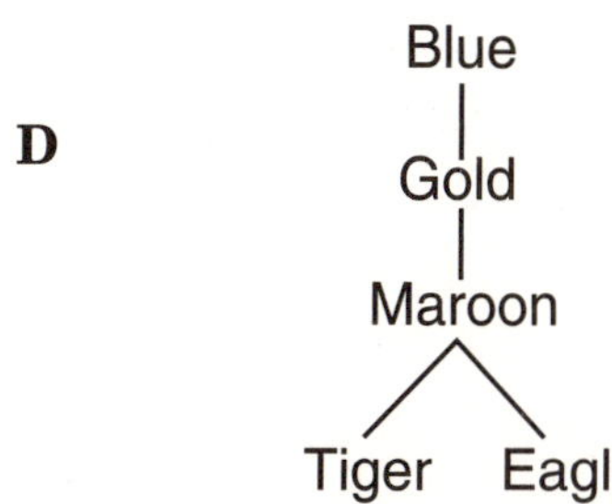

8 How many possible combinations of one class color and one mascot are there?

F 3

G 4

H 6

J 12

9 Sherri is making and decorating a wedding cake. The bottom layer will have a radius of 6 inches. She wants to place a daisy chain around the bottom edge of the cake. About how long should the daisy chain be?

A 18 in.

B 25 in.

C 36 in.

D 40 in.

10 A community group conducts a survey to determine public support for building a new high school. They ask people if they are for, against, or undecided. Which type of graph would best show this?

F Circle graph

G Line graph

H Bar graph

J Stem-and-leaf plot

11 Sheila is doing a report on chocolate for her class. As part of the report, she wants to demonstrate making Mexican hot chocolate. She wants each student and her teacher to have a 6-ounce serving. There are 26 students in the class, counting herself. About how many quarts of milk does she need?

A 27 qt

B 20 qt

C 6 qt

D 3 qt

Use the cards below to answer Questions 12–13.

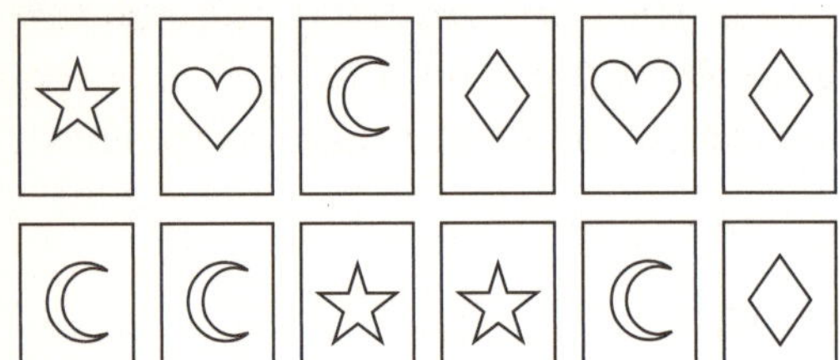

12 What is the probability of drawing a heart?

F $\frac{1}{6}$

G $\frac{1}{12}$

H $\frac{1}{5}$

J $\frac{1}{10}$

13 What is the probability of NOT drawing a moon?

A $\frac{2}{3}$

B $\frac{1}{4}$

C $\frac{1}{3}$

D $\frac{1}{2}$

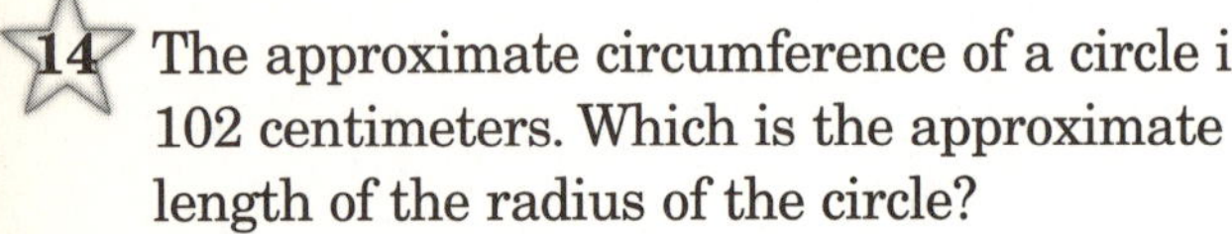

14 The approximate circumference of a circle is 102 centimeters. Which is the approximate length of the radius of the circle?

F 9 cm

G 17 cm

H 34 cm

J 51 cm

Use Quadrilateral *ABCD* to answer Questions 15–16.

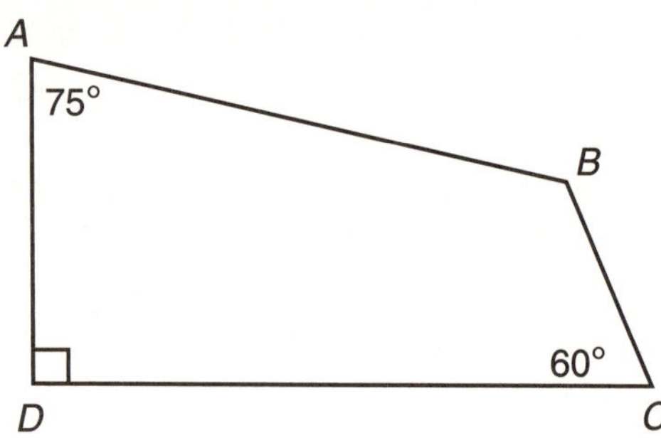

15 What is the measure of angle *B*?

A 60°

B 120°

C 135°

D 180°

16 Use a centimeter ruler to measure the perimeter of Quadrilateral *ABCD*. About how many centimeters is the perimeter?

F 6 cm

G 10 cm

H 16 cm

J 20 cm

17 Which is NOT always true of a rhombus?

A The sides are all the same length.

B Opposite pairs of angles are equal.

C The pairs of opposite sides are parallel.

D One pair of angles is less than 90° and the other pair is greater than 90°.

18 Osmar and Tommy are playing a game in their math class. Osmar chose the angle measures of 23 and 65 degrees. Tommy must choose a third angle measure to complete a triangle. Which angle measure should he choose to complete the triangle?

F 23°

G 42°

H 88°

J 92°

19 Each week Rita works from 10:30 A.M. to 4:15 P.M. Monday through Thursday without a lunch break. How many hours does she work each week?

Record your answer and fill in the bubbles on the grid below. Be sure to use the correct place value.

				.		
0	0	0	0		0	0
1	1	1	1		1	1
2	2	2	2		2	2
3	3	3	3		3	3
4	4	4	4		4	4
5	5	5	5		5	5
6	6	6	6		6	6
7	7	7	7		7	7
8	8	8	8		8	8
9	9	9	9		9	9

20 Mrs. Johnson uses 4 ounces of shelled pecans to make a pecan pie. She wants to give pies to 6 of her neighbors and keep 2 for herself. How many pounds of shelled pecans does she need to buy?

F 2 lb

G 4 lb

H 8 lb

J 12 lb

21 Mrs. Armstrong walks around her block 6 times in the evening. The distance once around the block is 300 yards. About how far does she walk in a week if she takes her walk 5 times during the week?

A Less than 1 mi

B Between 2 mi and 4 mi

C Between 3 mi and 4 mi

D More than 5 mi

22 Which is the best estimate of the perimeter of the figure?

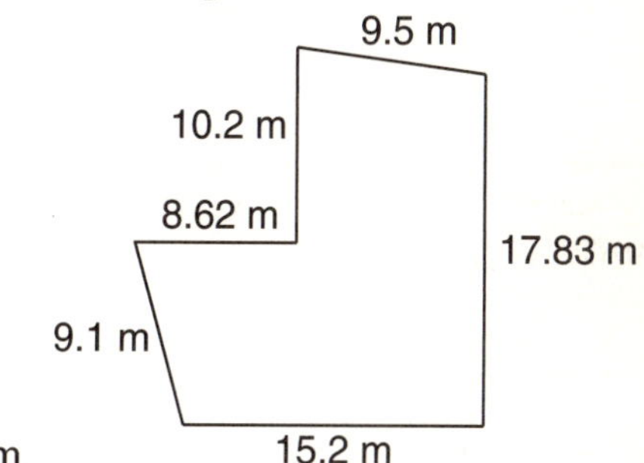

F 40 m

G 50 m

H 60 m

J 70 m

23 Which is an isosceles triangle?

A

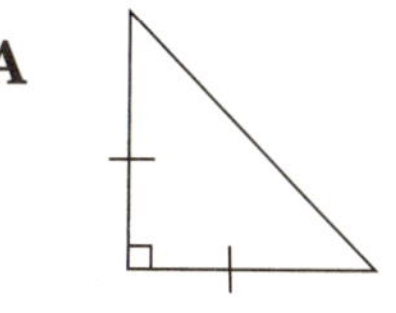

B

C

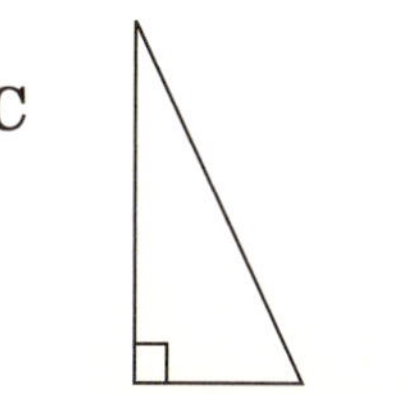

D Not Here

24 Luis hit 26 out of 50 balls at batting practice. Which is the best prediction of the number of balls he will hit out of 400 balls?

F 52

G 154

H 208

J 280

Use the table below to answer Questions 25–26.

Player	Total Shots Attempted	Baskets
Charlie	50	17
Loren	50	32
Nick	40	19
Michael	60	27

25 The table shows the attempted free throws by four players. Who is most likely to make a basket?

A Charlie

B Loren

C Nick

D Michael

26 If Nick throws 200 times, which is the best prediction of the number of baskets he will make?

F 38

G 57

H 89

J 95

27 Janet, Michelle, Sergio, and Zack are the four fastest runners on the track team. Janet is faster than Sergio, but not the fastest runner. The fastest runner is a boy and the slowest of the four is a girl. What is the order from slowest to fastest?

A Michelle, Janet, Sergio, Zack

B Michelle, Sergio, Janet, Zack

C Janet, Sergio, Zack, Michelle

D Zack, Janet, Sergio, Michelle

28 Mrs. Gomez is making triangular-shaped pennants to decorate the Renaissance Festival.

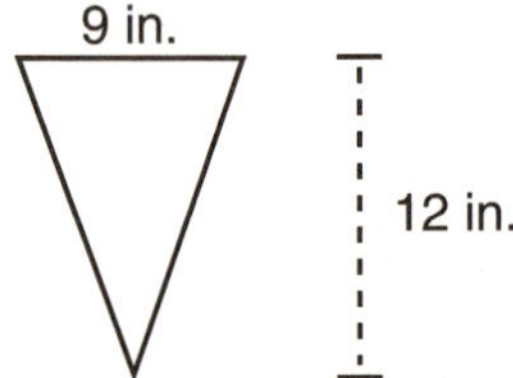

Which expression shows the area of the pennant?

F $\frac{1}{2}(9 \times 12)$

G $9^2 \times 12^2$

H $9 + \frac{12}{2}$

J Not Here

29 The cafeteria needs to make 112 sandwiches. Each sandwich will have 1 ounce of cheese and $2\frac{1}{2}$ ounces of sliced turkey. The cheese and turkey is ordered by the pound. How many pounds of each need to be ordered?

A 7 lb of cheese, 14 lb of turkey

B 7 lb of cheese, 16 lb of turkey

C 7 lb of cheese, 18 lb of turkey

D 8 lb of cheese, 20 lb of turkey

30 If you toss a number cube labeled 1–6 and a penny, which of the following shows the sample space?

F

All Possible Outcomes
1H, 2H, 3H, 4H, 5H, 6H

G

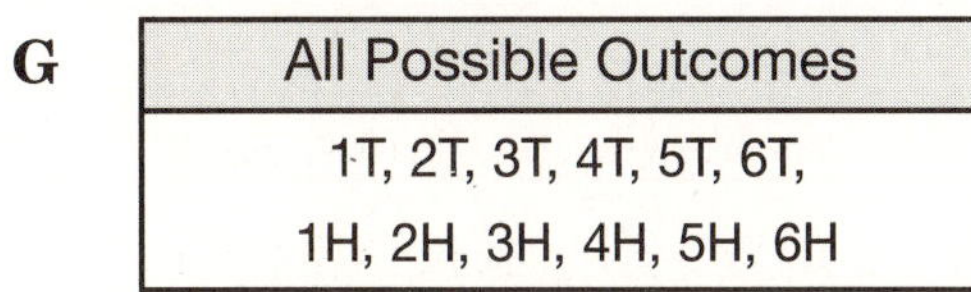

All Possible Outcomes
1T, 2T, 3T, 4T, 5T, 6T, 1H, 2H, 3H, 4H, 5H, 6H

H

All Possible Outcomes
1T, 2T, 3T, 4T, 5T, 6T

J Not Here

31 Michael is packing for a trip. He packs 3 T-shirts: one red, one black, and one white. He also packs a pair of shorts and a pair of jeans. How many different outfits are possible?

A 3

B 5

C 6

D 8

32 Which is the best estimate of the volume of the box?

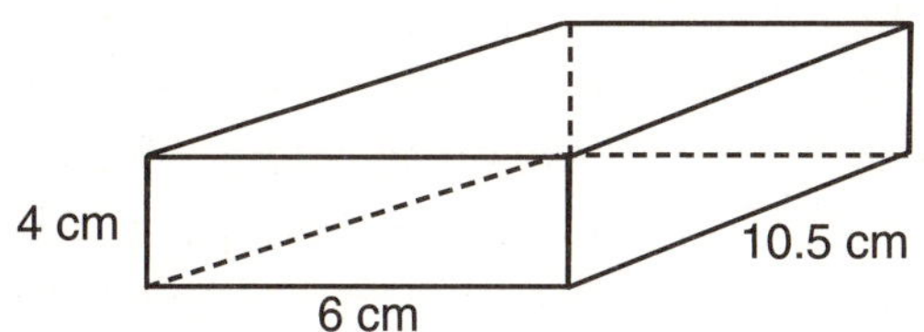

F 2 cm^3

G 24 cm^3

H 240 cm^3

J 2,400 cm^3

33 Sarah is making quilt squares using the geometric shapes shown in the drawing below.

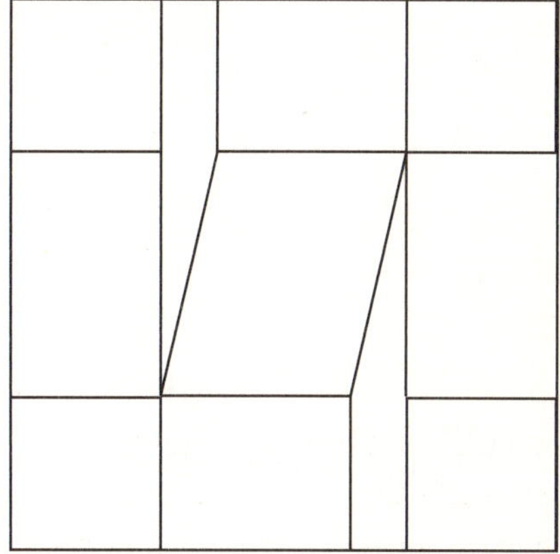

She uses a different color for each shape. The parallelograms are yellow. The squares are black. The trapezoids are orange and the rectangles are blue. How many pieces of each color are in each quilt square?

A 2 black, 6 blue, 3 orange, 1 yellow

B 4 black, 4 blue, 2 orange, 1 yellow

C 4 black, 3 blue, 1 orange, 2 yellow

D 4 black, 2 blue, 4 orange, 1 yellow

34 A circular fishpond has a circumference of 15 feet. What is the approximate diameter of the fishpond?

F About 4 ft

G About 5 ft

H About 10 ft

J About 45 ft

35 A circle has a 10-inch diameter. What is the radius of the circle?

A 5 in.

B 10 in.

C 15 in.

D 20 in.

Use the line graph below to answer Questions 36–37.

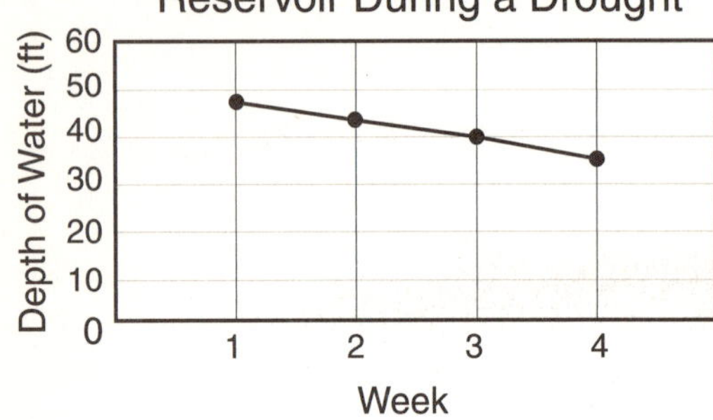

36 Which best describes the trend shown in the graph?

F The depth of the water has been steadily increasing.

G The depth of the water has stayed the same.

H The depth of the water has been steadily decreasing.

J The depth of the water has been rapidly decreasing and increasing.

37 Based on the graph, which is the best prediction for the depth of the water after 6 weeks of drought?

A 38 ft

B 36 ft

C 32 ft

D 28 ft

38 A recreation center has a game room that is $20\frac{1}{4}$ feet by 15.4 feet. There is a rectangular rug that is 12 feet by 8 feet. Approximately what area of the game room is NOT covered by the rug?

F 15 ft^2

G 100 ft^2

H 220 ft^2

J 300 ft^2

Use the table below to answer Questions 39–40.

Length (units)	Width (units)	Height (units)	Volume (cubic units)
5	3	2	30
10	6	2	120
20	12	2	480

39 The length, width, height, and volume of some boxes are shown above.
What happens when the width and length double, but the height stays the same?

A The volume stays the same.

B The volume doubles.

C The volume increases to four times the original.

D The volume increases to six times the original.

40 Which expression can be used to represent the volume of the boxes shown in the table?

F $l + w + h$

G $2(lwh)$

H lwh

J $\frac{1}{2}(l + w + h)$

41 The Party Now Company has two sizes of portable dance floors. One floor is 10 feet squared and the other is 8 feet by 16 feet. What is the area of the larger floor?

A 128 ft^2

B 100 ft^2

C 64 ft^2

D 16 ft^2

Use the list of data below to answer Questions 42–43.

Number of Days Until a Tomato Plant Had a Ripe Tomato

58	83	64	71	60	65
80	75	80	72	74	70

42 What is the mean value of the data?

F 65

G 71

H 76

J Not Here

43 Which has the greatest value in the list above?

A Range

B Median

C Mode

D The range, median, and mode are all the same for this list of data.

44 Which two values, if added to the list, will change the mode?

F 80 and 72

G 80 and 54

H 72 and 72

J 55 and 54

45 Chrissy measures the length of her pet rabbit, Chloe. Chloe is 44 centimeters long. How many millimeters long is the rabbit?

A 44 mm

B 404 mm

C 440 mm

D 4,400 mm

46 A circular garden has a flagpole at the center and paths crossing the garden as shown below.

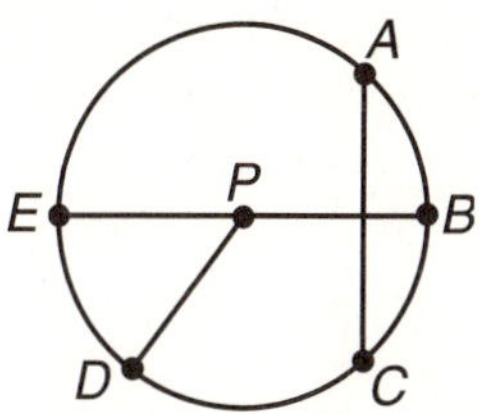

Which path is the diameter?

F $\overline{AC}$

G $\overline{EB}$

H $\overline{PD}$

J $\overline{EP}$

47 What is the volume of the figure shown below?

A 8 units^3

B 12 units^3

C 16 units^3

D 24 units^3

48 A new rectangular coyote enclosure at the zoo is 16 feet wide. To find the area of the enclosure, which value is also needed?

F The height of the enclosure

G The number of animals that will be in the enclosure

H The length of the enclosure

J Not Here

Use the graph below to answer Questions 49–50.

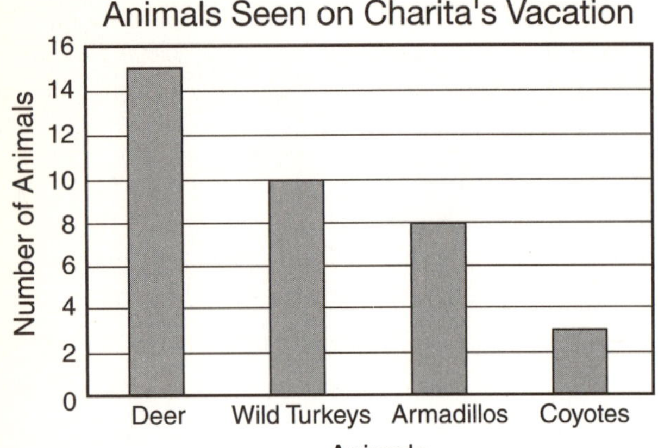

49 How many animals did Charita see in all?

Record your answer and fill in the bubbles on the grid below. Be sure to use the correct place value.

50 Last year Charita saw twice as many armadillos on her vacation as she did this year. How many did she see last year?

F 4

G 8

H 12

J 16

Use the graph below to answer Questions 51–53.

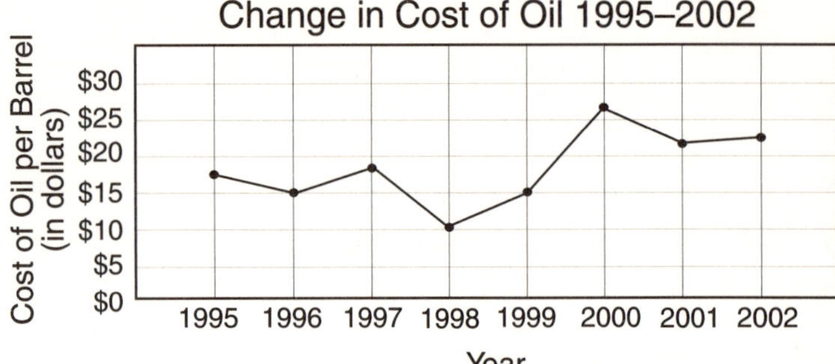

51 For the years shown, in which period was the average cost of a barrel of oil above $20 per barrel?

A 1997–1999

B 1998–2001

C 2000–2002

D Not Here

52 In which year was the average cost the lowest?

F 1995

G 1996

H 1997

J 1998

53 When did the greatest decrease in the price occur?

A From 1997 to 1998

B From 1999 to 2000

C From 2000 to 2001

D From 2001 to 2002

Use the graph below to answer Questions 54–55.

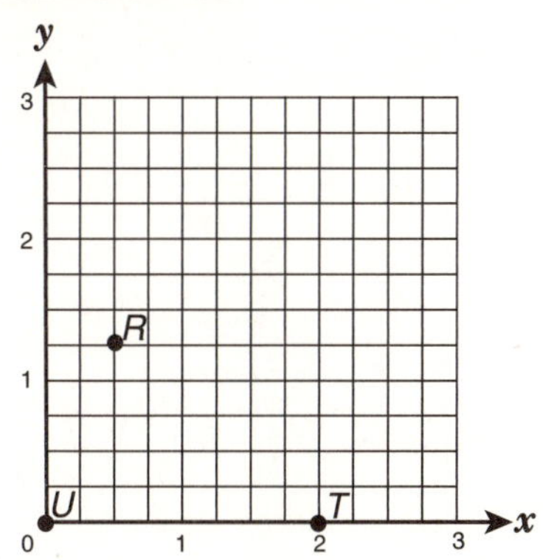

54 What are the coordinates of point R?

F $(1\frac{1}{4}, \frac{1}{2})$

G $(1\frac{3}{4}, 0)$

H $(\frac{1}{2}, 1\frac{1}{4})$

J $(0, 0)$

55 Which coordinates would form a parallelogram with points R, T, and U?

A $(1, 1\frac{1}{4})$

B $(2\frac{1}{2}, 1\frac{1}{4})$

C $(2, 1\frac{1}{4})$

D $(2, 2)$

56 A caterer needs 4 gallons of orange juice for a brunch. The orange juice comes in 48-ounce cans. What is the least number of cans the caterer should buy?

F 3

G 9

H 11

J 15

57 If the pattern below continues as shown, which figure will be the sixth figure?

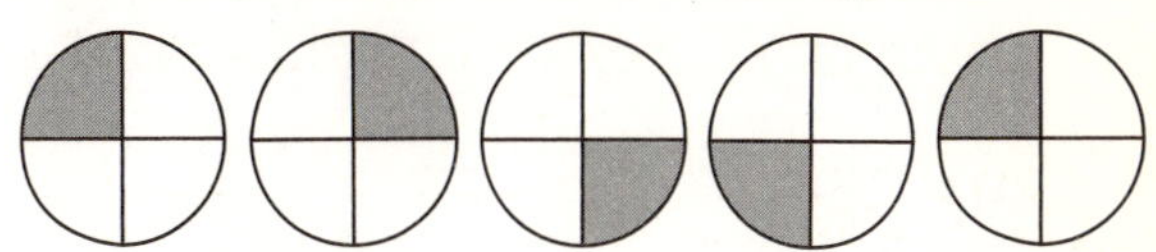

A

B

C

D

58 In the trapezoid shown here, the acute angle measures 40°.

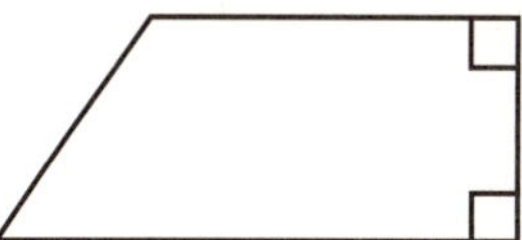

What is the measure of the obtuse angle?

Record your answer and fill in the bubbles on the grid below. Be sure to use the correct place value.

				.		
0	0	0	0		0	0
1	1	1	1		1	1
2	2	2	2		2	2
3	3	3	3		3	3
4	4	4	4		4	4
5	5	5	5		5	5
6	6	6	6		6	6
7	7	7	7		7	7
8	8	8	8		8	8
9	9	9	9		9	9

Use the stem-and-leaf plot below to answer Questions 59–60.

Number of Push-Ups Done by Students on the Football Team

Stem	Leaf
3	3 6 7 7
4	1 3 5 6 8
5	4 4 4 9
6	2 4

59 Which number is NOT shown in the stem-and-leaf plot?

A 36

B 45

C 55

D 62

60 What are the median and mode of the data?

F Median: 6, Mode: 4

G Median: 46, Mode: 54

H Median: 47, Mode: 54

J Median: 48, Mode: 44

61 A bookcase in Becky's room is 6 feet wide. The bookcase sits along a wall with twice as much space to the right of it as to the left of it. If the space to the left of the bookcase is 18 inches, which measure shows the length of the wall?

A 9 ft

B 10 ft

C 54 in.

D 126 in.

Use the thermometer below to answer Questions 62–63.

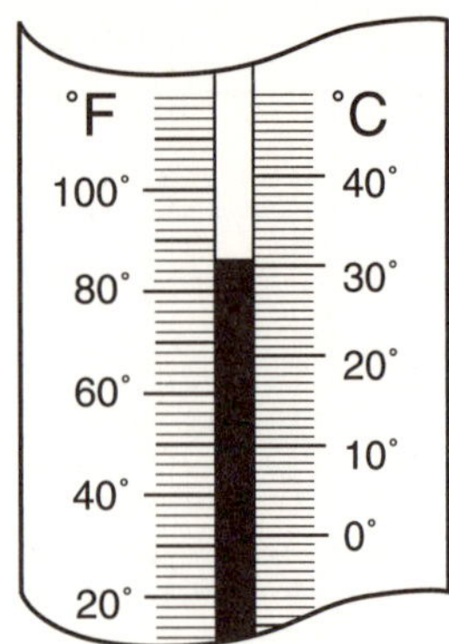

62 The thermometer shows the temperature at 4 P.M. If the temperature drops 4 degrees Fahrenheit each hour, what will the temperature be in degrees Fahrenheit at midnight?

F 73°F

G 69°F

H 54°F

J 21°F

63 The thermometer above shows the air temperature outside. A solar oven is placed outside on a picnic table. An oven thermometer inside the solar oven shows a temperature of 102°C. About how many degrees Celsius warmer is the air inside the solar oven than the air outside?

A 25°C

B 50°C

C 75°C

D 110°C

Use the circle graph below to answer Questions 64–65.

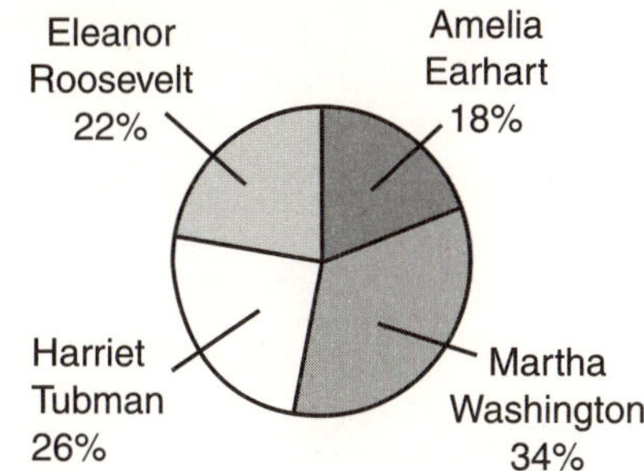

64 If 150 students were surveyed, how many voted for Amelia Earhart?

F 18

G 22

H 25

J 27

65 If 200 students were surveyed, how many more voted for Martha Washington than for Harriet Tubman?

A 16

B 24

C 52

D 68

66 Mr. Miller wants to show the class the distribution of the scores on the final exam. Which graph would best show this?

F Circle graph

G Line graph

H Bar graph

J Stem-and-leaf plot

67 Melanie swims for 45 minutes each morning. If she swims every day in July, how much time will she spend swimming in July?

A 315 minutes

B 15 hours 25 minutes

C 1,350 minutes

D 23 hours 15 minutes

68 Patti packed blue and white hats to wear on her vacation. She also packed red, green, and yellow shirts. If Patti picks a hat and shirt at random, which lists all the possible outcomes?

F

All Possible Outcomes
Blue hat, red shirt
White hat, red shirt
Blue hat, green shirt
White hat, yellow shirt

G

All Possible Outcomes
Blue hat, red shirt
White hat, red shirt
Blue hat, green shirt
White hat, green shirt
Blue hat, yellow shirt
White hat, yellow shirt

H

All Possible Outcomes
Blue hat, red shirt
Blue hat, white shirt
Blue hat, yellow shirt

J

All Possible Outcomes
White hat, red shirt
Blue hat, green shirt
White hat, green shirt
Blue hat, yellow shirt

Notes

End-of-Book
Building Stamina®

The End-of-Book Building Stamina® is a comprehensive review of all the TEKS covered in the lessons.
By practicing with these challenging, broad-based, higher-level thinking questions, you will be building up your stamina to succeed on the TAKS and in other academic endeavors that require higher-level thinking.

Building Stamina®

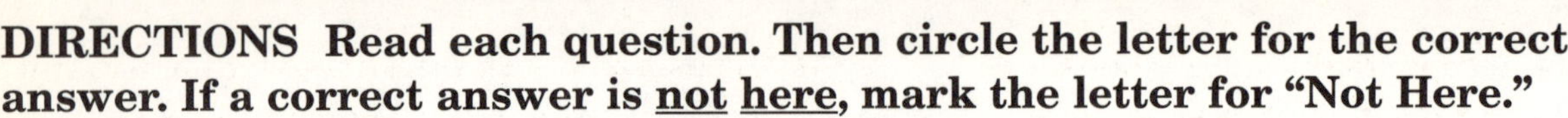

DIRECTIONS Read each question. Then circle the letter for the correct answer. If a correct answer is <u>not</u> <u>here</u>, mark the letter for "Not Here."

1 The distance from Dallas to Atlanta is approximately 1,322 kilometers. The distance from Dallas to New York City is about 2,516 kilometers. Approximately how much greater is the distance from Dallas to New York?

A 3,000 km

B 1,800 km

C 1,200 km

D 1,000 km

2 The table shows the number of visitors to a theme park.

Theme Park Visitors Last Year	
March	5,000,876
April	8,999,334
May	6,987,345
June	10,653,973
July	15,934,732

Which is the best estimate of how many more people visited the theme park in July than in March and April combined?

F About 500,000

G About 2,000,000

H About 4,000,000

J About 14,000,000

3 There are 2 neon signs on the same street. One sign blinks every 12 seconds. The other sign blinks every 15 seconds. Both signs are turned on at the same time. How many times will the first sign have blinked before they both blink at the same time?

A 8

B 6

C 4

D 3

4 Marvin vacuums the living room carpet every 6 days and mops the kitchen floor every 9 days. On February 23, he vacuumed the living room carpet and mopped the kitchen floor. On which previous date did he perform both household chores?

F Jan. 29

G Feb. 5

H Feb. 8

J Feb. 14

5 There are 40,012 seats in the baseball stadium that is home to the Mighty Buffaloes. The Mighty Buffaloes play 38 home games a year. An average of 19,210 fans attend each game. The general manager of the team wants to know how many additional seats could have been filled if each of the home games was sold out. Which expression can be used to find the approximate number of additional seats?

A $(40 \times 40{,}000) - 19{,}200$

B $40 \times (40{,}000 - 19{,}200)$

C $40{,}000 - (40 \times 19{,}200)$

D $(40 \times 19{,}200) - 40{,}000$

6 Lois rents a rehearsal studio. She is charged a flat fee of $250 and an additional hourly charge of $45. She rents the studio from 1 P.M. to 8 P.M. How much will she be charged?

F $295

G $315

H $565

J Not Here

7 Alex is planting 18 white roses and 45 red roses. How many rows can he plant if he wants each row to have the same number of white roses and red roses?

A 5

B 6

C 9

D 12

8 For which set of numbers is 8 the greatest common factor?

F 40, 80, 120

G 24, 56, 88

H 16, 32, 80

J 8, 88, 188

9 Which is NOT a prime factorization?

A $2^3 \cdot 5^4 \cdot 7^2$

B $11^3 \cdot 5^2$

C $3^3 \cdot 5^4 \cdot 7^2$

D $8^2 \cdot 3^2 \cdot 4^3$

10 A cat had 5 kittens. Three were black and the rest were calico. Which decimal represents the fraction of kittens that are calico?

F 0.25

G 0.4

H 0.6

J 0.75

11 A museum is planning to hold a fundraiser which 1,280 people are expected to attend. Each guest will be presented with a pin honoring the occasion. The pins are shipped in boxes of 50. What is the least number of boxes that need to be ordered in order to ensure that there is a pin for every guest?

A 12

B 25

C 26

D 30

12 Betsy is a salesperson. She earns a weekly salary of $650 and $7 for each cosmetic set she sells. Last week, she earned a total of $895. How many cosmetic sets did Betsy sell last week?

Record your answer and fill in the bubbles on the grid below. Be sure to use the correct place value.

				.		
0	0	0	0		0	0
1	1	1	1		1	1
2	2	2	2		2	2
3	3	3	3		3	3
4	4	4	4		4	4
5	5	5	5		5	5
6	6	6	6		6	6
7	7	7	7		7	7
8	8	8	8		8	8
9	9	9	9		9	9

13 Fred has a little less than $150. Which group of items does he NOT have enough money to purchase?

Ties	$12.00
Shirts	$29.95
Pants	$49.95
Overcoats	$125.00
Belts	$9.00

A 3 pairs of pants, a tie, a belt

B 3 shirts, 2 belts, 2 ties

C An overcoat, a belt, a tie

D 4 ties, 2 shirts, 2 belts

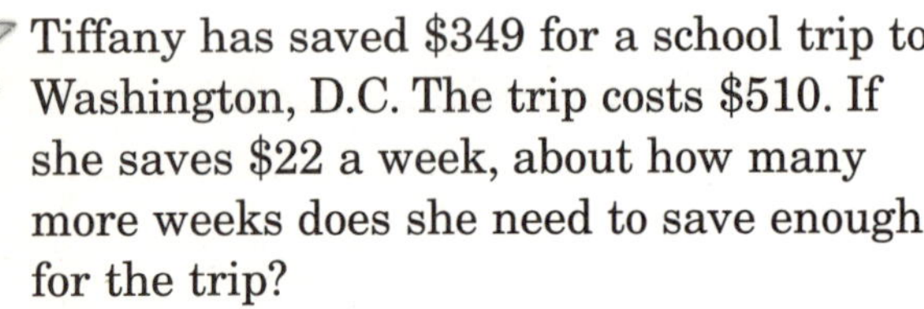

14 Tiffany has saved $349 for a school trip to Washington, D.C. The trip costs $510. If she saves $22 a week, about how many more weeks does she need to save enough for the trip?

F About 4 weeks

G About 6 weeks

H About 8 weeks

J About 10 weeks

15 Which integer is 4 units to the right of -5 on a number line?

A -9

B -1

C 1

D 4

16 Which of the following is NOT equivalent to the ratio 4:5?

F 1:5

G 8:10

H 12:15

J 40:50

17 There are 8 guests at a party standing in a circle. Each person is an equal distance from the person on either side. Martha is the seventh person in the circle. When she looks directly across, which person faces her?

Ken: second person in the circle
Louise: third person in the circle
Arnold: fourth person in the circle
Eugene: fifth person in the circle

A Ken

B Louise

C Arnold

D Eugene

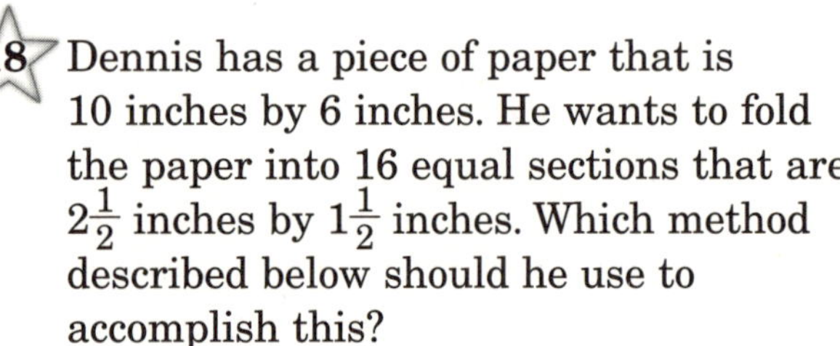

18 Dennis has a piece of paper that is 10 inches by 6 inches. He wants to fold the paper into 16 equal sections that are $2\frac{1}{2}$ inches by $1\frac{1}{2}$ inches. Which method described below should he use to accomplish this?

F Fold the paper in half four times. Fold twice horizontally and twice vertically.

G Fold the paper in half four times vertically.

H Fold the paper in half three times. Fold once horizontally and twice vertically.

J Fold the paper in half two times. Fold once horizontally and once vertically.

19 Which experiment does the tree diagram represent?

A Spin the spinner 1 time and toss the coin 1 time.

B Spin the spinner 1 time and toss 3 coins.

C Spin the spinner 2 times and toss 2 coins.

D Spin the spinner 3 times and toss the coin 1 time.

20 The table shows the winning times for the 440-yard hurdles at a state high school track meet.

Year	Time (seconds)
1999	52.50
2000	53.14
2001	53.33
2002	52.96
2003	53.39
2004	53.01

In which year was the winning time the second slowest?

F 2000

G 2001

H 2003

J 2004

21 Which addition expression has a sum less than \$50 and greater than \$40?

A \$24.22 + \$20.85 + \$13.97

B \$5.11 + \$9.44 + \$17.62

C \$35.15 + \$19.46 + \$4.75

D \$16.32 + \$19.63 + \$11.45

22 The table shows the number of people, in millions, who watched local news on different nights during a certain week.

Night	Males	Females
Monday	1.69	1.80
Tuesday	1.45	1.74
Wednesday	1.94	2.01
Thursday	1.67	1.56
Friday	1.50	1.30

A total of how many males watched the local news on Monday and Tuesday evenings?

F 3,140,000

G 3,040,000

H 314,000

J Not Here

23 What is the value of the expression $(18 + 12) \div 3 + 3$?

A 25

B 20

C 13

D 5

24 The table shows the number of kilometers hiked for each day of a hiking club's annual backpacking trip. On which two days is the difference between the distances hiked about 4 miles?

Day	Distance (Kilometers)
1	8.93
2	7.44
3	11.32
4	10.18

F Day 1 and Day 2

G Day 1 and Day 3

H Day 2 and Day 3

J Day 2 and Day 4

25 You went to the beach with a friend. You spent half of your money on the bus ticket. You forgot to bring sunglasses. After spending half of the remaining money on a pair of sunglasses, you then spent the rest, which was $6, on lunch. How much money did you take to the beach?

A $64

B $48

C $32

D $24

26 How many times do you need to jog around a $\frac{1}{4}$-mile track in order to jog $6\frac{3}{4}$ miles?

F 21

G 27

H 36

J 63

Use the bar graph below to answer Questions 27–28.

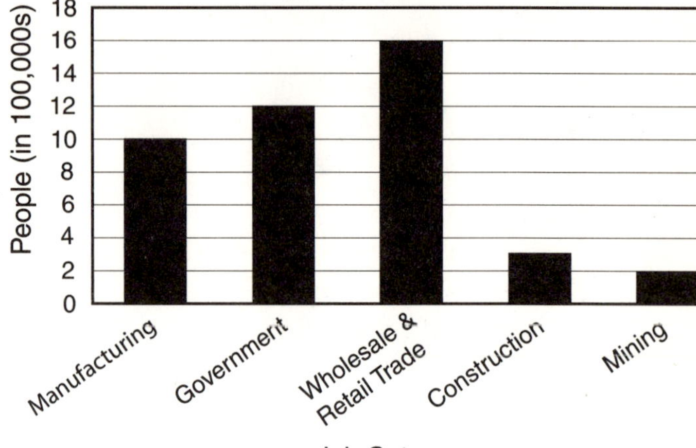

27 In which type of job are the most people employed?

A Manufacturing

B Government

C Wholesale and retail trade

D Construction

28 Fewer people are employed in agriculture than in construction, but more people are employed in agriculture than are employed in mining. Which could be the number of people employed in agriculture?

F 175,000

G 217,000

H 315,000

J 432,000

29 A restaurant seats 200 people. One hundred fifty seats are currently taken by diners. Which fraction shows the number of available seats?

A $\frac{1}{4}$

B $\frac{1}{3}$

C $\frac{2}{3}$

D $\frac{3}{4}$

30 In the set below, all fractions are equivalent. What are the values of a and b?

$\frac{7}{12}, \frac{14}{24}, \frac{a}{36}, \frac{56}{b}$

F $a = 28, b = 94$

G $a = 28, b = 64$

H $a = 21, b = 96$

J $a = 21, b = 84$

31 Matt threw a pizza party. He ordered 6 pizzas. Each pizza was cut into 8 slices. The guests at his party ate $4\frac{1}{4}$ pizzas. How many slices were NOT eaten?

Record your answer and fill in the bubbles on the grid below. Be sure to use the correct place value.

				.		
⓪	⓪	⓪	⓪		⓪	⓪
①	①	①	①		①	①
②	②	②	②		②	②
③	③	③	③		③	③
④	④	④	④		④	④
⑤	⑤	⑤	⑤		⑤	⑤
⑥	⑥	⑥	⑥		⑥	⑥
⑦	⑦	⑦	⑦		⑦	⑦
⑧	⑧	⑧	⑧		⑧	⑧
⑨	⑨	⑨	⑨		⑨	⑨

32 Which shows the number of days that are equivalent to 64 hours?

F $6\frac{1}{4}$ days

G $5\frac{1}{3}$ days

H $2\frac{3}{4}$ days

J $2\frac{2}{3}$ days

33 Which is the prime factorization of 800?

A $8 \cdot 10^2$

B $8 \cdot 5^2 \cdot 2^2$

C $5^2 \cdot 2^5$

D $25 \cdot 4^3$

34 Barbara bought a steak that weighs $4\frac{5}{6}$ pounds. The butcher's scale gives a decimal readout of the weight to the nearest hundredth. What did the scale display for the weight of Barbara's steak?

F 4.38

G 4.56

H 4.83

J 4.88

35 Which statement is NOT true of a trapezoid?

A The sum of the measures of the angles is 360°.

B Opposite sides are parallel.

C One pair of sides is not parallel.

D Sometimes two of the angles are right angles.

36 The table shows the days Cathy worked last week. It shows when she began and finished each day.

Day	Began	Finished
Monday	9:00 A.M.	2:30 P.M.
Tuesday	9:30 A.M.	2:30 P.M.
Wednesday	8:30 A.M.	3:00 P.M.
Thursday	9:00 A.M.	3:00 P.M.
Friday	9:00 A.M.	2:30 P.M.

If Cathy takes $\frac{1}{2}$ hour each day for lunch, which equation shows the total number of hours she worked on Monday, Tuesday, and Wednesday?

F $5\frac{1}{2} + 5\frac{1}{2} + 5\frac{1}{2} = h$

G $5 + 4\frac{1}{2} + 6 = h$

H $5\frac{1}{2} + 4 + 6 = h$

J $6 + 5 + 6\frac{1}{2} = h$

37 Which expression does NOT have a sum that is greater than 8 and less than 11?

A $4\frac{1}{8} + 3\frac{7}{9} + 2\frac{4}{5}$

B $2\frac{1}{8} + 3\frac{2}{5} + 3\frac{1}{3}$

C $6\frac{7}{8} + \frac{3}{4} + 1\frac{11}{12}$

D $5\frac{1}{6} + 3\frac{1}{2} + 3\frac{1}{12}$

38 The fraction bars show that the sum of $\frac{3}{4}$ and $\frac{2}{3}$ is the same as—

1

$\frac{1}{4}$

$\frac{1}{3}$

$\frac{1}{12}$

F the sum of $\frac{7}{12}$ and $\frac{8}{12}$

G the sum of $\frac{8}{12}$ and $\frac{9}{12}$

H the sum of $\frac{8}{12}$ and $\frac{10}{12}$

J the sum of $\frac{9}{12}$ and $\frac{10}{12}$

39 A walking path goes around the perimeter of a triangular park. One side of the park is $1\frac{3}{4}$ miles long. Another side is $\frac{1}{2}$ mile longer. If the entire length of the path is 6 miles, which expression can you use to find the length of the other side of the park?

A $6 - (1\frac{3}{4} + \frac{1}{2})$

B $(6 - 1\frac{3}{4}) + 2\frac{1}{4}$

C $6 - (1\frac{3}{4} + 2\frac{1}{4})$

D Not Here

40 What is the first step you need to perform in order to subtract $\frac{3}{5}$ from $\frac{7}{8}$?

F Find the least common multiple of the numerators.

G Find the least common multiple of the denominators.

H Subtract the smaller numerator from the larger denominator.

J Subtract the smaller denominator from the larger denominator.

41 Benji sleeps $6\frac{3}{4}$ hours each night. Esther sleeps $7\frac{1}{4}$ hours each night, and Brad sleeps $7\frac{2}{3}$ hours each night. Which statement below is true?

A Benji sleeps $\frac{1}{2}$ hour more than Esther each night.

B Brad sleeps $\frac{11}{12}$ hour more than Benji each night.

C Esther sleeps $\frac{1}{2}$ hour less than Brad each night.

D Esther sleeps $\frac{3}{4}$ hour more than Benji each night.

42 Lucas bought two large cakes that were exactly the same size. He cut one cake into 27 pieces. He cut the second cake into 36 pieces. When his father walked by and saw how Lucas cut the cakes, he told Lucas that both cakes need to be sliced so that each piece is exactly the same size. Lucas cuts the cakes again, doing as his father asked. What is the least number of pieces that Lucas can cut each cake into?

Record your answer and fill in the bubbles on the grid below. Be sure to use the correct place value.

				.		
0	0	0	0		0	0
1	1	1	1		1	1
2	2	2	2		2	2
3	3	3	3		3	3
4	4	4	4		4	4
5	5	5	5		5	5
6	6	6	6		6	6
7	7	7	7		7	7
8	8	8	8		8	8
9	9	9	9		9	9

43 A round pie can be cut into 7 pieces with 3 straight cuts. What is the greatest number of pieces that the pie can be cut into with 6 straight cuts?

A 16

B 18

C 22

D 29

44 How many squares are in this figure?

F 9

G 10

H 12

J 14

45 Which sequence follows this rule: Multiply by 2 and subtract 1?

A 3, 6, 12, …

B 3, 5, 9 , …

C 3, 7, 15 , …

D Not Here

46 Which expression can be used to find the nth term of this sequence?

Position	1	2	3	4	…	nth
Value of Term	3	5	7	9	…	

F $n + 2$

G $2n$

H $2n + 1$

J $2n - 1$

47 Kenisha saved \$1 the 1st week, \$2 the 2nd week, \$4 the 3rd week, and \$7 the 4th week. If the pattern continues, how much money should she expect to save in the 10th week?

Record your answer and fill in the bubbles on the grid below. Be sure to use the correct place value.

				.		
0	0	0	0		0	0
1	1	1	1		1	1
2	2	2	2		2	2
3	3	3	3		3	3
4	4	4	4		4	4
5	5	5	5		5	5
6	6	6	6		6	6
7	7	7	7		7	7
8	8	8	8		8	8
9	9	9	9		9	9

48 Margot is doing a report on the climate along the Gulf Coast of Texas. She wants to include information about the amount of rainfall over one year. Which would be the best type of graph for her to use?

F Line graph

G Bar graph

H Stem-and-leaf plot

J Circle graph

49 Michelle has 3 times as many model horses as Gina. Michelle has 12 model horses. Which equation could you use to find how many horses Gina has?

A $g \div 3 = 4$

B $3g = 12$

C $g = 4 + 3$

D $g + 4 = 12$

50 Bob had 15 fish. On Thursday he added more fish to the tank. Now he has 24 fish. If f represents the number of fish he added, $24 - f = 15$ can be used to represent the situation. Which is an equivalent equation?

F $f = 15 - 24$

G $f = 15 + 24$

H $f = 24 \div 15$

J $f + 15 = 24$

51 The table shows the amount of savings of Marx and Jung at different times.

Marx's Savings	Jung's Savings
$4	$ 7
$7	$13
$10	$19
$13	$25

If m represents Marx's savings and j represents Jung's savings, which formula represents the relationship between their savings?

A $m = j - 3$

B $m = j - 9$

C $j = 2m - 1$

D $j = 2m + 1$

52 The side lengths and volumes of some regular prisms are shown in the table below.

Side Lengths and Volumes of Regular Prisms

Side Length (inches)	Volume (cubic inches)
2	8
3	27
4	64
6	216
x	

Which expression can be used to find the volume, in cubic inches, of a similar prism with a side length of x inches?

F $4x$

G $x^2 + 4$

H x^3

J $6x^2$

53 The values of x and y are related in the following table.

x	4	7	10	13
y	8.8	15.4	22	28.6

Which formula could you use to find the value of y?

A $y = x + 4.4$

B $y = x - 2.2$

C $y = 2.2x$

D $y = x - 4.4$

54 The table below shows how the price of rice per pound is related to the number of pounds bought.

Rice (lb)	1	2	3	4
Total Price	$0.75	$1.50	$2.25	$3.00

Which equation shows how to find p, the price of n pounds of rice?

F $p = \frac{n}{0.75}$

G $p = n + 0.75$

H $p = 0.75n$

J $p = 75n$

55 What is the mean, median, and mode of this data set?

{4, 4, 5, 7, 7, 7, 9, 13}

A Mean: 7, Median: 7, Mode: 4

B Mean: 4, Median: 6, Mode: 7

C Mean: 7, Median: 7, Mode: 7

D Mean: 7, Median: 7, Mode: 9

56 The table below shows the electricity bills paid by the Keller family for the months of April through July.

Month	April	May	June	July
Amount	$32	$67	$102	$137

If the pattern continues, how much will their electricity bill be for August?

F $172

G $162

H $102

J $51

57 Four out of a litter of 12 kittens were calico. What is the ratio of calico to noncalico kittens?

A 3:1

B 1:2

C 1:3

D 1:4

58 To make a bleach solution, the teacher uses the ratio of 3 parts water to 1 part bleach. If she uses 2 cups of bleach, how many cups in all will there be in the bleach mixture?

F 1 c

G 3 c

H 4 c

J 8 c

Use the line graph below to answer Questions 59–61.

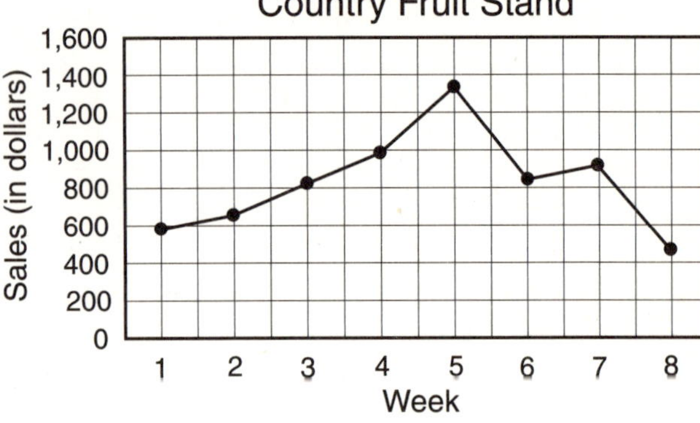

59 About how much were the sales in Week 6?

A $700

B $850

C $900

D $1,000

60 Between which 2 weeks did the greatest change in sales occur?

F Week 2 to Week 3

G Week 3 to Week 4

H Week 4 to Week 5

J Week 5 to Week 6

61 If operating expenses for the farm stand run about $350 a week, approximately what was the total profit for the summer?

A $300

B $1,000

C $2,000

D $4,000

62 A recipe calls for 3 cups flour to $1\frac{1}{2}$ cups sugar to $\frac{1}{2}$ cup brown sugar. What is the ratio of flour to brown sugar?

F 1 to 3

G 3 to 1

H 6 to 1

J 1 to 6

63 Sabrina can buy 3 tennis balls for $4.99. What is the greatest number of tennis balls she could buy for $20?

Record your answer and fill in the bubbles on the grid below. Be sure to use the correct place value.

				.		
0	0	0	0		0	0
1	1	1	1		1	1
2	2	2	2		2	2
3	3	3	3		3	3
4	4	4	4		4	4
5	5	5	5		5	5
6	6	6	6		6	6
7	7	7	7		7	7
8	8	8	8		8	8
9	9	9	9		9	9

64 Which of the following is NOT a true proportion?

F 1:3 = 4:12

G 2:4 = 1:2

H 4:9 = 16:36

J 4:3 = 5:4

65 On a scale drawing of a park, $\frac{1}{8}$ inch = 1 foot. How many feet are represented by a length of $13\frac{5}{8}$ inches?

Record your answer and fill in the bubbles on the grid below. Be sure to use the correct place value.

				.		
0	0	0	0		0	0
1	1	1	1		1	1
2	2	2	2		2	2
3	3	3	3		3	3
4	4	4	4		4	4
5	5	5	5		5	5
6	6	6	6		6	6
7	7	7	7		7	7
8	8	8	8		8	8
9	9	9	9		9	9

66 There are 400 students in sixth grade. Of these students, 180 are boys. What percent of sixth graders are girls?

F 30%

G 45%

H 55%

J Not Here

67 Which of the following statements is NOT true?

A 0.9% = 0.09

B 20% = 0.2

C 39% = 0.39

D 230% = 2.30

68 Which 2 whole numbers have a product of 108 and a sum of 21?

F 1 and 108

G 2 and 51

H 4 and 27

J 9 and 12

69 Alex wants to line the 4 shelves in his room. Each shelf is 44 inches in length. The shelf lining comes in 6-foot-long rolls. How many rolls will he need to buy to line the shelves?

A 2

B 3

C 4

D 5

70 Nikki scored 80% on her math test. Alvin scored 80% on his reading test. Nikki answered 8 more questions correctly than Alvin did. Together, their correct answers totaled 72. How many questions were on each test?

F Nikki's test, 40; Alvin's test, 50

G Nikki's test, 45; Alvin's test, 45

H Nikki's test, 50; Alvin's test, 40

J Nikki's test, 40; Alvin's test, 40

Use the figure below to answer Questions 71–72.

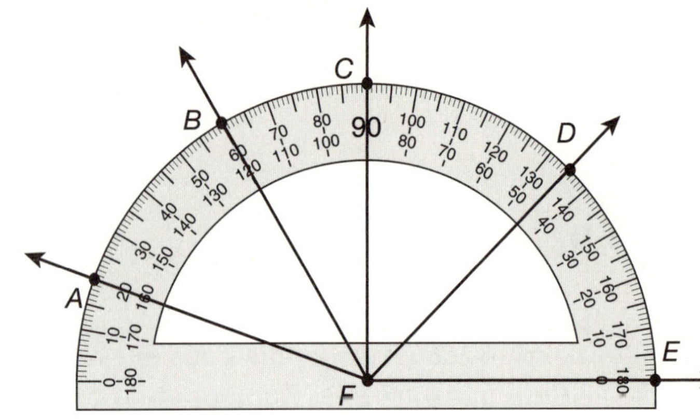

71 Which angle is an acute angle?

A $\angle AFE$

B $\angle BFE$

C $\angle CFE$

D $\angle DFE$

72 What is the measure of $\angle AFB$?

Record your answer and fill in the bubbles on the grid below. Be sure to use the correct place value.

				.		
0	0	0	0		0	0
1	1	1	1		1	1
2	2	2	2		2	2
3	3	3	3		3	3
4	4	4	4		4	4
5	5	5	5		5	5
6	6	6	6		6	6
7	7	7	7		7	7
8	8	8	8		8	8
9	9	9	9		9	9

73 Which graph best represents the following statement? "The sales of DVDs increased slowly, and then more rapidly."

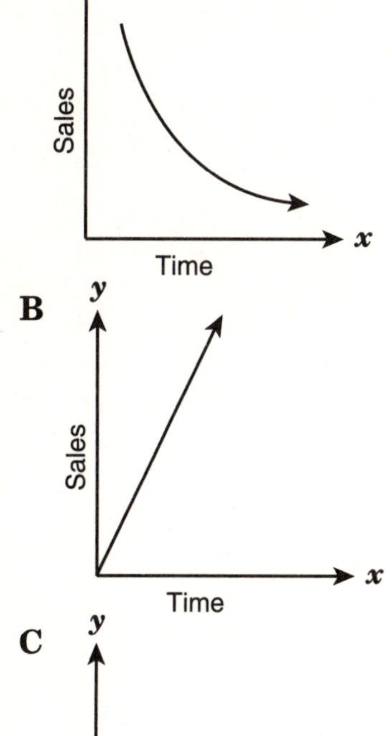

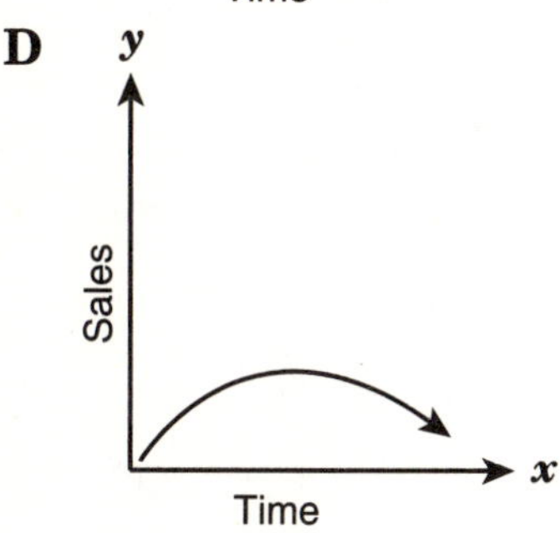

D

y

Sales

Time

x

74 Which of the following has an acute angle?

F

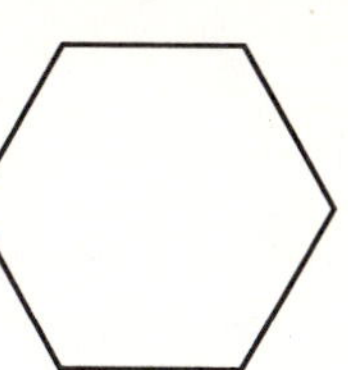

G

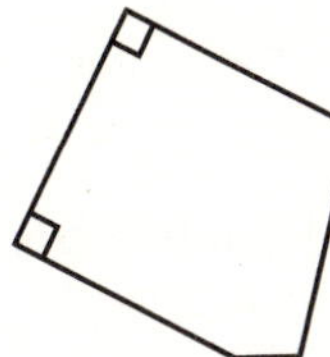

H

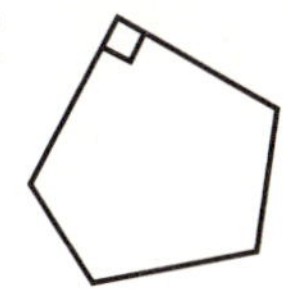

J

75 Fabio made this sign in woodshop.

What is the best description of the shape of the sign?

A Regular parallelogram

B Equilateral quadrilateral

C Parallelogram

D Rhombus

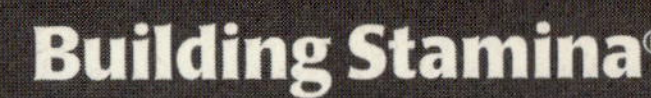

Use the figures below to answer Questions 76–77.

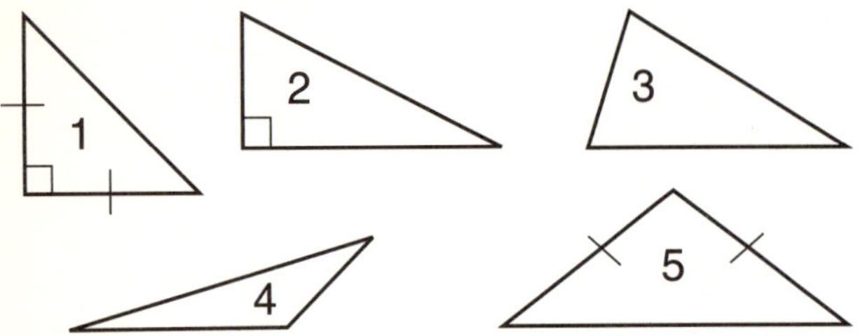

76 Which triangle or triangles are isosceles?

F 1 and 5

G 1 and 2

H 5

J 1, 4 and 5

77 Which triangle or triangles are scalene?

A 1, 2, and 3

B 2, 3, and 4

C 3

D 4

78 The circumference of a beach ball is about 24 centimeters. How does the circumference compare to the radius of the beach ball?

F The circumference is about $\frac{1}{6}$ the radius.

G The circumference is about $\frac{1}{3}$ the radius.

H The circumference is about 3 times the radius.

J The circumference is about 6 times the radius.

79 On a surveyor's map, a piece of property has this shape.

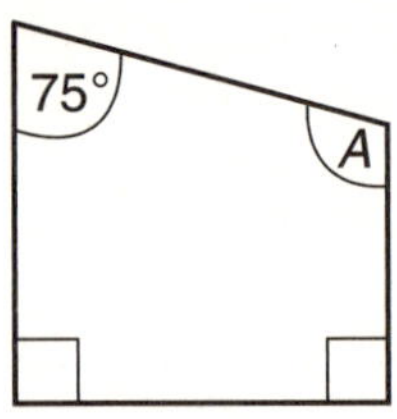

What is the measure of the angle *A*?

A 75°

B 90°

C 105°

D 360°

80 Lin made the kite shown below. What is the measure of the angle at the tail of the kite?

F 40°

G 60°

H 170°

J 190°

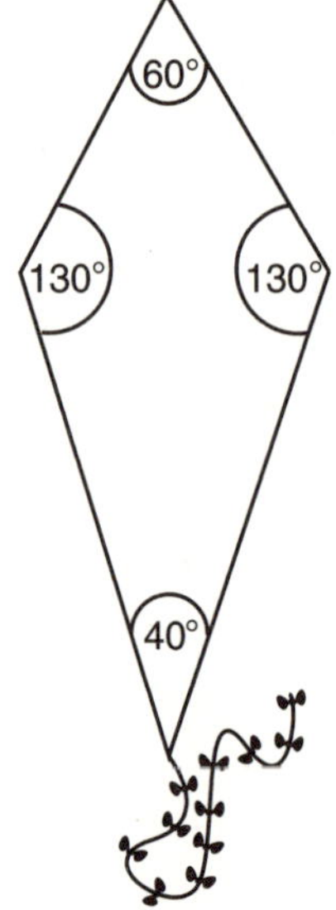

81 Which fraction is equivalent to 0.875?

A $\frac{3}{5}$

B $\frac{7}{8}$

C $\frac{4}{15}$

D $\frac{5}{16}$

Use the figure below to answer Questions 82–83.

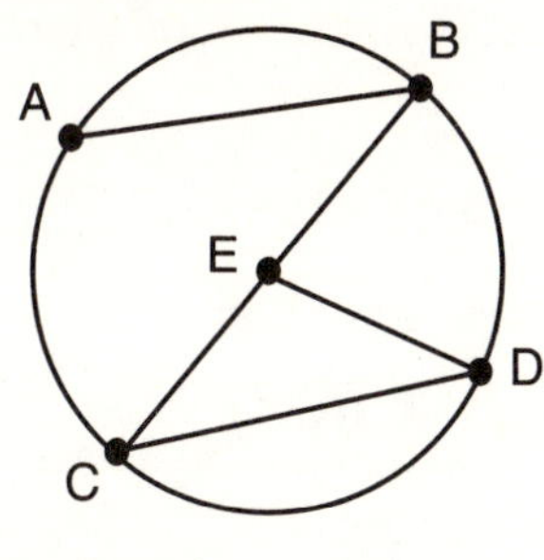

82 Which is NOT a radius?

F *AB*

G *BE*

H *CE*

J *DE*

83 If the measure of *ED* is 2.5 meters, what is the measure of *BC*?

A 2.5 m

B 5.0 m

C 7.5 m

D 25 m

Use the graph below to answer Questions 84–85.

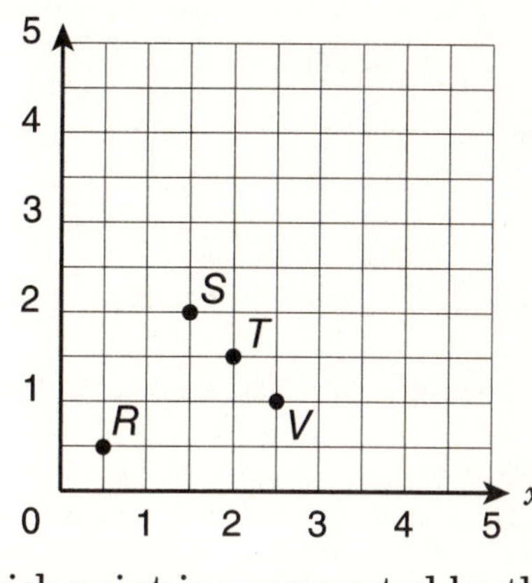

84 Which point is represented by the ordered pair $(2, 1\frac{1}{2})$?

F Point *R*

G Point *S*

H Point *T*

J Point *V*

85 Which coordinate pair best represents point *V* on the coordinate grid above?

A $(1, 2\frac{1}{2})$

B (2, 1)

C (5, 2)

D $(2\frac{1}{2}, 1)$

86 If the pattern in the sequence below is continued, how many squares will be shaded in the next figure?

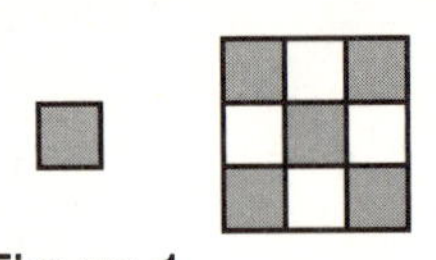

Figure 1 Figure 2 Figure 3

F 12

G 13

H 25

J 36

87 Figure 1 relates to Figure 2 as Figure 3 relates to which of the figures below?

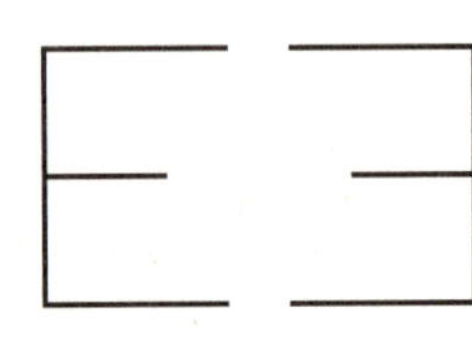

Figure 1 Figure 2 Figure 3

A

B

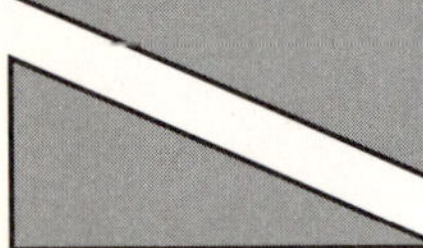

C

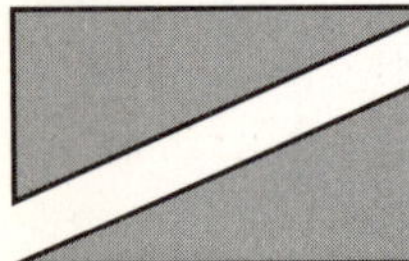

D

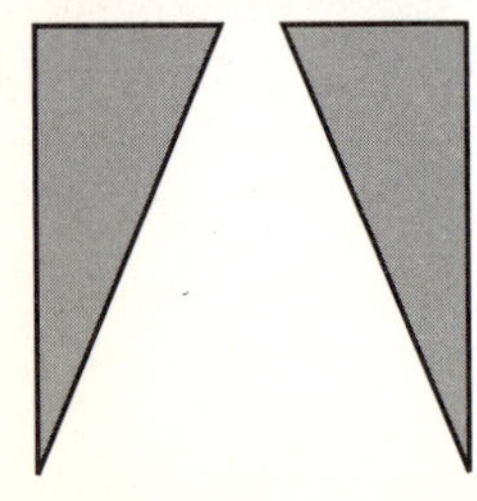

88 Janice has $2.70 in quarters and dimes. She has five times as many quarters as she has dimes. How many of each coin does she have?

F 12 dimes, 6 quarters

G 10 quarters, 2 dimes

H 10 dimes, 2 quarters

J 20 dimes, 4 quarters

89 Michael is working in the school garden. He measures a ladybug and a grasshopper. The ladybug measures 7 millimeters in length. The grasshopper measures 6 centimeters in length. About how many ladybugs would equal the length of the grasshopper?

A About 2

B About 9

C About 13

D About 42

90 Shawna is on the swim team. She can swim 100 yards in 2 minutes. At that speed, how many feet can she swim in 5 minutes?

F 1,500 ft

G 750 ft

H 300 ft

J 250 ft

91 The food service director of a summer camp ordered a 5-gallon container of maple syrup. How many 10-ounce jars can be filled from the container?

A 84

B 64

C 50

D 20

92 Alonzo needs 96 ounces of white paint and 160 ounces of blue paint to paint his grandmother's porch. The white paint costs $8.95 a quart and the blue paint is on sale for $6.75 a quart. About how much is the cost of the paint?

F $15

G $45

H $60

J $100

93 A cafeteria uses a number 8 dipper to serve macaroni and cheese. The number 8 dipper serves a portion that is 5 ounces. How many portions can be served from a steam tray that holds 10 pounds of macaroni and cheese?

Record your answer and fill in the bubbles on the grid below. Be sure to use the correct place value.

				.		
0	0	0	0		0	0
1	1	1	1		1	1
2	2	2	2		2	2
3	3	3	3		3	3
4	4	4	4		4	4
5	5	5	5		5	5
6	6	6	6		6	6
7	7	7	7		7	7
8	8	8	8		8	8
9	9	9	9		9	9

94 Mrs. Moore bought 5 pounds 12 ounces of chocolate chip cookies and 3 pounds 12 ounces of peanut butter cookies. Each cookie weighs 2 ounces. How many cookies did she buy?

F 12

G 32

H 76

J 152

Use the thermometer below to answer Questions 95–96.

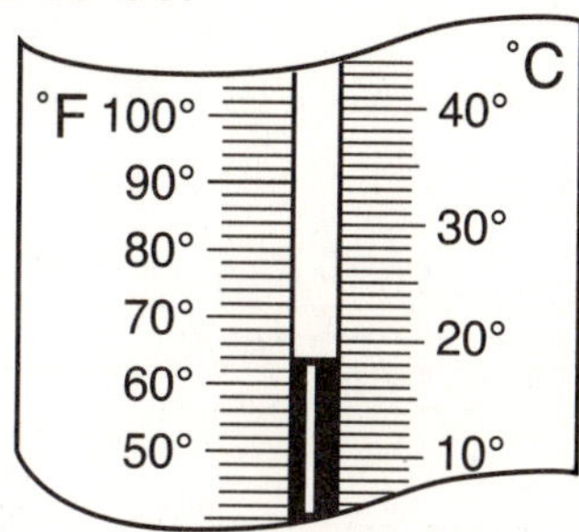

95 The thermometer shows the temperature at 6 A.M. If the temperature rises 6 degrees Fahrenheit each hour, what will the temperature be in degrees Fahrenheit at noon?

A 28°F

B 70°F

C 94°F

D 100°F

96 The thermometer above shows the air temperature outside. Inside Marinda's house, the temperature is about 6 degrees Celsius warmer. What is the temperature in degrees Celsius inside Marinda's house?

F 18°C

G 24°C

H 30°C

J 70°C

97 Every Saturday, Tommy does yard work for a neighbor from 9:30 A.M. to 12:45 P.M. The neighbor pays him $8 an hour. How much does Tommy earn in four weeks?

A $24

B $96

C $104

D Not Here

98 A rectangular swimming pool is 10 feet by 20 feet.

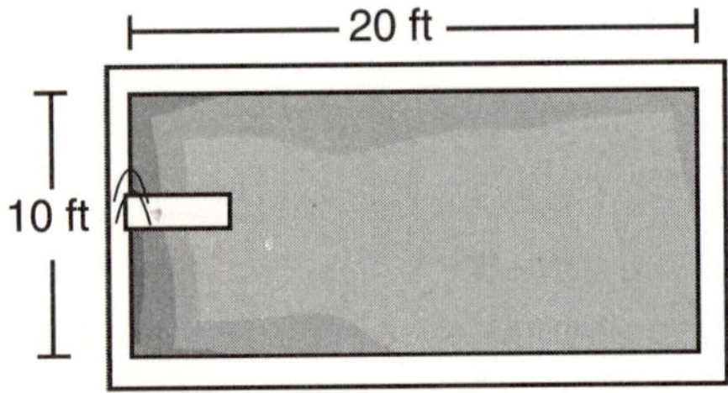

There is a 1-foot-wide border of tiles around the pool. Each tile is 1 square foot. The corner tiles are green. The tiles along the width alternate blue and white. The tiles along the length alternate blue and black. How many blue tiles are there?

F 10

G 15

H 30

J 40

99 An elephant's heart beats about 25 times a minute. How many times does an elephant's heart beat in a day?

A About 1,500

B About 1,750

C About 36,000

D About 100,800

100 Dawn walks 3 blocks east from home to Sara's house. Together, Dawn and Sara walk 4 blocks south to the grocery store. At the store, they meet their friend Rachel and walk 2 blocks west to Rachel's house. At Rachel's house, Dawn realizes that she needs to get home as quickly as possible to babysit for her little brother. What is the least number of blocks Dawn needs to walk to get home as quickly as possible?

F 1

G 5

H 7

J 11

101 What is the perimeter of the figure shown below?

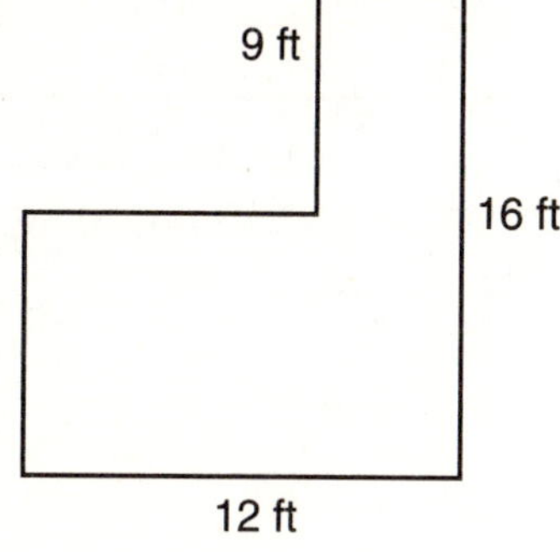

A 25 ft

B 28 ft

C 40 ft

D 56 ft

Use the figure below to answer Questions 102–103.

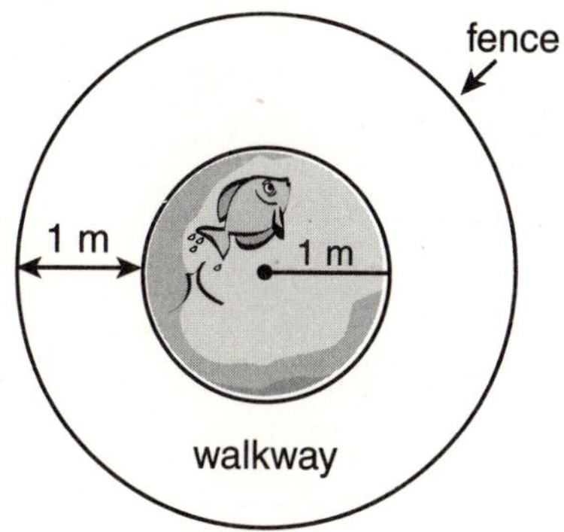

102 What is the approximate circumference of the fishpond?

A 2 m

B 3 m

C 5 m

D 6 m

103 What is the approximate length of the fence surrounding the walkway?

F 4 m

G 6 m

H 12 m

J 25 m

104 Mr. Emery places a photo that is 8 inches by 10 inches in a frame that is 12 inches by 14 inches.

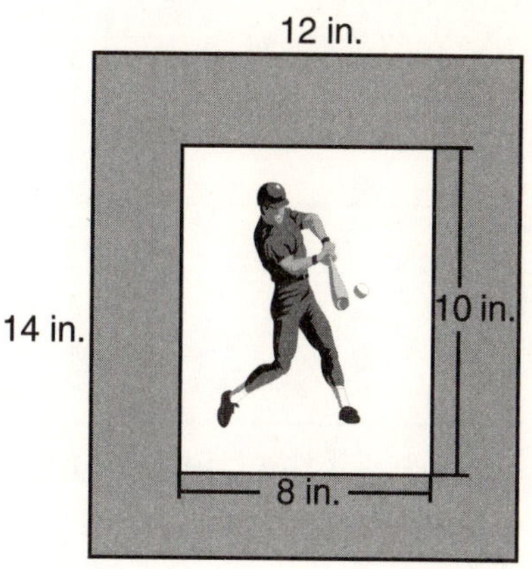

What is the area of the mat around the photo?

A 88 in.^{2}

B 128 in.^{2}

C 168 in.^{2}

D 248 in.^{2}

105 For a craft project, Alice cut a hexagon from a piece of gray felt. Each side on the hexagon measures 8 inches. She wants to glue a border of black trim around the edge. How many feet of trim does she need?

F 3 ft

G 4 ft

H 5 ft

J 6 ft

Use the diagram of a quilt square below to answer Questions 106–107.

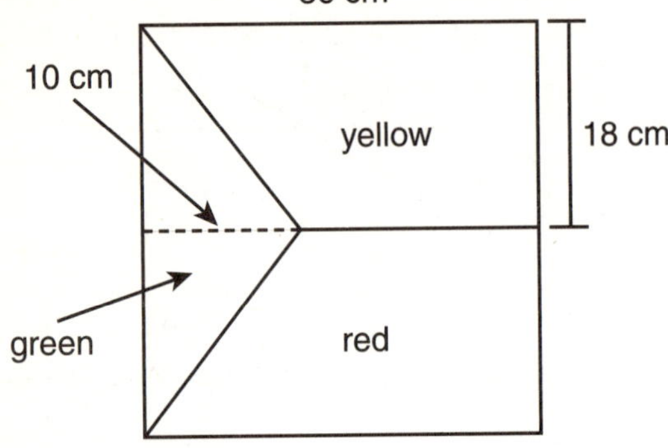

106 What is the area of the triangular part of the quilt square?

F 180 cm^2

G 260 cm^2

H 360 cm^2

J 900 cm^2

107 What is the red area of the quilt square?

A 360 cm^2

B 558 cm^2

C 1,116 cm^2

D 1,296 cm^2

108 Kari has a cube-shaped photo holder on her desk. It measures 4 inches on each edge. What is the volume of the photo holder?

F 4 $in.^3$

G 8 $in.^3$

H 16 $in.^3$

J 64 $in.^3$

Use the table below to answer Questions 109–110.

Storage Shed Dimensions

Model	Height	Width	Length
A	8 feet	8 feet	10 feet
B	10 feet	12 feet	10 feet

109 What is the volume of Model A?

A 80 ft^3

B 640 ft^3

C 800 ft^3

D 1,064 ft^3

110 If the price of the Model A storage shed is $50 a month, which would be a reasonable price for Model B?

F No more than $60

G Between $60 and $95

H Between $100 and $120

J More than $120

111 For which figure or figures is there enough information to find the area?

Figure A—a triangle with a base of 15 centimeters and a height of 8 centimeters
Figure B—a rectangle with a perimeter of 60 inches
Figure C—a square with a perimeter of 24 inches

A Figures A and B

B Figures B and C

C Figures A and C

D Figure A

112 Phyllis bought this aquarium for $70.

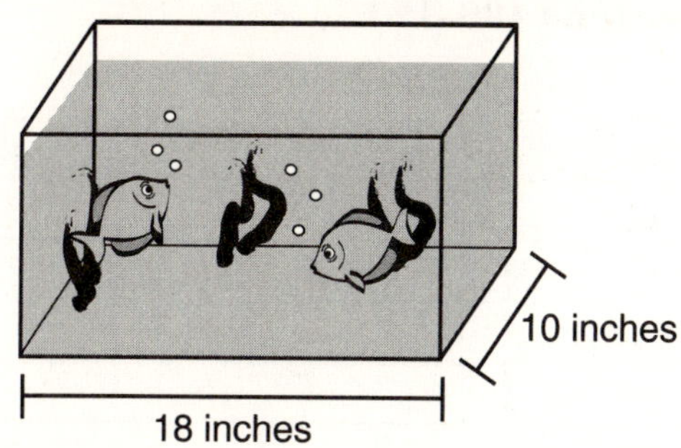

Which problem can be solved with the information given?

F The area of the tabletop that the aquarium will occupy

G The volume of the aquarium

H The total cost of the aquarium and 2 fish

J The volume of space available per fish if she puts 3 fish in the aquarium

113 If you spin each spinner below once, which list represents the sample space?

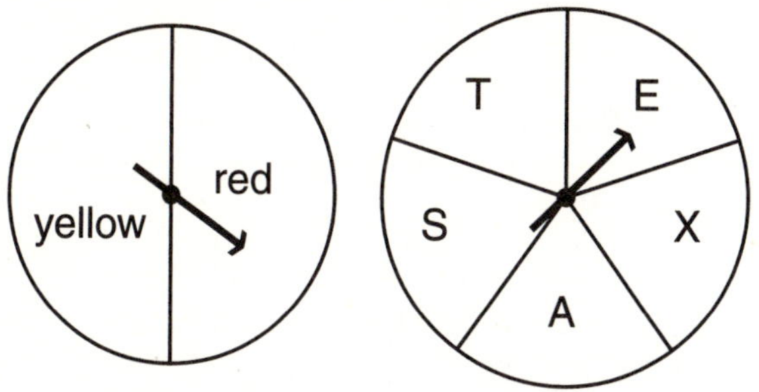

A Red, T; red, E; red, X; red, A; red, S; yellow, T; yellow, E; yellow, X; yellow, A; yellow, S

B Yellow, X; yellow, A; yellow, S; yellow, T; yellow, E

C Red, A; red, S; red, T; red, E; red, X

D Not Here

114 Kaitlyn spins this spinner once.

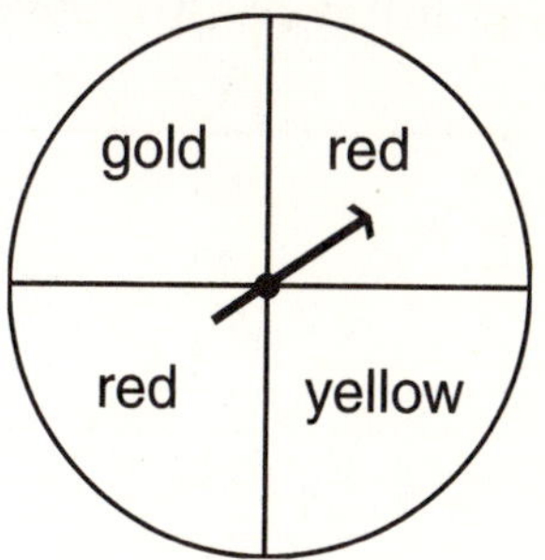

What is the probability that she spins red?

F $\frac{1}{4}$

G $\frac{1}{2}$

H $\frac{3}{4}$

J $\frac{2}{2}$

115 What is the greatest number between 4 and 4.5 that can be written using the digits 1, 3, 4, and 7?

A 4.713

B 4.371

C 4.317

D 4.173

116 If a game is played by drawing a card from a set of cards A–L and tossing a coin, which is a possible outcome?

F A, Z

G Heads, heads

H Z, tails

J C, tails

Use the set of data and the stem-and-leaf plot below to answer Questions 117–119.

Advanced Mathematics Test Scores					
43	63	52	44	58	62
58	46	53	49	59	45
48	61	66	54	47	46

Advanced Mathematics Test Scores

Stem	Leaf
4	3 4 5 6 6 7 8 9
5	2 3 4 8 9
6	1 2 3 6

117 Which score was left out of the stem-and-leaf plot?

A 44

B 53

C 58

D 66

118 Which is the range of the scores?

F 23

G 24

H 25

J 30

119 The mean score on a previous test with the same number of items was 55. What was the change in the mean on this test?

A −3

B −2

C +1

D +2

Use the table below to answer Questions 120–122.

Batting Practice

Player	Number of Pitches	Number of Hits
Conor	20	13
Joey	25	5
Brittany	24	7
Lupe	30	11

120 What is the experimental probability of Joey NOT making a hit?

F $\frac{4}{5}$

G $\frac{13}{20}$

H $\frac{5}{36}$

J $\frac{25}{99}$

121 Who is most likely the best hitter?

A Conor

B Joey

C Brittany

D Lupe

122 If Lupe bats 45 times, what is the best prediction of the number of hits she will make?

F 11

G 17

H 22

J 33

123 The lunch special at the Taste of Texas Café includes a salad, an entrée, and a dessert.

Salads	Mixed green Spicy Texas coleslaw
Entrees	Macaroni & cheese Turkey & gravy Texas burger
Dessert	Pecan pie Brownie

How many different ways can the lunch special be ordered?

A 3

B 6

C 8

D 12

124 Ms. Giddle asked her 20 students what they like best for breakfast from a list of 5 choices. Which type of graph would best represent the percentages of students that like each of the 5 choices?

F Line graph

G Bar graph

H Stem-and-leaf plot

J Circle graph

Use the data below to answer Questions 125–127.

Julian's Swim Times (in seconds)
67 75 72 71 82
66 71 71 77 88

Garth's Swim Times (in seconds)
76 79 74 78 78
73 70 72 78 69

Boyd's Swim Times (in seconds)
73 88 72 89 70
88 79 84 73 81

Carlos' Swim Times (in seconds)
88 88 85 83 96
84 98 93 86 95

125 Which swimmer's set of times had the greatest range?

A Julian

B Garth

C Boyd

D Carlos

126 Which swimmer had the fastest median time?

F Julian

G Garth

H Boyd

J Carlos

127 For which swimmer's set of times is the mode and median the same?

A Julian

B Garth

C Boyd

D Carlos

Grade 6

Mathematics Chart

LENGTH

Metric	Customary
1 kilometer = 1,000 meters	1 mile = 1,760 yards
1 meter = 100 centimeters	1 mile = 5,280 feet
1 centimeter = 10 millimeters	1 yard = 3 feet
	1 foot = 12 inches

CAPACITY AND VOLUME

Metric	Customary
1 liter = 1,000 milliliters	1 gallon = 4 quarts
	1 gallon = 128 ounces
	1 quart = 2 pints
	1 pint = 2 cups
	1 cup = 8 ounces

MASS AND WEIGHT

Metric	Customary
1 kilogram = 1,000 grams	1 ton = 2,000 pounds
1 gram = 1,000 milligrams	1 pound = 16 ounces

TIME

1 year = 365 days
1 year = 12 months
1 year = 52 weeks
1 week = 7 days
1 day = 24 hours
1 hour = 60 minutes
1 minute = 60 seconds

Centimeters
0 1 2 3 4 5 6 7 8 9 10 11 12 13 14 15 16 17 18 19 20

Inches
0 1 2 3 4 5 6

Continued on next page

Mathematics Chart

Perimeter	square	$P = 4s$
	rectangle	$P = 2l + 2w$ or $P = 2(l + w)$
Circumference	circle	$C = 2\pi r$ or $C = \pi d$
Area	square	$A = s^2$
	rectangle	$A = lw$ or $A = bh$
	triangle	$A = \frac{1}{2}bh$ or $A = \frac{bh}{2}$
	trapezoid	$A = \frac{1}{2}(b_1 + b_2)h$ or $A = \frac{(b_1 + b_2)h}{2}$
	circle	$A = \pi r^2$
Volume	cube	$V = s^3$
	rectangular prism	$V = lwh$
Pi		$\pi \approx 3.14$ or $\pi \approx \frac{22}{7}$

Problem-Solving Guide

To solve some mathematics problems you need to think about the question in a different way. You need to use special problem-solving skills like the ones below. You can use these four steps to solve any problem. Just follow the steps one at a time. Now you're on your way to becoming a good problem solver.

<table>
<tr><td>Step 1</td><td>Understand the problem.
Think about what you need to do to solve the problem.
• Read the problem carefully.
• What does the problem ask you to find?
• What information do you need to solve the problem?
• Do you need an exact answer or an estimate?</td></tr>
<tr><td>Step 2</td><td>Make a plan.
Choose a strategy that works best for the problem.
• Draw a picture
• Look for a pattern
• Guess and check
• Act it out
• Make a table
• Solve a simpler problem
• Work backwards
• Choose an operation</td></tr>
<tr><td>Step 3</td><td>Solve the problem.
Follow your plan to solve the problem.
• How can you use the strategy to help solve the problem?
• Write down the steps you need to follow.
• Show all your work.
• Record your answer.</td></tr>
<tr><td>Step 4</td><td>Check your answer.
• Look back at the problem.
• Did you answer the question that that problem asks?
• Does your answer make sense?
• How else could you solve the problem? Do you get the same answer?</td></tr>
</table>

Use the chart on page 289 to organize your thinking while solving problems.

Use this problem-solving organizer to help you solve problems.

Step 1 Understand the problem. Write what the problem asks you to find.
Step 2 Make a Plan. Write the steps you'll take to solve the problem.
Step 3 Solve the problem. Show your work and record your answer.
Step 4 Check your answer. Explain why your answer makes sense.

A

angle (ángulo) a shape formed when two rays meet at a vertex; Lesson 30

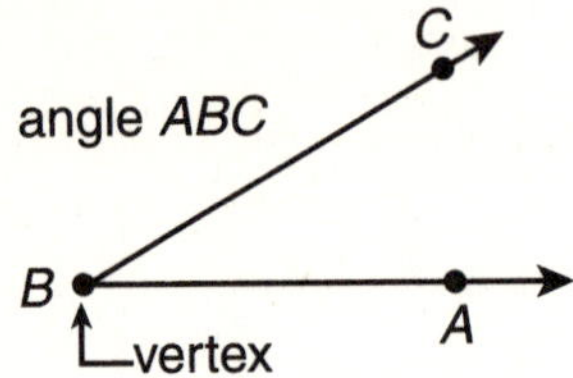

area (área) the number of square units used to cover a region. Area can be measured in standard or metric units such as the square inch (in.^{2}) or square centimeter (cm^2); Lesson 45

B

bar graph (gráfica de barras) a graph that shows data that can be counted. Bar graphs are used primarily to compare data. Bar graphs can have vertical or horizontal bars; Lesson 54

C

Celsius (°C) (Celsio) the metric unit for measuring temperature; Lesson 40

center point (punto central) a point lying in the middle of a circle that has the same distance from all points on the circle; Lesson 34

certain event (suceso seguro) an event that has a probability of 1 and will always occur; Lesson 50

chord (cuerda) a line segment whose endpoints are on the circle; Lesson 34

circle (círculo) a closed figure having all points the same distance from the center point; Lesson 34

chord
diameter (*d*)
radius (*r*)
center
circumference (*C*)

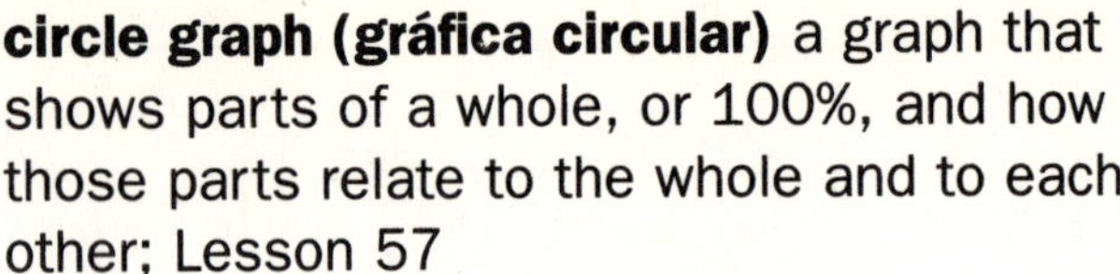

circle graph (gráfica circular) a graph that shows parts of a whole, or 100%, and how those parts relate to the whole and to each other; Lesson 57

circumference (circunferencia) the distance around a circle; Lessons 34, 44

common factor (factor común) a number that is a factor of two or more given numbers; Lesson 4

common multiple (múltiplo común) a multiple of two or more given numbers; Lesson 2

composite number (número compuesto) a whole number greater than 1 with more than two factors; Lesson 5

coordinate plane (cuadrícula de coordenadas) a grid that uses coordinates to show the location of points in space; Lesson 35

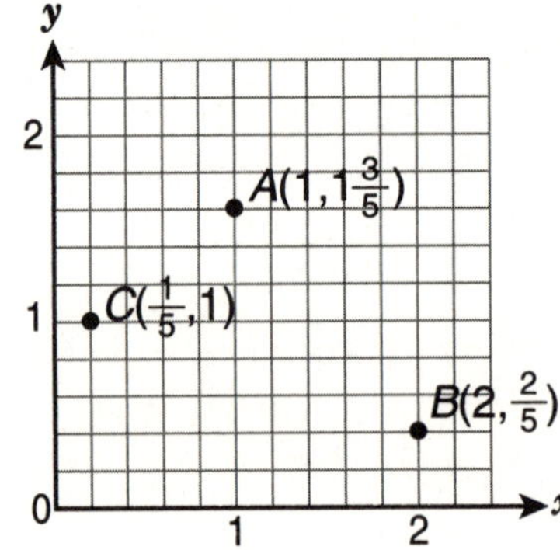

cross products (productos cruzados) multiplying on the diagonals of a proportion to determine equality; Lesson 27

D

decimal (decimal) a number that has one or more digits to the right of a decimal point; Lesson 17

diagonal (diagonal) a line segment that joins two vertices of a polygon, but is not a side of the polygon; Lesson 33

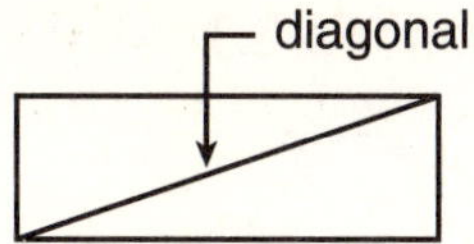

diameter (diámetro) a line segment that passes through the center of a circle and has both endpoints on the circle. The length of the diameter is twice the radius; Lessons 34, 44

dividend (dividendo) the number being divided in a division problem; Lesson 6

divisor (divisor) the number you divide by in a division problem; Lesson 6

E

equation (ecuación) a number sentence with an equal symbol (=); Lesson 22

equivalent fractions (fracciones equivalentes) fractions that name the same amount. To find equivalent fractions, you can multiply or divide the numerator and denominator by the same nonzero number; Lesson 15

equivalent ratios (razones equivalentes) different ratios that have the same value, such as $\frac{2}{3}$ and $\frac{4}{6}$; Lesson 26

experimental probability (probabilidad experimental) a ratio based on experimental data that is found by repeating the experiment several times; Lesson 51

$$P(E) = \frac{\text{number of times an event happens}}{\text{number of times the experiment is done}}$$

expression (expresión) a mathematical statement using numbers, variables and operations. A variable is a letter or symbol used to represent an unknown; Lesson 21

F

factors (factores) the numbers you multiply o get a product; Lessons 3, 4

Fahrenheit (°F) (Fahrenheit) the customary unit for measuring temperature; Lesson 40

fair game (juego justo) a game in which all the players have the same chance of winning; Lesson 48

formula (fórmula) an equation stating a relationship among variables; Lesson 23

G

greatest common factor (máximo común divisor) the greatest whole number that is a factor of each of the numbers; Lesson 4

I

impossible event (suceso imposible) an event that has a probability of 0 and will never occur. If $P(E)$ is the probability of an event occurring, the probability that the event will not occur is $1 - P(E)$; Lesson 50

improper fraction (fracción impropia) a fraction with a numerator greater than or equal to its denominator; Lesson 16

isosceles trapezoid (trapecio isósceles) a quadrilateral with one pair of parallel sides called bases and nonparallel sides, called legs, that are equal in length; Lesson 33

L

least common denominator (mínimo común denominador) the least common multiple of the denominators of two or more fractions. When adding and subtracting fractions with unlike denominators, use the least common denominator to find equivalent fractions; Lessons 18, 19

least common multiple (mínimo común múltiplo) the least number that is a common multiple of two or more given numbers; Lesson 2

line graph (gráfica lineal) a graph that is used primarily to show how one item of data changes over time. Coordinate points are plotted and then joined by a line; Lesson 55

lowest terms (mínima expresión) a rate or ratio that has no common factors other than 1; Lesson 26

M

mean (media) the sum of the data items divided by the number of addends, or data items; the *average* of a set of data; Lesson 53

median (mediana) the middle number or the average of the two middle numbers in a set of data that is arranged in numerical order; Lesson 53

mixed number (número mixto) a number made up of a whole number and a fraction; Lesson 16

mode (modo) the number that occurs most often in a data set. The data set may have no mode, one mode, or more than one mode; Lesson 53

multiple (múltiplo) a number that is a product of a number times any whole number greater than zero; Lesson 2

N

negative numbers (números negativos) numbers less than zero. Zero is neither positive nor negative; Lesson 8

O

origin (origen) the point where the *x*-axis and *y*-axis intersect on a coordinate grid; Lesson 35

P

parallelogram (paralelogramo) a quadrilateral with opposite sides that are parallel and the same length; Lessons 33, 45

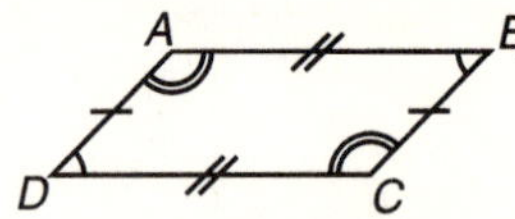

partial product (producto parcial) when multiplying a three-digit number, the product after multiplying by ones, after multiplying by tens, or after multiplying by hundreds is called a partial product; Lesson 3

percent (porcentaje) a ratio that compares a number to 100; Lesson 28

perimeter (perímetro) the distance around a figure. Perimeter can be measured in standard units such as the inch, foot, yard, and mile. It can also be measured in metric units such as the millimeter, centimeter, meter, and kilometer. To find the perimeter of a figure, add the lengths of its sides; Lesson 43

pi (π) the ratio of the circumference of any circle to its diameter. The ratio $(\frac{C}{d})$ is always the same, about $\frac{22}{7}$, or 3.14. The formula for finding the circumference of a circle is: Circumference $(C) = \pi d$ or $C = 2\pi r$; Lesson 44

polygon (polígono) a plane figure formed by joining three or more line segments. A polygon is named for the number of sides it has. Polygons have the same number of angles as sides. Polygons are named by capital letters, starting at one vertex and going in order, either clockwise or counterclockwise; Lesson 31

positive numbers (números positivos) numbers greater than zero; Lesson 8

prime factorization (descomposición en factores primos) a composite number written as the product of prime numbers; Lesson 5

prime number (número primo) a whole number greater than 1 with only two factors, itself and 1; Lesson 5

product (producto) the answer in multiplication; Lesson 3

proportion (proporción) an equation stating that two ratios are equal; Lesson 2

Q

quadrilateral (cuadrilátero) a polygon with four sides and four angles; Lesson 33

quotient (cociente) the answer in a division problem; Lesson 6

R

radius (radio) a line segment that connects the center of a circle and an endpoint on the circle; Lessons 34, 44

range (rango) the difference between the greatest and least numbers in a set of data; Lesson 53

rate (tasa) a ratio that compares two different kinds of quantities, such as miles and hours; Lesson 26

ratio (razón) a comparison of two quantities. A ratio can compare part-to-part, part-to-whole, or whole-to-whole; Lesson 25

ray (rayo) a part of a line which continues forever in one direction and has one endpoint; Lesson 30

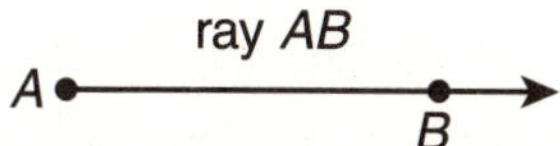

rectangle (rectángulo) a quadrilateral with four right angles; Lessons 33, 45

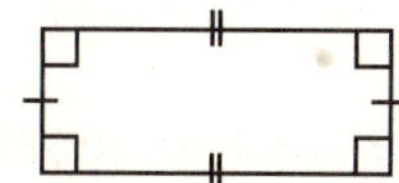

regular polygon (polígono regular) a plane figure with sides of equal measure and angles of equal measure; Lesson 31

remainder (residuo) the amount left over after dividing; Lesson 6

rhombus (rombo) a parallelogram with four sides of equal length; Lesson 33

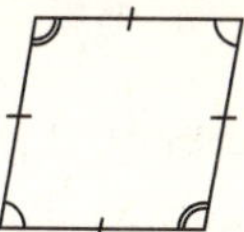

S

sample space (espacio muestral) a list of all possible outcomes for an event; Lessons 48, 49

sequence (secuencia) a set of numbers that is arranged in a pattern; Lesson 21

simplest form (mínima expresión) a fraction is in its simplest form when the numerator and the denominator have no common factors other than 1; Lesson 17

square (cuadrado) a rectangle with four sides of equal length; Lessons 33, 45

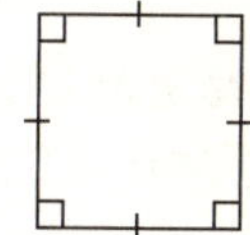

stem-and-leaf plot (diagrama de tallo y hojas) a graphical display of data items in numerical order. The leaf shows each data item's last digit on the right. The stem shows the digits to the left of the leaf; Lesson 56

T

term (término) a value within a sequence; Lesson 21

theoretical probability (probabilidad teórica) a ratio of how likely it is that an event will happen based on all the possible outcomes. Read $P(E)$ as "the probability of event E"; Lesson 50

$$P(E) = \frac{\text{number of favorable outcomes}}{\text{number of possible outcomes}}$$

trapezoid (trapecio) a quadrilateral with exactly one pair of parallel sides; Lessons 33, 45

V

variable (variable) a letter or symbol used to represent an unknown number in an equation; Lessons 20, 22

volume (volumen) the number of cubic units a container can hold. Volume can be measured in cubic units, such as cubic centimeters (cm^3) or cubic inches ($in.^3$); Lesson 46

X

***x*-axis (eje de las x)** the horizontal number line of a coordinate grid; Lesson 35

Y

***y*-axis (eje de las y)** the vertical number line of a coordinate grid; Lesson 35

Copy Masters

Use these copy masters to assist students throughout the year.

Name ______________________________

Copy Master 1
Hundred Chart

1	2	3	4	5	6	7	8	9	10
11	12	13	14	15	16	17	18	19	20
21	22	23	24	25	26	27	28	29	30
31	32	33	34	35	36	37	38	39	40
41	42	43	44	45	46	47	48	49	50
51	52	53	54	55	56	57	58	59	60
61	62	63	64	65	66	67	68	69	70
71	72	73	74	75	76	77	78	79	80
81	82	83	84	85	86	87	88	89	90
91	92	93	94	95	96	97	98	99	100

Name ______________________________

Copy Master 2
Place-Value Charts

Billions			Millions			Thousands			Ones		
hundred billions	ten billions	one billions	hundred millions	ten millions	one millions	hundred thousands	ten thousands	one thousands	hundreds	tens	ones

ones	.	tenths	hundredths	thousandths

Name ____

Copy Master 3
Number Lines

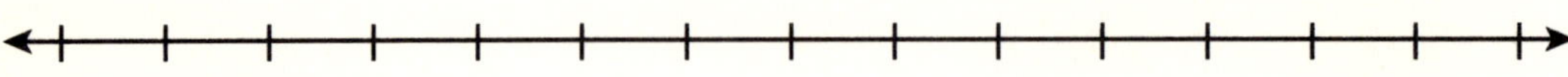

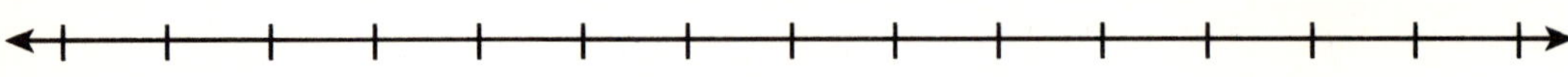

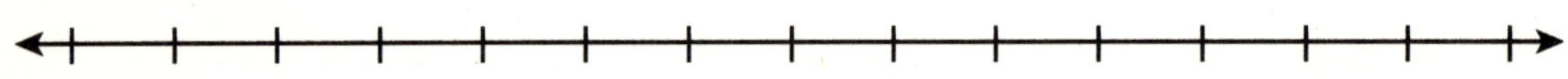

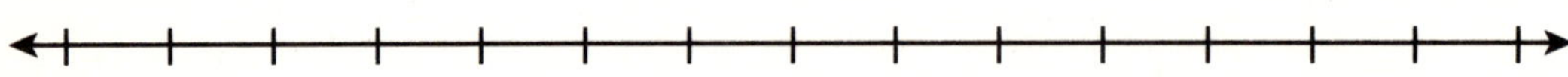

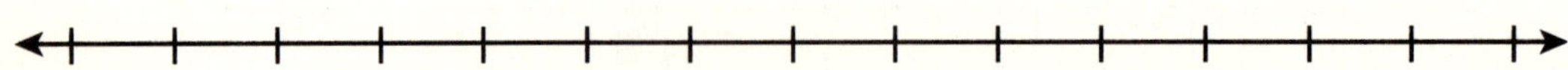

Name ____

Copy Master 4
Fraction Bars

Name ______________________________

Copy Master 5
Coordinate Grids

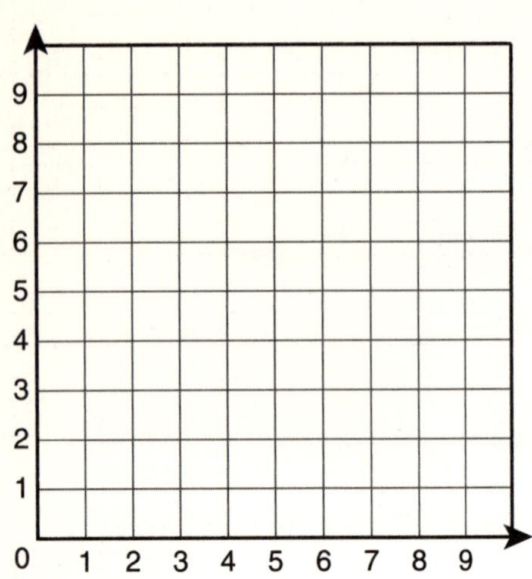

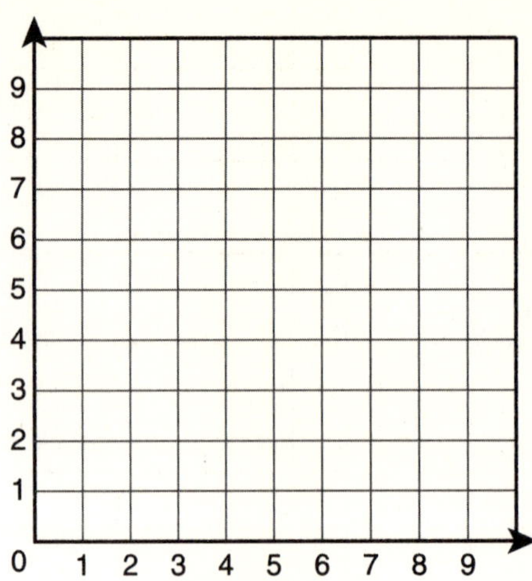

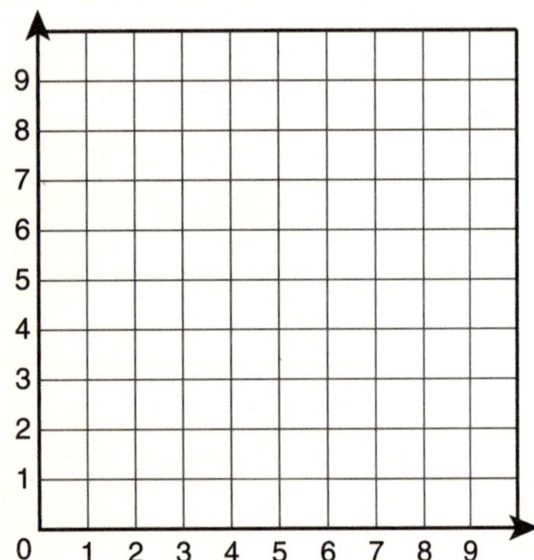

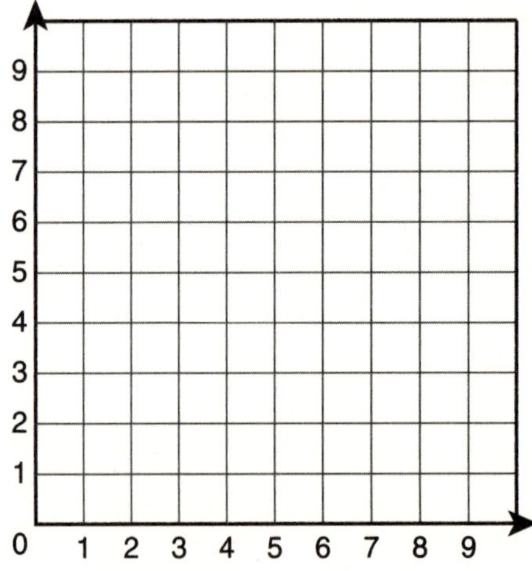

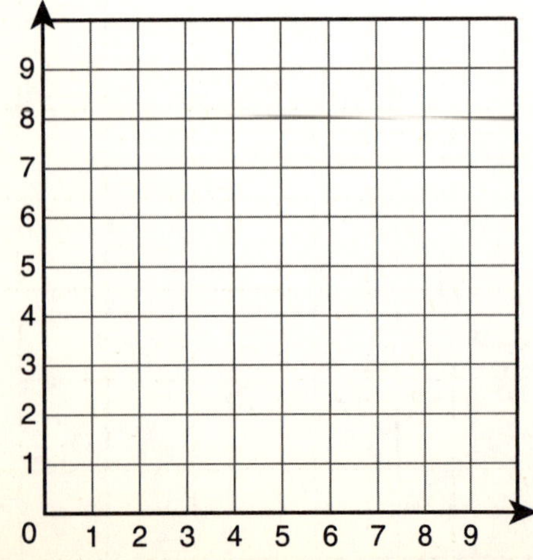

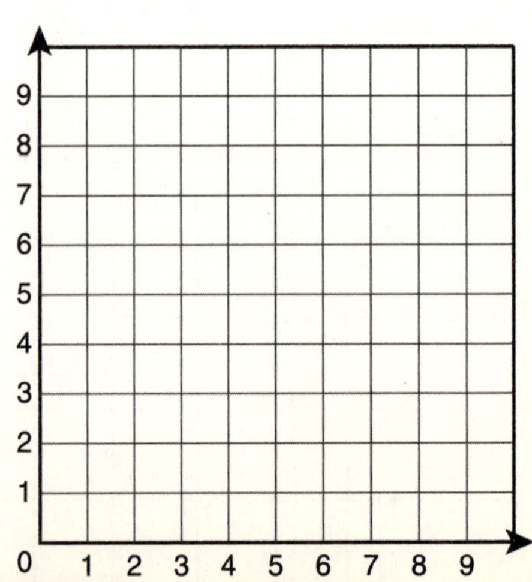

Name ______________________________

Copy Master 6
Centimeter Graph Paper

Name ____________________

Copy Master 7
Line Graphs

Title: ____________________

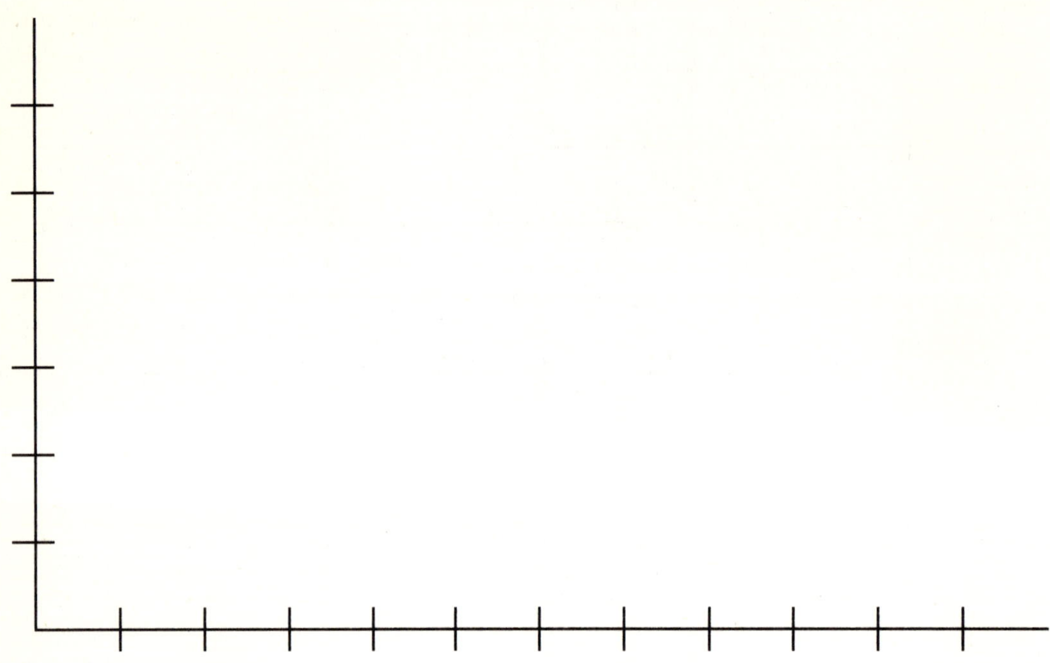

Title: ____________________

Notes

Notes

Notes

Notes

Notes

Notes